The

The Immigration Reader
America in a Multidisciplinary Perspective

Edited by David Jacobson

BLACKWELL
Publishers

The right of David Jacobson to be identified as editor of this work has been asserted in accordance with the Copyright, Designs and Patents Act 1988.

First published 1998

Blackwell Publishers Inc.
350 Main Street
Malden, Massachusetts 02148
USA

Blackwell Publishers Ltd
108 Cowley Road
Oxford OX4 1JF
UK

Library of Congress Cataloging-in-Publication Data
The immigration reader/edited by David Jacobson.
    p.   cm.
  Includes bibliographical references and index.
  ISBN 0–631–20776–7
        1–557–86916–2 (pbk)
    1. United States—Emigration and immigration.   2. United States—Emigration and immigration—Government policy.   I. Jacobson, David, 1940–   .
  JV6483. I555   1998
  304.873—dc21   97–20376
                                                                  CIP

British Library Cataloguing in Publication Data
A CIP catalogue record for this book is available from the British Library.

Typeset by Pure Tech India Ltd, Pondicherry
Printed and bound in Great Britain by MPG Books Ltd, Bodmin, Cornwall

This book is printed on acid-free paper

Contents

Contributors

David Jacobson, the Editor of this volume, teaches sociology at Arizona State University. He studied at the Hebrew University of Jerusalem, the London School of Economics, and Princeton University. He was born in Kimberley, South Africa. He is the author of *Rights Across Borders: Immigration and the Decline of Citizenship* (Johns Hopkins University Press, 1996) and editor of *Old Nations, New World: Conceptions of World Order* (Westview, 1994).

William S. Bernard was Director of the Center for Migration Studies at Brooklyn College of the City University of New York.

George J. Borjas is Professor of Public Policy at the John F. Kennedy School of Government at Harvard University.

Roy Simón Bryce-Laporte is the John D. and Catherine T. MacArthur Professor of Sociology and director of Africana and Latin American Studies at Colgate University.

Kitty Calavita is Associate Professor of the Department of Criminology, Law and Society at the University of California, Irvine.

Joseph H. Carens is Professor of Political Science at the University of Toronto.

Roger Daniels is Charles Phelps Taft Professor of History at the University of Cincinnati.

Thomas J. Espenshade teaches in the Department of Sociology and the Office of Population Research at Princeton University.

Francis Fukuyama is Hirst Professor of Public Policy at the Institute of Public Policy at George Mason University.

Jamie Goodwin-White is in the graduate program in the Department of Geography at Arizona State University.

Bill Ong Hing is Associate Professor at the School of Law at Stanford University.

Donald L. Horowitz is Charles S. Murphy Professor of Law and Professor of Political Science at Duke University.

Christian Joppke is Associate Professor of Sociology at the European University Institute, Florence (Italy).

Ivan Light is Professor of Sociology at the University of California, Los Angeles.

Douglas S. Massey is the Dorothy Swaine Thomas professor of Sociology at the University of Pennsylvania.

Alejandro Portes is Professor of Sociology at Princeton University.

Saskia Sassen is on the faculty of the School for International and Public Affairs at Columbia University.

Daniel J. Tichenor is an Assistant Professor of Political Science at Rutgers University, New Brunswick.

Reed Ueda is Associate Professor of History at Tufts University.

Michael Walzer is a permanent faculty member at the Institute for Advanced Study in Princeton.

William H. A. Williams is Professor at the College of Undergraduate Studies at the Union Institute, Cincinnati Center.

Acknowledgments

This is perhaps one of the most interesting times to be studying immigration. Preparing and working on this reader gave me the opportunity to make what felt like an exhaustive survey of the field of immigration in the different disciplines; it is an area that is lively and stimulating. And I could not complete this reader without the help of the lively and stimulating people who work in it.

I am very grateful to Zeynep Ozgen for her extensive help in collecting material. Jamie Goodwin-White not only wrote a chapter for this reader, but gave extensive and insightful suggestions as this project developed. I am grateful to Christian Joppke, Kitty Calavita, Thomas Espenshade and Daniel Tichenor for their gracious aid in working on their respective chapters. I am indebted to Simon Prosser who in his editorial capacity not only initiated this project, but gave some critical thoughts on the shape of the anthology. I am also indebted to Susan Rabinowitz for her aid. A number of anonymous reviewers also gave very useful suggestions.

As always, my greatest debt is to my family and our newest source of joy, Noam.

David Jacobson
Tempe, Arizona

George J. Borjas. "The Impact of Immigrants on Employment Opportunities of Natives." Reprinted by permission of the publisher from *The Changing Course of Migration*, published by Organization for Economic Cooperation and Development. Copyright © 1993 by OECD.

Roy Simón Bryce-Laporte. "Voluntary Immigration and Continuing Encounters between Blacks," *ANNALS of the American Academy of Political & Social Science*, 530, pp. 29–41, copyright © 1993 by Sage Publications, Inc. Reprinted by permission of Sage Publications.

Kitty Calavita. "Gaps and Contradictions in U.S. Immigration Policy: An Analysis of Recent Reform Efforts." Adapted from Calavita, *Controlling Immigration: A Global Perspective* edited by Wayne E. Cornelius, Philip L. Martin, and James F. Hollifield with the permission of the Publishers, Stanford University Press. © 1994 by The Board of Trustees of the Leland Stanford Junior University.

Joseph H. Carens. "Aliens and Citizens: The Case for Open Borders," *The Review of Politics*, vol. 49, no. 2, Spring 1987, pp. 251–73. Reprinted with permission.

Roger Daniels. "Ethnicity and Race in American Life" from Daniels, *Coming to America*. Copyright © 1990 by Visual Education Corporation. This material may not be reproduced without permission from the publisher, HarperCollins. Reprinted by permission of HarperCollins Publishers, Inc.

Francis Fukuyana. "Immigrants and Family Values," reprinted from *Commentary*, May 1993, by permission; all rights reserved. Reprinted by permission of International Creative Management, Inc. © 1993 by Francis Fukuyama.

Bill Ong Hing. "Asian Immigrants: Social Forces Unleashed After 1965." Excerpted from *Making and Remaking Asian America Through Immigration Policy, 1850–1990* by Bill Ong Hing with the permission of the publishers, Stanford University Press. © 1993 by the Board of Trustees of the Leland Stanford Junior University.

Donald L. Horowitz. "Immigration and Group Relations in France and America." This article originally appeared in Donald L. Horowitz and Gérard Noiriel (eds), *Immigrants in Two Democracies. French and American Experience*. © 1992, reprinted with permission by New York University Press.

Christian Joppke. "Multiculturalism and Immigration: A Comparison of the United States, Germany, and Great Britain," *Theory and Society*, vol. 25, no. 4, August 1996, pp. 449–500. © 1996, reprinted with kind permission from Elsevier Science-NL, Sara Burgerhartstraat 25, 1055 KV Amsterdam, The Netherlands.

Ivan Light. "Immigrant Entrepreneurs in America: Koreans in Los Angeles." This article originally appeared in Nathan Glazer (ed.), *Clamor At The Gates. The New American Immigration*. Reprinted with the permission of the author.

Douglas Massey. "The Social Organization of Mexican Immigration to the United States," *ANNALS of the American Academy of Political & Social Science*, 487, September 1986, pp. 102–13, copyright © 1986 by Sage Publications, Inc. Reprinted by permission of Sage Publications.

Alejandro Portes. From *Immigration Reconsidered: History, Sociology and Politics*, edited by Virginia Yans-McLaughlin. Copyright. Used by permission of Oxford University Press.

Saskia Sassen. "Foreign Investment: A Neglected Variable." This chapter originally appeared in Sassen, *The Mobility of Labor and Capital. A Study in International Investment and Labor Flow.* © 1988 by Cambridge University Press. Reprinted with permission.

Daniel J. Tichenor. "Inclusion, Exclusion, and the American Civic Culture." This article is a revised version of Tichenor, "Immigration and Political Community in the United States," *The Responsive Community*, vol. 4, no. 3, Summer 1994, pp. 16–28. © 1994 by The Responsive Community, 2020 Pennsylvania Ave., NW, Suite 282, Washington, D.C. 20006. Reprinted by permission of the Responsive Community.

Reed Ueda. "The Changing Face of Post-1965 Immigration." Excerpted from Ueda, *Postwar Immigrant America: A Social History.* Copyright © 1994. Reprinted with permission of St. Martin's Press, Inc.

Michael Walzer. "Membership." This chapter originally appeared in Walzer (ed.), *Spheres of Justice: A Defense of Pluralism and Equality*. Copyright © 1983 by Basic Books, Inc. Reprinted by permission of Basic Books, a division of HarperCollins Publishers, Inc.

William H. A. Williams. "Immigration as a Pattern in American Culture." This article originally appeared in *Proteus: A Journal of*

Ideas, Fall 1994, Shippensburg, PA 17257–2299. © 1994 by Shippensburg University. Reprinted with permission.

Introduction: An American Journey

David Jacobson

The often heard statement that America is a nation of immigrants conjures up an image of a collection of peoples, of ethnic groups, of religions tossed together as a "melting pot," a mosaic or a "salad bowl," depending on the political proclivities of the time. But America is a nation of immigrants in a much deeper sense than that. America was not only a place but an idea, and as such the migrant's destination was always just beyond the horizon; a nation of sojourners in a nation itself on a journey. In this respect, the distinction between immigrant and native is not so sharp, not only in that natives were all of immigrant origins (including, ultimately, American Indians), but that all are on a journey, collectively and individually, to an America as a promise, even as the Promised Land. Even the native is restless, as William H. A. Williams (chapter 1) writes, constantly reliving the immigrant's uprooting, as Americans move from farm to city, city to suburb, East to West, from rustbelt to sunbelt, and back again. Immigration is the beating heart of America.

In many respects, every modern nation is defined and constituted through immigration and through the selective inclusion and exclusion of outsiders. In modern German history, for example, immigration laws have favored ethnic Germans, reinforcing the notion that German national identity is rooted in a specific blood-line of people, the *Volk*. In United States history we see the use of both ethnic and political, as well as economic, criteria, a point that will be returned to later. Thus the act of determining the "character" of a nation involves regulating who may and may not come in, who are "family" and who are strangers. In this regard, immigration is a peculiarly modern phenomenon, even if migration as such is as old as human history itself. Immigration, with the implicit notion of bimodal movement from one fixed territory to another and, until recently at least, involving the explicit exchange of loyalties from one state to another, is characteristic of the modern nation-state. In medieval Europe, in contrast, kingdoms "migrated," such as the kingdom of the West Goths which moved from the Baltic area to the Black Sea to the Bay of Biscay in a few generations (Strayer 1970).

Still, the United States is unusual among modern nations to the degree that the "myth" of immigration – in the sense that immigration is integral to the way Americans imagine themselves – is woven into the social fabric. The United States is constantly *becoming*, rather than "to be," or so it likes to think of itself. Movement in time and place, individually and collectively, is the "normal" condition. Americans also, almost as a whole, proudly proclaim their immigrant origins, even if that migration was forced. For most other modern countries, to be "at home," so to speak, and relatively stable in time and space is the essence of normality. Travel is a transitionary phase between places, a phase to be quickly passed over for travel is, as its root meaning describes it, a *travail*.

Americans are rooted to the land, and like other nations and nationalisms there is a strong territorial component. The "People" are identified with a specific land, that of the United States. That land is, or has been, sacred in the American imagination, powerful enough in the national consciousness to mobilize millions in its defense (and for hundreds of thousands to be sacrificed). Consequently, the metaphor, as well as the reality, of the American as immigrant can be taken too far. Americans are not after all nomads for whom travel is the normal condition and to be stationary is to be immobile, and is the transitionary phase. Still, the relationship of the "American people" to the land is a nuanced one.

The Puritans, for better and for worse viewed as a historical source of American political institutions, are illuminating in this regard. For the Puritans the New World represented an "asylum" from persecution of the Old World, but also much more than that, it represented the promise of Eden, a supposedly unsullied and virgin terrain to begin anew. However, while in Puritanism we can see the inklings of the sacralization of land and an association of a certain people (the Puritans themselves) with that land, this association was not viewed as harmonious by the Puritans, let alone by native Americans. New England and the other colonies were terrains in which to continue the Reformation, to transform the Earthly kingdom and to bring heaven to earth. The Puritans had an "errand" in America's wilderness, to create anew, to build, to change the moral as well as the physical landscape. There was a close relationship with the land, but the land had to be cleared, metaphorically and literally. The Puritans were at home in the New World but not at peace with themselves; God's work still had to be done. The Puritans' "Great Migration" did not end, then, in Massachusetts Bay or in any of the other colonies in North America. In a sense, the journey just began when these immigrants arrived, a journey that was religious and spiritual, a journey to direct history. For the Protestant, wrote H. Richard Niebuhr (1961), life was "a pilgrim's progress which, whether made in solitary or in company, proceeds through unpredictability and crises toward the destination beyond life and death where all trumpets blow." America was a journey as much as a place, and it was a journey to an ever receding destination.

Much has changed, of course, since the Puritans came to the New World. Calvinist Puritanism has largely dissipated as a coherent force in American life (going back to the mid-nineteenth century). But the motif of a people collectively and individually on a journey, a "migration," be it spiritual, historical, or physical, has endured.

The concept of a "nation of immigrants" tends to suggest that America, the United States, is an inclusive country, captured in the image of the Statue of Liberty beckoning to the world, to the poor, the miserable, the destitute, to come to her open arms. In fact, the immigration motif is more subtle in its effects, creating questions of "belonging," and consequently who should be welcomed and to whom the door should be shut. This tension is evident in the very birth certificate of the country, the Declaration of Independence.

Immigration and American Identity

The Founders were a remarkable group in that not only did they "invent" a nation but they defined it in moral terms and as a moral enterprise. This is evident in the language of the Declaration of Independence which talks of, at least in the opening paragraphs, universal principles that apply to all nations. This new nation's specificity is as the vessel and carrier of universal values, as a chosen, redeemer nation: a nation defines itself in terms of universal criteria – identity is not primordial. The political revolution and the national revolution, Yehoshua Arieli (1964) points out, coincided. The political identity *was* the American identity. Consider, for example, what is perhaps the most familiar part of the Declaration:

> We hold these truths to be self-evident, that all men
> are created equal, that they are endowed by their Creator
> with certain unalienable Rights, that among these are Life,
> Liberty, and the pursuit of Happiness.
> That to secure these rights, governments are instituted
> among Men deriving their just powers from the consent
> of the governed.
> That whenever any Form of Government becomes
> destructive of these ends, it is the Right of the People to
> alter or to abolish it, and to institute new Government...

There is nothing specifically American about these words, in that any people could make these claims, except for the fact that the United States was to be defined by its moral mission, a mission to change the world – a moralism that goes back to the Puritans. As Tom Paine wrote in *Common Sense* in 1776, "But admitting we were all of English descent, what does it amount to? Nothing." American identity in principle was not primordial as such and all could become American. Indeed, reference is made directly to the immigrant roots of the country with complaints that the Crown "endeavored to prevent the population of these States; for that purpose obstructing the Laws of Naturalization of Foreigners; refusing to pass others to encourage their migrations hither..." In the colonialists' attempts to make the English reasonable, "We have reminded them of the circumstances of our emigration and settlement here."

And yet this moral, redeemer quality is in conflict with the very act of separation symbolized and stated by the Declaration of Independence, anticipating an isolationist thread in American life. The new republic could prosper only if freed of all ties with European despotism. "The attempt to realize a better social order," writes Felix Gilbert (1961:4), "presupposed a critical view of the values of the Old World and aroused a fear of ties which might spread the diseases of Europe to America." If being an American demanded a certain moral "quality," the question became, What was that quality? Similarly, outsiders and potential immigrants could be suspiciously scrutinized and their credentials examined, as the Federalists did in 1798 and as Congress did directly and through immigration legislation in the 1950s when the fear of communism was at its height.

But there was another tension at the very start, one that was much more insidious: the promise of these new American values and the much poorer practice in racial and ethnic terms. As Roger Daniels notes (chapter 2), the revolutionaries spoke of one people, but it was essentially a "white country." The Declaration itself refers to "merciless Indian Savages" from whom the king had failed to protect the colonialists. Slavery would be legally institutionalized in the Constitution to be arrived at 11 years later. And in a law enacted in 1790, Congress enabled "free white persons" to become citizens after two years residence. Other ethnic biases, if not formally legalized until the early twentieth century, faced immigrants, such as the Irish, to the New World. Thus the United States, from its very beginnings, was wrought with tensions between who should or should not belong, and between proclaimed ideals and actual practices.

Immigration and Citizenship

These contrasting elements in American national identity are reflected in the flux and shifts in immigration law, involving political, ethnic and economic concerns, particularly after the regulation of immigration and the naturalization of aliens became a function of the federal government after the Civil War, after, in other words, the United States became an unambiguously unitary nation. Prior to the late nineteenth century the regulation of immigrants and their naturalization was in the jurisdiction of the respective states. States performed naturalization procedures under a law passed in 1790, though naturalized immigrants were considered to be citizens in all the United States, with the rights and duties of one state enforceable by courts in all the states (Kettner, 1978). Despite this ambiguity – whether one's loyalties lay primarily with one's state or with the federal government was not legally clarified until the Civil War – the notion of citizenship figured prominently in the American Revolution.[1]

The American Revolution sought to form a nation, a nation that was to be based on the active consent of its citizens instead of the passive allegiance of subjects to the Crown. This concept of citizenship created terms of membership and, by implication, created a category of nonmembers, or aliens. Under early English law, there was a continum of social ranks and rights and no distinction was made between member and alien. Though with the rise of national states from the seventeenth century the concept of alien arose, the older notions had remained ensconced. The Revolution of 1776 would play a large role in breaking away from this practice (see Schuck and Smith, 1985).

Citizenship became the linchpin of the modern nation-state. It tied the citizen to the nation with the presumption of a singular loyalty. Citizenship ensured certain rights, and promoted the active participation of the citizenry in the process of government. And citizenship – this point is much less noticed – was also about "belonging in space," that is, the people were tied to a particular land (see Goodwin-White, chapter 20 in this volume). Membership, rights, territory – these are the three interlocking dimensions of citizenship. Citizenship located the individual in the nation and, by extension, in the world. In this context, naturalization has been a fundamental act, both for the immigrant and for the host society. The immigrant took on, so to speak, a new persona; for the host society the (welcomed) immigrant mirrored what that society, that nation, wanted to be – ethnically, religiously or politically.

Yet in recent decades, the traditional notion of citizenship has been buffeted by certain challenges, bringing into question the degree of its significance. Rights increasingly came to be predicated on residency not citizenship (with the major exception of the vote). Interest in naturalization was consequently rather low, leading to the argument that citizenship had been devalued (Jacobson, 1996; Schuck, 1984). Indeed, rights claims increasingly came to be made on the basis of human rights rather than citizen status (and the courts from the 1970s were increasingly ready to recognize human rights claims). This was significant because human rights do not presume any necessary acculturation into the host society, in this case the United States, as human rights inhere in "personhood" and not in nationality. This phenomenon (of devaluing citizenship) was accentuated by the growing flows of illegal and undocumented immigrants, particularly from the 1970s, and the growing illegal resident population; estimates are that about 350,000 people settle illegally each year in the United States (compared to, in 1994, about 804,000 legal immigrants).[2] Unauthorized immigrants bypass the process whereby the "desirable" future citizen is selected; furthermore, as the government extends rights to undocumented populations, so the phenomenon of basing rights on residency is reinforced. The perception that the United States had "lost control" of its borders had sociological as well as literal meaning: illegal immigration challenged the presumption that the nation could be defined and constituted through the regulation of who could and could not come to live in the United States.

However, from about 1995 naturalization requests grew dramatically in absolute numbers apparently in response to, in part, fears that immigrants who were permanent residents but not citizens would have their rights (*vis-à-vis* citizens) scaled back.[3] And, indeed, the welfare law enacted by Congress in 1996 did limit access of noncitizens to certain welfare benefits (see Espenshade, chapter 11). This raises the intriguing question of whether citizenship is being "revalued." However, this new surge of naturalizations is taking place in a different environment from the past, such that the very meaning of citizenship may be being transformed. For example, dual citizenship is being increasingly legalized, or immigrants have been anticipating legalization, in countries like the Dominican Republic, Mexico and Turkey to name a few. This obviously subverts presumptions of singular loyalties which framed classic understandings of citizenship. In a world which has become increasingly "compressed" and where people are increasingly aware of global linkages and maintain linkages with their "home" societies – in other words, where diasporic and transnational communities are increasingly the norm – people feel comfortable with multiple memberships (see Robertson, 1992).

To fully clarify this question, we still need to find out if the very recently naturalized citizens mirror those of the past: do they integrate into "mainstream" organizations and associations (as opposed to ethnically or nationally segmented groups); do they participate actively in civic politics (voting, political parties and the like) or are their claims made through judicial forums and on the basis of human rights claims; are the naturalizations driven by concern to participate politically or by a concern of the loss of certain "entitlements"; and finally, does naturalization still involve "belonging in space" in the national sense, or do we see instead the continuing and growing stress on transnational and diasporic links and "spaces"?

Overview of the Volume

The notion that membership and citizenship was a function of consent; the principle that being an American presupposed certain political values and characteristics; and the close association between immigration (voluntary and coerced) and ethnic identity, formation and conflict, are themes that thread throughout the history of immigration to the United States. These themes are implicated in debates about the "melting pot" and "multicultural-ism"; about whether immigrants are a benefit to, or a burden on, the economy; and about philosophical debates about immigration policy and whether the door to immigrants should be opened more or, if not closed, left only ajar. The chapters that follow are broken into sections on history, contemporary ethnicity, the economy, cross-national comparisons, and political debate. All the chapters on different levels analyze the role of immigration in "constitut-ing," or shaping, American society and politics and, implicitly at least, illustrate the intrinsic importance of immigration in stitching the fabric of the United States, be it a seamless, woven cloth or a roughly sown quilt.

Part I, on the history of immigration to the United States, con-siders both thematic and chronological aspects of American immig-ration history.

William H. A. Williams (chapter 1) considers immigration as the quintessential American experience. The immigration experience, he says, is woven into almost every aspect of American life: the uprooting from one's home and family; the restlessness; the encounters with strangers; the changing sense of self as well as location. American history cannot be told solely in terms of immig-ration, writes Williams, but in Americans' "embrace" of the future and the "endless" diversity countered by this shared national experience of migration, the patterns of immigration can be dis-cerned deeply within American history, culture, and identities.

Roger Daniels (chapter 2) analyzes the historical role of ethnicity and race in the constitution of colonial and, after 1776, national identity. He notes the dissonance between the notion that Amer-ican national identity transcended ethnic distinctions with actual practices and prejudices. Still, he notes, immigration in the early Republic was largely welcomed and when it was opposed, it was generally on ideological rather than on ethnic and religious grounds.

William Bernard (chapter 3) looks at immigration policy over five periods. In the colonial period (1609–1775) immigration was encouraged by labor needs and the toleration for a diversity of Christian denominations (except in New England). One of the grievances that precipitated the Revolution and the Open Door era (1776–1881) was the British government's refusal to allow greater "population of these states." Authority over immigration in this period was largely in the hands of state and local government. Federal control begins with the Era of Regulation (1882–1916). Restrictive measures begin in the latter half of the nineteenth century against Chinese and Japanese immigrants, and become more comprehensive in the Era of Restriction (1917–1964). "Quotas" were enacted by Congress to limit admission of southern and eastern Europeans, among others, as these aliens were deemed to be less "assimilable" than northern Europeans. In the postwar period, and in the context of the Cold War struggle against communism, the focus turned to restricting those with "alien beliefs," rather than nationality as such. However, the national origins quota system was not abolished until 1965, with the Hart-Celler Act, which begins the Era of Liberalization.

The dramatic changes in the demography of immigration after 1965 to the United States is described by Reed Ueda (chapter 4). The liberalization of immigration law reversed the dominance of immigration from Europe; by the 1980s only 11 percent of immigrants came from Europe, compared to 90 percent in 1900. Latin American and Asian immigrants made up the great majority of immigrants after 1970, with Mexicans the largest single source of immigrants (even excluding unauthorized immigrants). The changes (though unanticipated by the architects of the Hart-Celler Act) were due to the priority given to "family reunification" of the 1965 immigration law. Ueda also considers the post-1965 changes in the sex ratios of immigrants and, in addition, refugees, West Indian and Haitian immigration and the regional and urban concentration of immigrants.

In the final chapter in the history of immigration section, Kitty Calavita (chapter 5) analyzes the Immigration Reform and Control Act of 1986 (IRCA) and the Immigration Act of 1990. She argues that there has been a gap between the intended purposes of American immigration policy and their practical effect. This gap is a result of "paired oppositions" between the interests of American workers and employers, between the economic needs of a time and conflicting political attitudes, and between liberal democratic principles and police functions necessary to control the border. IRCA, which was designed to control illegal immigration (but failed to), and the Immigration Act of 1990, which increased the number of visas for people with special skills deemed necessary for the American economy, reflect this gap. While the rhetoric about immigration in this period has often been restrictionist, the actual outcomes have been expansionist; in this sense, immigration law has been largely symbolic rather than practical.

Part II concerns immigration and contemporary ethnicity. Ethnicity is, of course, part and parcel of the immigrant experience in the United States, and the ethnic dimension weaves through almost any discussion on immigration. Indeed, ethnicity is an important ingredient in all the discussions appearing in this anthology on the history, economics, comparative perspectives, and political debate on immigration. In this section, the specific focus is on groups that became much more noticeable following the 1965 immigration legislation.

Alejandro Portes (chapter 6) writes about Hispanic minorities in the United States, particularly Mexicans, Puerto Ricans, and Cubans. Portes notes that the sending countries of major Hispanic groups in the United States were objects of US expansion and intervention. This expansion preceded the onset of migration and, in a sense, members of these societies were Americanized before actually becoming immigrants. Portes considers labor market trends and socioeconomic performance among different Hispanic groups, and their political behavior (such as degree of activism and positions on political issues) and citizenship (particularly regarding rates of naturalization).

Asian–American immigration in the post-1965 period is the subject of Bill Ong Hing's discussion (chapter 7). Hing looks at the changing population characteristics of Chinese, Filipino, Korean and Asian Indian groups, the dynamics driving their immigration, and their different demographics (particularly, in this chapter, their socioeconomic profiles). He also considers Asian American political participation, challenging the apparently popular belief of political passivism.

Though voluntary immigration is central to the self-image of the United States, it has only exceptionally been associated with people of African descent. The slave trade tends to be the overwhelming motif of black migration. But, Roy Simón Bryce-Laporte writes (chapter 8), African American history (and American immigration history in general) would be incomplete without fuller recognition of black migration (voluntary as well as coerced), crossover, flight, and encounter. Laporte considers new black immigrants, whose volume, variety and visibility increased significantly after 1965, from areas such as the Caribbean and Latin America. These immigrants highlight the fact that black Americans are not monolithic, and that in some circumstances ethnicity such as, say, Dominican, can be more important then race. Conversely, black immigrants with a strong national identity find themselves labeled, and bond, along racial lines.

Douglas Massey (chapter 9) discusses the social networks that have facilitated Mexican migration, including illegal and undocumented migration. (Mexico is the biggest single source of immigrants, legal and illegal.) Economic conditions alone cannot explain the large flows from Mexico. Massive Mexican migration today reflects the earlier development of social networks that sustain it. These networks of family and friends link sending communities in Mexico with specific destinations in the United States. People from the same town or family are tied together in a set of reciprocal obligations that new migrants can draw on to enter and find work in the United States. These networks reduce the psychological and economic costs of migration and, as they become more extensive, become self-perpetuating.

In part III, four issues that have been at the center of discussion on immigration and the United States economy are discussed, namely the impact of immigrants on employment of natives; the extent immigrants are, or are not, a welfare burden; the impact of foreign investment on migratory flows to the US; and ethnic entrepreneurship.

George Borjas (chapter 10) addresses the question of whether immigrants hurt the income and employment opportunities of natives. He states that there is no such empirical evidence to support the argument that immigrants are detrimental for natives in this regard. Immigrants are neither "good" nor "bad" for natives, economically speaking.

The net fiscal cost (or gain) of immigrants – the difference between taxes paid by immigrants and the benefits they receive in return – is analyzed by Thomas Espenshade (chapter 11). Espenshade briefly reviews the literature on this debate. He notes that recent welfare reforms have the effect of reducing the public costs of immigration by eliminating or restricting the access of immigrants to public benefits. He discusses the combination of fiscal conservatism and the "anti-immigrant tone" that led up to the welfare reforms *vis-à-vis* immigrants. The tensions between state governments and the federal government over who should shoulder the cost of immigrants are also discussed.

The belief has been that foreign investment would foster development and create jobs in poorer countries and, consequently, dampen the desire of people to migrate to the highly industrialized countries, particularly the United States. In fact, Saskia Sassen (chapter 12) argues the opposite has happened. Increases in immigration from the Caribbean Basin and South East Asia to the United States occurred in periods of high economic growth in the sending countries and, similarly, of massive increases in foreign investment. Instead, Sassen describes in detail how direct foreign investment from highly industrialized countries has mobilized new segments of the population of sending countries into regional and long-distance migrations and migration networks. Migration is aided by the objective and ideological links established with the highly industrialized countries as a consequence of foreign investment.

Ethnic entrepreneurship has been a venerable theme in writings about immigration. Ivan Light (chapter 13) considers the case of Korean entrepreneurship in Los Angeles, noting both its benefits and its costs. Korean-owned firms have serviced low income, non-white neighborhoods that have been largely ignored by big retail corporations. Furthermore, these Korean businesses brought foreign capital into the Los Angeles economy, employed Americans and injected money into the general economy, helping other businesses. On the other hand, Light writes, Korean garment firms employed undocumented workers. Furthermore, Korean entrepreneurship sometimes involved the violation of laws protecting labor standards, public health, and morals (such as labor and sanitary codes in restaurants, or message parlors fronting for prostitution). Light also briefly discusses theories and causes of ethnic entrepreneurship.

Migratory flows are a global phenomenon, of course, and have been the subject of debate in Europe – another highly industrial zone and the destination of extensive migration – every bit as much as in the United States. Yet, the "prism" through which immigration is viewed, and the patterns of incorporation (or lack thereof) varies among the host societies, as a result of differing political and cultural traditions. In part IV, two chapters examine the United States in comparison to European countries that account for the great majority of immigrants and foreign residents in Western Europe.

Christian Joppke (chapter 14) considers immigration and multiculturalism in the United States, Germany and Great Britain. Multiculturalism, as Joppke describes it, is a challenge to the "premier cultural community" of the modern era, the nation; multiculturalism instead stresses multiple communities existing within national borders. Multiculturalism is also a quest for compensatory treatment of historically disadvantaged groups. Finally, it is a form of anti-colonial discourse and struggle. The linkage between immigration and multiculturalism differs across these three societies, shaped by different notions of nationhood, by the context in which immigration took place, and by the ethnic groups themselves. In the American case, multiculturalism is a relatively weak challenge to prevailing civic conceptions of nationhood which for some time accepted multiple ethnic identities. In Germany and Britain multiculturalism, in different ways, is a more direct challenge to established ideas of nationhood.

Both France and the United States share a belief that immigrants can and should be integrated into their respective societies and political communities. Yet, as Donald Horowitz (chapter 15) writes in his comparative study of these two nations, whereas the Americans celebrate ethnic pluralism and "hyphenated identities," France promotes the common citizen and a unitary national identity. In France, identity is dichotomized: immigrants who have naturalized and are no longer "foreigners" are assumed to have exchanged their former identities for French identity. Horowitz compares, in this context, education, religion, and political institutions in the two countries.

Immigration gets to the core of who "we" are, to conceptions of national and communal identities, and to the obligations citizens have to one another and to noncitizens. Immigration cuts across issues of citizenship, membership, and human rights. Immigration can be constitutive of, or undermine, primordial and felt associations of nationhood. No wonder it is a topic of intense debate, dispute, and contention. In part V, political theorists make arguments for: upholding the right to selectively accept outsiders; treating citizens and resident aliens essentially alike; accepting immigrants because they promote core American values; and accepting immigrants but in a way that is not at the economic or civic cost of natives. Clearly, "liberal" and "conservative" are not synonymous with, respectively, open and restricted approaches to immigration, and the debate on immigration is a nuanced one.

Michael Walzer (chapter 16) argues that the right of the state, as the institutional representative of the people, to choose an admissions policy is a basic right. Admission and exclusion are at the very heart of communal independence and self-determination. Without such admissions policies, there could be no "communities of character," associations of people with a special commitment to one another and a sense of a shared, meaningful life. But the principle of self-determination, Walzer says, is not absolute and is subject to the moral demands of "mutual aid." Refugees are a case in point, whose desparate situation morally demands that a country grant them asylum.

What is the justification for excluding the entry of people into a country? For most, the right to determine who comes in and who does not is inherent in sovereignty and essential for maintaining a sense of national community. But Joseph Carens (chapter 17) challenges this view and argues that borders should be generally open. People should normally be free to leave their own country and settle in another; this argument, Carens says, is strongest when applied to the migration of people from the third world. Citizenship has become, in the West, the equivalent of a feudal privilege, an inherited status, that is hard to justify. Carens draws on contemporary political theories in making this argument.

Francis Fukuyama (chapter 18) accepts that culture and values are important to social cohesion and to economic success. The question is whether contemporary immigration to the United States threatens those values? Fukuyama argues on the contrary: third-world immigrants, specifically Asian and Latino, have on the whole a deep devotion to family and a strong work ethic. Ideologies that threaten core American values such as, Fukuyama says, multiculturalism are western and American inventions. The problem is not the culture that third-world immigrants bring with them, but the contemporary "elite culture" of Americans.

The expansion of alien admissions and rights in the 1980s and early 1990s, together with the break from a nativist tradition (in 1965) that had favored certain ethnic groups over others, revealed, according to Daniel Tichenor (chapter 19), a promising inclusiveness. On the other hand, it also illustrated an enervation of the bonds between Americans themselves. We must ask ourselves, Tichenor says, whether certain obligations to disadvantaged Americans must be met before newcomers are granted membership "goods." Immigrants may hurt the underclass even if they do not hurt American economic opportunities in the aggregate: Tichenor points to studies that suggest employers were generally more willing to employ third-world immigrants than native blacks. Tichenor also makes an argument for involving local communities more centrally in debates about immigration policy.

In the concluding chapter, Jamie Goodwin-White examines the continuing interplay of space and identity in a nation of immigrants. Citizenship is considered as a specific spatial identity, a "belonging in space." Space in this sense is not only physical but communal: spaces of belonging indicate rights and roles as well as settlement and mobility, and delineate immigrants from citizens. The current period, Goodwin-White says, provides evidence that the relevant scales and qualities of spatial identities are changing, and as such require new conceptions of American citizenship.

The themes and issues covered in this volume do not, of course, come close to exhausting all the topics in the rapidly expanding immigration literature. Anthologies, such as this one, are inherently selective and inevitably some worthy issues could have been considered more fully, such as refugees and gender. Still, many of these issues, like refugees, would need a volume of their own to be treated justifiably. Other issues, like gender, are well treated elsewhere. Instead, the emphasis here is on the main concerns in the immigration debate in both the general public sphere and in the academy. Furthermore, the stress in this volume is on substantial, even lengthy, chapters on the chosen topics, rather than on relatively cursory and short chapters on a broad variety of subjects.

Studying immigration provides a cornucopia of intellectual delights, cutting as it does across so many disciplines and interests – from history to philosophy, sociology to economics, anthropology to law, political science to cultural studies to geography, to name a few. Let the feast begin.

Notes

1 This section draws on Jacobson (1996: 44–6).
2 Figure from US Immigration and Naturalization Service (1996).
3 The different factors that accounted for the increase in naturalization requests were presumed to be Proposition 187 in California, which would place limits on benefits to *illegal* immigrants, the presumption that Mexico would legalize dual citizenship (affecting the single largest body of immigrants in the United States), the effects of a large cohort of persons eligible for citizenship under the Immigration Reform and Control Act of 1986, bureaucratic streamlining and changes at the Immigration and Naturalization Service, and, of course, the new welfare law enacted in 1996. Still the differential impact of these factors has yet to be clarified and we do not yet know to what extent we are witnessing cohort effects (which would not affect *rates* of naturalization) and to what extent we are seeing changing rates, rather than increased absolute numbers, of naturalization.

References

Arieli, Yehoshua. 1964. *Individualism and Nationalism in American Ideology.* Cambridge, Mass.: Harvard University Press.

Gilbert, Felix. 1961. *To the Farewell Address: Ideas of Early American Foreign Policy.* Princeton: Princeton University Press.

Jacobson, David. 1996. *Rights across Borders: Immigration and the Decline of Citizenship.* Baltimore: The Johns Hopkins University Press.

Kettner, James H. 1978. *The Development of American Citizenship, 1608–1870.* Chapel Hill: University of North Carolina Press.

Niebuhr, H. Richard. 1961. "The Protestant Movement and Democracy in the United States." In *The Shaping of American Religion,* ed. J. W. Smith and A. L. Jamison. Princeton: Princeton University Press.

Robertson, Roland. 1992. *Globalization: Social Theory and Global Culture,* London: Sage.

Schuck, Peter H. 1984. "The Transformation of Immigration Law." *Columbia Law Review* 84, 1:1–90.

Schuck, Peter H., and Rogers M. Smith. 1985. *Citizenship without Consent.* New Haven: Yale University Press.

Strayer, Joseph R. 1970. *On the Medieval Origins of the Modern State.* Princeton: Princeton University Press.

U.S. Immigration and Naturalization Service. 1996. *Statistical Yearbook of the Immigration and Naturalization Service, 1994.* Washington, D.C.: U.S. Government Printing Office.

PART I

HISTORY OF IMMIGRATION TO THE UNITED STATES

1 Immigration as a Pattern in American Culture

William H. A. Williams

The idea of the United States as a nation of immigrants is a long-standing cliché. All of us born in this country are descended from people who were born somewhere else – across the Atlantic or the Pacific or below the Rio Grande. Only those called "Indians" are native to the place, and even their far distant ancestors migrated from Asia across the Aleutian land bridge. Yet, as John Higham once pointed out, on one level this "mythic" concept of a nation of immigrants claims too much. If we define immigrants, in Higham's words, as those "who chose America," then we should exclude from that term the Dutch and English settlers who colonized what they regarded as empty wilderness, African slaves forcibly transported here, and the Native Americans and Spanish settlers incorporated as conquered peoples (1968, 92). If, however, we consider not *categories* of people but the *effects* of the physical, social, and cultural series of acts involved in abandoning home and homeland, crossing the ocean, and settling in a new place amid strangers, then we might conclude that the *impact of immigration is the quintessential American experience, establishing a pattern that is replicated in almost every aspect of American life.*

Wherever we look we find the imprint of immigration, our primal cultural experience. The essentials of that experience involve physical separation – the uprooting from one's home, family, and past; the encounter with strangers and strangeness; the adaptation to change, of one's sense of self as well as of location; and the tensions between unity and diversity.

Consider the most obvious example of the ongoing influence of immigration: the restless character of American life with its accompanying high degree of physical mobility. As J. Hector St. John de

Crèvecoeur (himself an eighteenth-century French immigrant) noted, European immigrants quickly adjusted their sense of scale to American size and opportunity; "... two hundred miles formerly appeared a very great distance, it is now but a trifle..." (1957, 54). Things have changed little since Crèvecoeur's day. Whether one or ten generations removed from our immigrant ancestors, we, as a people, have always tended to move about at a remarkable rate, repeating the immigrant's original uprooting, as we move from farm to city, from city to suburb, East to West, criss-crossing back and forth across the continent. Concerning what he once called our "motion sickness," George W. Pierson claimed that "Ours has been the great spatial carelessness. We've been the footloose folk – and the scars of the experience show on our land. It has even warped our national character" (1968, 107).

Even those groups which at first seemed isolated from the immigrant momentum eventually picked up the pattern, often responding to the similar types of economic and social pressures that prompted European immigration. From the late colonial period until the end of the nineteenth century, African Americans, first as slaves and then as tenant farmers and sharecroppers, lived primarily in the rural South. However, with the cut-off of European immigration after World War I, African Americans became the principal newcomers to the city, gradually turning themselves into an urban people.[1] Similarly, Appalachians, who were once one of the most rooted groups in our population, have left their mountain homes in increasing numbers, pushing the boundaries of Appalachia into lowland cities, such as Cincinnati (Pickard 1991, 123).

Whatever it is that sets us moving, many of us, like immigrants, experience at some level the sense of loss of the old and familiar and the sometimes disturbing encounter with the new and different. Varying kinds of "culture shock" still await even those of us who have been born here, as we move from one part of America to another. A Pennyslvanian of German descent, leaving the green hills of his state for the desert vastness of Phoenix, Arizona, will encounter more alien surroundings, social as well as natural, than did his eighteenth-century ancestors when they exchanged the hills of Hesse or the Palatinate for the Valley of the Lehigh. Even when we do not move out of town, we change houses, leaving behind one neighborhood for another. The "ancestral home" is as rare a concept in America as is the family coat of arms.[2]

Today, jet planes, interstate highways, and telephones minimize the sense of uprooting for immigrants and internal migrants alike, whether from Accra in Ghana or Fox Hollow in Kentucky. Modern transportation and communication blur distances, perhaps even differences, between the old home and the new. The process of leave-taking no longer need be abrupt and traumatic. Visits, phone calls, video and cassette tapes, even E-Mail allow us to keep in touch across thousands of miles. As a result, today's immigrants may be neither fully here nor there, neither "back home" nor "at home" in their new locations. Even as it minimizes the uprooting, technology may make putting down roots even more difficult.

Ever on the move, we Americans frequently find ourselves in the midst of strangers, a prospect that so appalled the first generations of nineteenth-century immigrants that they huddled together in their ghettos, building ethnic enclaves of Irish, Germans, Jews, and Italians. When even these proved too porous to outsiders, immigrants formed social clubs made up of friends and neighbors who came from the *same* glens, counties, and cities in the Old Country. Ironically, this in-gathering of ethnic groups against the sea of strangers surrounding them helped to instill the pattern of migration within the second and third generations. The American-born children, anxious to become "American" in speech, dress, and habits, found the crowded ethnic enclaves suffocating and their families too inward looking and confining – too Old World. Just as the parents had left their families behind in Europe or Asia for a new life in America, so their American children repeated the process. Their journeys were often shorter, from the city to suburbs, but were undertaken for much the same reasons the parents had left Europe: to establish their own lives away from the confines of the past.

And so the process continues as a kind of "generational immigration," resulting in the weakening or, sometimes, even the sundering of family ties, as grown children leave their home town, state, or region. A glance at the folklore of many peoples reminds us that this phenomenon, taken for granted by Americans, has not always been the norm of human experience. In many of the Old World folk tales, children do not leave the family as a matter of course but only when banished from home by a wicked step-parent or forced by poverty to seek their fortunes elsewhere. That they survive and succeed only through great courage, wit, .and, frequently, the aid of magic suggests how unnatural the physical separation of families has seemed to many cultures.

Within the context of the family, even divorce can be seen as one more reiteration of the immigration experience working its way through the culture. Instead of bidding farewell to the limitations of one's home land, we now say good-by, sometimes with less trauma and inconvenience, to the limitations of a marriage. Some of us continue the process, migrating from one connubial arrangement to another, ever in search of the promised land of the heart.

It is in this continual search for the new life, the good life, that we can sense how deeply the underlying force of the immigrant experience has imprinted itself into the structure of our culture, molding the American sense of individualism. It is not merely a matter of believing that we all have a right to life, liberty, and the pursuit of happiness. Unbounded by history, family, and even our own experiences, we are supposedly free to be "ourselves," providing we first *find* "ourselves" – thus, our need to be always on the move, immigrating physically, socially, culturally, sexually, and/or spiritually in search of new shores of selfhood.

This state of mind, so American in its contours, did not originate here. The seeds of the "actualized self," as Abraham Maslow christened it, were first sown back in the Old World by men and women who wanted something better and who thought they had to leave home to find it in America. "What attachment," asked Crèvecoeur, "can a poor European emigrant have for a country where he had nothing?" (1957, 39). Thus, the act of emigration was a rejection of the *ancien regime*, more profound, in its way, than that of the revolutionaries who stayed home and went to the barricades. Since the French Revolution, the Old World has sought to remake man by first remaking society. In America, we get right to work on the individual. We close the door on the old self, throw away the key, and embark on our journey in search of the "green light, the orgiastic future" that lured F. Scott Fitzgerald's Great Gatsby. And if some of us end up like Jay Gatsby, dying enroute, the same fate sometimes overtook our immigrant ancestors.

A society and culture based on an internalized, repeated pattern of immigration will never be complete, any more than a self which can always be remade will ever be fully finished, except in death. Alexis de Tocqueville's comment on the average American of Andrew Jackson's day still rings true: "Death at length overtakes him, but it is before he is weary of his bootless chase of that complete felicity which forever escapes him" (1945, 145). Our unfinished society, the proper domain for our unfinished selves, is itself the inevitable product of the very act of immigration. In leaving the European hamlet, the African kraal, or Asian village, the immigrant left behind not merely friends and relations. He/she left structure, discipline, form, and context. What was not dictated by the state was set by tradition: what to eat, how to dress, whom to marry, how to earn a living, what to think, even the name and face of God. Although the immigrants willingly left much of the baggage of tradition behind, they did try to bring some of their Old World culture with them. No matter. Plants and animals, pests and people may be sometimes successfully transplanted from one place to another. Forms, customs, and mentalities, however, rarely flourish unaltered in alien ground, especially, as in the New World, where the cultural soil is cultivated to produce freedom from, not adherence to, tradition.

Even when groups came to America for the expressed purpose of establishing their European-conceived institutions and social structures, they found that the New World could be unexpectedly inhospitable to even the most radical designs of the Old. Free to make concrete their Old World dreams, immigrants and their children were also free to abandon them for other, very different dreams.

The example of the New England Puritans is paradigmatic. The in-gathering of the Saints in their transplanted English villages began to dissipate even during the first generation as farmers first moved their barns to the fields outside the village and then moved their houses out to the barns beyond the immediate and never-tiring gaze of the congregation (Lockridge 1970, 83). On the theological side, in the seemingly limitless atmosphere of America, the doctrine of predestination, which had appeared so dynamic and revolutionary back in Europe, came to appear gloomy and eventually undemocratic. It seemed more American for the individual to choose salvation than to have God, like an Old World despot, decide such matters Himself. In America, the Old Lights eternally give way to New Lights; congregations fragment; new sects and denominations appear, even new religions establish themselves, only to produce in turn their own set of "come-outers."

As individuals migrate, physically and culturally, from their immigrant beachheads, the institutions they or their parents bring with them, or invent in America, also change, some evolving in unexpected ways. The path from Puritanism to Congregationalism to Unitarianism may be an extreme case in point. Yet even those institutions which do not fragment, or stray too far beyond their original concepts, can accumulate a great deal of unanticipated internal diversity. The Roman Catholic Church has shown a remarkable ability to maintain its structure and cohesion while absorbing vast numbers of people representing many ethnic groups. Yet, today the Church enjoys a greater amount of internal debate on important issues than do some Protestant denominations.[3] These "American" qualities set it dramatically apart from large sections of the Church in other countries.

It was once fashionable among American historians to attribute the ever-changing nature of our institutions to factors indigenous to the New World: the abundance of "empty" land and the unstructured nature of the frontier. Such factors are certainly important. Yet given a culture whose primal, endlessly repeated founding act has been the immigrant's physical rejection of the past for an unrealized, even indefinable future, what else but constant change and diversity could define it? Even if all of the immigrants to America had been only English Puritans or Irish Catholics or German Lutherans or Russian Jews, the basic character of American life probably would have been much the same as it is today.

Admittedly, it is hard to imagine an America settled exclusively by blond, blue-eyed Swedes recapitulating the degree of diversity which immigrants from almost every place on earth have produced here. We are one of the most diverse nations (as opposed to empires) in history – a great historical joke on immigrants and American-born alike. Almost no one comes to America for the joy of interacting with other races and other faiths. Nor do many native-born Americans rise in the morning praying that they may hear yet one more accent, see yet one more strange face. This is the paradox of both immigration and internal migration: one leaves home to promote one's self interest (less often, the interests of one's group) and, sooner or later, comes face to face with multiples of the "Other." The cream of this jest is that if the immigrant were not a minority before coming here, he might suddenly find such status bestowed upon him on arrival.

Diversity – pluralism, multiculturalism, whatever we call it – is the unanticipated, unplanned bonus of American immigration. However, we have been slow to appreciate this gift and to incorporate our appreciation of it into our culture. Discrimination, both in the sense of recognizing difference and of treating those who are different unequally, became a common feature of American life early in our history – not that discrimination or prejudice are peculiarly American phenomena, as a glance at today's headlines will demonstrate. And while the tensions and conflicts arising from competition among groups certainly lie at the center of our culture, other countries are even more fixated upon "the Other." Consider

Northern Ireland or Israel or South Africa or Bosnia. Unique to America is the amazing variety of people and the number of factors involved in our diversity. We Americans constantly adjust and readjust the boundaries between "us" and an ever evolving sea of "thems."

E pluribus unum is a simple concept when applied to a box of marbles. It becomes more problematic when applied to a diverse population that must somehow function as a society and share something of a common culture. At the beginning of this century the apparent resolution to the tensions between homogeneity and heterogeneity lay in conformity, encouraged or enforced, to a white, Anglo-Saxon, Protestant, middle-class America as defined by the male members of the "dominant" group. Diversity was at best a bewildering variety of paths that, nevertheless, were supposed to converge at the common caldron of Americanism. However, the famous "melting pot" was expected to produce only a white broth; it was never intended for peoples for color.[4]

The "liberal" culture that began to take shape during the 1930s sought to replace unity through conformity with an assumed unity of purpose. Accordingly, ethnic pluralism was to be tolerated for two reasons. First, regardless of their apparent differences, all Americans supposedly shared the same socioeconomic goals: jobs, homes, education for the kids, etc. They would, then, work together to realize their mutually held dreams. Then, as economic differences between Americans narrowed, so would the cultural differences which divided them because (and here the liberals were a bit circumspect) the bases for these differences – religion and Old World customs – were not *that* important. Jews, for example, could enter the social and economic mainstream of the American life because, as they did so, they would leave behind the more extreme manifestations of their Jewishness. Broad-brimmed black hats, beards, and pasachs were fine for the Hassidim – religious exotics who, like their Christian counterpart, the Amish, had a right to remain on the social fringe if they wished. But surely, those choosing to enter the mainstream would voluntarily give up extremes of dress, behavior, and belief. Many liberals were probably never aware of the extent to which they assumed that WASP-dom dethroned would reappear as a culture of choice among a broadened middle class of diverse ethnic backgrounds. And again, non-whites were not high on this agenda.

In the 1950s, African Americans, descendants of our most prominent *involuntary* immigrant population, insisted that liberal practice, as well as theory, break down the walls of racism. Yet, a decade later, as Blacks strove to enter the mainstream, they passed an outflow of middle-class white kids embarked on a cultural migration to an uncharted land of absolute freedom, a kind of America of the imagination. Almost religiously hirsute, and much more bizarrely dressed than their immigrant grandparents when they landed here at the turn of the century, the hippies and yippies of the 1960s helped extend the debate about diversity beyond questions of ethnic equality and economic opportunity. Feminists then took up the debate, and by the end of the 1970s the concept of diversity was beginning to include respect for cultural difference. Today, our ideas of multiculturalism have broadened to include issues of gender, sexual preference, lifestyle, physical and mental disability, even philosophy and morals, as well as race.

While we debate whether or not to celebrate the fact that Heather has two mommies, the whole process of diversification continues. New immigrants, legal and illegal, arrive from Asia, Africa, Latin America, and the Middle East, as well as from Europe. According to the 1990 census, one in twelve Americans is foreign born (Roberts 1993, 64). And the convection current of the American-born continues, circulating from East to West, North to South, and back again. We denounce yet again the tyranny of the past, leave the old worlds of family, faith, habit, or convention for the liberating promise of the future. As a result, America continues to be new and unfamiliar, even to those of us whose families have been here for generations. Responding to continual change and defending ourselves against it, we go on generating new organizations, new therapies, new lifestyles, new religions, as, inevitably, new minorities appear to assert new rights.

Today we try out new metaphors to help us grasp the nature of our continually evolving society. With the idea of the melting pot overturned, we speak of America as a "tossed salad" or a "smorgasbord," metaphors at once inclusive (everyone can be in the salad or on the table) and exclusive (the borscht is here, the tamales there, and don't dribble sour cream on the collard greens). As we near the end of this century, we search for the sources that will unite us while honoring diversity. How to spin unity out of diversity has been the primary dilemma of our immigrant nation and will remain so. Our task may be lightened somewhat if we can keep in mind that it is the ongoing effort to find unity, while respecting differences, that defines us as a people. As Werner Sollors suggests in *Beyond Ethnicity*, "Americanness" is achieved "at the point of its emergence, and how it is established again and again as new-comers and outsiders are socialized into the culture – a process which inevitably seems to revitalize the culture at the same time" (1986, 7).

In arguing for the centrality of immigration to the American experience, I am not suggesting that the whole of American history and culture can be explained solely in terms of immigration. There is a point at which the forces suggested in this essay so interact with other basic patterns of our culture that the imprint of immigration blurs and may seem lost amid a welter of other factors. Never-theless, in our leave taking and our arriving; in our loss and our discovery; in our rejection of the past and our embrace of the future; in our surrender of the familiar and our confrontation with the new – in our bewildered efforts to see in the mirror of our endless diversity the unifying effects of sharing this strange national experience – in all of this we can discern the patterns of immigration deep within our culture, deep within ourselves.

Notes

1 Movements of African Americans within the South and the North still tend to be toward the cities. However, the recent movement of Blacks *back* into the South has been toward nonmetropolitan areas (Fosler 1990, 72–3).
2 According to Sam Roberts, "Since 1960, nine in ten American households packed up for another home." In the years following World War II, one fifth of Americans moved annually. This percentage has been slowly declining. In 1990, one sixth of the nation changed houses (1993, 136–7).
3 In his 1977 book on American Catholicism, Andrew Greeley predicted that diversity of opinion within the church, especially on the issue of contra-ception, might result in the "emergence of many different styles of affilia-tion" within the Catholic community (150).
4 See John Higham's essay, "Ethnic Pluralism in American Thought" (1984).

References

Crèvecoeur, J. Hector St. John de, *Letters from an American Farmer*, New York: Dutton, 1957.
Fosler, R. Scott, et al. *Demographic Change and the American Future*. Pittsburgh: University of Pittsburgh, 1990.
Greeley, Andrew. *The American Catholic: A Social Portrait*. New York: Basic Books, 1977.
Higham, John, *Send These to Me: Immigrants in Urban America*. Rev. ed. Balti-more: The Johns Hopkins Press, 1984.
——"Immigration." In *The Comparative Approach to American History*, edited by C. Vann Woodward. New York: Basic Books, 1968.

Lockridge, Kenneth A. *A New England Town: The First Hundred Years: Dedham, Massachusetts, 1636–1736*. New York: W. W. Norton, 1970.

Maslow, Abraham H. *Toward a Psychology of Being*. 2nd edn. New York: Van Nostrand Reinhold, 1965.

Pickard, Jerome, "Appalachia's Decade of Change: A Decade of Immigration." *Appalachia: Social Contest Past and Present*. 3rd edn. Edited by Bruce Ergood and Bruce E. Kure. Athens: Ohio University, 1991.

Pierson, George W. "Mobility." In *The Comparative Approach to American History*. Edited by C. Vann Woodward. New York: Basic Books, 1968.

Roberts, Sam. *Who We Are: A Portrait of America Based on the Latest US Census*. New York: Random House, 1993.

Sollors, Werner, *Beyond Ethnicity: Consent and Descent in American Culture*. New York: Oxford University, 1986.

Tocqueville, Alexis de *Democracy in America*. Trans. by Henry Reeve. Edited by Phillips Bradley. Vol 2. New York: Vintage, 1945.

2 What Is An American? Ethnicity, Race, the Constitution and the Immigrant in Early American History

Roger Daniels

Perhaps the most persistent rhetorical question in our history is, What is an American? The most famous – and misleading – answer to that question was published in the year before the American Revolution ended. Its French author, a Norman petty nobleman, Michael-Guillaume-Jean de Crèvecoeur (1735–1813), is a most curious person for Americans to accept as a definer of their nationality, but it has become almost obligatory to do so. Crèvecoeur came to America with the French army and, after Montcalm's defeat, toured extensively in the British colonies and settled and was naturalized in Orange County in upstate New York. A Loyalist during the Revolution, he abandoned the United States in 1780, although his book, published two years later under his American pseudonym, J. Hector St. John, was titled *Letters from an American Farmer*. In 1783 he returned to the United States as French consul in New York, where he stayed for seven years before returning permanently to France. In the most quoted passage in his book he asked:

> What then is the American, this new man? He is either an European or the descendant of an European, hence that strange mixture of blood, which you will find in no other country. I could point out to you a family whose grandfather was an Englishman, whose wife was Dutch, whose son married a French woman, and whose present four sons have now four wives of different nations. *He* is an American, who, leaving behind him all his ancient prejudices and manners, receives new ones from the new mode of life he has embraced, the new government he obeys, and the new rank he holds. He becomes

an American by being received in the broad lap of our *Alma Mater*. Here individuals of all races are melted into a new race of men, whose labours and posterity will one day cause great changes in the world.

Although even casual students of intellectual history will recognize that effusion as a product of French romanticism rather than American experience, it is easy to see why it became and has remained so popular. In the first place it was flattering – "will one day cause great changes in the world" – and, to later generations, the almost uncanny prefiguration of the myth of the melting pot makes Crèvecoeur seem prophetic. The polyethnic family he describes, while certainly possible, especially in New York, was clearly not representative. And the notion that an immigrant could shed his culture the way a snake sheds his skin is nonsense. More than a century later a lesser known immigrant from Romania, Marcus Eli Ravage (1884–1965) wrote a much more realistic analysis of the problem of acculturation.[1]

> The alien who comes here from Europe is not the raw material that Americans suppose him to be. He is not a blank sheet to be written on as you see fit. He has not sprung out of nowhere. Quite the contrary. He brings with him a deep-rooted tradition, a system of culture and tastes and habits – a point of view which is as ancient as his national experience and which has been engendered in him by his race and his environment. And it is this thing – this entire Old World soul of his – that comes into conflict with America as soon as he has landed.

Neither of these nearly polar views is, of course, a substitute for modern social analysis. During the eighteenth century and before, there was an intermediate step between being a European and an American: It was being a colonial. Nicholas Canny and Anthony Pagden have analyzed what they call the development of "colonial identity in the Atlantic world" in the three centuries before 1800. They describe a process in which colonizing individuals and groups come to see themselves as distinct and different *both* from people back home and from indigenous persons in the place of settlement. Thus Lowland Scots transplanted to England's first plantation in Ireland quickly differentiated themselves from stay-at-home Scots on the one hand and the native Irish on the other.[2] Yet if we imagine two immigrant Ulstermen, one Presbyterian Scotch Irish and the other Catholic Irish, on the Carolina frontier in the 1760s, both would be likely to make primary distinctions, not between themselves, but between settlers and Indians, between settlers and slaves, and perhaps between backcountry people and coastal gentry.

This is not to say that there was no ethnic conflict in the colonies or that it was not important. Maldwyn Jones was correct in devoting an entire chapter of his survey, *American Immigration* (1960), to what he called "Ethnic Discord, 1685–1790."[3] But before we discuss and detail that discord, we must spend some time looking more closely at the attitudes of the most numerous ethnic group in the American colonies, the English.

English Attitudes

Toward the end of the seventeenth century, probably about 90 percent of all the settlers in British North America were of English birth or descent. The development of African slavery and the increased immigration of non-English groups caused this percentage to drop steadily, so that, as we have seen, by the first census a century later, that percentage was down to 48 percent of the total, 60 percent of the white population. In two of the original states, New Jersey and Pennsylvania, English were actually a minority of the white population, an estimated 47 percent in New Jersey and barely more than a third – 35 percent – in Pennsylvania. There the minority English founded immigrant protective societies: In Philadelphia in 1772 self-conscious English residents founded the Society of Sons of St. George for the "Advice and Assistance of Englishmen in Distress," emulating similar organizations founded there by Scots (1749), Irish (1759), and Germans (1766). Majorities, or those who psychologically feel themselves to be majorities, don't really need to organize, and nowhere else in colonial America were such groups established by English people. Even in the nineteenth and twentieth centuries, new English immigrants organized few such groups.

The dominance of English culture and institutions was even more overwhelming than that of English and English-descended persons: language, law, the predominance of English and later British economic power, were overwhelming, and have left indelible marks on American society. But very soon after settlement began native-born Americans – second-generation English Americans – came to outnumber the immigrant generation, the founding fathers and mothers. In New England, for example, the most English part of the American colonies, there was relatively little immigration from anywhere after the English Civil War of the mid-seventeenth century, and the tremendous population increase in New England from less than twenty-five thousand in 1650 to just over a million at the first census is almost entirely due to natural increase. All things considered there may have been as much or more emigration from New England as immigration to it in that period. Whole groups, as we have seen, went to Long Island (and to other parts of New York), some individuals, the most famous of whom was Benjamin Franklin, went to other colonies or to Great Britain and, in the aftermath of the Revolution, many Loyalist exiles found havens in Canada and England.

It is quite clear that, even before the Revolution produced a crisis in loyalty, there were conflicting claims of loyalty for most English Americans and a colonial identity was evolving. On the one hand, persons who had never seen it referred to England as "home," and among the elite, education in England – at the Inns of Court, for example – and travel there, were common. On the other hand, the very different conditions of American life, differing views of what today we call national security, and, eventually, economic conflict all helped to produce an American, as opposed to an English American, outlook. These differences, as we shall see, came to a head during and after the American Revolution, which has been called the crucible of American nationalism. But less than twenty years before the Revolution a fourth-generation English American like John Adams (1735–1826) could refer to himself enthusiastically as a "British American," a description he would avoid once the Revolution began.

But long before the Revolution began – in fact, from the earliest days of English colonization – there were conflicts between English and other groups and between non-English groups in the colonies. For convenience we can divide these into "race relations" and "ethnic relations." The term *race relations* sounds modern and is in fact of twentieth-century coinage, but the fact of race relations, between English and Indians, between English and blacks, and, eventually, between all whites and Indians and blacks, was a fundamental if largely ignored aspect of colonial life.

Race Relations

The relationships between European settlers and Native Americans can be described in a very narrow spectrum. Early on, in Jamestown, Plymouth, and elsewhere, the settlers learned essential agricultural techniques from Indians, techniques that were probably crucial to their survival. Soon after the initial peaceful coexistence, conflict broke out, usually stemming from Indian resistance to white aggrandizement. The conflicts usually resulted either in the extermination of the Indians of a given locality or their expulsion to the west. In Massachusetts what we can call proto-Indian reservations – areas in which the remaining Indians were to be segregated – were developed as early as the mid-seventeenth century. The colonists called such places "Indian plantations," "Indian villages," or "praying towns." As the last designation suggests, Christianization was often part of the "taming" process.

Until very recently, most of what writing there has been about Indian-white relations in the Colonial Era – and after – had assumed, implicitly or explicitly, that however brutal and rapacious most whites in direct contact with Indians had been, the purposes of the missionaries who went among them were benign and benevolent. The path-breaking work of Robert Berkhofer a quarter century ago has destroyed this notion: he, and a number of other scholars since, have shown clearly that Christian missionaries had little regard – to put it mildly – for the Indian's culture and that they consciously advanced the political and economic goals of settler society.[4] From John Eliot (1604–90), the Puritan "apostle to the Indians," through the recently canonized Junipero Serra (1713–84), who established missions in California, the martyred Marcus and Narcissa Whitman (1847), missionary-settlers in Oregon, and the clerical reformers who helped the federal government run its reservations in the late nineteenth and early twentieth centuries, there persisted one constant demand: that Indians cease being Indians, that they commit cultural suicide, or what has been termed ethnocide. This racial policy established a fateful pattern for American ethnic relations. In years to come this same kind of demand – what has been called the demand for Anglo-conformity – would be made of European ethnic groups: assimilate on the terms of the prevailing norms.

Not surprisingly, some Indians were enslaved, and although the subject has been little studied, Indian slavery in North America seems to have been practiced most extensively in South Carolina. Even there, however, it did not last long. Since Indian wars, smallpox, and other epidemics greatly reduced the available Indian population, the number of Indian slaves fell drastically after 1719, and African slavery came to dominate. Reliable data are hard to come by. One report of the governor and council in 1708 lists 4,080 whites – 3,960 free and 120 servants; 4,100 Negro slaves – 1,800 men, 1,100 women, and 1,200 children; and 1,400 Indian slaves – 500 men, 600 women, and 300 children. Thus slaves were 57 percent of the population, and a quarter of the slaves were Indians. The leading student of the subject, John Donald Duncan, has counted the advertisements about slaves in the *South Carolina Gazette* for a period beginning in 1732. In the next ten years some 3,343 Negroes, 15 white servants, and only 4 Indians were advertised for sale; during 1732–52 the paper ran ads seeking the return of 678 runaway blacks, 191 whites, and 14 Indians. Clearly Indian slavery was no longer a statistically significant factor; nonetheless it had existed and is but another indication of the state of race relations in the American colonies.[5]

White-black race relations, of course, are even less ambiguous; Christian missionaries were not much interested in black souls, although most masters did see that their slaves became Christianized. Unlike Indians, who were largely sloughed off – the Constitution's dismissive "excluding Indians not taxed" is typical – Negro slavery and thus white-black race relations were very much a matter of law. Although the English common law did not recognize slavery and in the celebrated Somerset case, Lord Mansfield, a British judge, ruled in 1772 that all slaves held in England must be set free, with the double standard that came to characterize British imperialism on racial matters, slavery in British colonies took on the full color of law.[6] Slavery existed in the North and South from the seventeenth century, but only in the states from Delaware south were elaborate slave codes developed. While in the southern states slaves, whether red or black, were primarily rural and, as we have seen, of increasing and eventually paramount importance in southern agriculture, in the North slaves and free blacks were almost all urban residents. Only in very recent years have historians, most significantly Gary Nash, begun to explore the dimensions of black life in northern cities before the Civil War. In only one northern city, New York, was slavery well established. In 1740, when the city's population was some 12,000 there were about 2,000 slaves, one-sixth of the population. New York's brief slave code was nearly as strict as those of the Deep South, and it was in New York that the most appalling atrocity of northern urban race relations of the colonial period occurred: the so-called New York slave revolt of 1741. As a result of judicial proceedings that lasted more than a year, 150 slaves were imprisoned, 18 hanged, 13 burned, and more than 70 shipped to the West Indies; since the "conspiracy" supposedly involved a Negro-Catholic plot to take over the city, 25 whites were also imprisoned and four of them hanged. Was there a revolt? Probably not. The pioneer Negro historian George Washington Williams wrote in 1883 that it was "one of the most tragic events in all the history of New York or the civilized world."[7] Contemporary historical opinion is more likely to doubt the conspiracy while recognizing that there were criminal elements at work. Much of the evidence involved a series of arsons that were used as a cover for burglaries. As in most conspiracies, real and imagined, the testimony of co-conspirators was vital. New York had had a real slave rebellion in 1712, in which nine whites were killed, which probably helped account for the degree of hysteria.[8] But perhaps the most instructive thing about the 1741 slave revolt is the way in which this example of mass hysteria has been almost totally ignored, except by specialists, as opposed to the continuous examination and reexamination of the other great example of colonial hysteria – the Salem witchcraft trials of 1692 – the details of which are known, as Macaulay would say, by every schoolboy. The American mythos does not include the notion of race relations in the colonial North, although religious hysteria is admissible.

No full account of the majority of black Americans in colonial cities who were not slaves can be given here, but their status can be summarized: They were neither slave nor free. In Massachusetts, where there may have been 1,300 blacks in a population of 62,000 in 1710 – about 2 percent – a number of laws regulating black behavior had been enacted by then. Black slaves and servants – along with similarly enslaved Indians and mulattoes – were subject to curfew; interracial marriage and sexual intercourse between blacks and whites were forbidden, and free Negroes were forbidden to entertain or harbor nonwhite servants in their homes without the consent of the latter's masters. Yet free blacks could testify in courts, own and transfer property, and were otherwise given status by the law. Since assimilationist pressures upon blacks were largely absent in both North and South, the direct analogy with treatment of European immigrants does not exist. But when, in the mid-nineteenth century, immigrants began to come from Asia in significant numbers, the same kinds of patterns of race relations developed in the Far West as had existed on the East Coast. It also seems clear that having long-established discriminatory legal codes of behavior to govern race relations made discriminatory ethnic relations seem more "natural."

Ethnic Relations

During the era of the American Revolution – as in other great crises in our history – ethnic differences were played down. In the *Federalist Papers*, for example, John Jay was thankful that

> Providence [had] been pleased to give this one connected country to one united people – a people descended from the same ancestors, speaking the same language, professing the same religion, attached to the same principles of government, very similar in their manners and customs.

As we have seen, this was nonsense, and New Yorker John Jay (1745–1829) knew it better than most: He not only lived in the polyglot city but was himself of Huguenot ancestry. In the nearly two centuries before the Revolution, the attitudes of the predominant English Americans blew hot and cold about "foreign immigrants," prefiguring an ambivalence that has continued to prevail in American society up to the present day.

We must not imagine that there was a uniform ethnic attitude among the English-descended colonists: Differences of geography and class were also important, as were differences of religion. Attitudes in Massachusetts were not the same as those in South Carolina; an employer of indentured labor would not have the same views as a wage earner. A member of a religious minority would often be more tolerant of "strangers" than would a member of whichever group happened to constitute the local majority religion.

But there were similarities, the most fundamental of which was an emergent and growing English nationalism, which, especially when mixed with militant Protestantism, produced an extreme cultural arrogance. While English Americans in the colonial period at one time or another expressed hostility toward every other European ethnic group present in North America, the greatest and most long-lasting animus was directed, not surprisingly, against the two largest such groups: the Irish and the Germans.

Prejudice against the Irish was more general, if for no other reason than the fact that Irish were distributed throughout the colonies and the Germans more concentrated. Even in Massachusetts, where 90 percent of the ethnically identifiable white people were believed to be of English descent, some 4 percent of the same population – fifteen thousand persons – were believed to be of Irish heritage. There were at most, twelve hundred persons of German origin or heritage in a state that had nearly three hundred seventy-five thousand inhabitants. The widespread prejudice against the Irish was, as we have seen, unmixed with distinctions about where in Ireland they hailed from: Persons who today would be classified as Scotch (or Ulster) Irish, southern Irish, or English Irish were all just Irish to eighteenth-century Americans. Yet we must understand that this prejudice was not reflected in statute law. Except for the anti-Catholic legislation, which at one time or another existed on the statute books of every colony – even, as we have seen, in Maryland – no legal distinctions were made among free white persons. We must also remember that much of the anti-Catholicism of colonial America was, by definition, rhetorical. Since there were by the end of the era only about twenty-five thousand practicing Catholics in the colonies – and almost all of those in Pennsylvania and Maryland – most Americans had never seen a Catholic, which perhaps made them all the more frightening when they did begin to come a couple of generations later.

Discrimination against Germans was another matter: Its focus was, naturally enough, in Pennsylvania, where Germans were a third or more of the population from the middle of the eighteenth century. John Higham has argued that "the first major ethnic crisis American history" involved the Pennsylvania Germans whose settlements seemed to be an unassimilable alien bloc to many of Pennsylvania's non-German majority. Included among the latter was Benjamin Franklin, who, it could be argued, was a founding father of non-religious American nativism. His complaints about "German boors" are notorious and his only-half-humorous suggestion that his fellow English-speaking Pennsylvanians learn German so that they would not become strangers in their native land sounds very much like the anti-Spanish arguments of the zealots of the contemporary organization called U.S. English.

Franklin, who tried to boss colonial Pennsylvania politics, was angry with the Germans because, in one of the earliest examples of ethnic bloc voting in our history, they had voted the wrong way and supported his enemies in a series of elections. The Philadelphia German Lutheran leader, Henry M. Mühlenberg, described the marshaling of ethnic voters in one colonial election: Some six hundred German voters assembled at the German schoolhouse and then "marched in procession to the *courthouse* to cast their votes."[9] Franklin's pamphlet, *Observations Concerning the Increase of Mankind* (1751), shows him not only anti-German but, like so many of his fellow Americans, imbued with a broad racism.[10]

> Why should the Palatine Boors be suffered to swarm into our Settlements, and by herding together establish their Language and Manners to the Exclusion of ours? Why should Pennsylvania, founded by the English, become a Colony of *Aliens*, who will shortly be so numerous as to Germanize us instead of our Anglifying them, and will never adopt our Language or Customs, any more than they can acquire our Complexion.
>
> Which leads me to add one Remark: That the Number of purely white People in the World is proportionally very small. All Africa is black or tawney. Asia chiefly tawney. America (exclusive of the new Comers) wholly so. And in Europe, the Spaniards, Italians, French, Russians and Swedes, are generally of what we call a swarthy Complexion; as are Germans also, the Saxons only accepted, who with the English, make the principal Body of White People on the Face of the Earth. I could wish their numbers were increased. And while we are, as I may call it, *Scouring* our Planet, by clearing America of Woods, and so making this side of our Globe reflect a brigher Light to the eyes of Inhabitants of Mars or Venus, why should we in the Sight of Superior Beings, darken its people? Why increase the Sons of Africa, by Planting them in America, where we have so fair an Opportunity, by excluding all Blacks and Tawneys, of increasing the lovely White and Red? But perhaps I am partial to the Complexion of my Country, for such Kind of Partiality is Natural to Mankind.

Nor were Germans the only ethnic target group in Pennsylvania. The Quaker establishment, Gary Nash tells us, was particularly concerned, not about the Germans who were often its allies, but about the Scotch Irish, who they feared would take over the colony. Quaker pamphleteers attacked Presbyterians complaining of an almost global conspiracy, "a perpetual Presbyterian holy war against the mild and beneficent government of the Kings of England."[11] The Scotch Irish, in turn, attacked Germans and Quakers, as, among other things, being soft on Indians.

Other kinds of ethnic resentments found their way into the language: The phrase "Dutch treat" – meaning no treat at all – for example, describes the alleged stinginess of the Dutch and probably expressed resentment at their generally superior status – they had, after all, got in on the ground floor – in New York and New Jersey.

That there was not more ethnic conflict than there was may well be attributable, as George Frederickson and Dale T. Knobel have suggested, to the fact that so many of the non-English were on the frontier: "Physical space effectively inhibited interethnic tension or at least impeded active discrimination against disapproved minorities."[12]

In any event, John Jay's propaganda about ethnic unity to the contrary, there was significant ethnic discord before the American Revolution. And although the Revolution is, quite properly, viewed as the crucible of American nationality, it also created important fracture lines not only in the American people but in every ethnic group in the new nation.

The most obvious evidence of these fractures is the incidence of emigration from the new United States, emigration being the most profoundly un-American act that one can imagine. Although American historians have enjoyed dwelling on the consensual nature of American society in general and the American Revolution in particular, proportionally speaking, the eighty to one hundred thousand persons who fled the country – mostly to Canada or Britain – were a larger segment of the American people than the perhaps half a million who left France after 1789 were of the French people. The American loyalists, in addition, helped to ensure that Canada would not be drawn into the political orbit of the new nation. As we have seen in the last chapter, loyalists came from many ethnic groups, and non-English or English-descended persons may well have been overrepresented among them. Very recent – post-1763 – immigrants certainly were. Some twenty-eight thousand of various ethnicities went to Nova Scotia, most of them taken to Halifax by British ships. Scots Highlanders, from the Mohawk Valley and elsewhere, who had fought on the losing side, were settled *en bloc* in what they named Glengarry County in Ontario; smaller ethnic enclaves were created by Scots Presbyterians, Dutch, and Germans, who each settled along the Saint Lawrence or on the shores of Lake Ontario. There were Huguenot and Jewish loyalists as well; particularly notable were the De Lanceys of New York who fled to Canada and whose vast estates were seized.[13]

The revolutionaries not only tried to play down ethnic discord, but sometimes wrote as if no ethnic differences existed. Jefferson, in the Declaration of Independence, spoke blithely of "one people," prefiguring Jay's line in *The Federalist*, and in the Declaration of the Causes and Necessity of Taking Up Arms of a year earlier, which he coauthored with John Dickinson, a bald reference was made to

"our forefathers, inhabitants of the island of Great-Britain."
(George Washington, in his 1796 Farewell Address, partially
written by the West Indian-born Alexander Hamilton, was more
circumspect: He used the "one people" line but carefully noted
that Americans were either "citizens by birth or choice of a common country" and that, "with slight shades of difference," they
had "the same religion, manners, habits, and political principles.")

Jefferson did make reference to immigration in the Declaration.
Part of his bill of particulars against "the present King of Great
Britain" was that "[h]e has endeavored to prevent the population
of these States; for that purpose obstructing the Laws of Naturalization of Foreigners; refusing to pass others to encourage their
migration hither." He also commented on race relations, making
it clear that his United States was a white man's country, further
charging that the king had excited "domestic insurrections amongst
us, and has endeavoured to bring on the inhabitants of our
frontiers, the merciless Indian Savages, whose known rule of
warfare, is an undistinguished destruction of all ages, sexes and
conditions."

Immigrants and the Constitution

The revolutionary consensus continued into the era of the Constitution. The Articles of Confederation, agreed to in 1777 and
adopted in 1781, did not deal with the crucial questions of immigration, naturalization, and citizenship, but provided only in Article
4, that "the free inhabitants" of each state "shall be entitled to all
privileges and immunities" in other states, "paupers, vagabonds
and fugitives from Justice excepted." (The right of poor migrants
to cross state lines would not be fully established until the Supreme
Court's ruling in *Edwards* v. *California* in 1941.)

The Constitution, ratified in 1788, was more specific. Its only
direct mention of immigration – and the only direct mention to
date, as immigration is not discussed in any of the amendments –
referred to a very special kind of migration, the slave trade. In Article
1, Section 9, dealing with the powers of Congress, it provided:

> The Migration or Importation of such Persons as any of the States
> now existing shall think proper to admit, shall not be prohibited by
> the Congress prior to the Year one thousand eight hundred and

eight, but a Tax or duty may be imposed on such Importation not exceeding ten dollars for each person.

The words *slave* and *slavery* do not appear in the original Constitution, although the subject was a bone of contention at the Constitutional Convention. In the famous three-fifths compromise, slaves are "other persons." Gouverneur Morris (1752–1816), who did the final polishing of the language, did not approve of slavery and kept that word out. He did permit the word "Indian" to be used. "Slavery" only appears in the Thirteenth Amendment (1865), which abolished the institution. Congress did abolish the slave trade as quickly as it legally could, in March 1807. Jefferson had invited it to do so in his message of December 1806:

> I congratulate you, fellow-citizens, on the approach of the period at which you may interpose your authority constitutionally to withdraw the citizens of the United States from all further participation in those violations of human rights which have been so long continued on the unoffending inhabitants of Africa!

Despite the prohibition, perhaps fifty thousand slaves were illegally imported from Africa and elsewhere in the New World after the 1807 prohibition.

The Constitution also empowered Congress, in Article 1, Section 7, "to establish an uniform Rule of Naturalization" but provided no particulars, so that naturalization has been a kind of political litmus test of the national climate of opinion about immigrants and immigration. The Constitution made certain distinctions between native-born and naturalized citizens. In Article 1, Section 2, it ordained that "no Person shall be a Representative [in Congress] who shall not have...been seven Years a Citizen" and set the requirement higher for senators who had to have been "nine Years a citizen." And Article 2, Section 1, barred any future immigrant from the presidency, restricting that office to "natural born citizens" and persons who were citizens at the time of the Constitution's adoption. This provision, of course, applies to the vice-presidency as well. But rather than emphasizing the negative nature of these provisions, what should be noted is that the founding fathers not only expected immigration to continue but also enabled immigrants to hold all but the very highest office in the land. Immigrants have, in fact, held every office in the American government to which they are eligible, save only Chief Justice of the United States.

Changing Standards of Naturalization

The first Congress in 1790 took advantage of the specific constitutional empowerment and passed a naturalization statute. In keeping with the revolutionary consensus, which was still in effect, it was the most generous in our history, at least for white people who were not indentured servants. It provided that "free white persons" who had been in the United States as little as two years could be naturalized in any American court. However this meant that immigrant blacks – and later immigrant Asians – were not supposed to be naturalized; it said nothing about the citizenship status of persons who were not white and born here: their status, until 1870, would depend on the law in the individual states, as no national citizenship was created until that time. Whether free blacks were citizens or not depended on which state they lived in.[14]

Even more perplexing was the status of American Indians. From the time of Chief Justice John Marshall's decision in the case of *Cherokee Nation* v. *Georgia* (1831), it was established that Indian tribes were, in Marshall's words, "domestic dependent nations," and that Indians therefore were aliens, and not citizens. Marshall based his ruling on the brief but potent commerce clause, part of Article 1, Section 8, which empowered Congress "to regulate Commerce with foreign Nations, and among the several States, and with the Indian Tribes." And since Indians were not "free white persons," they were aliens who could not be naturalized. In practice many states and localities treated acculturated Indians as if they were citizens – allowed them to vote, hold office, and so on – and, as early as the Grant administration, Eli Samuel Parker (1828–95), an American Indian and a former general in the Union Army, held office as commissioner of Indian affairs. In 1887 Congress, in the Dawes Act, conferred citizenship on acculturated Indians not living on reservations, citizenship that many western states and localities refused, in practice, to recognize. Finally, in 1924, Congress made all native-born American Indians citizens.

But the revolutionary consensus soon began to break down as American politics was polarized around those two archetypical figuers, Alexander Hamilton and Thomas Jefferson, and our first political parties, the Federalists and what became known as the

Democratic-Republicans. The Federalists perceived that many of the staunchest supporters of their opponents were recent immigrants from Ireland and France, immigrants who were essentially political exiles in the era of the French Revolution. It was not ordinary immigrants who most concerned the Federalists but, rather, distinguished ones who became anti-Federalist editors and pamphleteers. These included such men as the English scientist Joseph Priestly (1733–1804) and Jefferson's friend Victor Marie Du Pont (1767–1827). The anti-immigrant feeling, which had arisen toward the end of Washington's second term, came to a head during the administration of John Adams (1797–1801) and was exacerbated by the first undeclared war in our history, the so-called quasi war with France of 1798–1800 – which was fought entirely at sea. The second Naturalization Act, in 1795, only five years after the first, increased the necessary period of residence to five years. Three years after that, as part of the package of bills known to history as the Alien and Sedition Acts, the now-desperate Federalists, realizing that they were about to lose political power, required an alien to file a declaration of intention to become a citizen at least five years before becoming a citizen and increased the period of residence to fourteen years. In addition, all aliens were required to register with federal officials. Other parts of the Alien and Sedition package, all of which were enacted in less than a month in the summer of 1798, included the Aliens Act, the Alien Enemies Act, and the Sedition Act (which need not concern us here, as it applied to everyone). The Aliens Act gave the president unlimited power to order out of the country any alien "whom he shall judge dangerous to the peace and safety of the United States." The Alien Enemies Act, which would have gone into effect only if the United States had declared war, empowered the apprehension and confinement of male enemy aliens fourteen years of age and older.[15]

In the event, the Aliens Act was never enforced against anyone, although some who felt threatened left the country and others went into hiding. When the turn of the political tide put the Jeffersonians in power in 1801, they rolled back most, but not all, of the Federalist anti-alien legislation. The Naturalization Act of 1801 restored the residence requirements of 1795 (but not of 1790), and five years has remained the period of residence until this day. The registration requirements of that law were repealed and aliens did not have to register again until 1940, when the United States again felt threatened from abroad. The Aliens Act simply expired, as it had a two-year limit and was never renewed.

Not until the passage of the Internal Security Act of 1950 was a president given power, in peacetime, to incarcerate persons, and that statute applied to citizens as well as aliens. Nor were the Jeffersonians immune from a xenophobia of their own. During the War of 1812, Congress amended the Nationality Act to provide that no British alien who had not declared the intention to become a citizen before the war began could be naturalized – a provision that was repealed after the war was over.

American Nationalism

One can make too much of the xenophobia and prejudice of the revolutionary era and the early republic. The victory in the Revolution produced in the new nation an overwhelming feeling of confidence that all battles could be won, all obstacles overcome. And most Americans were concerned, as Jefferson put it, with "the population of these states" and, to that end, welcomed immigration. When immigration was opposed, it was largely on ideological rather than ethnic or religious grounds. Federalists opposed radical immigrants from England, France, or Ireland; Jeffersonians in Congress, unduly concerned about the migration and settlement here of exiled nobility from France, got a provision put into the 1795 Naturalization Act requiring an applicant for citizenship to foreswear any hereditary titles of nobility.

The very circumstances of the Revolution tended to defuse religious prejudice, at least for a time. Not only were the Americans allied with Catholic France, but they wished to gain the support of French Catholic Quebec. Canada was given pride of place in the Articles of Confederation: It could join the new nation at any time. Any other new adherent was dependent on the agreement of nine states. When the Continental Congress sent a delegation to Canada in a vain attempt to get it to join in the Revolution, its leaders had the wit to persuade the only Catholic signer, Charles Carroll of Carrollton, to join it, and he persuaded his cousin, Father John Carroll, later to become the first American Roman Catholic bishop, to join them. The priest was reluctant, noting in a memorandum that:[16]

> I have observed that when the ministers of religion, leave the duties of their profession to take a busy part in political matters, they generally fall into contempt, and sometimes even bring discredit to the cause in whose service they are engaged.

Later in the Revolution, when the French fleet used Philadelphia as a home port, priests became a common sight on its wharves and streets. On two occasions in Philadelphia, the French minister had Te Deums said in the small Catholic church to celebrate the third anniversary of the Declaration of Independence and the victory at Yorktown. Many members of Congress, even some from pope-hating New England, attended. If they were not more tolerant, at least their public demeanor was.

In addition, the natural-rights philosophy that inspired so many of the leaders of the revolution tended them toward tolerance and nonsectarianism. In the Declaration, Jefferson spoke of "Nature's God"; the more politically minded draftsmen of the Articles of Confederation spoke of "the Great Governor of the World"; and Washington in his first inaugural spoke, appropriately enough for the Father of his Country, of "the benign Parent of the Human Race." These statements by leaders were paralleled by legislative actions. The Virginia and Massachusetts Bills of Rights (1776 and 1780), the Virginia Statute of Religious Liberties (1786) and, above all the "no establishment" clause of the First Amendment ("Congress shall make no law respecting an establishment of religion, or prohibiting the free exercise thereof"), all set a laudable and unprecedented standard of religious liberty – though it was one many or most Americans did not really believe in.

In the revolutionary period and the years immediately afterward, the tolerance and nonsectarianism engendered during and after the struggle for independence were not seriously challenged or put to the test. Relatively few immigrants came – perhaps an average of ten thousand a year from the time of Yorktown to the end of the War of 1812, and the vast majority of these were Protestant Britons. The rapid population growth of those years – it grew more than two and a half times between 1790 and 1820 (3.9 to 9.6 million) – was almost entirely due to natural increase. And, because the nation annexed so much territory during the period, the number of persons per square mile barely increased, going from 4.5 to 5.6.

In these circumstances early American nationalism could be, and was, almost entirely positive. It did not attack – as later aspects of it would – ethnic, national or racial groups or single out certain ideological strands as "un-American." It was, as Philip Gleason has cogently argued, characterized by three elements: its ideological quality, its newness, and its future orientation. Because it was ideological, it did not stress national or ethnic origin or any denomination, although there was, both in rhetoric and in the laws of

many states, a distinct bias toward Christianity. The obvious newness of American nationality – the closeness of most Americans to
the great events of their past – lent it an essentially positive aspect,
while its future orientation – the conviction of most Americans that
the future would not resemble but greatly outstrip the past – only
served to strengthen its positiveness.[17]

Much of this would change in the decades after 1820. Immigration would increase to reach its highest incidence in the mid-
1850s. The bulk of that immigration would not be English but Irish
and German, and much of it would be Catholic. In addition, the
nation would face, in the 1860s, the greatest crisis of its existence.
Under these pressures, one strain of American nationalism would
turn ugly and produce, not the sporadic nativism and xenophobia
of the colonial period, but a full-blown movement that exalted
bigotry to a matter of principle.

Shortly after the end of the War of 1812, John Quincy Adams
(1767–1848) caught the spirit of early American nationalism nicely.
Writing to a European, Adams, who had as much intimate knowledge of Europe as any American of his generation, made this
point:[18]

> That feeling of superiority over other nations which you have
> noticed, and which has been so offensive to other strangers, who
> have visited these shores, arises from a consciousness of every indi-
> vidual that, as a member of society, no man in the country is above
> him; and, exulting in this sentiment, he looks down upon those
> nations where the mass of the people feel themselves the inferiors
> of the privileged classes, and where men are high and low, according
> to the accidents of their birth.

And we should not forget that such sentiments as Adams describes
were not restricted to American natives. Many immigrants quickly
took on the ideological accents of their adopted land. As my mentor,
Theodore Saloutos, one of the pioneers of American immigration
history, used to say, when an immigrant becomes an American
patriot, he is often not satisfied to become a 100 percent American
but tries to be a 200-percenter. Adams, in the letter quoted above,
described how he thought immigrants should behave, echoing, in
some ways, the remarks of Crèvecoeur at the end of the Revolution.

> [Immigrants] must cast off the European skin, never to resume it.
> They must look forward to their posterity rather than backward to
> their ancestors; they must be sure that whatever their own feelings

may be, those of their children will cling to the prejudices of this country.

This hyperassimilationist ideal, as we have seen, was never realistic; immigrants generally died in the skins they were born with. And, while most immigrants were, almost by definition, future oriented, their visions of both the present and the future would be modified significantly by the cultural environment of their past.

Notes

1 Marcus Eli Ravage, *An American in the Making: The Life Story of an Immigrant* (New York, 1917), p. 60 ff.
2 Nicholas Canny and Anthony Pagden, eds., *Colonial Identity in the Atlantic World, 1500–1800* (Princeton, 1988).
3 Maldwyn A. Jones, *American Immigration* (Chicago, 1960).
4 Robert R. Berkhofer, Jr., *Salvation and the Savage* (Lexington, Ky., 1965).
5 John Donald Duncan, "Indian Slavery," in Bruce A. Glasrud and Alan M. Smith, eds., *Race Relations in British North America, 1607–1783* (Chicago, 1982), pp. 85–106.
6 *Somerset* case in Helen Catterall, ed., *Judicial Cases Concerning American Slavery and the Negro* (Washington, D.C., 1926), pp. 4–5.
7 George Washington Williams, *History of the Negro Race in America* (New York, 1882).
8 The best account of the New York slave revolt is Ferenc M. Szasz's "The New York Slave Revolt of 1741: A Re-Examination," *New York History* 48 (1967): 215–30.
9 Henry M. Muhlenberg, as quoted in Gary B. Nash, *The Urban Crucible* (Cambridge, Mass., 1979), p. 509, n. 54.
10 Franklin's pamphlet from Leonard W. Labaree, ed., *The Papers of Benjamin Franklin*, vol. 4 (New Haven, 1961), p. 234.
11 Nash, *Urban Crucible*, p. 284.
12 George M. Frederickson and Dale T. Knobel, "History of Prejudice and Discrimination," *HEAEG*, p. 840.
13 For American loyalism, see Wallace Brown's *The King's Friends* (Providence, R.I., 1965) and Mary Beth Norton's *The British-Americans: The Loyalist Exiles in England, 1774–1789* (New York, 1972).
14 For naturalization, see James H. Kettner's *The Development of American Citizenship, 1607–1870* (Chapel Hill, N.C., 1978).
15 For the Alien and Sedition Acts, see John C. Miller's *Crisis in Freedom* (Boston, 1952).
16 For Bishop Carroll, see John Tracy Ellis's *American Catholicism*, 2nd edn (Chicago, 1969), pp. 36–7.
17 Philip Gleason, "American Identity and Americanization", *HEAEG*.
18 John Quincy Adams, letter of June 4, 1819, cited in Moses Rischin, ed., *Immigration and the American Tradition* (Indianapolis, 1976), pp. 48–9.

3 Immigration: History of U.S. Policy

William S. Bernard

In the nearly four centuries since the English first settled in Jamestown, immigration has been of concern to the makers of public policy. Americans have sought to stimulate and regulate the flow of newcomers in a variety of ways. U.S. immigration policy has been a sensitive barometer both of the achievements and of the problems of national development, for it has been quick to respond to changing economic, political, social, and diplomatic circumstances. The history of American immigration policy falls into five distinct periods: the colonial era (1609–1775); the Open Door era (1776–1881); the era of regulation (1882–1916); the era of restriction (1917–1964); and the era of liberalization (1965 to the present).

The Colonial Period, 1609–1775

In the 17th century the English drive for overseas empire shaped the patterns of immigration and settlement in the North American colonies. The process of peopling the American continent was deliberate and organized, for population was needed to cultivate the virgin lands of the New World – population that would enable colonies to supply raw materials to the mother country and would consume its manufactured goods.

From the early 17th century to the American Revolution, colonial immigration policy was carried out on two levels: on one, the government of the empire – the Crown, Parliament, the Board of Trade – regulated the activities of the North American colonies; on the other, the colonial governments – legislatures, proprietors, and local officials – enacted and enforced laws within the imperial framework. On occasion the two levels came into conflict. In the 1660s, for example, when Parliament approved the transportation of convicted felons to the Chesapeake Bay area – considering that putting them to work in the labor-short colonies was more productive than executing or imprisoning them – the Virginia assembly, fearful of social disturbances, decreed that "no person trading with Virginia, either by land or sea, should bring in any 'jailbirds'." Maryland in 1676 enacted a similar exclusionary law, but Parliament overruled the restrictions, and private contractors continued to arrange the transportation of convicts to those colonies into the 18th century.

On the whole, however, the consensus at both levels of government was that the goal of immigration policy was the recruitment of labor. It was left to colonial governments and entrepreneurs to devise schemes to attract people to the colonies and thereby increase property values, rents, and profits. To do this they advertised the opportunities of the New World to the people of the British Isles and Europe in a variety of ways. In 1609 the Virginia Company launched a publicity drive in London; its advertisements, preached from the pulpits, generated a flurry of gentry investment and volunteering for colonization. In the late 17th century, Anthony Ashley Cooper, the proprietor of the Carolinas, publicized throughout the West Indies and Europe the abundant land and the religious toleration that could be found there. William Penn made Pennsylvania the most widely advertised of all the colonies: he himself went to Europe to supervise recruitment campaigns and distributed hundreds of pamphlets and advertisements in English, French, German, and Dutch announcing that Pennsylvania had given all males the right to vote, had enacted a humane penal code, and required no military service.

Colonial governments provided not only information about, but transportation to, the colonies and subsidized purchase of lands and tools for new settlers as well. The Puritans of Massachusetts Bay helped pay for the transportation, food, and equipment of recruits to their Holy Commonwealth. The Calverts of Maryland, Cooper of the Carolinas, and Penn dipped into family fortunes to stock the colonists with equipment and supplies, and sold land to new arrivals at low prices. By extending this helpful hand to enterprising immigrants, they provided them from the very beginning with a substantial stake in the settlement.

Colonies also offered "bounties" to recruiting agents who provided settlers. As early as 1678 South Carolina was paying bounties to importers of white servants, sometimes to the master of a vessel who brought the newcomers, and sometimes to immigration agents called "importers." These schemes for recruitment and transportation stimulated the first great wave of colonization in the Chesapeake Bay area. The Virginia Company pioneered the practice of indentured servitude, and in the 17th century brought an average of 1,500 bonded laborers each year to the Chesapeake Bay. An indentured servant bound himself to the company or to a planter for four to seven years; in return he received free passage, a year's provisions, a house and tools, and a share of the crops he produced. When his contract expired, he gained all the rights of a freeman and the opportunity to hold title to his own land. In 1619 the company established the "headright" system to promote still more immigration. The headright conferred upon a person a title to 50 acres of uncultivated land upon arrival in Virginia or, if he was already there, for paying the transportation costs of another settler who would discharge the obligation by working on his land.

Dedicated to reforming the English church and to building a regenerate society, the Puritans of the New England colonies limited their recruitment to fellow religious communicants of the gentry, yeoman, tradesman, and artisan classes of England. They sought family men with useful skills who could help build the community; they excluded or expelled itinerants, adventurers, Quakers, and members of other religious sects of which they did not approve. They spurned the mass advertising employed by the proprietary colonies and Virginia, relying for selection instead on the quiet working of religious inspiration. Since the Puritan polity tied civil government to ecclesiastical goals, full political and civil rights were granted only to the members of their church. The Puritan New England colonies were the most socially homogeneous settlements in America; religious orthodoxy functioned both as a process of selection and as a restriction on the numbers who came.

By 1700 nearly all the colonies were employing some combination of advertising, grants of land, employment incentives, transportation payment, and guarantee of rights and freedoms to increase the flow of immigrants; informal naturalization laws permitted aliens to secure freehold land (land without restrictions on transfer) once they had arrived. Like a giant magnet, the colonies drew farmers, workers, artisans, and tradesmen who had been dislodged by a changing European economy. Although the availability of work was the primary inducement, the religious policy of most of the colonies was an additional attraction. Outside New

England's restrictive establishment, toleration of all Christian denominations, and even of Judaism, was gradually established. Some proprietors marked their colonies as havens for particular groups seeking protection from religious persecution: Lord Calvert made Maryland an asylum for England's Catholics; William Penn turned Pennsylvania into a sanctuary for Quakers and others; the strict orthodoxy of New England made its settlements the destination of those seeking an uncompromisingly reformed English church – though even in New England a degree of tolerance had been accorded to non-Congregationalists by 1700. Religious conformity itself declined throughout the 18th century. Without coercive authority, secure leadership, and state sanctions, religion became a matter of choice with little formal relevance to civil status, and religious tests for entry into any of the colonies soon fell into disuse.

The attraction of the New World for non-British groups was increased after 1740 by a major shift in policy toward arriving aliens. Until that year, colonial governments granted deeds of "denization," or naturalization, to aliens that bestowed civil and property-holding rights preliminary to full British citizenship. To speed up settlement, letters of naturalization were even issued to aliens in England. These deeds, however, were not binding upon the imperial government and were often not honored by the colonies. In 1740 Parliament cleared the ambiguous status of aliens by passing a universal naturalization act that made all aliens in the colonies fully naturalized British subjects as soon as they could prove that they had resided continuously on British territory for seven years.

Changes in the land-distribution policy of the colonies in the 18th century further stimulated the flow of newcomers. The head-right system had concentrated an excessive amount of land in the hands of a few prosperous merchants and speculators, so in 1705 the Virginia legislature dismantled the program and introduced a system of direct government sale of land warrants to settlers at low prices; Maryland and the Carolinas soon followed the same course. In New England the practice of deeding land only to acceptable religious groups collapsed under the pressure of popular demand for new uncultivated areas. Land speculators obtained whole townships from the General Court of Massachusetts in the 1720s and, in the 1740s, held public auctions of New England land. The proprietors of the huge virgin land tracts in the Northern Neck of Virginia, the hinterland of Pennsylvania, the Carolinas, and Maryland distributed freehold land at public sales and opened settlement unconditionally to all comers.

Three features of immigration policy that would shape 19th-century patterns were established in the colonial period. First, it was local government that exercised jurisdiction over immigration and settlement. Second, the central government left it to local governments and entrepreneurs to recruit immigrants from other countries. Finally, the increasing demands of economic development led to a search for new sources of labor – a search that would spread in the 19th century into countries unimagined by Tudor Englishmen or colonial planters.

The Open Door Era, 1776–1881

The rejection by the British government of colonial demands for a more open immigration policy to attract newcomers was one of the many grievances that led colonists to take up arms against the British in 1775. The Declaration of Independence attacked the king and the Privy Council for endeavouring "to prevent the population of these states" by refusing to recognize general naturalization acts passed by colonial assemblies and by restricting westward settlement in the Proclamation of 1763 and the Quebec Act of 1774. As the Revolution progressed it also brought with it a new concept of national identity. In their struggle to separate themselves from Englishmen, Americans began to see themselves as a unique people bred from the frontier and from the mingling of several nationalities. The popular writer Tom Paine wrote in 1776, "Europe, and not England, is the parent country of America." By then more than a third of the country's white inhabitants were of non-English origin.

The Philadelphia convention that drafted the Constitution of the United States in 1787 debated the question of immigration. Alexander Hamilton, a West Indian by birth, argued that immigrants could make important contributions to the welfare of the nation and that they should be regarded as "on the level of the first citizens." George Mason of Virginia agreed, saying he "was for opening a wide door for emigrants," but hesitated "to let foreigners... make laws for us and govern us." Pierce Butler of South Carolina and Gouverneur Morris of Pennsylvania feared that immigrants would retain the political principles of the despotic countries they had left behind. Despite these reservations, however, the framers of the Constitution ended by making the foreign-born ineligible only for the presidency; senators had to be citizens for nine years or more, and representatives for seven. Congress was also empowered to establish a uniform naturalization law.

Many leaders of the new republic clearly expected the immigrant to play a major role in the development of the nation. In the Northwest Ordinance of 1787, Congress guaranteed religious freedom in the Northwest Territories, hoping that this liberty would be an added attraction for immigrants. "That part of America which has encouraged [the foreigners] most, has advanced most rapidly in population, agriculture and the arts," observed James Madison, while Hamilton declared that "a perfect equality of religious privileges will probably cause [immigrants] to flock from Europe to the United States," and Assistant Secretary of State Tench Coxe composed notes for the information of the immigrant which endorsed the freedom of religion in the United States and promised that freedom to all.

The American Revolution and the Napoleonic wars hindered the flow of immigration until 1815. In the intervening period Congress passed [1790] the first federal laws loosely defining a uniform rule for the naturalization of aliens: any free white person who resided for two years "within the limits and under the jurisdiction of the United States" could acquire American citizenship. The review of naturalization applications was to be made by "any common law court of record in any one of the States." These generous terms for citizenship and open immigration laid the basis for the massive growth of population that was to follow in the next century.

But the political struggles of the new nation also led to the first, though ultimately unsuccessful, effort to impede the assimilation of newcomers. In 1798 the Federalist party secured the passage of the Alien Act designed to harass immigrants who they suspected might become Republicans, and to deny them the vote by raising the residency requirement for citizenship to 14 years. Three years later, after the Republican victory in the election of 1800, the act was repealed in favor of a 5-year residency requirement.

Authority over immigration continued to be exercised mainly by state governments and local officials until after the Civil War. In practice the regulation of immigrant traffic was assumed by those states having large ports, such as Massachusetts, New York, Pennsylvania, and Maryland. From 1820 to 1860 these states passed laws to reduce the social and financial costs of monitoring immigration. New York, where two-thirds of all newcomers landed, pioneered inspection and welfare laws and required shipmasters to report the name, occupation, birthplace, age, and physical condition of each passenger. On the basis of these reports, the infirm and the destitute who might become wards of the state could be identified and deported. Bond had to be posted for any immigrant suspected of being a potential charity case. New York also charged each shipmaster $1.50 for cabin passengers and $1.00 for those in steerage; the fees paid were used to maintain a marine hospital. Massachusetts ordered shipmasters transporting immigrants to pay $2.00 for each passenger to the city of Boston; those fees were used for support of those foreigners who, after admission, became paupers. To execute these laws the coastal states established immigration boards; run by social reformers and humanitarians who served without pay; their enforcement procedures tended to be casual.

New York's state laws requiring the screening of immigrants were challenged in a landmark U.S. Supreme Court case, *City of New York v. Milne* (1837), in which the defendant Milne, the master of a ship that transported immigrants, argued that the New York regulations were an obstruction of interstate and foreign commerce. The Supreme Court, however, found that the laws derived from the legitimate right of states to exercise police power within their boundaries: "We think it as competent for a State to provide precautionary measures against the moral pestilence of paupers, vagabonds, and possibly convicts, as it is to guard against the physical pestilence which may arise from unsound or infectious articles imported, or from a ship, the crew of which may be laboring under an infectious disease," the opinion read. This decision authorized state governments to set criteria for the suitability of immigrants for admission and to reject arrivals who did not meet their standards.

The processing of new arrivals in the mid-19th century was best exemplified by the procedures used at Castle Garden, the immigration depot of New York City between 1855 and 1890. Converted from a former opera house at the southern tip of Manhattan, Castle Garden provided reception and orientation services, a hospital where sick passengers could recuperate before venturing forth, an inexpensive restaurant, free baths, baggage-carrying services, and a communal kitchen. The commissioners of Castle Garden served without pay, compiling employment listings, arranging for transportation, and even licensing numerous boarding houses to which they could direct immigrants who needed lodging. They gave a brief medical examination to all passengers, recorded names, ages, occupations, religions, and the value of the belongings they brought into the country. Castle Garden was run as if it were a protective charity foundation: it provided safety from swindlers and confidence men, a hospitable reception for the newcomers, practical advice, and social services. The spirit of benevolence guided the welfare workers on its all-volunteer staff.

During the first half of the 19th century the federal government did little to supervise, control, or promote immigration. Federal officials kept no records of immigrants until 1820, when the State Department first began to count the number of immigrant entrants each year. The tasks of recruiting immigrants and adjusting the newcomers to American life when they arrived were assumed by local governments and by entrepreneurs; the federal government simply relied on the open land market and other advantages and opportunities to attract immigrants.

The expanding frontier and industrializing cities continued to demand manpower. Several western states sent brochures and pamphlets overseas describing the opportunities to purchase public land at $1.25 an acre. In 1845 Michigan appointed an agent to recruit immigrants on the docks of New York City. Wisconsin followed suit, and also organized country committees to compile mailing lists of the settlers' friends and relatives still in Europe. Minnesota hired a clerk to draw up mailing lists and to send advertisements to Europe in English, Welsh, German, Dutch, Norwegian, and Swedish; it had a publicity agent covering Sweden and another stationed in Bremen, who visited shipping offices and emigrant boarding houses; and it awarded prizes for the essays that were judged best at describing opportunities in the state for the immigrant. These essays were published in seven languages and distributed in the appropriate countries of Europe.

In the second half of the 19th century, 33 state and territorial governments established immigration offices to attract newcomers. Their pamphlets extolled the virtues of the American frontier and of its allegedly salubrious climate. An Iowa pamphlet of 1870 described the beauty of an Iowan Indian summer; Minnesota pointed out that its death rate was only a fourth or a third of that in Europe. The theme most emphasized, however, was the contrast between American opportunity and European stagnation. The Iowa pamphlet declared that in the Midwest men could become prosperous and independent, while in Europe "the great majority ... must live out their days as dependent labourers on the land of others." Minnesota's pamphlet proclaimed, "It is well to exchange the tyrannies and thankless toil of the old world for the freedom and independence of the new . . . it is well for the hand of labour to bring forth the rich treasures hid in the bosom of the NEW EARTH." The competition for immigrants also inspired a fierce rivalry between states. Wisconsin charged that Minnesota was farther away, had fewer railroads, and more frequent natural disasters. Iowa and Minnesota disparaged the Dakotas, with their locusts, Indians, blizzards, and droughts.

As the flow of arriving immigrants increased, policy makers slowly began to realize that the federal government was going to have to devote greater attention to the new arrivals; in 1855 Congress directed officials of the U.S. Customs Service to compile both quarterly and annual immigration reports. In 1864 Congress passed a bill establishing a Bureau of Immigration, but in 1867 it transferred the job of keeping immigration records to the more technically capable Bureau of Statistics in the Treasury Department.

The first federal attempt at direct promotion of immigration was made in 1864, with a contract-labor law that authorized employers to finance the transportation of immigrant workers and to bind their services in advance, but the measure was repealed in 1868 in the face of protests from labor organizations.

The Republican party became the major advocate for a stronger federal immigration policy. The Republican platform of 1864 asserted: "Foreign immigration which in the past has added so much to the wealth, resources, and increase of power to this nation – the asylum of the oppressed of all nations – should be fostered and encouraged by a liberal and just policy"; in 1868 and 1872 the Republican party reaffirmed this plank.

A dispute in 1874 over the coming of Mennonite (Amish) immigrants nearly pushed Congress into an unprecedented policy, as congressmen debated a proposal to reserve a huge tract of western land for thousands of Mennonites as an inducement for them to come to the United States rather than to Canada. Opponents of the plan argued successfully that no group should receive preferential treatment on the basis of "a special right to compact themselves as an exclusive community." The controversy ended when three western states offered the Mennonites exemption from military duty and thereby lured most of them to the United States.

By the 1870s over 280,000 immigrants a year were disembarking at American ports. The highest levels of government could no longer afford to be diffident or to entrust to the states the management of the powerful force of immigration. In 1875, a United States

Supreme Court decision inaugurated a major revision in national immigration policy. In *Henderson* v. *Mayor of New York*, a case raising issues identical to those in *New York* v. *Milne*, the Supreme Court reversed its 1837 decision: the justices now declared that all existing state laws regulating immigration were unconstitutional on the grounds that they usurped the exclusive power vested in Congress to regulate foreign commerce. The justices concluded by calling for federal supervision of immigration:

> It is equally clear that the matter of these statutes may be, and ought to be, the subject of a uniform system or plan. The laws which govern the right to land passengers in the United States from other countries ought to be the same in New York, Boston, New Orleans, and San Francisco . . . We are of the opinion that this whole subject has been confided to Congress by the Constitution; that Congress can more appropriately and with more acceptance exercise it than any other body known to our law, state or national; that by providing a system of laws in these matters, applicable to all ports and to all vessels, a serious question, which has long been a matter of contest and compliant, may be effectually and satisfactorily settled.

This decision at first threw the burden of receiving foreigners and discouraging unfit immigrants onto private philanthropic organizations, because a federal agency to perform these functions had not yet been established. Overwhelmed by the growing volume of immigrants and the strain on their resources, charity workers soon petitioned Congress to authorize federal action. In the 1880s Congress enacted a series of statutes bringing immigration under direct federal control and – a measure that proved to be more significant – allowing the federal government to exercise its authority to restrict the entry of people thought to be undesirable.

The Era of Regulation, 1882–1916

In the late 19th century the federal government built the administrative and bureaucratic machinery that would operate this new federal immigration policy. Policy makers began to experiment with new ways of monitoring arrivals, so that only those thought to be most adaptable to American society would be admitted. As concern about social problems thought to be the result of immigration mounted, they gradually constructed regulations that admitted only those who were healthy and employable.

The drive for federal regulation of immigration originated in California, where Chinese immigrants had begun to arrive around the time of the gold rush of 1849; many more came to the West Coast in the ensuing years, largely as contract labor brought in to build the railroads. By 1869, 63,000 Chinese had come to the United States, and twice that number arrived in the course of the next decade. Public reaction to the mounting numbers led the government of California to experiment with laws that would cut down the rate of entry. As early as 1852 the governor and the state assembly were recommending restrictive measures; state courts declared the Chinese ineligible for naturalization on the grounds that they could not be categorized among the "free whites" stipulated by federal law. In 1855 California passed a law levying a $50 capitation tax on arriving passengers ineligible for citizenship. Two years later, however, the U.S. Supreme Court declared this act unconstitutional. In 1870 restrictionists, claiming that Asian prostitutes were being imported into the country, obtained a state law prohibiting the landing of any Mongolian, Japanese, or Chinese female who could not provide evidence of voluntary emigration and decent character. To curb the influx of contract labor, the law was subsequently extended to males.

Nearly all the Chinese who came were unskilled laborers who were willing to work for little pay and who therefore were thought to threaten the wages and working conditions of the locals. Labor organizations, led by the Mechanics State Council of California, decided that state regulation was not sufficient and appealed to the U.S. Congress to place national limits on the immigration of Chinese workers. Republicans and Democrats alike in the far-western states agreed that federal action was required, but this placed the administration in an awkward position: Chinese immigration rights had been formally guaranteed by the Burlingame Treaty between the United States and China (1868), by which, in exchange for certain trade concessions, the U.S. government pledged that it would not restrict the numbers of Chinese workers coming into the country. But in 1879 Congress gave way to pressure from the western states, and in direct violation of that agreement enacted legislation banning from American ports any vessel carrying more than 15 Chinese passengers. President Rutherford B. Hayes vetoed the measure as a violation of international agreement. But the next year a new treaty was negotiated with China which permitted the United States to "regulate, limit, or suspend," but "not absolutely prohibit," the immigration of Chinese laborers, and in 1882 Congress took advantage of the provision to suspend the entry of Chinese workers for ten years. The Chinese Exclusion Act of 1882 stated that restrictions were needed because "in the opinion of the Government of the United States the coming of Chinese laborers to this country endangers the good order of certain localities."

The most radical provision of the law was the one that barred all foreign-born Chinese from acquiring citizenship. The basis for this statute was the Naturalization Act of 1790 in which acquisition of citizenship by naturalization had been limited to "free white persons"; an act of 1870 had subsequently extended the privilege to "aliens of African nativity and persons of African descent." Now, for the first time, a federal statute was designating a group as specifically ineligible on the grounds of race. Chinese immigration had aroused a national effort to identify an unassimilable alien race and to ban it from entry. Although in the 1880s the Chinese issue was kept distinct from the problems arising from European immigration, it nonetheless firmly established the prerogative of the federal government to raise restrictive barriers against specific national groups.

In 1882 Congress enacted the first comprehensive federal immigration law and delegated authority to the Treasury Department for enforcing it, but the states were still left with primary responsibility for the inspection of immigrants to see that all those excluded by law – convicts, lunatics, idiots, and incapacitated persons who might become public charges – were turned back. Carrying on another earlier state practice, immigrant welfare was paid for out of a federal fund raised by levying a charge of 50 cents on each entering alien.

In 1885 Congress passed the Foran Act, another exclusionary law, this time lobbied through Congress by the Knights of Labor. It prohibited the recruitment of unskilled labor by prepaid passage and advance contracting, but it did not affect skilled workers, artisans, or teachers. It was followed in 1888 by a supplemental law that ordered the deportation of alien contract laborers within one year of entry; by this measure the federal government was empowered to specify regulations that could lead to deportation.

At the same time as the groundwork was being laid for the imposition of federal controls, the character of immigration also began to change, shifting in ways that aroused concern in some quarters and that led to demands for the government to find new solutions. Although immigrants from northern and western Europe remained in the vast majority in the 1880s, new comers from southern and eastern Europe were becoming increasingly numerous. They were referred to as "new immigrants," a label that soon acquired invidious connotations.

By the 1890s the new immigrants were in the majority – and in most years it was a large majority. Many natives saw them as having peculiar habits and alien cultures. Some began to believe that the Slavs, Jews, Magyars, Sicilians, and others included in the group were innately inferior and racially unassimilable. Popular journals were filled with hostile references to the newcomers. A large foreign-born population only gradually being acculturated was filling the major urban centers. The demands for a more systematic public policy increased. State authorities were calling for federal assistance to process the multitude of immigrants and to facilitate their adjustment. They demanded that minimal health and competency standards be set for the welfare of native and immigrant communities alike. The Progressive movement, bent on the reform of government and industry and the improvement of social services, popularized the notion that government regulation of immigration would make its management more efficient.

In 1891 Congress finally established a permanent administration for the national control of immigration in the form of a superintendent of immigration within the Treasury Department. Minimum health qualifications for immigrants were formulated, as was an effective method for deporting immigrants rejected by U.S. inspectors: steamship companies were now compelled by law to return all unacceptable passengers to their country of origin. Aliens who landed illegally or became public charges within one year of arrival were subject to deportation. The law of 1891 also added new categories to those to be excluded: polygamists were banned, along with "persons suffering from a loathsome or dangerous contagious disease." The exclusion of contract labor was extended by prohibiting employers from advertising abroad for laborers and by preventing laborers responding to illegal advertisements from entering the country.

The law of 1891 ushered in full-scale federal control of immigration. Although the regulatory mechanisms operated only on overseas immigrants and did not affect people crossing U.S. borders by land, the state governments were at least no longer responsible for monitoring the stream of foreigners arriving from abroad. Overtaxed charity organizations were relieved of their burden as federal agents began to provide reception services to newcomers.

About three-quarters of the newcomers entered at the port of New York City. The old welcoming station, Castle Garden, was no longer sufficient, so a new federal facility, Ellis Island, was built to take its place. Constructed on the site of an old naval arsenal in 1892, Ellis Island was the gateway to America for millions of immigrants until 1932, when it was turned into a detention center; it was closed in 1954, but refurbished and reopened in 1965 as an immigration museum administered as part of the Statue of Liberty National Monument.

In contrast to the casual paternalism of Castle Garden, Ellis Island was efficient and impersonal. After quarantine and customs procedures immigrants were hustled past doctors on an assembly-line basis, each doctor assigned to looking for one specific disease; three special inspectors decided on the doubtful cases. As health regulations were added to the exclusion clauses, the examinations grew more complex and time-consuming. Those who passed were then interviewed by registry clerks who recorded vital statistics and other background information. Finally, the immigrants were sent to special offices housed in the federal station for currency exchange, rail tickets, baggage handling, and telegrams.

If Ellis Island was a symbol of hope and opportunity to millions of newcomers, it was also the symbol of rejection for many others. In the late 1890s, the more stringent examination system annually debarred over 3,000 applicants for admission; by 1910 the number exceeded 24,000. About 15 percent of those sent back were rejected as having contagious diseases, another 15 percent as constituting contract labor, and the remainder as potential charity cases. An organized movement to establish stricter controls over the massive influx of foreigners began to form at about the same time that Ellis Island opened. From 1891 to 1929 Congress erected a complex body of law designed to narrow the range of immigrants who qualified for admission. The course of this evolution of policy was, however, far from smooth. Well into the 20th century, the Democratic party, speaking generally, was indifferent or strongly opposed to restriction. The urban electorate of the Northeast and Midwest pressured congressmen to keep immigration as open as possible. Steamship companies and industrialists lobbied for a liberal policy that would assure large cargoes of passengers and a steady supply of cheap labor. Several presidents, from Rutherford B. Hayes to Woodrow Wilson, vetoed congressional bills that would have tightened admissions standards or excluded whole national groups. The evolving immigration policies were the product neither of a coherent plan nor of a systematic philosophy. The total effect, however, was that step by step, requirements for entry were made more and more stringent.

By the turn of the century Congress had already begun to strengthen the administrative apparatus for controlling immigration. In 1893 boards of special inquiry were formed to handle immigration problems and to collect "a list or manifest of alien passengers" entering the United States. In 1906 authority over immigration was transferred from the overburdened Treasury Department to the newly created Department of Commerce and Labor, and a separate Bureau of Immigration and Naturalization was established within that department.

Further refinements and additions were made to the list of excluded. In part a reaction to the assassination of President William McKinley by an anarchist in 1901, but even more a reflection of a widespread fear of "radicals," Congress in 1903 barred anarchists and saboteurs from entry, along with epileptics and professional beggars. Repeated attempts were made to introduce literacy as a requirement for entry, although it would be a long time before these met with any success. The Immigration Restriction League, founded in 1894 by a small group of young Harvard-educated Boston Brahmins, made the literacy requirement its goal for twenty years. In 1896 Massachusetts Senator Henry Cabot Lodge sponsored a bill in Congress that would have excluded any immigrant unable to read 40 words in some language. It was passed by Congress but vetoed by President Grover Cleveland on the grounds that it violated the traditional American policy of free immigration. Other attempts were made in 1898, 1902, and 1906, when the bills did not get through Congress, and in 1913 and 1915, when they did not receive a presidential signature.

The most throughgoing restrictions remained those placed on Asian immigration. In 1902 congressmen from the far-western states finally succeeded in having the Chinese Exclusion Act renewed indefinitely, but almost simultaneously the Japanese began arriving in California in numbers as great as those of the Chinese immigrants in their peak years. In reaction, leading businessmen and civic leaders organized the Japanese and Korean Exclusion League in San Francisco (1905), and the movement quickly spread. But again considerations of international diplomacy intervened; the result was the 1907–1908 Gentlemen's Agreement between Japan and the United States that called for voluntary regulation by the Japanese in exchange for the ending of the segregation of Japanese pupils in San Francisco's schools.

At the same time, elsewhere in the country restrictionists were becoming equally disturbed by the numbers of immigrants coming from southern and eastern Europe. In 1910 a congressionally appointed commission headed by a moderate restrictionist, Senator William P. Dillingham of Vermont, issued a 42-volume report on the alarming effects of immigration. It began with the assumption that the new immigrants were racially inferior to the old immigrants from northern and western Europe and manipulated mountains of statistics to provide a "scientific" rationale for restricting their entry. The evidence in fact contradicted the conclusions, but the Dillingham report nonetheless convinced many that southern and eastern Europeans were incapable of becoming Americans and that the best mechanism for restricting their numbers would be the imposition of a literacy test.

The Era of Restriction, 1917–1964

The Immigration Act of 1917 was the first in a series of severely restrictive statutes based on the findings of the Dillingham Commission. A literacy test was finally enacted; all newcomers over 16 years of age who could not pass it were turned back. No laborers were allowed from the so-called Asiatic Barred Zone, which included India, Indochina, Afghanistan, Arabia, the East Indies, and other, smaller Asian countries, but not China and Japan, which were covered by other legal provisions. The act was the first step in establishing a federal policy of restriction wholly based on a rank order of eligible immigrants that favored national groups thought to be most assimilable. Congress overrode the veto of President Wilson, who denounced the act as a violation of American ideals and the traditional Open Door policy.

The literacy test, it soon became clear, would not have its desired effect. In 1921 over 800,000 arrivals were recorded – a total only slightly below the prewar average – and the proportion of southern and eastern Europeans among them remained high. Congress then proceeded to the next step. By the Quota Act of 1921 (the Johnson Act) it limited the annual number of entrants of each admissible nationality to 3 percent of the foreign-born of that nationality as recorded in the U.S. Census of 1910. Quotas were established for countries in Europe, the Near East, and Africa, and for Australia and New Zealand. No limits were placed on immigration from nations in the Western Hemisphere. Congress continued to allow free immigration from its neighbors, partly to maintain good relations and partly yielding to pressure from southwestern agricultural lobbies interested in maintaining the flow of cheap farm labor from Mexico. Southern and eastern European immigration, however, was sharply curtailed; the annual quotas for southern and eastern European countries were in every case less than a quarter of the numbers admitted before World War I.

The principle of special preferences introduced in 1921 was greatly expanded in succeeding years. Preferences – but only within quota limits – were given to "the wives, parents, brothers, sisters, or children under eighteen years of age, and fiancées . . . of citizens of the United States, . . . of aliens now in the United States who have applied for citizenship in the manner provided by law, or . . . of persons eligible for United States citizenship who served in the military or naval forces of the United States [during World War I]." Establishing priorities in the interests of maintaining family unity represented yet another new principle of immigration policy.

The 1921 act also introduced a new class, later referred to as the "nonquota" category, which included aliens returning from visits abroad, professional actors, artists, lecturers, singers, nurses, ministers, and professors. After 1924 all wives and dependent children of U.S. citizens were allowed to enter as nonquota immigrants, as were aliens belonging to any recognized learned profession or employed as domestic servants. All these would be admissible over and above the quotas for the national groups to which they belonged. The nonquota list was extended by subsequent legislation, but the essential point of the original act was its principle that admission could be based on individual characteristics rather that on national quotas. It was to that extent, at least, a liberalizing provision in a law otherwise known only for its restrictionist features.

The law of 1921 was still not rigorous enough for many restrictionists, who, led by Senator Albert Johnson of the state of Washington, soon secured a more draconian measure. The Immigration Act of 1924 (Johnson-Reid Act) reduced the admissible annual total to 165,000, less than a fifth of the average prewar level (see table 3.1), and the annual quota for each nation was set at 2 percent of the foreign-born of that nationality recorded by the 1890 Census. The choice of 1890 as the base year placed immigrants from southern and eastern Europe at a still greater disadvantage because few had come to the United States that early. The annual

Table 3.1 [*orig. table 7*] The effects of the quota acts on the volume and sources of immigration

Annual immigration	Immigrants from northern and western Europe	Other immigrants, chiefly from southern and eastern Europe
Average, 1907–1914	176,983	685,531
Under 1921 act	198,082	158,367
Under 1924 act	140,999	20,847
Under national-origins system[a]	127,266	23,235[b]

[a] The legal maximum of 150,000 has been exceeded slightly because the legal minimum per-country quota of 100 was in some cases a higher number than the strict application of the national origins formula would have allowed.
[b] Southern and eastern Europeans only.
Source: Based on the annual reports of the Immigration and Naturalization Service.

quotas for Italians, Greeks, Slavs, and others from that part of the world represented a mere 3 percent of their prewar annual immigration average. The Immigration Act of 1924 also barred from entry all aliens ineligible for citizenship – that is, it reaffirmed Chinese exclusion and banned many Asians who were declared racially ineligible. For example, the Japanese who had been made racially ineligible for citizenship by a 1922 U.S. Supreme Court ruling were now prohibited from immigrating. Secretary of State Charles Evans Hughes vigorously protested Japanese exclusion because it violated the terms of the 1907–1908 Gentlemen's Agreement, but his protests were ignored.

All immigrants now had to procure a visa from an American consul in their country of origin, a system that provided an opportunity for initial screening, since the thrust of the 1924 act was not only to limit the number of immigrants, but also to select those considered best suited to American society.

Senator Johnson summed up the case for restriction and invoked its broad basis of popular support. The American people, he said,

have seen, patent and plain, the encroachments of the foreign-born flood upon their own lives. They have come to realize that such a flood, affecting as it does every individual of whatever race or origin, cannot fail likewise to affect the institutions which have made and preserved American liberties. It is no wonder, therefore, that the myth of the melting pot has been discredited. It is no wonder that Americans everywhere are insisting that their land no longer shall offer free and unrestricted asylum to the rest of the world . . .

The United States is our land. If it was not the land of our fathers, at least it may be, and it should be, the land of our children. We intend to maintain it so. The day of unalloyed welcome to all peoples, the day of indiscriminate acceptance of all races, has definitely ended.

Finally, the Immigration Act of 1924 provided for a "national origins" system favoring northern and western European groups which was to replace the formal quota system in 1927. The foundation of restrictionist policy until 1965, the national origins system was designed to prevent further changes in the ethnic composition of American society that might come from a new infusion of immigrants. The total annual immigrant quota from all nations was fixed at 150,000; each country received the percentage of that number that was equal to the percentage of people in the U.S. population of 1920 who could be counted as having derived from that country by birth or descent. A minimum quota of 100 was allotted to every nation, but aliens ineligible for citizenship were barred from access even to these quotas; thus China and Japan theoretically received quotas of 100 each, but in practice the Chinese and Japanese people could not take advantage of them.

Since the U.S. Census did not classify Americans by descent beyond the second generation, national origins were determined by classifying and then counting surnames and by an intricate statistical analysis of the population since 1790 that was crudely adjusted for natural increase. For example, the surname "Smith" was assumed to indicate English ancestry, although it could as well be an Anglicized version of "Schmidt" or could belong to a black person. This dubious procedure gave Great Britain 57 percent of the total annual quota, whereas by using the 1890 Census, Britain would have received only 21 percent. Protests from Scandinavia and German-American civic groups caused the British figure to be recalculated and lowered in favor of other northern and western European countries, whose quotas were thus slightly increased. In the end, northern and western Europe (including the British Isles) received 82 percent of the total annual quota, southern and eastern Europe 16 per cent, with 2 percent left to the remaining quota-receiving nations.

Whether the quota system was based on national origins or on the U.S. Census, however, it had the same conceptual weakness. The effort to assign quotas to encourage "assimilable" groups was thwarted by the ethnic diversity of the political units upon which apportioned quotas were based. Both systems assigned quotas to sovereign countries, ignoring the reality that within common political borders a variety of groups might dwell – Czechs, Poles, and others born in Germany, for example, were eligible for entry under the German quota – and that those boundaries might also change; for instance, as Poland's boundaries expanded and contracted, Austrian, Russian, German, and Baltic nationals sometimes qualified, and sometimes did not, under Poland's national quota.

By 1929 the national origins quota system was fully operative. But almost simultaneously immigration to the United States began to drop with the onset of the Great Depression and the series of events that led to World War II, and large portions of most quotas went unfilled. As unemployment rose in 1930, consular officials, acting on instructions from President Herbert Hoover, began vigorously to apply the clause excluding those likely to become public charges, so that all but the relatively well-to-do were prevented from obtaining visas. President Franklin D. Roosevelt subsequently revoked this order (1936), but the failure of the 1924 law to distinguish between immigrants and refugees in tallying annual quota counts still effectively limited the entry of Jewish émigrés who were then fleeing the fascist regimes in Europe. As a result, between 1933 and 1944 fewer than 250,000 refugees were admitted as immigrants, many of them on a nonquota basis. In that period, popularly regarded as the time of refugee immigration, the United States in fact received the smallest influx of newcomers since the 1830s. For the first time in its history, in the 1930s the number of people leaving the United States exceeded the number entering.

By the end of the thirties, when war again appeared imminent, the federal government modified its immigration policy to meet what it defined as the security and defense needs of the nation. A 1941 law (the Smith Act) authorized American consuls to refuse visas to applicants who might endanger "the public safety" and empowered the president to deport any alien whose departure was "in the interest of the United States." The quest for Allied unity during the war resulted in a reversal of the government's hitherto restrictive policy toward the Chinese. On December 17, 1943, Congress repealed the Chinese Exclusion Act dating from 1882 and opened up citizenship to foreign-born Chinese. The salutary effects of the new law were in practice meager, however: the Chinese received only a token quota of 105 and remained the one exception to the policy that continued to exclude all other Asians.

The plight of millions of European refugees, uprooted by the ravages of the war, prompted the federal government to devise measures to help them migrate to the United States. Policy makers became concerned with this issue, in part from efforts to develop better relations with European national groups who might otherwise fall under Soviet influence. President Harry S. Truman issued an executive order in 1945 calling for the admission of 40,000 displaced persons to the United States, to be given priority under the regular quota system. In a more far-reaching move Congress passed the War Brides Act of 1946, which admitted on a nonquota basis some 120,000 alien wives and children and a few hundred husbands of armed-services personnel into the United States. Congress extended similar provisions to Chinese and Japanese spouses in 1947.

The first Displaced Persons Act (1948) provided for the admission for permanent settlement of more than 220,000 people over a two-year period, giving priority to applicants from the Baltic states and setting such an early date to qualify as a displaced person that Jewish and Catholic refugees from Poland, who came later, were largely excluded. Thirty percent of those admitted had to be farmers. Displaced persons were required to have sponsors who would guarantee their housing and employment; security screening was strictly mandated. The most controversial provision of the law – and a victory for moderate restrictionists – was the requirement that displaced persons were not to be admitted as non-quota immigrants. Instead, regular immigration quotas were to be "mortgaged" at 50 percent each year for as many years as it took to "pay back" the displaced persons allowed to enter under its terms. President Truman reluctantly signed the bill, but he found it "flagrantly discriminatory," criticized its restrictive clauses, especially the early cut-off date that "discriminated in callous fashion" against Jews and Catholics, and called for speedy and just amendment.

A revised Displaced Persons Act was passed in 1950 which liberalized the terms of admission and increased the annual quotas: the Baltic and agricultural preferences were removed and the technical provisions discriminating against Jews and Catholics eliminated. Other refugees created by the war's aftermath, such as Greeks and national minorities living inside German borders, were also given quotas. A new ceiling of 415,000 was set for a two-year period, but sponsorship requirements remained, and the mortgaging principle was retained. The mortgaging principle was dropped in the Refugee Relief Act of 1953, which admitted 205,000 refugees as nonquota immigrants.

The refugee acts showed that the exigencies of winning allies in the Cold War, combined with genuine humanitarian impulses, could loosen overall immigration policy. Annual quota limits were suspended, and in 1956 Congress allowed 20,000 refugees, mainly Hungarians, but also Chinese and Yugoslavs, to immigrate. In 1957 Dutch Indonesian refugees were admitted; in 1960 the World Refugee Year Law admitted displaced persons from Cuba and China. These were among the precedents for the recent program for the resettlement of refugees from Southeast Asia.

The Cold War also had its other side, however, bringing with it the Internal Security Act of 1950, which required the exclusion or deportation of all aliens who had been Communist party members or had belonged to so-called front organizations. National security was also given as the reason behind the need for a revaluation of the whole body of immigration law. Both restrictionists and those wanting a more open policy agreed that the statutes passed in the early 20th century had to be recodified and updated.

In 1952 Congress approved the Immigration and Nationality (McCarran-Walter) Act, which assembled in a unified code all previous legislation that had been developed haphazardly for the past century and retained the exclusionary principle of national origins in fixing quotas. Once more, Congress had occasion to pass a restrictive immigration act over a presidential veto, as President Truman refused to sign the bill. Under the provisions of the McCarran-Walter Act, northern and western European nations received no less than 85 per cent of the total annual quota. Tighter restrictions were placed on immigrants from the colonies of quota-receiving countries: their inhabitants could no longer qualify for admission under the quotas of the mother countries but were confined to a quota that was set for each colonial territory (a provision designed to cut the flow of black immigrants from the British West Indies, who had previously entered under the ample British quota).

Although the McCarran-Walter Act reaffirmed the old principle of national origins in its quotas, it abolished the category of aliens ineligible for citizenship and thereby loosened restrictions on immigration by Asians: Japan was given a quota of 185; China retained its quota of 105; and countries in an area designated the Asia-Pacific Triangle, including colonial areas such as Hong Kong, were given a quota of 100 each. Although these were small, token quotas, which lumped these people together with other "undesirable" groups, the practice of excluding Asian races and the ban on the naturalization of foreign-born Asians were at least ended.

The McCarran-Walter Act contained other liberalizing features. Special-preference categories were introduced into each quota for immigrants with extraordinary educational or technical training or other special abilities. The bill retained and enlarged the nonquota class, which included immediate relatives of citizens and of permanent-resident aliens. Thousands of wives from Europe and Asia were able to join their husbands in the United States. A measure of equal treatment of the sexes was obtained by the granting of nonquota status to alien husbands of American wives.

In the late 1950s the national origins quota system was beginning to look more and more incompatible with mid-century international relations. The practice of restricting certain national groups had been eroded by refugee acts, the more liberal provisions of the McCarran-Walter Act, and, more generally, by changing public attitudes toward foreign peoples. The system seemed incongruous as the United States proclaimed itself the leader of the "free world" and emphasized its traditional role as an asylum for the oppressed. President John F. Kennedy attacked the system in 1963, charging that it had no "basis in either logic or reason. It neither satisfies a national need nor accomplishes an international purpose." After Kennedy's death, President Lyndon B. Johnson urged Congress to reform it.

The Era of Liberalization, Hart-Celler Act of 1965

The movement to reform immigration policy culminated in the Hart-Celler Act of 1965 whose provisions took effect in 1968. Both cornerstones of restrictionist policy – the national origins quota system and the designation of the Asia-Pacific Triangle – were abolished. The ceiling on total annual immigration was raised to 290,000. The other countries of the Western Hemisphere had available 120,000 visas annually without limit for any one country; the Eastern Hemisphere had 170,000, of which no one country could use more than 20,000. Applicants were to be admitted on a first-come, first-served basis.

Nonquota admissions were retained in the 1965 act, as was the preferential treatment for certain quota immigrants, especially family members and individuals with particular skills, from the Eastern Hemisphere. No preferential system was provided for the Western Hemisphere. Refugees from both hemispheres were allotted only a small number of visas, but the new law allowed them to be admitted under parole with no numerical limitations.

The act of 1965 increased immigration from countries whose quota allocations had previously placed them at a disadvantage. In the decade before the Hart-Celler Act, China had sent a quota and nonquota total of 1,000 immigrants per year; in 1975 9,000 Chinese immigrants arrived. In 1965 India, Greece, and Portugal supplied 300 immigrants, 4,400 immigrants, and 2,200 immigrants, respectively; by 1975 these numbers had increased to 14,000; 9,800; and 11,000, respectively. Between 1920 and 1960, of all U.S. immigration, Europe as a whole accounted for 60 percent, South and Central America for 35 per cent, and Asia for 3 percent. In 1975 Europe accounted for 19 per cent, South and Central America for 43 percent, and Asia for 34 percent.

The lack of a preferential-treatment system for the Western Hemisphere nations was a source of complaint. Some immigrants seeking to join relatives who had already immigrated often had to wait a year or two before their numbers came up in the processing pattern that enabled their admission. A solution was reached in the Western Hemisphere Act of 1976 which distributed preferences equally to Eastern and Western Hemisphere nations, and gave Western Hemisphere immigrants with special training, family ties, and skills priority over other immigrants. The 20,000-visa limit for countries in the Eastern Hemisphere was henceforth also applied to the West.

Since the colonial period American immigration policy has been determined by a variety of public institutions and governmental bodies – local until the late 19th century, and thereafter federal – as a result of a movement toward greater centralization of public policy. When the federal government assumed control over immigration, it began to establish criteria for admissions. Restrictive measures were installed and systematically enforced to ensure that only limited numbers and only those foreigners found acceptable by American society would be given entry. In the mid-20th century these exclusionary measures were gradually dismantled; the requirements of a diplomacy based on a closer international order and a growing tolerance for ethnic diversity eventually opened immigration on an equal basis to all national groups.

4 The Changing Face of Post-1965 Immigration

Reed Ueda

An Imbalanced Worldwide Immigration

The liberalization of immigration policy following the 1965 Hart-Celler Act did not produce geographic balance in immigration sources; instead it reversed the former imbalance in which Europe predominated over other regions. In the 1960s the traditional dominance of immigration from Europe began to decline. By the 1980s only 11 percent of the total immigration came from Europe, as compared with 90 percent in 1900.

Latin Americans and Asians made up a large majority of immigrants arriving after 1970. The Mexican influx remained the largest factor in Latin American immigration, even without undocumented aliens. But immigration grew faster from other Hispanic nations such as the Dominican Republic, El Salvador, Peru, and Ecuador. Immigration from Asia grew fastest of all. Immigration rose spectacularly from the Philippines, Korea, China, Vietnam, and India – the principal sources of Asian immigration after the Hart-Celler Act. By the early 1980s, nearly half of all immigrants came from Asian points of origin. The number of nations producing immigrants also grew, making the variety of arriving nationalities the largest in history.[1]

The reassignment of highest preference to family reunification after the 1965 Hart-Celler Act had important repercussions for the patterns of immigration. Because most immigrants would qualify for admission through family relationship, the family preference had an unprecedented potential to multiply admissions from the major immigrant-sending countries. Thus it tended to heighten the numerical dominance of immigration from particular Latin American and Asian nations.[2]

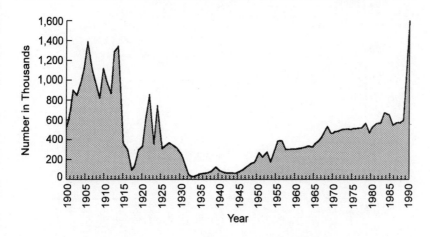

Figure 4.1 [*orig. figure 3.2*]   Immigrants admitted, *1900–1990*.
Annual immigration formed peaks in the early and late twentieth century.

Source: *1990 Statistical Yearbook of the immigration and Naturalization Service* (Washington,
D.C.: U.S. Government Printing Office, 1991), Chart C, p.38.

Annual immigration rebounded after 1965 (figure 4.1), rising
gradually from an average of 450,000 immigrants in the 1970s to
730,000 in the 1980s. International diversity coupled with economic and demographic complexity in the wave of immigration
from 1965 to the 1990s. Although annual immigration rose after
1970 to very high levels, it was far more heterogeneous and
balanced in its demographic aspects than at the turn of the century.
In part, this was because post-1965 immigration was a continuation
of immigration patterns established from 1924 to 1965.

The increased proportions of white-collar personnel, females,
and children that began after 1924 persisted after 1965. Because
in the 1970s and 1980s employment opportunities for females
improved, while heavy manual labor jobs historically attracting
male immigrants dwindled, female immigrants continued to
outnumber males. The unlimited class of visas for immediate relatives of citizens and preferences for immediate relatives of resident
aliens paved the way for the admission of spouses, parents, and
children to rise steadily (figure 4.2). Indeed, experts on immigration
demography found that marriage became the principal route
to obtaining visas by the 1980s. Family migration and
reunification contributed to continuing low levels of return migration. Low levels of return combined with high levels of immigration in the 1980s to make net immigration in that decade the
highest in history.[3]

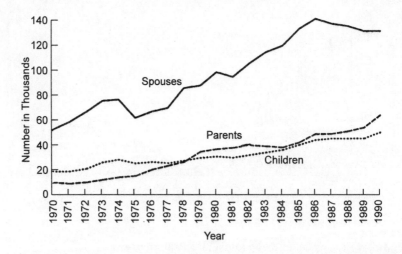

Figure 4.2   [*orig. figure 4.2*]   Immigrants admitted as immediate relatives of U.S. citizens, 1970–1990. With the 1965 Hart-Celler Act, which expanded opportunities for family reunification, admissions of immediate relatives rose steadily.

Source: *1990 Statistical Yearbook of the Immigration and Naturalization Service* (Washington, D.C.: U.S. Government Printing Office, 1991), Chart D, p. 43.

The global immigrants of the 1970s and 1980s could be divided into two economic classes, whereas the immigrants before the Great Depression were almost uniformly working class. The post-1965 influx possessed the largest contingents of human capital – highly educated and trained workers – in history, reflecting the development of admission preferences that favored newcomers in fields requiring a high level of training. In the 1970s, 25 percent of immigrants were professionals and more than 40 percent were white-collar workers. These rates of human capital migration continued into the early 1980s. From 1976 to 1990, more than 35 percent of employed immigrants were in professional and other white-collar jobs, and 12 percent were in skilled crafts. Many who worked in these areas brought capital, entrepreneurial skills, and ethnic and familial networks to support new business ventures.[4]

The human capital migration was counterbalanced by a large contingent of low-skilled workers. Service workers, laborers, and semiskilled operatives composed about 46 percent of employed immigrants arriving from 1976 to 1990. Poor and transient illegals, estimated at somewhere between three and six million in the early 1980s, sought low-paid, labor-intensive jobs. The flow of the low-skilled and undereducated rose in numbers and in percentage of arrivals in the 1980s and 1990s. Hispanic, Asian, and West Indian workers moved into the service and semiskilled job markets in big cities like Los Angeles and New York City, causing increasing friction and conflict with native black workers.[5]

In the 1980s, the social class division in immigration corresponded to two different sets of nationality groups. The first consisted of groups possessing large numbers and shares of white-collar and highly educated workers. It included nationalities from India, the Philippines, Korea, Taiwan, and China, as well as from Great Britain and Canada. These groups often exhibited close to even sex ratios and had a median age near thirty. The second group of nationalities had large totals and proportions of less-skilled and less-educated operatives, laborers, and service employees. Some had a higher percentage of male immigrants or a lower median age than the first group. These were from Mexico, Central America, Southeast Asia, and the Caribbean: specifically, Haiti, the Dominican Republic, Cuba, the West Indies, and Puerto Rico.[6]

Mexican immigration in many ways was the bellwether of changes in immigration patterns after 1965, becoming the preeminent example of the rising influx of poor migrants from the third world. More immigrants came from Mexico than from any other country. The share of low-skilled workers was higher from Mexico than from the large majority of countries in the world. More than 70 percent of employed Mexican immigrants in the 1970s and 1980s were laborers, farmers, and service workers. Finally, Mexicans constituted the largest share of illegal immigrants in the United States – as much as 60 percent in one estimate.[7]

The new Asian immigrants

After World War II, the door to Asian immigration began to reopen slightly. The repeal of Chinese and Asian Indian exclusion had been the first wedge in the door, and the passage of the McCarran-Walter Act in 1952 opened it still wider by providing token quotas to all Asian nations, as did the enactment of displaced persons and "war brides" policies.[8]

Asian mass immigration returned fully with the liberalization of the quota system under the Hart-Celler Act of 1965. Old Asian communities were transformed, and a multitude of new Asian ethnic colonies sprouted in the backwash of an immense wave of Asian arrivals. The Asian America that had long been constituted chiefly by Chinese and Japanese communities derived from the turn of the century was infused with new diversity by groups from East and South Asia. The variety of national and ethnic Asian subpopulations rose to rival that found historically among immigrants from Europe. By the 1970s, Asians constituted the largest share of newcomers admitted yearly from a continental region: one and one-half million immigrants from Asia arrived in that decade, compared with 840,000 from Europe. After 1965, the fastest-growing ethinic groups were Asians who had virtually no significant previous representation in the American population. Immigrants arrived from South Korea, Cambodia, Vietnam, Laos, Thailand, Indonesia, Burma, Sri Lanka, Singapore, Malaysia, Pakistan, India, and Bangladesh, while others came from areas where immigrant Asian communities had been established earlier in the century, such as the West Indies and Latin America.[9]

The social complexity of Asian mass immigration after 1965 contrasted sharply with the laborer influx of the late nineteenth and early twentieth centuries. A human capital migration of professionals and highly educated technical workers from homeland elites grew into a large influx. Arrivals from the Philippines and India included an unusual number of health care professionals. In the late 1980s, immigrants from India, the Philippines, China, and Korea ranked in the ten nationalities with the largest representation of professional and managerial workers. In 1975, three-quarters of employed Indian immigrants were professional, technical, or managerial workers. Highly trained elites often came through a two-stage process in which they first entered the United States on temporary visas as students in American universities and later applied successfully for permanent residency.[10]

Large waves of low-skilled and impoverished immigrants also arrived from Asia, consisting of two distinct groups. The first were immigrants who moved to big cities such as New York, Boston, Chicago, and Los Angeles to take jobs in service industries and light manufacturing. The Chinatowns of the United States, particularly the burgeoning Chinese community of New York City, received a huge influx of newcomers from Hong Kong seeking jobs in the sweatshop garment industries, restaurants, and hotels. The second group of poor newcomers from Asia were the one million refugees who fled from war, persecution, and political upheaval in the troubled homelands of Northeast and Southeast Asia from the end of World War II to 1990. The Chinese became the first Asian refugee population in the aftermath of World War II. The ending of the Vietnam War brought new refugee populations from

Cambodia, Laos, and Vietnam, including minority subgroups such as the ethnic Chinese from Vietnam and the ethnic Hmong from Laos. The tide of Asian refugees mounted higher from the 1970s to the 1980s; the pace of refugee arrivals stepped up from 20,000 admissions a year in the 1970s to nearly 100,000 admissions annually in the early 1980s. By 1990, 800,000 refugees from Indochina, constituting half of all refugees from that region, were resettled in the United States.[11]

The refugees suffered a traumatic uprooting and were equipped with the fewest resources to make the difficult transition to American life. Some groups had more advantages than others in the struggle to rebuild their lives. Many refugees from Vietnam came from urban centers where educational opportunities and better jobs had been available. They had historic ties with French and American culture and familiarity with English that in some cases aided adjustment. In comparison, the refugees from Cambodia and Laos were poorly suited to the conditions of American life and were by far the most disadvantaged of the new Asian refugees. With very little education and job skills, they encountered the most difficult entrance to American society, and by necessity they made their adjustment through the welfare system.[12]

The discipline of migrating in family units determined the movement of human capital elites, poor laborers, and refugees alike in the Asian immigration after 1965. In sharp distinction with transient Asian labor migrants early in the twentieth century, post-1965 Asian immigrants by and large were determined to settle permanently in the United States. Thus the transference of families was a critical necessity, and many Asians immigrated in whole families and used the family preference. Other Asians capitalized heavily on the right of naturalized citizens to bring family members to the United States as "immediate relatives" above annual visa limitations. Asian immigrants were quick to take out citizenship papers and composed a disproportionate share of the newly naturalized in the 1970s and 1980s. They began a spiral of chain migration: the numerous spouses, children, and parents who entered in the unlimited class of "immediate relative" in turn sponsored their "immediate relatives," and so on. Consequently, annual admissions from each Asian country greatly exceeded the visa allotment of 20,000. These factors caused total immigration from Asia to skyrocket.[13]

Female immigrants from Asia achieved increasing representation as a result of policies that promoted family reunification. Wives

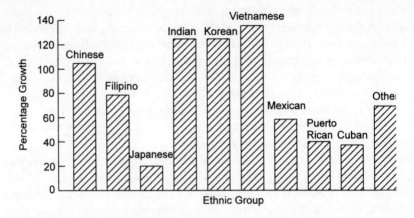

Figure 4.3 [*orig. figure 4.3*] Population growth of Asian and Hispanic ethnic groups, 1980–1990. After passage of the Hart-Celler Act in 1965, Asian and Hispanic immigrants became the fastest-growing ethnic groups.

Source: Derived from *Statistical Abstract of the United States, 1992* (Washington, D.C.: U.S. Government Printing Office, 1992), table 16, p. 17.

planned their moves with the intention of obtaining gainful employment because of the new job opportunities of the 1970s and 1980s for female workers in light manufacturing, personal service, and industrial service in hotels, restaurants, and hospitals. After 1965, the numbers of female immigrants admitted annually from Asia equaled the numbers of male immigrants, altering the historic overrepresentation of males in Asian immigration.

The Asian ethnic populations of the United States grew rapidly from the swelling tide of immigration. The growth rate of the Chinese population, measured by decade, increased from the 1950s to the 1970s from 58 percent to 85 percent and for the Filipino population from 44 percent to 126 percent. Certain Asian populations increased with exceptional speed from the arrival of immigrants. The number of foreign-born in the Filipino population grew 171 percent from 1970 to 1980, in the Korean population 649 percent. In the 1980s, the Koreans, Indians, and Vietnamese surpassed other Asian nationalities in the rate of population growth (figure 4.3). Despite the fact that Asian ethnic groups grew faster than all others, they still constituted less than 3 percent of the U.S. population in 1990 because of their small representation in the population before 1965.[14]

Population growth became a revolutionary force that started a new generational cycle in Asian ethnic communities. The small historic enclaves of Chinese, Koreans, and Filipinos evolved from earlier migrations were galvanized into new life by the injection of newcomers with families. Along with the families in the new communities from southern Asia, they formed the beginnings of a new progression of generations among Asian Americans.

The new Latin American immigrants

Central America and South America contributed a rapidly increasing portion of immigrants who arrived after 1965. Although labeled by nationality – as Hondurans or Colombians, for example – these groups were not homogeneous and included important subelements because they came from Latin American nations that were multiethnic in character. Italians, Spaniards, Germans, Chinese, Japanese, and Jewish immigrants came from various countries in Central and South America. *Mestizo* Hondurans, black Panamanians, and mulatto Colombians (*costeños*) arrived in rising numbers. A particularly large share of Panamanians and Hondurans were nonwhite: 28 percent of all foreign-born Hondurans and 59 percent of foreign-born Panamanians, according to the 1970 federal census.[15]

Notwithstanding the ethnic and racial diversity of immigrants from Latin America, the overwhelming majority of these immigrants reported themselves as white in the federal census. In 1970, more than 90 percent of all foreign stock from Costa Rica, Guatemala, El Salvador, and Nicaragua were white. But since all Central American nations, with the possible exception of Costa Rica, possessed a majority or a large proportion of *mestizos*, many who identified themselves as whites on the 1970 census probably were *mestizos*.

From the 1950s to the 1970s, an average of a few thousand immigrants each year arrived from Costa Rica, El Salvador, Guatemala, Honduras, Nicaragua, and Panama. In 1970, the Panamanians, numbering 48,000, and the Hondurans, numbering 31,000, constituted the largest Central American groups in the United States. By the 1980s, however, the populations from El Salvador and Guatemala grew faster as a result of an exodus from war and civil strife.[16]

Many of the immigrants from Central America were women in service or low white-collar jobs who came on their own to earn income that they periodically sent back in remittances to their families. They responded to the growing demand for workers who could provide household help, child care, elder care, and maintenance service in office buildings, hotels, and hospitals. The percentage of employed newcomers who were domestic servants remained high, ranging between 15 and 28 percent annually from each country. The number of immigrant males per hundred females was quite low in the late 1960s, falling to sixty for Nicaragua and fifty-one for Panama.[17]

The social and demographic features of immigration from South America differed in important respects from those of the wave from Central America. Immigration from South America was larger, and it began to rise earlier, in the 1950s. The population of South Americans in the United States in 1970 was 389,000, well over twice as many as the total of Central Americans. During the 1970s and 1980s again, immigration from South America was nearly twice as large as immigration from Central America.

The various migrant streams from Central and South America were differentiated by key social and demographic characteristics from the 1960s to the mid-1970s. The sex ratios among migrants from many South American countries were significantly more balanced than those for Central American countries. An average of eighty to more than one hundred males per one hundred females came from Argentina, Ecuador, Colombia, Peru, and Venezuela at various intervals from the 1950s to the 1960s. In the 1970s, the ratio remained almost even for immigrants from most South American countries.

Differences in age patterns could be found between the waves from Central America and South America. Male immigrants from Central America were younger on the average than those from South America. Also, the age distribution among South Americans tended to remain the same from the 1960s to the 1970s, while among Central Americans it shifted more toward the young.

Immigrants from South America contrasted with those from Central America in occupational distribution, especially in the areas of professional work and domestic service. The percentages of professionals from South American nations in most cases were twice as great or more as among arrivals from Central American countries. Professionals constituted over 30 percent of the immigrants from South American nations such as Bolivia, Chile, and Venezuela; entrepreneurs and managers made up a comparatively small portion of the "brain drain" from South America. Also, every South American country sent an appreciably smaller percentage of domestic workers than did the Central American countries. For example, from 1968 to 1975, 27 percent of immigrants from Honduras and 22 percent from El Salvador were domestic workers, but only 4 percent and 5 percent were domestic workers from Argentina and Venezuela, respectively.[18]

South American migrations displayed unusual and individual features according to country of origin. The volume of immigration from South America varied enormously from country to country, with Colombia, Ecuador, and Argentina sending by far the greatest numbers of immigrants in the 1960s and 1970s. Brazil was several times more populous than these nations, yet it sent fewer immigrants to the United States. By the 1980s, however, immigration from Brazil was rising. Venezuelan immigrants were much younger than those from any other South American country, probably because they included large numbers of wives and children. An unusually high proportion – over one-third – of Bolivians were professionals. Bolivia and Venezuela sent the largest percentages of clerical workers from South American countries. Argentina, Colombia, Ecuador, and Uruguay sent the highest percentages of skilled and semiskilled workers.[19]

The effects of human capital migration were somewhat beneficial to some Latin American nations. Many of the immigrants returned to their home countries, bringing ideas and techniques acquired while working in the United States. Thus, Colombian medical facilities and services were upgraded by the return of physicians and technicians who had acquired knowledge and training abroad.

Despite significant variations among the immigrant nationalities from Central and South America, they exhibited common social patterns and characteristics. First, because they possessed the education, occupational orientations, and lifestyles suited to urban society, they flocked to the metropolitan regions of the Northeast, Pacific Coast, and Gulf Coast states. Very few rural laborers and farmers migrated, although the economies of most Central and South American countries were greatly dependent on agricultural production. Thus the immigrants represented a mobile, urban-oriented part of their homeland societies. Second, New York City assumed a unique role in attracting nonwhite immigrants from both Central and South America. Third, a trend developed beginning in the 1970s toward migration of the less-educated and poorer elements, as the proportion of blue-collar workers among immigrants from Central and South America rose. The share of domestic and service workers, especially from Central America, increased, while the proportion of white-collar workers from a number of

Central and South American nations declined. In the 1980s, low-skilled immigrants were a half or more of arrivals and continued to include many women and young adults. Undocumented immigration from Central and South America, especially from El Salvador and Nicaragua, was substantial, according to impressionistic accounts and journalistic reports. The flow of low-skilled and undocumented immigrants intensified in the 1980s as people fled to the United States from turmoil and revolution in this region.

Two important new Hispanic groups arrived from Caribbean islands a generation apart in time. The Cuban immigrants who fled from Castro's Communist regime beginning in 1959 constituted the first large wave of refugees from Latin America. Many migrated in well-established families and thus displayed a broad range of age levels and a balanced sex ratio; they also were drawn from the professional and business classes. After 1965, however, the composition of Cuban immigrants changed as more laborers and young couples began to arrive. By the 1980s, Cubans were the single largest nationality of refugees in American history, with about 500,000 arrivals, as compared with 470,000 arrivals from the nation of Vietnam. In the 1980s, immigrants from the Dominican Republic began to arrive in rapidly rising numbers. They challenged the Puerto Ricans as the largest Hispanic group in New York City by the 1990s. Many Dominicans originated from rural communities as the Puerto Ricans did, but they tended to come from moderately well-off farming families. The majority, however, were workers and middle-class migrants from cities, many of whom obtained employment in the service and mass-production industries of the urban Northeast. Many young male immigrants came to establish an economic foothold without wives, but eventually they married other female immigrants, who by the 1980s increased in numbers as a result of the flow toward jobs in personal and industrial service.[20]

The West Indian and Haitian immigrants

With the growth of employment opportunities during and after World War II, black immigrants once more moved from the British West Indies to the United States. Twenty thousand immigrants arrived from Jamaica between 1948 and 1954. Many worked as contract laborers in Florida agriculture. This flow was halted by provisions of the McCarran-Walter Act that reduced the quotas for British territories in the Caribbean. From 1954 to 1965, British

West Indian immigrants moved chiefly to the United Kingdom, where they found entry easier.[21]

Political changes in the Caribbean, the United Kingdom, and the United States, however, stimulated a new rise in immigration from the British West Indies and Haiti. Beginning in the 1960s, many West Indian islands moved toward independence from Britain, thus also gaining an independent standing with respect to the immigration policies of the United States. In Haiti, the abuses of the dictatorial François Duvalier regime precipitated an exodus to the United States. At roughly the same time, in 1962, the United Kingdom enacted new policies to curb the influx of West Indian immigrants. In 1965, the Hart-Celler Act abolished colonial quotas and created equal access for the micro-nations of the West Indies. These developments in combination established the political and legal conditions for the upsurge of black West Indian immigration to the United States. In the decade after the passage of the Hart-Celler Act, more immigrants from the British West Indies and Haiti arrived than in the previous seventy years. The newly independent countries of Jamaica, Trinidad and Tobago, Guyana, the Bahamas, and Barbados supplied the bulk of the West Indian newcomers to the United States.[22]

Like Latin America, the West Indies and Haiti had rapid population growth in impoverished rural regions after World War II. The underemployed in the labor force, like the migrants from Puerto Rico, secured cheap and fast access to the United States by jet airways linking the West Indies with American international airports in cities such as Miami, New York, and Boston.

The rate of immigration accelerated. The number of Jamaican immigrants arriving yearly grew more than ten times from 1962 to 1970, when a total of 150,000 immigrants from the British West Indies arrived. An average of 20,000 West Indians entered the United States each year from the 1960s to the 1970s, while thousands more came as illegal immigrants. In the 1960s and 1970s, more females than males immigrated. Females were especially likely to migrate from Jamaica, where twice as many females as males left in the 1960s. Many were young adults who came to the United States for service and manufacturing work.[23]

While the majority of West Indian immigrants in the 1960s were young, unmarried adults, the share of children and adolescents rose sharply in the 1970s and more immigrants arrived as family dependents. Fifty percent of all immigrants arriving from Jamaica were under the age of twenty; in the 1980s, the average age of Jamaicans remained among the lowest of all immigrant groups. These trends along with growing sex-ratio balance showed that immigration from Jamaica included many people who were arriving in families or were joining family members already established in the United States.

As in the immigration from Latin America, the occupational concentrations of immigrants from black Caribbean nations shifted from those employed in white-collar and skilled jobs toward those and low-skilled occupations. During the early 1960s, half of the employed immigrants arriving each year from Jamaica, Barbados, Trinidad and Tobago, and the other British West Indies were professional, white-collar, and skilled workers. In the same period, wealthy and middle-class Haitians dominated in the movement to the United States. Unskilled workers constituted only one out of five immigrants from Jamaica and less than one out of three immigrants from the other islands. Beginning in the late 1960s, however, white-collar and skilled workers from the West Indies declined relative to the influx of low-skilled and poorly educated workers. In the 1980s and recurring intermittently into the 1990s, rural laborers poured out of Haiti. Because they could not afford the cost of transportation to the United States, they tried to enter illegally by taking small boats on a dangerous ocean voyage to Florida. Poor female labor migrants made up a rising share of the influx from the British West Indies and Haiti.[24]

The declining factor of European immigration

Once an overwhelmingly dominant demographic force, European immigration dwindled rapidly after 1965 (Figure 4.4). Whereas in the late 1950s and early 1960s Europeans composed half of all immigrants admitted, they amounted to less than 10 percent of immigrants in the late 1980s. The average number of annual arrivals from Europe declined from 80,000 in the 1970s to 70,000 in the 1980s. Immigrants from northern and western Europe, who once formed a huge majority of immigrants, accounted for only 3 percent of arrivals in 1990. The European countries sending the largest numbers of immigrants from the 1970s to the 1980s were the United Kingdom, Italy, Germany, and Portugal. With political collapse, war, and ethnic conflict in eastern Europe, a new wave from the former Soviet Union and eastern bloc countries arrived in mounting numbers in the 1990s. European immigrants were no longer a significant labor factor, as more than half of employed

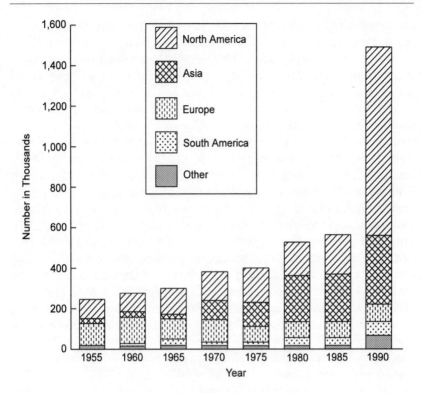

Figure 4.4 [*orig. figure 4.4*]   Immigrants admitted by region of birth, selected years, 1955–1990. While Europeans represented the bulk of immigrants until about 1960, more permissive admissions policies and economic forces in the developing world led to increased admissions from Asia and Latin America after 1965.

Source: 1990 Statistical Yearbook of the Immigration and Naturalization Service (Washington, D.C.: U.S. Government Printing Office, 1991), p. 36.

European newcomers were professional and white-collar employees. A small number of European immigrants were undocumented and employed in industrial or personal service occupations.[25]

Seeding the New Frontier of Immigrant Colonies

In the first half of the twentieth century, immigrants settled in distinctive regional constellations. Immigrants from Europe predominated in the urban Northeast and the Great Lakes region; immigrants from East Asia flocked to Hawaii and the Pacific Coast; Mexican immigrants settled heavily in the Southwest. Since the Great Depression, these regional concentrations began to spread out gradually as newcomers edged beyond the initial perimeter of settlement.[26]

Before 1920, Mexican migrants usually located in towns and farm districts near the Mexican border, specifically in the agricultural areas of southern California and the lower Rio Grande River of Texas. In the 1920s, however, the scope of movement widened as Mexicans traveled as far north as Chicago, Detroit, Cleveland, and Milwaukee to take factory jobs. Although Mexican colonies continued after World War II to flourish in the urban centers of the Midwest, the Mexican population still chiefly concentrated in the South and West, where about 90 percent of the Mexican American population lived. In 1970, one of every six persons in Arizona, California, Colorado, New Mexico, and Texas was of Mexican origin. In 1970, about 50 percent of all Mexicans in the Southwest lived in California, and 36 percent lived in Texas. Outside of Mexico City and Guadalajara, Los Angeles was the largest Mexican city in the world in 1970, home to more than one million Mexican Americans.[27]

Since World War II, urbanization has been the key to the forming of Mexican communities. In 1940 Mexicans were the most rural of the major ethnic groups in the United States, but by 1970 they were among the most urbanized. Sixty-six percent of all Mexican Americans lived in urban areas in 1950, while 85 percent did so in 1970.

The Puerto Ricans initially settled within a much smaller geographic space than the Mexicans, collecting mainly around the New York City metropolitan area. In fact, the regional concentration of Puerto Ricans was much higher than that of Mexicans. Although the Puerto Rican population fanned out to other cities in New Jersey and New England, 70 percent of all first-and second-generation Puerto Ricans lived in New York City in 1960. In 1970, most of the 820,000 Puerto Ricans on the mainland still resided in New York City, which housed the most sizable and important of all Puerto Rican communities on the mainland. The first neighborhoods grew up after World War I around the Brooklyn Navy Yard and East Harlem, which turned into the hub of the Puerto Rican community. After World War II, Puerto Ricans moved from there into the South Bronx, the Lower East Side and the Upper West Side of Manhattan, and the Williamsburg section of Brooklyn. Despite the historic geographic focus of Puerto Ricans in the Northeast, they settled increasingly in the 1970s in the north central, southern, and western regions of the country.[28]

The historic geographic clusters created by immigrant groups of the early twentieth century endured into the late twentieth century, but with the advent of the mass immigration after 1965 the old ethnic configuration was overlaid by colonies of immigrants from Asia, Latin America, the Caribbean, and the Middle East that spread over the entire nation, particularly into regions where few of these nationalities had lived before. Multicultural geography was being nationalized.

The residential distribution of the newest immigrants was highly selective. Overwhelmingly, they gravitated to several gateway metropolitan areas: New York City, Los Angeles, San Francisco, Chicago, Miami, Houston, San Diego, and Washington, D.C. These major entry points also appealed as places of settlement because they possessed host colonies and the fastest expanding areas of the economy and residential construction.[29]

The complex array of Central American nationalities displayed a more variegated pattern of settlement than either the Mexican or Puerto Rican population. By the 1970s, these newcomers had settled in urban areas of the New England, Middle Atlantic, Great Lakes, Gulf Coast, and Pacific Coast states. The largest populations of Central Americans clustered in New York City, Los Angeles, San Francisco, Miami, and Chicago. Central American groups displayed varying rates of concentration in these areas and cities. Costa Ricans, El Salvadorans, and Nicaraguans were most numerous in the West in 1970. Within California, El Salvadorans and Nicaraguans flocked to San Francisco, while Guatemalans favored Los Angeles. By contrast, Hondurans flocked to the urban centers on the Gulf Coast and in the Northeast, where Panamanians also tended to congregate. New York City possessed the largest population of Hondurans and Panamanians. *Mestizo*, black, and Indian Central Americans of all nationalities were more numerous in New York City than in any other U.S. city.[30]

The Cubans and Dominicans, two of the largest groups of new Hispanic immigrants, diverged with respect to geographic settlement. Cubans preferred to locate in areas close to their homeland, especially in Florida, where Miami became a focal point of Cuban arrival and permanent settlement. Dominicans flocked to New York City, but in the 1970s and 1980s they spread northward to New England and southward to Washington, D.C. A substantial migration also flowed to Florida. By the 1990s they vied with the Puerto Ricans for numerical dominance of Hispanic districts in New York City.[31]

The colonies of West Indians, like those of Puerto Ricans, were located initially in New York City. Earlier in the century, New York

State alone contained almost two-thirds of the Jamaican blacks in the United States; most resided in the Harlem section of New York City. But even then, West Indians were numerous in Massachusetts and Florida. After World War II, West Indian immigrants surged into the Midwest and the West Coast, settling in Michigan, Illinois, and California.[32]

Asian immigrants showed a new willingness to move outside of Hawaii and the West Coast, their historic zone of settlement from the late nineteenth century to World War II. Newcomers from China, Hong Kong, Taiwan, South Korea, and Vietnam migrated to the East Coast, the Midwest, and the South, settling in Washington, D.C., New Jersey, Massachusetts, Illinois, and Texas. The state of Virginia, which once had virtually no Asians, served as a significant indicator of this trend. Economist Thomas Muller noted that Virginia in the 1990s "rank[ed] eighth in the admission of immigrants" and was "a major center for Asian enterprises." Most Asians formed rapidly growing communities in metropolitan centers, but many Cambodian and Laotian immigrants could be found in rural areas and small cities. The geographic distribution of Asian ethnic groups shifted away from the Far West as a result of the creation of new enclaves. The percentage of population on the West Coast among the historic Asian groups shrank steadily from 1950 to 1980. So rapid was the nationwide spread of the Asian population that a major demographic study concluded in 1993 that the "spatial assimilation of Asian Americans may well happen at a greater speed than for either Hispanics or blacks."[33]

At the micro-level of community geography, clusters of third world immigrants formed out of the shift of population from central-city districts to suburbs. From metropolitan centers, the southern and eastern European stock moved increasingly into suburban areas, while the Hispanic, Asian, and Caribbean immigrants replaced them, rehabilitating commerce and housing in the declining urban neighborhoods abandoned by the Europeans. The third world immigrants assumed a central role in light manufacturing, service industries, and small shopkeeping. They became the new dynamic force in the metropolitan economy and society. But over time, they too appeared to be following the earlier waves of European immigrants along the "tenement trail" to the suburbs. An important clue to this movement was that the proportions of Mexicans, Central and South Americans, Cubans, and Puerto Ricans living in central cities tended to decline gradually in the 1980s and 1990s. In the long run, class and generation exerted growing control over geographic location. As the descendants of immigrants rose economically through better jobs and education, they moved into neighborhoods defined by higher income levels.[34]

The regional and community clusters of immigrant settlement formed distinctive patterns but did not become rigid. As a result of the fluidity of geographic movement, the United States possessed a lower degree of spatial isolation of immigrant groups than found in other societies. A changing ethnic geography reduced the potential for ethnic separatism and strengthened the forces of inclusion.[35]

Notes

1 Vernon M. Briggs, Jr., *Immigration Policy and the American Labor Force* (Baltimore: Johns Hopkins University Press, 1984), pp. 78–82; Frank D. Bean and Marta Tienda, *The Hispanic Population of the United States* (New York: Russell Sage Foundation, 1987), p. 119–21; Thomas Muller and Thomas J. Espenshade, *The Fourth Wave: California's Newest Immigrants* (Washington, D.C.: Urban Institute Press, 1985), pp. 14–15; U.S. Department of Commerce, *Statistical Abstract of the United States, 1990* (Washington, D.C.: U.S. Government Printing Office, 1991), table 7, p. 10.

2 Guillermina Jasso and Mark R. Rosenzweig, *The New Chosen People: Immigrants in the United States* (New York: Russell Sage Foundation, 1990), p. 38.

3 Ibid., pp. 185–86; Muller and Espenshade, *The Fourth Wave*, p. 14.

4 Alejandro Portes and Ruben G. Rumbaut, *Immigrant America: A Portrait* (Berkeley: University of California Press, 1990), pp. 14–23.

5 Briggs, *Immigration Policy*, ch. 5; Bean and Tienda, *The Hispanic Population*, p. 119; Jack Miles, "Blacks versus Browns: The Struggle for the Bottom Rung," *The Atlantic*, October 1992, pp. 41–68.

6 Portes and Rumbaut, *Immigrant America*, pp. 58–72.

7 Bean and Tienda, *The Hispanic Population*, p. 121.

8 David M. Reimers, *Still the Golden Door: The Third World Comes to America* (New York: Columbia University Press, 1985), Table 1.1, pp. 24–5.

9 Herbert R. Barringer, Robert W. Gardner, and Michael J. Levin, *Asians and Pacific Islanders in the United States* (New York: Russell Sage Foundation, 1993), p. 44; Reimers, *Still the Golden Door*, ch. 4; Laurence H. Fuchs, *The American Kaleidoscope: Race, Ethnicity, and the Civic Culture* (Hanover, N.H.: University Press of New England), pp. 291–2; Peter I. Rose, "Asian Americans: From Pariahs to Paragons," in Nathan Glazer, ed., *Clamor at the Gates: The New American Immigration* (San Francisco: Institute for Contemporary Studies, 1985), pp. 196–203; Peter Kwong, *The New Chinatown* (New York: Hill and Wang, 1987), pp. 38–41.

10 Barringer, Gardner, and Levin, *Asians and Pacific Islanders*, p. 195; Reimers, *Still the Golden Door*, pp. 100–02, 107, 114; Portes and Rumbaut, *Immigrant America*, pp. 58–72.

11 Roger Daniels, *Coming to America: A History of Immigration and Ethnicity in American Life* (New York: HarperPerennial, 1991), pp. 354–5, 368–70; Valerie O'Connor Sutter, *The Indochinese Refugee Dilemma* (Baton Rouge: Louisiana State University Press, 1990), p. 165.

12 Barringer, Gardner, and Levin, *Asian and Pacific Islanders*, pp. 32–5; Nathan Caplan, John K. Whitmore, and Marcella H. Choy, *The Boat People and Achievement in America: A Study of Economic and Educational Success* (Ann Arbor: University of Michigan Press, 1989), and *Children of the Boat People: A Study of Educational Success* (Ann Arbor: University of Michigan Press, 1991); Reimers, *Still the Golden Door*, pp. 173–84.

13 Elliott R. Barkan, *Asian and Pacific Islander Migration to the United States: A Model of New Global Patterns* (Westport, Conn.: Greenwood Press, 1992), pp. 74–6; Daniels, *Coming to America*, p. 343.

14 Richard T. Gill, Nathan Glazer, and Stephan Thernstrom, *Our Changing Population* (Englewood Cliffs: Prentice-Hall, 1991), Table 19–6, pp. 339–40; U.S. Bureau of the Census, *1990 Census of Population and Housing*, Summary Tape File 1C, "Detailed Race."

15 Ann Orlov and Reed Ueda, "Central and South Americans," in Stephan Thernstrom, ed., *Harvard Encyclopedia of American Ethnic Groups* (Cambridge: Harvard University Press, 1980), pp. 210, 212.

16 Because their numbers were relatively small until after World War II, the United States Census Bureau did not record statistics for individual Central and South American nationalities until 1960. The bureau had hitherto aggregated all data concerning these groups under the rubric "Central and South Americans" and it continued this practice in publications such as its series of *Current Population Reports* on persons of Spanish origin. The Immigration and Naturalization Service began to report immigrants from specific Central and South American countries in the mid-1950s.

17 These and following statistical data on Central and South American immigrants come from the author's tabulation of demographic characteristics published in the *Annual Reports* of the U.S. Immigration and Naturalization Service.

18 Ian R.H. Rockett, "Immigration Legislation and the Flow of Specialized Human Capital from South America to the United States," *International Migration Review* 19 (1976): 47–61.

19 Ines Cruz and Juanita Castano, "Colombian Migration to the United States," Part 1, and Elsa M. Chaney, "Colombian Migration to the United States," Part 2, in *The Dynamics of Migration* (Washington, D.C.: Smithsonian Institution, 1976).

20 Reimers, *Still the Golden Door*, pp. 164–73; Nancy Foner, ed., *New Immigrants in New York* (New York: Columbia University Press, 1987), pp. 2, 4, 9, 18, 28, 55, 62, 65–7. Also see in Foner, Patricia R. Pessar, "The Dominicans: Women in the Household and the Garment Industry," pp. 104–7. Also see Lisandro Perez, "Cubans," and Glenn Hendricks, "Dominicans," in Thernstrom, *Harvard Encyclopedia*.

21 Aspects of British West Indian immigration since World War II have been examined in the following articles in the journal *Social and Economic Studies*:

W. F. Maunder, "The New Jamaican Immigration," 4 (1955): 39–63;
G. E. Cumper, "Working Class Emigration from Barbados to the U.K.,
October 1955," 6 (1957): 77–83; R. W. Palmer, "A Decade of West Indian
Migration to the United States, 1962–1972," 23 (1974): 571–87; and G. W.
Roberts, "Emigration from the Island of Barbados," 4 (1955): 245–87. For a
synopsis of West Indian group history see Reed Ueda, "West Indians," in
Thernstrom, *Harvard Encyclopedia*. Thomas Sowell, *Essays and Data on Amer-
ican Ethnic Groups* (Washington, D.C.: Urban Institute Press, 1978), provides
useful data on the socioeconomic features of the West Indian population.

22 Philip Kasinitz, *Caribbean New York: Black Immigrants and the Politics of Race*
(Ithaca: Cornell University Press, 1992), pp. 26–7.

23 Reed Ueda, "West Indians." The demographic tabulations for this article,
both published and unpublished, are used in this sketch of the characteristics of West Indian immigrants. Also see Nancy Foner, "The Jamaicans:
Race and Ethnicity among Migrants in New York City," in Foner, *New
Immigrants*, p. 199.

24 Ueda, "West Indians'; Michel S. Laguerre, "Haitians," in Thernstrom,
Harvard Encyclopedia; Reimers, *Still the Golden Door*, p. 148; Susan Buchanan
Stafford, "The Haitians: The Cultural Meaning of Race and Ethnicity," in
Foner, *New Immigrants*, pp. 104–7.

25 These data are derived from *1990 Statistical Yearbook of the Immigration and
Naturalization Service* (Washington, D.C.: U.S. Government Printing Office,
1991), table B, p. 39; and *Statistical Abstract of the United States, 1992*
(Washington, D.C.: U.S. Government Printing Office, 1992), table 8, p. 11.

26 David Ward, "Immigration: Settlement Patterns and Spatial Distribution,"
in Thernstrom, *Harvard Encyclopedia*.

27 Bean and Tienda, *The Hispanic Population*, table 5.1, p. 139; Joan W. Moore,
Mexican Americans, 2d edn. (Englewood Cliffs, N.J.: Prentice-Hall, 1976),
pp. 55, 112.

28 Joseph Fitzpatrick, *Puerto Rican Americans: The Meaning of Migration to the
Mainland* (Englewood Cliffs, N.J.: Prentice-Hall, 1971), pp. 10–11, 15–16,
53–57; Joseph Fitzpatrick, "Puerto Ricans," *Harvard Encyclopedia*, pp. 858–
59; Bean and Tienda, *The Hispanic Population*, table 5.1, p. 139.

29 Thomas Muller, *The Immigrant and the American City* (New York: New York
University Press, 1992), pp. 111–14.

30 Bean and Tienda, *The Hispanic Population*, table 5.1, p. 139.

31 David Gonzalez, "Dominican Immigration Alters Hispanic New York," *New
York Times*, 1 September 1992, p. 1.

32 Ira deA. Reid, *The Negro Immigrant: His Background, Characteristics, and Social
Adjustment, 1899–1937* (New York: AMS Press, 1939), pp. 85–9.

33 Muller, *The Immigrant and the American City*, p. 65; Gill, Glazer, and Thernstrom, *Our Changing Population*, table 19–6, pp. 339–40; Barringer, Gardner,
and Levin, *Asians and Pacific Islanders*, p. 133.

34 Bean and Tienda, *The Hispanic Population*, table 5.6, p. 147.

35 Stanley Lieberson and Mary C. Waters, *From Many Strands: Ethnic and Racial
Groups in Contemporary America* (New York: Russell Sage Foundation, 1988),
p. 83.

5 Gaps and Contradictions in U.S. Immigration Policy: An Analysis of Recent Reform Efforts

Kitty Calavita

Introduction

Since the first federal immigration laws in the U.S. in the nineteenth century through to the Immigration Act of 1990, U.S. immigration policies tend to be characterized by a pronounced gap between their purported intent and their practical effect. Some have explained this gap as due to the difficulty of controlling through legislation that which is essentially an economically driven phenomenon (Bach 1978; Lopez 1981). Others have explained it as an indication of the incompetence of the Immigration Service and the failure of its enforcement policies (Crewdson 1983; U.S. Congress 1972; 1980). Still others have observed that it stems from the difficulties of balancing competing, and equally compelling exigencies – "right versus right" (Teitelbaum 1980).

It seems unlikely that this gap is the product of a single set of factors or underlying dynamic. Rather, it is proposed here that a number of tensions, or "paired oppositions," taken together help explain the pattern of apparent failure of immigration policies to achieve their purported intent, and recreate what is often referred to as the immigration "problem." First, there is the opposition of employer and worker interests on the issue of immigration, making a "national" economic interest difficult to identify, much less to pursue. In the late nineteenth century, industrialists praised the stream of immigrants from Europe as they provided the cheap labor with which to fuel the burgeoning factories of the Industrial Revolution in the U.S. Domestic labor was far less enthusiastic, *precisely because* the new immigrants allowed employers to stabilize wages and break the grip of union labor.

As the Vice President of a Jersey City local put it in 1884 as his union was defeated in its strike efforts, "It's that... Castle Garden [where the bulk of European immigrants landed] that's killing us" (New Jersey Bureau of Industry and Labor, 1884). In 1885, Congress responded to organized labor's demands to curtail immigration from Europe with the "Anti-Alien Contract Labor Law." This law, touted as the "salvation" of American labor against impoverished immigrant labor and the "greedy capitalists" who imported it (*Congressional Record*, 1884: 5349), was carefully crafted not to interrupt the "golden stream" that was so appreciated by Carnegie and his fellow industrialists. Pronounced "a sham" and "a sop to Cerberus" by opponents in Congress (*Congressional Record*, 1885:1839), the law was a symbolic measure with which to appease workers while not interfering with the labor supply.

A century later, the employer sanctions provision of the Immigration Reform and Control Act repeats the pattern. Pressed to do something to control illegal immigration, but reluctant to "harass" employers, Congress passed a symbolic measure with little meaningful potential. The point here is not so much that illegal immigration is difficult to control through legislative measures (although it is), nor that Congress is somehow inept or incapable of designing effective policies. Rather, the far more fundamental issue relates to the very nature of the immigration "problem." Specifically, the inability of Congress to respond effectively has less to do with the difficulties of finding a *solution* than it does with arriving at a consensus as to what the *problem* is.

Second, the structure and composition of labor force needs are clearly economic in nature, but they have profound political implications. Furthermore, a tension often exists between the real needs of the economic structure at a given point in time, and the political ability or willingness to recognize those needs. It is proposed here that the gap between official immigration policies and *de facto* policies may reflect this discrepancy. Since the 1950s, illegal immigration to the U.S. has been high, as undocumented immigrants perform much of the low-wage labor in certain sectors of the economy, such as in agriculture, construction, hotels, and restaurants. Wages and working conditions in these sectors are often insufficient to attract U.S. workers to these jobs in which third-world immigrants are concentrated. While policymakers have been unwilling to improve enforcement of labor standards as a strategy for reducing the appeal of undocumented immigrant workers, neither are they prepared to send the message that the U.S. economy systematically produces jobs that only third-world workers find attractive, by officially endorsing the importation of workers to fill those jobs. The result is a clandestine movement – illegal immigration – with which to satisfy an economy, the margins of which are politically unpalatable.

Finally, it may be that the liberal democratic principles upon which western democracies are grounded are at odds with the police functions necessary to control and regulate immigration and refugee flows. Even in the absence of the political ambiguities and class divisions described above, it may be that controlling the movement of the economically destitute and politically persecuted requires measures antithetical to basic constitutional and human rights. While it is true, for example, that "Operation Wetback" in 1954 succeeded in deporting most of the illegal Mexican immigrants in the Southwest, at least temporarily, it also resulted in the deportation of a not insignificant number of U.S. citizens and legal residents (Morgan, 1954). The difficulties the Clinton Administration has had in devising a policy for handling the Haitian refugee problem is a further illustration of this tension. Having stated in his electoral campaign that he would not violate Haitians' right to apply for asylum, President Clinton was then faced with the very real tension between human rights on one hand and border control on the other.

It is suggested here that the discrepancy between the stated purpose of U.S. immigration policies and their practical consequences is at least in part the product of these three sets of tensions of "paired oppositions." In other words, the contradiction in immigration policies between their stated intent and their outcome may reflect these basic underlying contradictions in the political economy of immigration.

The remainder of this chapter examines the most recent immigration reforms in the United States from this perspective, specifically the Immigration Reform and Control Act of 1986 (IRCA) and the Immigration Act of 1990.

IRCA and its Impacts

"America must regain control of her borders" was the battlecry of immigration reformers in the early 1980s. By 1986, apprehensions

of illegal immigrants by the Border Patrol reached over 1.5 million
(U.S. Immigration and Naturalization Service, 1986: 95).[1] Some
immigration scholars maintain that the increase in illegal immigration was the result of Immigration and Naturalization Service
(INS) policies. Citing the lack of funding to the INS, and an attitude
of benign neglect both in Congress and in the agency itself, it has
been argued that the economic advantages of illegal immigration
have historically encouraged a hands-off stance (Hadley, 1956;
Kirstein, 1973; Bach, 1978; Lopez, 1981). More captive and vulnerable than U.S. citizens or permanent residents, the undocumented
"work scared and hard," as former Secretary of Labor Ray Marshall
(1978: 169) once put it. Indeed, there is substantial evidence, that
the INS has actively, even officially, tolerated undocumented
immigration during periods when it was a critical source of farm
labor (Calavita, 1992).

Since the Irish immigration of the mid-1800s, the appreciation of
the economic role of the immigrant has almost always been accompanied by anti-immigrant nativism and public pleas for restriction.
Based on varying combinations of racism, visions of tax increases,
cultural and political protectionism, and organized labor's concerns
over bargaining power, these anti-immigrant backlashes have
tended to intensify in periods of uncertainty, such as economic
crisis and/or perceived threats to the national security (Higham,
1955; Cornelius, 1982).

In the last two decades, immigrants have been the targets of
renewed public concern. As in the past, a vocal minority has
blamed the new immigrants for virtually every social ill affecting
American society, including crime, environmental deterioration,
and urban uprisings. And, as in the past, it is in large part *because*
immigrants supply a cheap labor force (i.e., precisely that which
employers and policymakers have appreciated) that they provide
an easy target of backlash by wary taxpayers and domestic workers.
The predominantly illegal nature of the contemporary flow
enhances the reaction. As the fear spread in the early 1980s that
the U.S. had "lost control of its borders," immigration restrictionism and antagonism against those who personified this lack of
control intensified. IRCA can best be understood within this historical context, as an attempt to respond to the contradiction between
the economic motor of illegal immigration and the new nativism
that generates political demands for restriction.

IRCA consisted of three fundamental components. First, the
legalization provision allowed undocumented immigrants who

had been in the U.S. in illegal status since before January 1, 1982, to apply for legal residence. Second, employer sanctions made it illegal for an employer to knowingly hire undocumented workers. Finally, the Special Agricultural Worker program allowed certain undocumented workers in the agricultural sector to apply for legalization, and provided for additional farm workers to be admitted, should a shortage of farm labor develop.

The most significant consequence of this law, which had been touted as the answer to an uncontrolled border, was the legalization of millions of undocumented immigrants who had for years lived and worked in the shadows. A total of 3 million immigrants applied to one of IRCA's two legalization programs, far more than policymakers had expected. Approximately 1.7 million applicants filed for the general legalization program (LAW), with the approval rate at close to 98 per cent (Bean, Vennez, and Keely, 1989: 68). Another 1.3 million applied for legalization through the Special Agricultural Worker program (SAW). Despite claims that fraud was widespread (U.S. Commission on Agricultural Workers, 1992), the approval rate for the SAW program was approximately 94 per cent (Bean et al, 1989: 68). This SAW program vastly exceeded the original projections, with policymakers having predicted no more than 210,000 applicants (Baker, 1990: 165). The majority of these legalized immigrants came from Mexico (69.8% of LAW applicants; 81.9% of SAW applicants), with a significant minority coming from other Central American countries (13.4% of LAW; 4.2% of SAW), and from Asia (4.3% of the LAW applicants, and 5.4% of SAW applicants) (Bean, Vennez, and Keely, 1989: 69). Five states – California, Texas, Illinois, New York, and Florida– accounted for over 80 per cent of the applications (Baker, 1990: 165).

Ironically, the political centerpiece of IRCA – employer sanctions – had little concrete effect. Section 101 of IRCA makes it illegal to knowingly employ aliens not authorized to work in the U.S. The provision applies to all types of employers, including those who subcontract all or part of their work, and all kinds of workers, including day laborers and temporary workers. Further, the law requires that employers ask all new employees for documentation proving their identity and eligibility to work in the U.S., that they fill out and sign an "I-9" form for each new hire, listing the specific documents seen and their expiration dates, and that they keep this form on file. Penalties for violations of the "knowing hire" provision range from $250 for the first offense to $10,000 for repeated offenses. A "pattern or practice" of violations may bring criminal penalties, including six months in prison. Fines for paperwork violations related to the I–9 form range from $100 to $1,000 per violation.

The INS published its final Rules and Regulations on IRCA in the *Federal Register* on May 1, 1987 (U.S. Immigration and Naturalization Service, 1987). These regulations gave employers three business days after the date of hire to complete 1–9 forms, with those who employ workers for fewer than three days being required to complete the paperwork in 24 hours (8 C.F.R. 274a.2). Finally, employers are to be given three days' notice before inspections by the INS (8 C.F.R. 274a.2)

During the debates preceding the enactment of employer sanctions, its advocates in Congress and in the INS maintained that most employers would voluntarily comply with this law. Admitting that the INS would be able to monitor only a tiny fraction of the nation's approximately 7 million employers each year, employer sanctions proponents argued that this was of little consequence. The deterrent effect of the law, this argument went, would be based on voluntary compliance and the example set by a few well-publicized fines.

After passage of employer sanctions, INS Commissioner Alan Nelson (personal communication, 1988) stated that most employers were abiding by the law simply because it was the law. INS District Counsel in San Diego, Martin Soblick, has spoken enthusiastically of "the success we've had across the board in securing voluntary compliance from employers nationwide" (quoted in the *San Diego Union/Tribune*, February 1, 1989). The Western Regional Commissioner of the INS, Harold Ezell, maintained that the fines imposed under employer sanctions operated as a deterrent on those few employers who might not otherwise comply voluntarily (*San Diego Union*, August 31, 1988: B-2).

Border apprehension statistics in the first three years of the new law at first glance seemed to validate the official optimism concerning employer compliance and the deterrent effect of the law. From fiscal year 1986 to fiscal year 1989, INS Border Patrol apprehensions along the southern border, where the overwhelming bulk of illegal aliens are apprehended, went from 1,615,854 to 854,939. However, a dramatic reversal of this decline began in the second quarter of 1989. After an initial sharp decline in the first quarter of 1989, apprehensions increased more than 32 percent in the last two quarters of the year compared to the same period in 1988 (U.S.

Immigration and Naturalization Service, cited in Dillin, 1989b: 7), leading one usually more circumspect reporter to suggest that the border was "spinning out of control" (Dillin, 1989a: 8). The figures for fiscal year 1990 show an even steeper rise in apprehensions. In the San Diego sector where the greatest number of apprehensions are made, an 89 percent increase over the same month the previous year was registered for December 1989; January 1990 saw an increase of 51 percent and the number for February was up 78 percent (U.S. Border Patrol, cited in Brossy, 1990: B3). Confronted with these statistics, INS spokesperson Duke Austin admitted, "[t]he trend is not in the right direction" (quoted in ibid., p. B2). The most comprehensive study to date of the effect of employer sanctions on the volume of illegal border crossings (Crane et al., 1990) concludes that the initial reductions in apprehensions were less a product of employer sanctions than they were a consequence of the IRCA's legalization provisions, which legalized close to three million immigrants, many of whom had periodically crossed the border illegally prior to their change of status. The study further demonstrates that the three-year apprehension figures do not indicate any substantial deterrent effect from the law. The U.S. Department of Labor's study of the impact of employer sanctions on the labor market similarly concludes that "the drop in apprehensions in the immediate post-IRCA years may have been more of a pause than a change in behavior" (U.S. Department of Labor, 1991: 62). The Commission on Agricultural Workers, established by Congress to trace the effect of IRCA on agricultural conditions, reaches similar conclusions (U.S. Commission on Agricultural Workers, 1992), as do most academic studies (see, for example, Bean, Vennez, and Keely, 1989; Fix, 1991).

In part, it may be that employer sanctions has had little deterrent effect because the provision is not systematically enforced. In its first report to Congress on the impact of employer sanctions, the General Accounting Office (GAO) noted that the INS expected to audit approximately 20,000 employers in fiscal year 1988 – in other words, one-third of one percent of the approximately 7 million employers in the United States (U.S. General Accounting Office, 1987: 27). INS records showed that it fell short of even this goal, having completed 12,319 inspections, or less than one-fifth of one percent of the nation's employers (U.S. Immigration and Naturalization Service, 1988). In the first five months of fiscal year 1989, the INS conducted 5,000 inspections, almost exactly replicating the 1988 figures (Bean, Vennez, and Keely, 1989: 43). The selection procedure for inspections reduces even further the chances of an offending employer being detected. In order to "demonstrate that the Service is not engaging in selective enforcement of the law" (U.S. Immigration and Naturalization Service, 1987: IV–9), a substantial portion of inspections is initiated on the basis of a random selection process (referred to as the General Administrative Plan, or GAP) generated by a listings of five million employers across the country. By early 1989, 25 percent of employer sanctions were based on this random procedure, while 75 percent were based on leads (Bean, Vennez, and Keely, 1989: 43). By 1990, the proportion of GAP inspections had risen to 35 percent (U.S. General Accounting Office, 1990: 94). Even though the GAP procedure nets far fewer offenders than lead-based inspections, the goal is to increase to 40 percent the number of inspections based on random selection (Bean, Vennez, and Keely, 1989: 43).

However, the most potent ingredient affecting employers' continued hiring of the undocumented despite employer sanctions may be their perception of the protection accorded them by the I–9 form. As we have seen, IRCA requires employers to request documentation from all new hires and to fill out I–9 forms, which attest to having seen these documents. In one in-depth study of 100 employers in Southern California (summarized in Calavita, 1990), almost universal compliance with this requirement was found. All but five of the employers interviewed systematically requested documentation and completed the required paperwork. Rather than seeing the paperwork requirement as burdensome, many of these employers view the I–9 form as an effective barrier between violation and prosecution. The Director of Human Resources at a large plant who later told the interviewer. "Evidently we have people who are illegal," pointed out that "It [the I–9] would help protect us."

These employers have tapped the source of a paradox in the employer sanctions law. Despite admitting to employing undocumented workers, these employers will probably not be subject to fines under employer sanctions; instead, those who have completed the paperwork (the vast majority) are labeled "compliers." A garment shop personnel director who confided to the interviewer that he had instructed his undocumented workers to "fix" their patently false documents, explained the paradox this way: "The I–9," he said, "takes a lot of responsibility off of me and puts it back on the employee." To understand fully the prevalence of this illegal activity and employers' relative impunity, it is necessary to

untangle the dynamics of this shift of responsibility via the I–9
form, a shift that had its source in the law itself.

In 1982, a "good faith" clause was inserted in the bill that was to
become IRCA. This clause stipulated that if employers check workers' documents, regardless of the validity of those documents, they
will be assumed to have complied with the law. During the debate
of the final bill in the Senate, Senator Alan Simpson reiterated the
theme that had pervaded the lengthy proceedings. "I can assure my
colleagues," he said, "that an innocent employer will be protected
by following the verification procedures" (quoted in Montwieler,
1987: 255). By the time IRCA was passed in 1986, this protection
was spelled out carefully. It included a provision that the required
document check, conducted in "good faith" (Section 101), would
constitute an "affirmative defense that the person or entity has not
violated [the 'knowing hire' clause]." Equally important, it released
employers from the responsibility for detecting fraudulent documents, stating that "a person or entity has complied with the
[document check] requirement...if the document reasonably
appears on its face to be genuine."

These protections were designed to minimize employer opposition to the law. As early as 1981, when the Senate Subcommittee
held hearings on "The Knowing Employment of Illegal Aliens," the
acting Commissioner of the INS, Doris Meissner, stressed that
"[i]mplementation of the law is not designed to be and will not
be anti employer.... Unlike a number of State statutes concerning
employer sanctions, the Federal law relative to the knowing hiring
of illegal aliens will not require employers to make judgments
concerning the authenticity of documentation..." (U.S. Congress,
1981: 5). At the same hearing, Senator Simpson repeated, "It
[employer sanctions] must be the type of program which does not
place an onerous burden upon the employer with respect to what
he has to do to avoid a penalty" (p. 86). In 1985, the Chamber of
Commerce, convinced that employer sanctions would not pose an
"onerous burden," officially *endorsed* the measure.

The affirmative defense clause and the "good faith" document
check for all practical purposes redefined compliance. Gerald Riso,
Deputy Commissioner of the INS at the time, unwittingly summarized this *de facto* transformation in the meaning of compliance
before the House Subcommittee in 1983 when he said, "We have
made some assumptions that most employers will voluntarily comply *if we make compliance pragmatically easy for them*" (U.S. Congress,
1983: 265; emphasis added). The Senate Judiciary Committee was

more specific, stating confidently, "The Committee believes that the affirmative defense which results from compliance...will encourage the majority of employers to elect to comply" (U.S. Congress, 1985: 32).

During the legislative process, a semantic transformation had taken place in which compliance with the paperwork requirement had come to stand in for compliance with the real heart of the employer sanctions law–the "knowing hire" provision. This transformation in the definition of compliance was critical in eliminating employer opposition to the law. Simultaneously appeasing the public that demanded an employer sanctions law and employers who derived economic benefits from immigrant workers, IRCA was a carefully crafted response to an underlying contradiction between political and economic forces.

The rhetoric of employer compliance with the spirit of the law facilitated this sleight of hand. The important role played by the expressed assumption of voluntary compliance is revealed by the fact that the move to "protect" employers was often couched in terms of the discrimination potential of the law. The concern was regularly expressed that without an "affirmative defense," well-intentioned employers in their effort to comply with the law, might refuse to hire those who "look or sound foreign" (Select Commission on Immigration and Refugee Policy, 1981: 67). The Senate Judiciary Committee explained the need for a "good faith" clause based on a similar assumption of employer compliance: "If employers, recruiters, and referrers are given no protection, they will feel insecure and seek to avoid penalties by avoiding persons they suspect might be illegal aliens, in other words, those who 'look or sound foreign' to them" (U.S. Congress, 1985: 8–9).

Not only did the rhetoric of employer compliance facilitate the transformation in what "compliance" meant, but it allowed Congressional sponsors to counter an increasing volume of data suggesting that employer sanctions had never worked. Two General Accounting Office studies (1982; 1985) documented the difficulties of employer sanctions enforcement in 19 countries around the world, and concluded that only in Hong Kong had sanctions actually reduced undocumented migration. Twelve states (including California) had already experimented with sanctions during the 1970s, and in no case had they had any measurable effect, and only a handful of employers had ever been convicted and fined (for the California case, see Calavita, 1982). Immigration policymakers, committed to this law that effectively reconciled conflicting demands, countered the mounting evidence with the assurance that US employers would voluntarily comply with employer sanctions simply because it was the law.

The move to make compliance "pragmatically easy" for the employer was based on political necessity and justified on the grounds that "most employers, as generally law-abiding citizens, will uphold the law" (U.S. Congress, 1981: 4). This assumption of the law-abiding nature of employers not only made it important to protect the employer through the affirmative defense provision, but apparently made it unnecessary to worry lest this protection become a loophole through which employers could circumvent the law – a possibility that was left virtually unexplored through five years of Congressional debate. The employer sanctions law that resulted, grounded as it was in assumptions about voluntary compliance, virtually guaranteed widespread employer violations. Facing a contradiction between political and economic forces, legislators produced a law whose effect was to be solely symbolic. The point here is not simply that Congress passed a toothless law by making compliance easy through the incorporation of loopholes. Rather, the law made *violations* "pragmatically easy." Through the affirmative defense and good faith provisions, Congress guaranteed that conformity with the paperwork requirements would be taken as an indication of compliance, thereby ensuring that violations of the "knowing hire" provision – the real meat of the law – would be virtually risk free.

Perhaps not surprisingly, the number of fines levied for violations of employer sanctions has been relatively low. An Urban Institute study of ten major cities covering all four INS regions found that in El Paso, where the most employer sanctions fines were served, only one fine was levied "for every two months of agent service" (Fix and Hill, 1990: 89). The rate in Chicago was one fine per *two years* of agent service. The study concludes with an understatement, "INS enforcement activity could not be characterized as hyperactive" (ibid., p. 89). When fines are issued, they are relatively light, varying from $9,459.00 in the Northern Region, to $2,060.00 in the Southern Region. According to a General Accounting Office study, these fines are usually further reduced by about 59 per cent through negotiations (cited in ibid., p. 86).

The Immigration Reform and Control Act of 1986 has been hailed both as landmark legislation that will "regain control of our borders," and as an ingenious creation painstakingly fashioned through the political art of compromise and concession. This simplified depiction of IRCA is wrong on both counts. First, while the mandate to regain control of the borders did provide the political motor of the reform effort, the sole restrictive provision of the law – employer sanctions – will remain a symbolic measure with little impact on immigration flows. At the same time, other provisions of IRCA, such as the Special Agricultural Worker program, will predictably add to the stock of immigrant workers. Thus, not only does IRCA pull both ways at once, but the long-term impact of this reform, which originated in and was fueled by restrictionist fervor, is likely to be a continued increase in immigration, both documented and undocumented.

The Immigration Act of 1990

Once the problem of illegal immigration had been addressed – if not solved – by IRCA, the attention of policymakers turned to reforming policies related to legal immigration. Driven primarily by a concern that U.S. immigration policies did not reflect the shifting economic and labor force needs of the post-industrial period, Congress passed the Immigration Act of 1990 (IA; PL 101–649). As described by Papademetriou (1992: 9–12), three fundamental factors were integral to the debate surrounding this latest immigration reform. First is the transformation of the US economy, such that the proportion of the workforce engaged in manufacturing has fallen as the proportion working in services has increased. Related to this shift is the concern that the US workforce can supply neither the highly skilled technicians and professionals required in the new service sector, nor the large number of entry-level workers that this sector depends on. Second, in the past the bulk of legal immigrants to the US has settled in urban areas of the Northeast corridor; yet, it is precisely these locations that have been hardest hit by the shift to a service-oriented economy, and the global competition which has hastened the move of manufacturing out of these areas in search of cheaper, more flexible labor elsewhere. Third, there has been a steady decline in US fertility rates, such that immigration now accounts for a substantial portion (30%) of population growth in the US, as well as providing over 33 percent of new workforce entrants. Within the context of these background factors, the Congressional debate focused on how to provide workers for the US economy, thereby to enhance its global competitiveness without, however, jeopardizing the interests of US workers by displacing them, depressing wages, or debilitating their bargaining position.

Although the debate centered around these economic issues, this latest immigration reform once again made family unification a central priority. The Immigration Act leaves unchanged the unlimited visa provision for immediate relatives of US citizens. In addition, it introduces a ceiling or "cap" on overall immigration whereby the immigration of more distant relatives under the family preference system is limited to 465,000 minus the number of *immediate* relatives (admitted under the unrestricted visa provision) who were given visas the previous year. In 1995, the number of such visas for relatives was 480,000, minus the number of visas allocated for immediate relatives the previous year. If, for any reason, the number of visas allocated in this manner is fewer than 226,000 in any given year, up to 55,000 visas for the spouses and children of IRCA-legalized residents will be made available. In another nod to the principle of family unity, and in an effort to reduce backlogs for visas for Mexican nationals, the Act made available at least 77 per cent of second preference visas (allocated to the spouses and minor children of legal residents) on a first come/first served basis, eliminating the per country ceiling (*Interpreter Releases*, 1990).

One of the major changes in the new law consists of an expansion in the proportion of visas set aside specifically for economic purposes. Indeed, the number of such "economic" visas will almost triple, rising from 54,000 under previous immigration law to 140,000 under this Act. In addition to this quantitative change, the law substantially changes qualification procedures and administrative mechanisms. First, it instructs the Department of Labor to set up a pilot program to determine if it is feasible to identify occupations in which there are labor shortages and issue categorical certifications for the immigration and employment of workers in those occupations, to replace the *ad hoc*, case-by-case approach currently used. Second, it stipulates that employers must inform their workers of their intention to import foreign workers. As Papademetriou (1992: 26) describes these provisions, "They offer employers easier and more predictable access to foreign workers . . . while creating additional requirements which employers must meet if they wish to employ foreign workers."

These employment-based visas will be issued according to a new preference system. In the first preference, 40,000 visas will go to people of "extraordinary ability" (such as scientists, artists, and athletes), "outstanding" researchers and academics, and executives of US multinationals. In the second preference, another 40,000 visas are allocated for immigrants with advanced degrees or "exceptional ability" who have received a concrete offer of employment, after certification from the Department of Labor that a labor shortage exists in that particular field. Another 40,000 visas go to third preference immigrants – an assortment of skilled workers, professionals, and "other workers." This latter category of "other workers" includes unskilled workers and is limited to 10,000 visas annually. Finally, fourth and fifth preferences provide 10,000 visas each, for "special immigrants" (religious workers, those with foreign medical degrees, US government employees, etc.) and investors, in cases in which their investment would create at least ten US jobs.

Overall, the Immigration Act will raise legal immigration from a current annual level of approximately 534,000, to a fixed ceiling of 714,000 annually in 1992–4 and 738,000 beginning in 1995. Despite the introduction of a "cap" on legal immigration, this ceiling may be exceeded beginning in 1995, depending on the amount of growth in the numerically unlimited "immediate relative" class. While this quantitative change is important, perhaps more significant is the emphasis in this law on shaping immigration flows to perceived economic needs – a principle that has often driven US immigration but has rarely been so explicitly pronounced in the legislative process.

Peter Schuck (1992: 91) concludes his discussion of the Immigration Act of 1990:

> The restrictionist road, along which U.S. immigration law had traveled for over six decades, well into the 1980s, again beckoned [in 1990], yet this time it was not taken. Many Americans believed that the 1965 and 1980 reforms had opened the front door too wide and that the immigrants passing through it added relatively little economic value to society. A recession had begun and the Persian Gulf war impended. In the end, however, those who wanted fewer and similar immigrants lost while those who sought more and different ones won.

While Schuck frames his analysis in terms of competing special interests, his description is consistent with the more structural model proposed here. Against a backdrop of restrictionist sentiment and an escalating recession, lawmakers passed the expansionist Immigration Act of 1990, increasing the size of the immigrant flow and tailoring it to perceived economic imperatives.

Conclusion

I have argued here that the recurring gap in US immigration policies between the stated intentions of the law and its practical effects is the result of contadictory interests between workers and employers; a political unwillingness either to eliminate or officially sanction bad working conditions in those parts of the economy where third-world immigrants are concentrated; and inherent tensions between border control and inalienable human rights. The gaps and contradictions both within and among IRCA, the Immigration Act of 1990, and more recent restrictionist efforts can best be understood within this context of conflicting economic and political imperatives.

This expansionist approach is now being challenged, as Congress not only reconsiders the advantages of large numbers of legal immigrants, but has moved to limit noncitizens' access to welfare and other forms of federal assistance. Just six years after Congress expanded the legal immigration flow with the Immigration Act of 1990, they have returned to the "restrictionist road" which, while contradicting long-standing economic realities, resonates clearly with political demands for tougher immigration controls.

Because these paired oppositions are structural in nature and inhere in the political economy of a capitalist democracy, their ramifications will continue to be felt in the future. The current anti-immigrant backlash, particularly strong in California where Proposition 187 passed by a landslide in 1994, has yielded some strong rhetoric and even some legislative changes that aim to "regain control of the borders." Some of these measures – such as Prop. 187 which would bar undocumented immigrants from attending public schools or receiving non-emergency medical care – have been found by the courts to violate basic human rights and constitutional principles. As the underlying contradictions of immigration control continue to play themselves out, the flow of undocumented immigrants is not likely to be substantially affected by legislative tampering, nor will the gap between the purported intent of immigration policies and their outcome disappear in the foreseeable future.

Note

1 Apprehension rates are not a precise measure of undocumented immigration. Not all undocumented border crossers are ascertained, some are apprehended more than once, some "undocumented" immigrants enter legally and overstay, and some variations in apprehension rates are the result of shifts in border patrol policies or resources. Nonetheless, most experts agree that by 1986, undocumented immigration in the U.S. had increased substantially over earlier decades (Bean, Vernez, and Keely, 1989; Fix, 1991; Martin, 1994).

References

Bach, Robert L. 1978. "Mexican Immigration and U.S. Immigration Reforms in the 1960s." *Kapitalistate*, vol. 7: 73–80.

Baker, Susan González. 1990. *The Cautious Welcome: The Legalization Programs of the Immigration Reform and Control Act*. Santa Monica: The Rand Corporation.

Bean, Frank D., Georges Vernez, and Charles B. Keely. 1989. *Opening and Closing the Doors: Evaluating Immigration Reform and Control*. Lanham, MD: University Press of America.

Brossy, Julie. 1990. "Aliens Entering without Papers Show Sharp Rise." *San Diego Tribune*, March 12.

Calavita, Kitty. 1982. "California's 'Employer Sanctions': The Case of the Disappearing Law." Research Report Series, 39. La Jolla: Center for U.S.–Mexican Studies, University of California, San Diego.

———. 1983a. "California's 'Employer Sanctions' Legislation: Now You See it, Now You Don't." *Politics and Society*, vol. 12, no. 2: 205–30.

———. 1984. *U.S. Immigration Law and the Control of Labor: 1820–1924*. London: Academic Press.

———. 1989. "The Contradictions of Immigration Lawmaking: The Immigration Reform and Control Act of 1986." *Law and Policy*, vol. 11, no. 1 (January): 17–47.

———. 1990. "Employer Sanctions Violations: Toward a Dialectical Model of White-Collar Crime." *Law and Society Review*, vol. 24, no. 4: 1041–69.

———. 1992. *Inside the State: The Bracero Program, Immigration and the INS*. New York: Routledge.

Congressional Record. 1884. 48th Congress. 1st Session.

———. 1885. 48th Congress. 2nd Session.

———. 1902. 57th Congress. 1st Session.

———. 1921. 66th Congress. 3rd Session.

———. 1954. 83rd Congress. 2nd Session.

Congressional Research Service. 1980. *History of the Immigration and Naturalization Service*. A Report prepared for the use of The Select Commission on Immigration and Refugee Policy. Washington, D.C.: U.S. Government Printing Office.

Cornelius, Wayne A. 1982. "America in the Era of Limits: Nativist Reactions to the 'New' Immigration." Research Report Series, 3. La Jolla: Center for U.S.–Mexican Studies, University of California, San Diego.

———. 1988. "The Role of Mexican Labor in the North American Economy of the 1990s." Presented at the Fourth Annual Emerging Issues Program for State Legislative Leaders: "The North American Economy in the 1990s," 7–10 Dec.

Cornelius, Wayne A. 1989. "The U.S. Demand for Mexican Labor," in W. A. Cornelius and J. A. Bustamante (eds), *Mexican Migration to the United States: Origins, Consequences, and Policy Options*. La Jolla: Center for U.S.–Mexican Studies, University of California, San Diego, for the Bilateral Commission on the Future of U.S.–Mexican Relations.

Crane, Keith, Beth Asch, Joanna Zorn Heilbrunn, and Danielle C. Cullinane. 1990. *The Effect of Employer Sanctions on the Flow of Undocumented Immigrants to the United States*. Lanham, MD: University Press of America.

Crewdson, John. 1983. *The Tarnished Door: The New Immigrants and the Transformation of America*. New York: Times Books.

Dillin, John. 1989a. "Illegal Immigration Surges in '89," *Christian Science Monitor*, December 27.

———. 1989b. "Stalking Illegal Immigrants." *Christian Science Monitor*, November 30.

Fix, Michael. 1991. *The Paper Curtain: Employer Sanctions' Implementation, Impact, and Reform*, Washington, D.C.: The Urban Institute Press.

Fix, Michael, and Paul T. Hill. 1990. *Enforcing Employer Sanctions: Challenges and Strategies*. Lanham, MD: University Press of America.

Galarza, Ernesto. 1964. *Merchants of Labor: The Mexican Bracero Story*. Sage Yearbook in Politics and Public Policy. Santa Barbara, California: McNally & Loftin, Publishers.

Greene, Sheldon L. 1972. "Public Agency Distortion of Congressional Will: Federal Policy Toward Non-Resident Alien Labor." *George Washington Law Review*, vol. 40. no. 3 (March): 440–63.

Hadley, Eleanor. 1956. "A Critical Analysis of the Wetback Problem." *Law and Contemporary Problems*. vol. 21: 334–57.

Higham, John. 1955. *Strangers in the Land: Patterns of American Nativism, 1860–1925*. New Brunswick, NJ: Rutgers University Press.

Interpreter Releases. 1990. "Recent Developments: Congress Approves Major Immigration Reform." vol. 67, no. 41. October 29, 1990.

Kirstein, Peter Neil. 1973. *Anglo Over Bracero: A History of the Mexican Workers in the United States from Roosevelt to Nixon*. Ph.D. Dissertation, Saint Louis University.

Levine, Daniel B., Kenneth Hill, and Robert Warren (eds). 1985. *Immigration Statistics: A Story of Neglect*. National Academy Press.

Lopez, Gerald P. 1981. "Undocumented Mexican Migration: In Search of a Just Immigration Law and Policy." *UCLA Law Review*, 28 (April): 615–714.

Marshall, Ray. 1978. "Economic Factors Influencing the International Migration of Workers," in Stanley Ross (ed.), *Views Across the Border*, pp. 163–80. Albuquerque, NM: University of New Mexico Press.

Miller, Mark J. and Philip L. Martin. 1982. *Administering Foreign-Worker Programs: Lessons from Europe.* Lexington, MA: Lexington Books.

Montwieler, Nancy Humel. 1987. *The Immigration Reform Law of 1986.* Washington, D.C.: Bureau of National Affairs.

Morgan, Patricia. 1954. *Shame of a Nation: A Documented Story of Police-State Furor Against Mexican-Americans in the U.S.A.* Los Angeles: Los Angeles Committee for the Protection of the Foreign Born.

New Jersey Bureau of Industry and Labor. 1884. *7th Annual Report*, p. 295.

New York Journal of Commerce. 1892. December 13, p. 2.

Papademetriou, Demetrios G. 1992. *International Migration in North America: Issues, Policies, Implications.* Immigration Policy and Research, Working Paper 14. U.S. Department of Labor. Bureau of International Labor Affairs.

Papademetriou, Demetrios and Mark Miller. 1983. *The Unavoidable Issue: Immigration Policy in the 1980s.* Philadelphia: Institute for the Study of Human Issues.

Reisler, Mark, 1976. *By the Sweat of Their Brow: Mexican Immigrant Labor in the United States, 1900–40.* Westport, CT: Greenwood Press.

Samora, Julian. 1971. *Los Mujados: The Wetback Story.* Notre Dame, Indiana: The University of Indiana Press.

Schuck, Peter H. 1975. *The Judiciary Committees: A Study of the House and Senate Judiciary Committees.* The Ralph Nader Congress Project. New York: Grossman Publishers.

———. 1992. "The Politics of Rapid Legal Change: Immigration Policy in the 1980s." *Studies in American Political Development,* 6 (Spring): 37–92.

Select Commission on Immigration and Refugee Policy. 1981. *U.S. Immigration Policy and the National Interest. Final Report and Recommendations.* March 1. Washington, D.C.: U.S. Goernment Printing Office.

Teitelbaum, Michael S. 1980. "Right Versus Right: Immigration and Refugee Policy – the United States." *Foreign Affairs,* (Fall) vol. 59, no. 1: 21–59.

U.S. Commission on Agricultural Workers. 1992. *The Final Report of the Commission on Agricultual Workers.* Washington, D.C.: U.S. Government Printing Office.

U.S. Congress. House. 1972. *Illegal Aliens: Hearings before the Subcommittee on Immigration, Citizenship, and International Law of the House Committee on the Judiciary.* Parts 4–5. 92nd Congress, 2nd Session.

———. 1980. *Dept. of Justice Authorization and Oversight for Fiscal Year 1981. Hearings Before the Senate Committee on the Judiciary.* 96th Congress, 2nd Session.

———. 1981. *The Knowing Employment of Illegal Immigrants: Hearings Before the Subcommittee on Immigration and Refugee Policy of the Senate Committee on the Judiciary.* 97th Congress, 1st Session.

———. 1983. *The Immigration Reform and Control Act of 1983: Hearings Before the Subcommittee on Immigration, Refugees, and International Law of the House Committee on the Judiciary.* 98th Congress, 1st Session.

———. 1985. *Senate Judiciary Committee Report on S.* 1200, Report 99–132, 99th Congress, 1st Session.

U.S. Department of Labor. Bureau of International Labor Affairs. 1991. "Employer Sanctions and U.S. Labor Markets: Second Report." Washington, D.C.: U.S. Government Printing Office.

U.S. General Accounting Office. 1982. "Information on the Enforcement of Laws Regarding Employment of Aliens in Selected Countries." GAO/GGD-82-86. Washington, D.C.: Government Printing Office (Aug. 31).

——. 1985. "Illegal Aliens: Information on Selected Countries' Employment Prohibition Laws." GAO/GGD-86-17BR. Washington, D.C.: Government Printing Office (Oct.).

U.S. General Accounting Office. 1987. "Immigration Reform: Status of Implementing Employer Sanctions After One Year." GAO/GGD-88-14. Washington, D.C.: Government Printing Office (Nov.).

——. 1988. "Immigration Reform: Status of Implementing Employer Sanctions After Second Year." GAO/GGD-89-16. Washington, D.C.: Government Printing Office (Nov.).

——. 1990. "Immigration Reform: Employer Sanctions and the Question of Discrimination." GAO/GGD-90-62. Washington, D.C.: Government Printing Office (March).

U.S. Immigration and Naturalization Service. 1986. *Statistical Yearbook of the Immigration and Naturalization Service 1985*. Washington, D.C.: GP.

——. 1987. "Implementation of the Immigration Reform and Control Act: Final Rules." *52 Federal Register*, No. 84, May. 1.

——. 1988. "Employer Activity Report Through October 31, 1988." Unpublished internal report.

U.S. Statutes at Large. 13 U.S. Stat. at Large, pp. 385–7.

PART II

IMMIGRATION AND CONTEMPORARY ETHNICITY

6 From South of the Border: Hispanic Minorities in the United States

Alejandro Portes

Hispanics are those individuals whose birth or declared ancestry locates their origin in Spain or in the Latin American countries. Until recently, this rubric did not exist as a self-designation for most of the groups so labeled, being essentially a term of convenience for administrative agencies and scholarly research. Thus, the first thing of note to be said about this population is that it is not a consolidated minority but, rather, a group-in-formation whose boundaries and self-definitions are in flux. The emergence of a Hispanic "minority" has depended more on the actions of government and the collective perceptions of Anglo-American society than on the initiative of the individuals so designated. The increasing attention gained by this category of people derives mainly from their rapid population growth during the past two decades, a consequence of high fertility rates among some national groups, and, more important, of accelerated immigration. The heavy concentration of this population in certain regions of the country has added to its visibility. Over 75 percent of the 14.5 million people identified by the 1980 census as Hispanics are concentrated in just four states: California, New York, Texas, and Florida; California alone absorbed almost one-third.[1]

The absence of a firm collective self-identity among this population is an outcome of its great diversity, despite the apparent "commonness" of language and culture that figures so prominently in official writings. Under the same label, we find individuals whose ancestors lived in the country since at least the time of independence and others who arrived last year; substantial numbers of professionals and entrepreneurs along with humble farm laborers and unskilled factory workers; whites, blacks, mulattoes, and mestizos; full-fledged citizens and unauthorized aliens; and finally, among the immigrants, those who came in search of employment and a better economic future and those who arrived escaping death squads and political persecution at home. Aside from divisions between the "foreign" and the native-born, no difference is more significant than that of national origin. Nationality not only stands for different geographic places of birth but serves as a code word for the very distinct histories of each major immigrant flow, which molded the patterns of entry and adaptation to American society. For this reason the literature produced by "Hispanic" scholars has tended until recently to focus on the origins and evolution of their own national groups rather than encompassing the diverse histories of all those falling under the official rubric.

Most members of the Spanish-origin population – at least 60 percent – are of Mexican origin, divided between native-born Americans and immigrants; another 14 percent come from Puerto Rico and are U.S. citizens by birth, whether they were born in the island or the mainland; the third group in size is Cubans, who represent about 5 percent and are, overwhelmingly, recent immigrants coming after the consolidation of a communist regime in their country. In addition to these major groups, there are sizable contingents of Dominicans, Colombians, Salvadorans, Guatemalans, and other Central and South Americans, with their own distinct histories, characteristics, and patterns of adaptation.[2]

The complexity of Hispanic ethnicity is a consequence, first of all, of these diverse national origins, which often lead to more differences than similarities among the various groups. Lumping them together is not too dissimilar from attempting to combine turn-of-the-century northern Italian, Hungarian, Serbian, and Bohemian immigrants in a unit based on their "common" origin in various patches of the Austro-Hungarian Empire. A second difficulty is that most Spanish-origin groups are not yet "settled"; they continue to expand and change in response to uninterrupted immigration and close contact with events in the home countries. This dense traffic of people, news, and events between U.S.-based immigrant communities and their not-too-remote places of origin offers a far more challenging landscape than, for example, the condition of European ethnic groups, whose boundaries are generally well defined and whose bonds with the original countries are becoming increasingly remote.[3]

Migration and Settlement Patterns

Ethnic groups come into being in one of three ways: conquest, immigration, or political settlements. The third way is exceptional and is based on the agreement of spatially contiguous nationalities to cooperate in the creation of a common nation-state. Through such settlements, countries like Switzerland, Belgium, and Yugoslavia have emerged, and individual nationalities within each – especially the less numerous ones – have become ethnic minorities.[4] U.S. history does not register a single significant instance of this pattern of "negotiated" ethnicity, and thus ethnic groups have generally emerged through the other alternatives: conquest or immigration.[5]

Spanish-origin groups are well represented under each rubric because the historical events that created today's largest communities involved a mix of both conquest and immigration. To anticipate the argument: the migration flows that consolidated these communities reflect, almost mirrorlike, the expansion of the United States into its immediate periphery. The countries that supplied the major Spanish-origin groups in the United States today were, each in its time, targets of this expansionist pattern. U.S. intervention undermined the social and economic fabric constructed under Spanish colonial domination and reoriented it toward the new hegemonic power. This internal imbalancing of postcolonial societies, which preceded the onset of migration, has created today's ethnic communities. In a sense, the sending populations were Americanized before their members actually became immigrants to the United States.

Mexicans

Mexico is the prime example of the creation of a Spanish-origin community through conquest and immigration. As Mexican-American scholars have frequently noted, their ancestors were already here before a war of conquest converted them into foreigners in their own land.[6] Like native Indians, Mexicans represent a classic example of ethnic-group formation through military conquest and occupation. Things did not stop there, however, because the rapid expansion of the U.S. economy into what had been northern Mexico reclaimed labor from the portion of the country south of the Rio Grande. Growers and railroad companies sent paid recruiters into the reduced Mexican republic to offer free rail travel and advances on wages as incentives for local workers to come north. Mexican immigration thus had its immediate origins in deliberate recruitment by North American companies, and was not a spontaneous movement.[7] Economic penetration followed political intervention in shaping what eventually became the largest Spanish-origin minority in the United States.

At the time of the labor-recruitment waves in the nineteenth and early twentieth centuries, the border was scarcely enforced. As original settlers of the land, Mexicans came with the territory, and the arrival of new contract laborers and the movement back and forth across the Rio Grande met with little official resistance. Hence, Mexicans were an integral part of the Southwest's population before they became immigrants and much before they became "illegal" immigrants. The latter term made its appearance after passage of the National Origins Immigration Act of 1924 and the creation of the Border Patrol (established to prevent the inflow of Asians and other elements deemed undesirable, rather than the crossing of Mexicans). In 1929, for example, the U.S. Supreme Court upheld an earlier administrative decree declaring individuals who commuted between residences in Mexico and their work in the United States to be legal immigrants.[8] It was only in the post-Depression era and especially after World War II that crossing the border became a formally regulated event leading to the criminalization of the traditional inflow.[9]

Thus, contrary to the conventional portrait of Mexican immigration as a self-propelled movement of foreigners across a well-defined border, the process had its origins in North American geopolitical and economic interests that first restructured the neighboring nation and then proceeded to organize dependable labor outflows out of it. Such movements across the new border were a well-established routine in the Southwest before they became redefined as immigration, and then "illegal" immigration.

Puerto Ricans

Puerto Rico, a long-neglected outpost of the Spanish Empire, came into U.S. hands as an outcome of the Spanish-American War. North American influence, which had a profound effect on this mostly rural society dedicated to coffee exports and simple subsistence agriculture, began shortly after the military occupation, when U.S. capital started pouring into new sugarcane plantations and mill construction. The land requirements of the new industry and the political power of its promoters led to the rapid displacement of subsistence peasants. Because the labor requirements of sugar growing fall mainly during the harvest season, an increasing number of dispossessed peasants were forced into the cities, where urban unemployment, previously unknown, became an established feature of Puerto Rican society.[10]

In 1917 the Jones Act gave the islanders U.S. citizenship along with the obligation of serving in the armed forces. Despite the absence of legal restrictions on immigration and the new economic conditions in Puerto Rico, migration to the mainland began slowly. In 1920 Puerto Ricans in the United States were estimated at only twelve thousand, and twenty-five years later, they were still fewer than one hundred thousand.[11] The inflow accelerated after World War II, owing to three principal causes. The first was the continuing industrialization and urbanization of the island under U.S. auspices, especially after initiation of "Operation Bootstrap" in the late 1940s. Touted as a comprehensive solution to underdevelopment, the new policy industrialized the country and brought the majority of its population into the cities, but the capital-intensive industries did not generate enough jobs to keep up with the urban inflow and with rapid population growth. Unemployment became acute at a time when modern consumption expectations from the mainland were being diffused widely among the urban population.[12] Second, the barrier of a long and expensive sea journey disappeared with the advent of inexpensive air travel. Just as new products and fashions were pouring in from the North, the means to travel there in order to acquire them became available to the mass of the population. Third, the increasing economic reasons to leave the island and facilities for doing so were directly activated by labor recruiters, a practice that began at the turn of the century but became widespread only during and after World War II.[13]

These were years of rapid expansion in the U.S. economy, which generated a strong demand for low-wage unskilled labor. Just as Mexicans coming under the Bracero program helped meet that demand in the Southwest and Midwest, Puerto Rican contract labor filled the gap in the East. Job opportunities available to members of both migrant groups were similar, except that the Puerto Rican inflow had a stronger urban bent, which accelerated rapidly during the 1950s and 1960s. Puerto Rican men became employed in increasing numbers as unskilled factory operatives and as menial help in hotels and restaurants; Puerto Rican women worked as domestics and were hired by the thousands as seamstresses in the garment industry.[14]

From their places of destination Puerto Rican migrants moved gradually west, finally meeting the outposts of the Mexican inflow. Chicago, in particular, became a major point of confluence of the two Spanish-speaking labor streams. It was in the East and primarily in New York City, however, that the largest Puerto Rican concentrations emerged. Settling in dilapidated neighborhoods left behind by older immigrants, Puerto Ricans added a new flavor to the city's ethnic mix. East Harlem became Spanish Harlem; the South Bronx, the Lower East Side of Manhattan (redubbed *Loisaida*), and other urban districts were also rapidly Hispanicized.[15]

The consolidation of these ethnic communities represented the end point of a process that began with the acquisition and economic colonization of Puerto Rico. Just as in Mexico, the migrations that gave rise to today's ethnic minority did not occur spontaneously but had their beginnings in political decisions and economic initiatives on the receiving side. The rise of Spanish-speaking working-class communities in the Southwest and Northeast may thus be seen as a dialectical consequence of past expansion of the United States into its immediate periphery. The process of internal restructuring after intervention was more thorough in Puerto Rico than in Mexico, given direct political control by the United States and the weakness of the prior political and economic structures, a difference that stands at the core of the diverging paths of economic adaptation followed by immigrants from the two places.

Cubans

Cuban immigration, which also had its roots in the history of relations with the United States, took a different and more dramatic form. One effect of the Cuban War of Independence in the late nineteenth century was to create sizable émigré communities on the mainland, especially in New York, Key West, and Tampa. With the economic support of these three communities, the Cuban Revolutionary party launched the last and successful war of independence against Spain.[16] After three years of conflict, the United States intervened, and when the Spanish-American War ended, Cuba formally became a republic. However, the island was occupied by U.S. troops and governed by military authority from 1900 to 1902 and again in 1908–1909. The Platt Amendment, approved by the U.S. Congress as an addendum to the Cuban constitution, guaranteed the United States the right to intervene in Cuban internal affairs. Politically and economically, the island became a protectorate. North American capital flowed into the sugar industry and into iron and nickel mining shortly after the first occupation, although the growing of tobacco, coffee, and other agricultural exports remained in Cuban hands.[17] Despite domination by North American interests, Cuba never became a recruiting ground for cheap agricultural labor, mainly because of the somewhat higher level of development of the island's economy, relative to its neighbors, and the division of the rural labor force into small commercial farmers in tobacco, fruits, and coffee, and an organized rural proletariat in the cane fields. Both factors reduced the size of the subsistence peasantry and hence the pool of readily available workers. In addition, Cuba did not share a land border with the United States, as did Mexico, and was not a full U.S. possession, as was Puerto Rico.[18]

The Platt Amendment was formally abolished in the 1930s, but the heavy tutelage over Cuban internal and foreign affairs continued. In 1941, for example, Cuba declared war against the Axis powers on the same day as the United States, and voted consistently on the U.S. side in all international meetings during and after World War II. The North American hegemony shaped a local bourgeoisie that was profoundly Americanized in its outlook and behavior. The Cuban upper class relied on the North for political guidance and imitated American ways of doing business and patterns of consumption. This hegemony also promoted strong feelings of anti-imperialism in other segments of the population, especially among young intellectuals, whose desire to escape U.S. tutelage grew with the years.[19]

These contradictory trends were to culminate in the revolution against Fulgencio Batista. All segments of the nation participated in this struggle, but their visions of the future were quite different. For the Cuban bourgeoisie, Batista represented a throwback to a primitive era, which had to be overcome in order to consolidate liberal democracy. For the young intellectuals who led the fight, however, Batista was a U.S. puppet whose defeat would mark the beginnings of a genuine struggle of national liberation.[20] Opposition to imperialism became a rallying cry of the triumphant revolution as it pressured the Cuban upper and middle classes into submission. Deprived of political power and suffering wave after wave of confiscations, these groups saw their only escape in moving north to secure U.S. help for reconquering the island. True to their origins and past, the Cuban bourgeoisie relied on U.S. leadership and firmly believed that a communist regime so close to U.S. shores was an impossibility.[21]

The waves of exiles drastically transformed the character of the U.S. Cuban community. From a small group of descendants of the nineteenth-century émigrés and some occasional immigrants, Cubans became one of the most rapidly growing and most concentrated foreign minorities in the country. The political origins of this inflow gave it quite distinct characteristics compared to those initiated by labor recruitment. The first waves of Cuban refugees were strongly committed to return after the overthrow of Castro's regime, and were supported in this goal by the U.S. government.[22] The commitment waned after the Bay of Pigs defeat, especially after resolution of the Missile Crisis of 1962, which committed the U.S. government to restrain exile organizations in exchange for removal of Soviet missiles from the island. An adaptation process then began, which saw subsequent refugee cohorts become progressively less oriented toward immediate return and more toward family reunification and a new life in the United States.

The Kennedy and Johnson administrations attempted to resettle the Cubans away from Miami but met stubborn resistance. Gradually, resettled refugees drifted back to Miami, making Cubans one of the most spatially concentrated immigrant groups. Proximity to the island and climate may have something to do with this behavior, but the principal reason appears to have been the framework for daily life and economic opportunity created by the earlier cohorts of exiles, which generated a context of incorporation quite different from that awaiting other Latin immigrants.[23] Consequences of these patterns will be examined below.

Despite its unique history, Cuban immigration was also influenced decisively by the earlier hegemony exercised by the United States over the island. In this case, it was not deliberate recruitment that triggered large-scale migration but a major political upheaval that confronted the classes adapted to and prospering under U.S. hegemony with groups irreconcilably opposed to it. The victory of the latter led to an exodus of formerly dominant classes in the only direction that, given past history, they could possibly take.

Nonimmigrants

More recent migrations also illustrate the same general pattern of U.S. political and economic intervention. For instance, the present sizable inflow from the Dominican Republic did not start until the 1960s, in the wake of direct U.S. intervention to stem a leftist military uprising. The country had been occupied by U.S. troops earlier in the century but, during the decades of the Trujillo dictatorship, it remained an isolated backwater. The assassination of Trujillo and reassertion of U.S. hegemony in the country coincided with rapid increases in out-migration, as a consequence of which Dominicans represent today the seventh-largest immigration contingent to the United States and one of the most concentrated.[24] Unlike Cubans, they have chosen not south Florida but the New York metropolitan area as their principal place of settlement, where in 1985, they were the single largest immigrant nationality, accounting for 17 percent of the New York-bound inflow.[25]

The absolute and relative sizes of immigrant national cohorts drop rapidly as we leave the immediate periphery of the United States and the countries that experienced its intervention most directly. Despite its size, for example, Brazil has been a minor contributor to U.S.-bound immigration. In 1980 there were slightly more than forty thousand Brazilian-born persons in the United States, who represented only 0.3 percent of the foreign-born and less than one-tenth of 1 percent of the Brazilian population. The same is true of immigrants from Argentina, who amounted to 0.5 percent of the foreign-born, and whose weight relative to the Argentine population was less than one-third of 1 percent.[26] Geographical distance alone does not account for these patterns, however. For example, Costa Rica is a small country relatively close to the United States, yet in 1980 there were only 29,639 Costa Ricans in the United States. Unlike other Caribbean nations and several of its Central American neighbors, Costa Rica has been able to avoid, at least until recently, direct U.S. intervention and thus retain a measure of national autonomy. Neighboring El Salvador, however, which has experienced such intervention in its domestic life, has seen an accelerated process of out-migration, mainly to the United States.[27]

Charles Tilly argues for the importance of networks in the process of immigration. There is little doubt that immigration is a network-mediated process and that networks account for the continuity of these flows, even when the original conditions have changed,[28] but questions remain as to what forces initiate the process, why it originates in certain countries and locations and not in others, and what accounts for the different compositions and patterns of incorporation of various groups. Attempts to explain specific outflows must therefore rest on the identification of broader structural determinants. In this respect the contrasting experiences of Latin American countries offer a valuable clue because they show that contrary to much journalistic lore, the flows do not arise spontaneously out of poverty. Equally undeveloped countries and regions may have different migration histories, and sizable outflows may originate in more-developed areas rather than less-developed areas. The reason is that the beginnings of these movements are rooted in the history of prior economic and political relationships between sending and receiving countries. In particular, contemporary migration patterns tend to reflect precisely the character of past hegemonic actions by regional and global powers.

Labor Market Trends

The literature on labor-market performance and the socioeconomic condition of the major Spanish-origin groups in the United States has sought to answer three questions: Are there significant differences in the condition of these groups both in comparison with the U.S. population and among themselves? Are there significant differences in the *process* by which education, occupation, and income are achieved? If there are differences in this process, what are their principal causes?

Table 6.1 presents a summary of descriptive statistics drawn from the 1980 census. Aside from age and nativity, included as background information, the rest of the figures indicate that the socioeconomic performance of Spanish-origin minorities is generally inferior to that of the U.S. population as a whole and, by extension, of the white non-Hispanic majority. This is true of education, occupation, income, and entrepreneurship (measured by rates of self-employment), although less so of labor force participation, especially among females.

The same figures also indicate major disparities among Spanish-origin groups. In general, Puerto Ricans are in the worst socioeconomic situation, as manifested by high levels of unemployment, female-headed families, and poverty, and correspondingly low levels of education, occupation, and income. Mexicans occupy an intermediate position, although consistently below the U.S. population. Note that Mexicans are the majority of all Hispanics and have a disproportionate weight in aggregate figures that purport to describe the Spanish-origin population as a whole. Cubans are in a better situation, as are the "Other Spanish." Both groups have rates of occupation, family income, and self-employment closer to the U.S. average. ("Other Spanish" consists of immigrant groups too small to be counted individually plus those that declared Spanish-origin ancestry without further specification. The conflation of groups make it difficult to provide a meaningful interpretation of the absolute condition of the category or the processes that have led to its creation.)

Table 6.1   [*Orig. table 6.1*] Selected characteristics of Spanish-origin groups, 1980

Variable	Mexicans	Puerto Ricans	Cubans	Other Spanish	Total U.S.
Number (in millions)	8.7	2.0	0.8	3.1	226.5
Median age	21.9	22.3	37.7	25.5	30.0
Percentage native born	74.0	96.9	22.1	60.5	93.8
Percentage female-headed families	16.4	35.3	14.9	20.5	14.3
Median years of school completed[a]	9.6	10.5	12.2	12.3	12.5
Percentage high school graduates[a]	37.6	40.1	55.3	57.4	66.5
Percentage with 4+ years of college[a]	4.9	5.6	16.2	12.4	16.2
Percentage in labor force[b]	64.6	54.9	66.0	64.6	62.0
Percentage females in labor force[b]	49.0	40.1	55.4	53.4	49.9
Percentage married women in labor force[c]	42.5	38.9	50.5	45.7	43.9
Percentage self-employed[d]	3.5	2.2	5.8	4.5	6.8
Percentage unemployed	9.1	11.7	6.0	8.0	6.5
Percentage professional specialty, executive, and managerial occupations:					
males	11.4	14.1	22.0	19.0	25.8
females[d]	12.6	15.5	17.9	17.2	24.7
Percentage operators and laborers:					
males	30.4	30.9	23.1	23.8	18.3
females[d]	22.0	25.5	24.2	19.9	11.7
Median family income	14,765	10,734	18,245	16,230	19,917
Median income of married couples with own children	14,855	13,428	20,334	16,708	19,630
Percentage of families with incomes of $50,000+	1.8	1.0	5.2	3.6	5.6
Percentage of all families below poverty level	20.6	34.9	11.7	16.7	9.6

[a] Persons twenty-five years of age or older.
[b] Persons sixteen years of age or older.
[c] Women sixteen years of age or older; husband present and own children under six years of age.
[d] Employed persons sixteen years of age or older.

Sources: Bureau of the Census, *General Population Characteristics, United States Summary*, 1983a: tables 39, 48, 70; Bureau of the Census, *General Social and Economic Characteristics, United States Summary*, 1983b: tables 141, 166–71.

The existence of differences in the socioeconomic position of the Spanish-origin population, a phenomenon well known to researchers in the field, must have some cause or causes.[29] As framed in current research efforts, the issue is whether the condition of a specific minority is explainable entirely on the basis of its background characteristics or, rather, derives from other factors. If members of a given group attain socioeconomic positions comparable to those of native-born Americans with similar human-capital endowments, the observed differences can be imputed to the group's current average levels of education, work experience, and other significant causal variables. If, on the other hand, differences persist after statistically equalizing the minority's background, other factors must come into play. If the gap is disadvantageous, discrimination is generally assumed to play a role; if the gap is advantageous, collective characteristics of the group are explored in search of a possible explanation.

Several analyses, especially those of educational attainment, tend to support the "no-difference, no-discrimination" hypothesis. This is the conclusion reached, for example, by Hirschman and Falcón after a broad-gauged study of educational levels among "religio-ethnic" groups in the United States.[30] However, these authors also report that after controlling for all possible relevant predictors, the Mexican educational attainment still falls 1.4 years below the norm. Similarly, in a study of occupational attainment based on the 1976 Survey of Income and Education (SEI), Stolzenberg concludes that the causal process is essentially the same among all Spanish-origin groups and that, after standardizing individual background characteristics, no evidence of discrimination remains. However, Stolzenberg includes in the analysis a series of state dummy variables in order to control for the possible confounding of geographic location and ethnicity. What he does, of course, is to insure a priori that ethnic differences would be insignificant because of the high concentration of particular groups in certain states. Including "Florida" as a causal predictor, for example, pretty much eliminates the distinct effect of Cuban ethnicity because this group is highly concentrated in that state; the same is true for New York and the Puerto Ricans. Even with state dummies included, significant ethnic effects on occupational attainment remain in Stolzenberg's analysis of the Mexican and Cuban groups. The Mexican coefficient is negative, indicating lower occupational levels than those expected on the basis of the group's average characteristics; the Cuban effect is positive, however, indicating above-average attainment, and becomes stronger when state controls are deleted.

A subsequent and more carefully specified analysis of SEI wage data by Reimers yields conclusions similar to Stolzenberg's. After controlling for selection bias and human-capital predictors, Reimers finds that male Puerto Rican wage levels fall 18 percent below the average for white non-Hispanic men; those of Mexicans and other Hispanics are 6 and 12 percent below, respectively. These sizable differences are interpreted as evidence of labor-market discrimination. Cuban men, however, receive wages 6 percent above white non-Hispanics of similar human-capital endowment. These differences lead Reimers to conclude that "the major Hispanic-American groups differ so much among themselves...that it makes little sense to lump them under a single 'Hispanic' or 'minority' rubric for either analysis or policy treatment."[31] Studies based on different and more recent data sets also tend to replicate the finding of significant disadvantages in occupational and earnings attainment for Mexicans and, in particular, Puerto Ricans, and a small but consistent advantage for Cubans relative to their human-capital levels.[32]

In attempting to explain the differences, we are not helped by arguing that there is discrimination in the labor market because that does not clarify why discrimination operates differentially among culturally similar groups and sometimes not at all. The only course is to examine the particular characteristics and history of each group. To do this, we must not only abandon the general label "Hispanic" but also leave behind the residual category "Other Spanish," which is too heterogeneous to permit a valid summary explanation. Left are the three major Spanish-origin minorities: Mexicans, Puerto Ricans, and Cubans.

When the socioeconomic performances of these groups are compared, two major riddles emerge. First, why do Mexicans and Puerto Ricans differ so significantly in such characteristics as labor force participation, family structure, and poverty, as well as in levels of wage discrimination; and second, why do Cubans register above-average occupations and family incomes relative to their levels of human capital? The below-average socioeconomic condition of the first two groups is *not* itself a riddle because their migration and settlement histories reveal the roots of exploitation and discrimination. What historical accounts do not explain is why the present condition of these groups should differ so markedly. Similarly, the absolute advantage of Cubans relative to other

Spanish-origin groups is not mysterious because, as seen above, this minority was formed largely by upper- and middle-class persons who left Cuba after the revolution. The puzzle is rather why the collective attainment of Cubans should sometimes exceed what can be expected on the basis of their average human-capital endowment. A fairly common explanation is that Cubans were welcomed in the United States as refugees from a communist regime, receiving significant government aid denied to other groups. This explanation, mentioned in passing by Jasso and Rosenzweig, and vigorously defended by Pedraza-Bailey[33] in her comparative study of Cuban and Mexican immigrants, runs against evidence from other refugee groups that have received substantial federal benefits but remain in a precarious socioeconomic condition. Southeast Asian refugees, for example, benefited from the extensive aid provisions mandated by the 1980 Refugee Act, more comprehensive and generous than those made available to Cubans during the 1960s, yet levels of unemployment, poverty, and welfare dependence among most Southeast Asian groups continue to exceed those of almost every other ethnic minority.[34]

Although the favorable governmental reception of Cubans in the United States certainly contributed to their adaptation, it must be seen as part of their distinct mode of incorporation. This interpretation calls attention to the social and economic context in which successive immigrant cohorts are received. A sociological explanation to the above riddles can be found in the distinct modes of incorporation of the three major Spanish-origin groups. Mexican immigrants and new Mexican-American entrants into the labor force tend to come from modest socioeconomic origins and have low average levels of education. In addition, however, they enter labor markets in the Southwest and Midwest, where Mexican laborers have traditionally supplied the bulk of unskilled labor. As noted by Tilly, social networks within the ethnic community tend to direct new workers toward jobs similar to those of their coethnics, a pattern reinforced by the orientation of employers. Lacking a coherent entrepreneurial community or effective political representation, Mexican wage workers must fall back on their own individual resources, "discounted" by past history and present discrimination against their group. Because many Mexican workers are immigrants and a substantial proportion are undocumented, employers continue to view them as a valuable source of pliable low-wage labor, a "preference" that may account for the relatively low average rates of Mexican unemployment, yet it also creates barriers for those who seek upward mobility.[35]

Puerto Rican migrants fulfilled a similar function for industry and agriculture in the Northeast during an earlier period, but with two significant differences. First, Puerto Ricans often entered labor markets that were highly unionized, unlike those of the Southwest; second, they were U.S. citizens by birth and thus entitled to legal protection and not subject to ready deportation. These two factors combined over time to make Puerto Rican workers a less pliable, more costly, and better organized source of labor. When employers in the Northeast began gradually to shift to other immigrant groups – West Indian contract workers in agriculture, and Dominican, Colombian, and other mostly undocumented immigrants in urban industry and services – Puerto Ricans on the mainland were shunted aside in the labor market but lacked an entrepreneurial community to generate their own jobs.[36] During the past two decades they have migrated back to the island in record numbers, and those remaining in the Northeast have experienced levels of unemployment and poverty comparable only to those of the black population.[37]

The Cuban pattern of adaptation is different because the first exile cohorts created an economically favorable context of reception for subsequent arrivals. The bulk of early Cuban migration, composed of displaced members of the native bourgeoisie rather than laborers, brought the capital and entrepreneurial skills with which to start new businesses; later arrivals followed a similar course, leading eventually to the consolidation of an ethnic enclave economy in south Florida.[38] The strong entrepreneurial orientation of the earlier Cuban cohorts is illustrated by census figures on minority-business ownership in table 6.2. In 1977, when these data were collected, black- and Mexican-owned businesses were the most numerous in absolute terms, reflecting the size of the respective populations. In per capita terms, however, Cuban-owned firms were by far the most numerous and the largest in gross receipts and number of employees. Figures in the bottom rows of table 6.2 suggest that the relative weight of Miami Cuban firms among Hispanic-owned businesses has continued to grow since 1977. By 1984 five of ten largest Hispanic-owned firms in the country and four of the ten largest banks were in Miami, at a time when the Spanish-origin population of the area represented barely 5 percent of the national total.

Table 6.2   [*orig. table 6.2*] Spanish-origin and black-owned firms in
the United States

Variable	Mexicans	Puerto Ricans	Cubans	All Spanish	Black
Number of firms, 1977	116,419	13,491	30,336	219,355	231,203
Firms per 100,000 population	1,468	740	3,651	1,890	873
Average gross receipts per firm (thousands of dollars)	44.4	43.9	61.6	47.5	37.4
Firms with paid employees, 1977	22,718	1,767	5,588	41,298	39,968
Firms with employees per 100,000 population	286	97	672	356	151
Average employees per firm	4.9	3.9	6.6	5.0	4.1
Average gross receipts per firm with employees (thousands of dollars)	150.4	191.9	254.9	172.9	160.1
Ten largest Hispanic industrial firms, 1984: Percentage located in area of group's concentration[a]	40	10	50	100	
Estimated sales (millions of dollars)	402	273	821	2,317	
Number of employees	5,800	1,100	3,175	10,075	
Ten largest Hispanic-owned banks and savings banks, 1984: Percentage in area of group's concentration[a]	40	20	40	100	
Total assets (millions of dollars)	1,204	489	934	2,627	
Total deposits (millions of dollars)	1,102	434	844	2,380	

[a] Southwest locations for Mexicans; New York and vicinity for Puerto Ricans; Miami metropolitan area for Cubans.

Sources: Bureau of the Census, *1977 Survey of Minority-Owned Business Enterprises*, 1980; Hispanic Review of Business, *Annual Survey of Hispanic Business*, 1984, 1985.

This helps explain how successive cohorts of Cuban immigrants
have been able to make use of past human-capital endowments and
exceed their expected level of attainment. Employment in enclave
firms allows new arrivals to use their occupational skills and experience without having them "discounted" by discrimination or unfamiliarity with the receiving culture, and it creates opportunities for
upward mobility within existing firms or through self-employment.
The bond between co-national employers and employees helps
fledgling immigrant enterprises survive by taking advantage of the
cheap and generally disciplined labor of the new arrivals; the latter
may benefit over the long term, however, by availing themselves of
mobility opportunities within the enclave that are generally absent
elsewhere.

A longitudinal study of Cuban and Mexican immigrants conducted during the 1970s illustrates different patterns of adaptation,
conditioned by the presence or absence of an enclave mode of
incorporation. By the early 1970s the middle-class immigration
from Cuba had ceased and new arrivals came from more modest
socioeconomic origins, comparable to those of Mexican legal immigrants. The study interviewed samples of Cuban refugees and Mexican legal immigrants at the time of their arrival during 1973–1974,
and followed both samples for six years, interviewing respondents
twice during that interval.[39] Table 6.3 presents data from the last
follow-up survey, which took place in 1979–1980. The first finding
of note is the degree of concentration of Cuban respondents, 97
percent of whom remained in the Miami metropolitan area. By
comparison, the Mexican sample dispersed throughout the Southwest and Midwest, with the largest concentration – 24 percent –
settling in the border city of El Paso.

Table 6.3 [*orig. table 6.3*]   The socioeconomic position of Cuban and
Mexican immigrants after six years in the United States

Variable	Mexicans (N = 455)	Cubans (N = 413)
Percentage in city of principal concentration	23.7	97.2
Percentage speaking English well	27.4	23.7
Percentage home owners	40.2	40.0
Percentage self-employed	5.4	21.2
Percentage employed by other Mexicans/Cubans	14.6	36.3
Average monthly income[a]	$912	$1,057
Average monthly income of employees in large Anglo-owned firms[a]	$1,003	$1,016
Average monthly income in small nonenclave firms[a]	$880	$952
Average monthly income in enclave firms[a]	–	$1,111
Average monthly income of the self-employed, Cubans[a]	–	$1,495

[a] 1979 dollars.

Source: A. Portes and R. Bach, *Latin Journey: Cuban and Mexican Immigrants in the
United States* (Berkeley: University of California Press, 1985), chaps 6, 7.

Otherwise, samples were similar in their knowledge of English – low for both groups after six years – and their rates of home ownership. They differed sharply, however, in variables relating to their labor-market position. More than one-third of 1973 Cuban arrivals were employed by Cuban firms in 1979, and one-fifth had become self-employed by that time; these figures double and quadruple the respective proportions in the Mexican sample. Despite their concentration in a low-wage region of the United States, after six years the Cubans had an average monthly income significantly greater than that of Mexicans. However, a closer look at the data shows no .major differences among either Mexicans or Cubans employed in large Anglo-owned firms, commonly identified as part of the "primary" labor market. Nor are there significant differences among those employed in the smaller firms identified with the "secondary" sector; Mexicans and Cubans in both samples received lower wages than primary-sector employees. The significant difference between Cuban and Mexican immigrants lies with the large proportion of the former employed in enclave firms, whose average income was actually the highest in both samples. In addition, self-employed Cuban immigrants exceeded the combined monthly incomes of both samples by approximately $500, or one-half of the total average.

Regarding Mexicans and Puerto Ricans, there is no comparable empirical evidence to support the mode of incorporation hypothesis as an explanation of observed occupational and income differences. Few studies compare Puerto Rican patterns of attainment and those of other minorities, but the available information points to the gradual supplanting of Puerto Ricans by newer immigrant groups as sources of low-wage labor in the Northeast.[40] This evidence is congruent with the interpretation of the current situation of one group – Mexicans – as an outcome of its continued incorporation as a preferred source of low-wage labor in the Southwest and Midwest and that of the other – Puerto Ricans – as a consequence of its increasing redundancy for the same labor market in its principal area of concentration.

Political Behavior and Citizenship

Differences among Spanish-origin groups are again highlighted by their political concerns, organizations, and effectiveness. Regardless of national origin, a major gap separates the native-born, whose interests are always tied to their situation in the United States, and immigrants, whose political allegiance and organized actions often relate to events in the country of origin. The political sociology of Hispanic-Americans can thus be conveniently summarized under two main categories: first, the goals and actions of established groups, including the native-born and naturalized citizens; and second, the political orientations, particularly the problematic shift of citizenship, among immigrants.

Ethnic politics

The political history of Mexican-Americans bears considerable resemblance to that of American blacks. Both groups endured subordination and disenfranchisement and then attempts to dilute their electoral power through such devices as literacy tests, gerrymandering, and co-optation of ethnic leaders, and both groups have had similar reactions to past discrimination. Mexican-Americans differ from black Americans, however, in one crucial respect, namely, their proximity to and strong identification with the country of origin. Attachment to Mexico and Mexican culture correlates strongly with a sense of "foreignness," even among the native-born and, hence, with lower rates of political participation.[41] The reluctance to shift national allegiances appears to have presented a major obstacle in the path of effective organizing by Mexican-American leaders.

Despite these difficulties, a number of organizations have emerged that articulate the interests of one or another segment of the minority. These range from the earlier *mutualistas* and the Orden de Hijos de America to the subsequent League of United Latin American Citizens (LULAC) and the G.I. Forum, created to defend the interests of Mexican-American World War II veterans.[42] The 1960s marked a turning point in Mexican-American politics. Inspired in large part by the black example, a number of militant organizations emerged that attempted to redress past grievances by means other than participation in the established parties. Many radical student and youth organizations were created, and a third party, La Raza Unida, won a series of significant electoral victories in Texas. Although the more militant demands of these organizations were never met and most of them have ceased to exist, they succeeded in mobilizing the Mexican-American population and creating a cadre of politicians who could forcefully defend its interests before national leaders and institutions. Today, LULAC and the

Mexican-American Legal Defense Fund (MALDEF) are among the most powerful and active Hispanic organizations. In 1984 ten of the eleven members of the Hispanic Caucus in Congress represented districts with a heavy Mexican-American population.[43]

Unlike Mexicans, Puerto Ricans are U.S. citizens by birth and do not face the obstacle that naturalization proceedings pose to political participation. In addition, the Puerto Rican migrant population is concentrated in New York, where both the city and state have a long tradition of ethnic politics. A number of factors have conspired, however, to reduce the political weight of this population over the years; these include lack of knowledge of English, generally low levels of education and occupation, and the resistance of established political "clubs" led by Jews, Italians, and other older immigrants. The strong sojourner orientation of many migrants has also reduced their interest and attention to local politics. For many years, Puerto Rican activism on the mainland aimed at improvements in the economic and political status of the island rather than of the New York community.[44]

Although concern for the welfare of Puerto Rico has not diminished, the needs of the mainland communities have gradually gained attention since World War II. During the 1960s Puerto Rican politics paralleled the course followed by Mexicans and blacks, with the appearance of militant youth organizations like the Young Lords and the Puerto Rican Revolutionary Workers' Organization. There were also significant advances in mainstream politics as a number of Puerto Ricans won local and state offices; like Mexicans, Puerto Ricans have voted overwhelmingly Democratic. By 1982, when the joint Black and Puerto Rican Caucus had been established, there were six Puerto Rican state legislators. During the 1970s Puerto Ricans also elected their first state senator and first congressman. At present Robert Garcia (the Bronx, 18th District) is the eleventh member of the Hispanic Caucus in the U.S. House and the sole Puerto Rican representative.

Like Mexicans, first-generation Cuban immigrants face the riddle of naturalization, and like Puerto Ricans, they tend to remain preoccupied with events in their country. Cubans, like both Mexicans and Puerto Ricans, usually speak little English on arrival, which also conspires against effective participation. Despite these obstacles, Cuban-Americans have become a potent political force in south Florida, and now hold mayoral offices in the largest cities in the area, Miami and Hialeah, and in several smaller municipalities. Cuban-Americans are influential in the local Republican party and have elected a substantial delegation to the state legislature. A political action group funded by exile businessmen – the Cuban-American National Foundation – has lobbied effectively in Washington for such causes as the creation of Radio Martí and the appointment of Cubans to federal offices.[46] The loyalty of Cuban-Americans to the Republican party dates from two events of the Kennedy administration: the defeat of the Bay of Pigs invasion in 1961 and the Soviet-American agreement of 1962 that reined in the exiles and prevented their launching new military attacks. Cubans have blamed the Democrats for these two events, which destroyed chances for a victorious return to the island. As hopes for return became dimmer and the refugee community turned inward, Cubans naturalized in record number and lined up solidly behind the Republican party, which has become an increasingly serious contender in Florida politics.[47] The trend culminated in the election of the Spanish-origin Republican mayor of Tampa as the new governor in 1986.

There are recent indications, however, that the monolithic conservatism of the Cuban vote may be more apparent than real. It is true that Cubans overwhelmingly supported Ronald Reagan and other Republican candidates for national office in 1980 and 1984, and that they continue to oppose any foreign policy initiative perceived as "soft" on communism. Nevertheless, the vote in local elections has become more progressive and guided by local concerns and issues. During a recent mayoral election in Miami, for example, the Republican candidate finished a distant last. The final race was between two Cuban-Americans, a conservative banker supported by the Latin and Anglo business communities and a more progressive, Harvard-trained lawyer. The latter won handily, primarily because of a heavy Cuban grass-roots vote. Similarly, indications are that Cuban representatives in the state legislature are more likely than their Republican colleagues to be concerned with populist issues, especially those involving ethnic minorities.

An important topic for future research is the apparent convergence of the political organizations representing major Spanish-origin groups. Although, as noted earlier, there is little similarity in the historical origins or present socioeconomic situation of these groups, political leaders see a basic community of interests on such issues as the defense of bilingualism and a common cultural image. If the term *Hispanic* means anything of substance at present, it is at the political level. An indication of this trend is the emergence of the National Association of Latin Elected Officials (NALEO), a

Table 6.4 [orig. table 6.4] U.S. citizenship acquisition for selected countries and regions, 1970–80

	Naturalized 1971–80	Percentage of total	Cohort of 1970[b]	Naturalized during next decade	Percentage of cohort	Peak year during decade[c]
Cuba	178,374	12	16,334	7,621	47	8th (2,444)
Mexico	68,152	5	44,469	1,475	3	9th (404)
Central and South America	40,843	3	31,316	6,161	20	9th (1,480)
Canada	130,380	9	13,804	856	6	8th (182)
Western Europe	371,683	25	92,433	17,965	19	7th (5,103)
Asia	473,754	32	92,816	44,554	48	7th (15,129)
Totals[a]	1,464,772		373,326	94,532	25	7th (27,681)

[a] All countries; column figures do not add up to row total because of exclusion of other world regions (Africa, Eastern Europe, and Oceania).
[b] Number of immigrants admitted for legal permanent residence.
[c] Year of most numerous naturalizations during the decade after legal entry; actual number naturalized in parentheses.

Source: Immigration and Naturalization Service, *Annual Reports*, various years.

strong organization consisting of Mexican, Puerto Rican, and Cuban congressmen, state legislators, and mayors.[48] So far, this organization has managed to function smoothly and effectively, despite major differences among its disparate constituents.

Citizenship

The first step for effective political participation by any foreign group is citizenship acquisition. Table 6.4 presents data showing the different rates of naturalization among the foreign-born in recent years. During the 1970s, naturalized Mexican immigrants represented only 6 percent of the total, even though they were the most numerous of all nationalities and represented close to 20 percent of all legal admissions during the preceding decade. By contrast, the much smaller number of Cuban immigrants contributed 12 percent of all naturalizations, exceeding the figure for Canada despite the much larger number of eligible Canadian immigrants. The rest of Latin America contributed only 3 percent, owing to the relatively small size of the cohorts of legal immigrants from the region before the 1970s.

The remaining columns of the table present data for the 1970 immigrant cohort that is representative of trends during recent years. The highest rates of naturalization are for Asian immigrants – mostly Chinese, Indians, South Koreans, and Filipinos – and Cubans. Citizenship acquisition among these groups represented close to one-half of the 1970 immigrant cohorts from the respective source countries. Intermediate rates – close to one-fifth of the 1970 immigrant cohort – are found among western Europeans and Central and South Americans. The lowest rates, less than 7 percent, are for immigrants from the two countries contiguous to the United States: Mexico and Canada. Mexican immigrants are also the slowest to naturalize, as indicated by their peak year of naturalizations during the decade – the ninth, two full years behind the norm for all countries.[49]

The analytical literature on determinants of these differences contains two separate strands: first, studies that attempt to explain variation among nationalities, and second, those that focus on proximate causes within a particular group. A pioneer contribution to the first or comparative literature is the study by sociologist W. Bernard, who identified literacy, educational attainment, and occupational prestige as major causes of differences in the rates of naturalization between "old" and "new" European immigrants, as defined in his time. Subsequent studies have generally supported Bernard's hypothesis.[50]

In addition, more recent quantitative studies have identified other variables, such as the political origin of migration and the geographical proximity of the country of origin. Refugees from communist-controlled countries naturalize in greater numbers, all things being equal, than other immigrants. Those from nearby countries, especially nations that share land borders with the United States, tend to resist citizenship change more than others. Both results seem to reflect the operation of a general factor, which may be labeled the potential "reversibility" of migration: immigrants for whom it is more difficult to return because of political conditions back home or the high cost and difficulty of the journey tend to naturalize at higher rates than those for whom return is a simple bus ride away.[51]

Studies of the proximate determinants of citizenship have generally focused on minorities with the lowest propensities to naturalize. Mexican immigrants are notorious in this respect, their collective behavior having given rise to a huge gap between the pool of potentially eligible citizens (and voters) and its actual size. Accordingly, several recent studies have sought to identify the principal determinants of both predispositions and behaviors with respect to U.S. citizenship within Mexican immigrant communities. This research includes both quantitative analyses and ethnographic observations.[52] Studies that focus on objective variables have identified such characteristics as length of U.S. residence, level of education, knowledge of English, age, marital status, citizenship of spouse, and place of residence as potentially significant. In general, the decision to naturalize appears to derive from a complex of determinants, including individual needs and motivations and facilitational factors. Mexican immigrants whose stake in the United States is limited to low-wage jobs have little motivation to obtain citizenship. Those, on the other hand, who have acquired property, whose spouses or children are U.S. citizens, and who begin to feel barriers to upward mobility because of their legal status have much greater incentives to begin the process.[53]

Motivation is not enough, however, because citizenship acquisition is not easy. It requires knowledge of English and some knowledge of civics to pass the naturalization test, which favors the better-educated immigrants and those who have lived in the country longer and know more about it. Finally, there is the question of external facilitation. The most significant factors in this respect are social networks and the conduct of official agencies in charge of the process. Networks, as noted earlier, play a variable role in this process because networks consisting solely of Mexican kin and friends tend to be unsupportive of the naturalization process and those that include U.S.-born or naturalized relatives and friends facilitate it.[54] The key governmental agency involved in the process, the U.S. Immigration and Naturalization Service (INS), has a decidedly ambiguous approach toward Mexican applicants. Indeed, ethnographic research has identified "fear of the INS" as a significant deterrent to naturalization among Mexican immigrants, and North, in *The Long Gray Welcome*, an in-depth study of the agency's naturalization procedures, describes the numerous obstacles – from heavy backlogs to arbitrary examiners – often thrown in the way of poor and poorly educated immigrants.[55] Confronted with such barriers, the appropriate question may not be why so few Mexicans naturalize but why so many succeed in doing so.

Conclusion

The history of the major Spanish-origin communities above the Rio Grande reveals a turning point with the expansion and intervention of a rising national power during the nineteenth and early twentieth centuries, and provides context for today's efforts to reach economic and political parity within American society. The success of these efforts depends on the material and educational resources of the different immigrant groups and on the social contexts that receive them. Workers coming to perform low-wage labor in agriculture and industry have faced the greatest obstacles because they lack the resources to move up quickly in the U.S. economy and have been subject to much discrimination. In addition, immigrant workers who see their journeys as temporary maintain strong expectations of return, which adds to their sense of "foreignness" and discourages active participation in mainstream American life.[56]

The contrasting history of the Cuban community is not likely to be repeated any time soon because the circumstances of its origin and initial reception in the United States are unique. Except for professionals migrating legally from several South American countries, whose patterns of adaptation tend to be fairly smooth, the most likely trend for future years is the continuation of manual labor immigration from Mexico, the Dominican Republic, and other countries of the Caribbean Basin. One reason for this trend is the resilience of networks of migration over time: migrant flows tend to become self-sustaining through the actions of kin and friends across space. A second reason is the continuing demand for immigrant labor by domestic employers. In the West, demand for Mexican workers remains strong both in agriculture and in industry. In the East, a similar demand exists for Colombians, Dominicans, West Indians, and other Caribbean nationalities.[57]

An exception to this trend is the situation of Puerto Ricans. For reasons discussed above, the condition of "preferred" low-wage labor shifted gradually from this minority to other Caribbean immigrant groups. As a result, the cities of the Northeast face the paradox of unemployment levels among their Puerto Rican communities twice as large as those of native whites, along with the influx of thousands of undocumented immigrants who face little trouble in finding employment. The situation of urban Puerto Ricans thus approaches the bleak one of inner-city blacks, except for the possibility of return migration to the island. Thousands have made use in recent years of this "reverse" escape valve away from the grim conditions of the mainland. In general, the diversity of Spanish-origin communities and the complexity of migration and settlement patterns is likely to continue. Although it is too soon to anticipate the outcome, the growing size of many of these groups, their concentration, and their increasing political and economic presence guarantee them a not insignificant role in American society.

Notes

1 Bureau of the Census, *Condition of Hispanics in America Today*, Special Release, September 13, 1983.
2 C. Nelson and M. Tienda, "The Structuring of Hispanic Ethnicity: Historical and Contemporary Perspectives," *Ethnic and Racial Studies*, 1985: 49–74; Immigration and Naturalization Service, *Annual Report* (Washington, D.C.: Government Printing Office, 1984).
3 N. Glazer, "Pluralism and the New Immigrants," *Society* 19 (1981): 31–6; R. D. Alba, *Italian Americans: Into the Twilight of Ethnicity* (Englewood Cliffs, N.J.: Prentice-Hall, 1985).
4 F. Nielsen, "Structural Conduciveness and Ethnic Mobilization: The Flemish Movement in Belgium," in *Competitive Ethnic Relations*, ed. S. Olzak and J. Nagel (Orlando, Fla.: Academic Press, 1986), pp. 173–98; K. Hill, "Belgium: Political Change in a Segmented Society," in *Electoral Behavior: A Comparative Handbook*, ed. R. Rose, (New York: Free Press, 1974), pp. 29–107.

5 S. Lieberson, "A Societal Theory of Race and Ethnic Relations," *American Sociological Review* 26 (1961): 902–10.
6 M. Barerra, *Race and Class in the Southwest: A Theory of Racial Inequality* (Notre Dame: Notre Dame University Press, 1980); A. Camarillo, *Chicanos in a Changing Society* (Cambridge: Harvard University Press, 1979).
7 J. Samora, *Los Mojados: The Wetback Story* (Notre Dame: University of Notre Dame Press, 1971); J. A. Bustamente, "The Historical Context of Undocumented Mexican Immigration to the United States," *Aztlán* 3 (1973): 257–81; M. J. Piore, *Birds of Passage: Migrant Labor and Industrial Societies* (New York: Cambridge University Press, 1979).
8 R. L. Bach, "Mexican Immigration and the American State," *International Migration Review* 12 (1978): 536–58.
9 Bustamente, "The Historical Context of Undocumented Mexican Immigration"; Barrera, *Race and Class in the Southwest*.
10 F. A. Bonilla and R. Campos, "A Wealth of Poor: Puerto Ricans in the New Economic Order," *Daedalus* 110 (1981): 133–76.
11 J. Moore and H. Pachón, *Hispanics in the United States* (Englewood Cliffs, N.J.: Prentice-Hall, 1985).
12 C. Rodriguez, *The Ethnic Queue in the U.S.: The Case of Puerto Ricans* (San Francisco: R & E Research Associates, 1976); Bonilla and Campos, "A Wealth of Poor."
13 E. Maldonado, "Contract Labor and the Origin of Puerto Rican Communities in the United States," *International Migration Review* 13 (1979): 103–21; Moore and Pachón, *Hispanics in the United States*.
14 V. Sanchez-Korrol, *From Colonia to Community* (Westport, Conn.: Greenwood Press, 1983); Bonilla and Campos, "A Wealth of Poor."
15 Sanchez-Korrol, *From Colonia to Community*; Bonilla and Campos, "A Wealth of Poor"; J. Fitzpatrick, *Puerto Rican Americans: The Meaning of Migration to the Mainland* (Englewood Cliffs, N.J.: Prentice-Hall, 1971).
16 J. Mañach, *Marti, El Apostol* (Hato Rey, P.R.: El Mirador, 1963).
17 F. Ortiz, *Cuban Counterpoint: Tobacco and Sugar* (New York: Knopf, 1947).
18 H. Thomas, *Cuba, the Pursuit of Freedom*, Book V (New York: Harper & Row, 1971).
19 N. Amaro, "Class and Mass in the Origins of the Cuban Revolution," Washington University Series in Comparative International Development, no. 10 (1969); M. Zeitlin, "Political Generations in the Cuban Working-Class," in *Latin America: Reform or Revolution?*, ed. J. Petras and M. Zeitlin (New York: Fawcett, 1968), pp. 235–48.
20 Thomas, *Cuba, the Pursuit of Freedom*, Book VIII; Amaro, "Class and Mass in the Origins of the Cuban Revolution."
21 S. Pedraza-Bailey, "Cuba's Exiles: Portrait of a Refugee Migration," *International Migration Review* 19 (1985): 4–34; T. D. Boswell and J. R. Curtis, *The Cuban-American Experience* (Totowa, N.J.: Rowman & Allanheld, 1984).
22 Pedraza-Bailey, "Cuba's Exiles"; N. Amaro and A. Portes, "Una Sociología del Exilio: Situación de los Grupos Cubanos en Estados Unidos," *Aportes* 23 (1972): 6–24.

23 S. Diaz-Briquets and L. Perez, "Cuba: The Demography of Revolution," *Population Bulletin* 36 (1981): 2–41; K. L. Wilson and W. A. Martin, "Ethnic Enclaves: A Comparison of the Cuban and Black Economies in Miami," *American Journal of Sociology* 88 (1982): 135–60.

24 S. Grasmuck, "Immigration, Ethnic Stratification, and Native Working-Class Discipline: Comparisons of Documented and Undocumented Dominicans," *International Migration Review* 18 (1984): 692–713; J. A. Moreno, "Intervention and Economic Penetration: The Case of the Dominican Republic," University of Pittsburgh Latin American Occasional Papers, no. 13 (1976).

25 Immigration and Naturalization Service, *Annual Report* (Washington, D.C.: Government Printing Office, 1985).

26 Bureau of the Census, *Annual Report* (1984).

27 P. W. Fagen, "Central Americans and U.S. Refugee Asylum Policies" (Paper presented at the conference on immigration and refugee policies sponsored by the Inter-American Dialogue and the University of California, San Diego, La Jolla, 1986, Mimeographed).

28 A. Portes and J. Walton, *Labor, Class, and the International System* (New York: Academic Press, 1981).

29 Nelson and Tienda, "The Structuring of Hispanic Ethnicity"; L. Perez, "Immigrant Economic Adjustment and Family Organization: The Cuban Success Story Reexamined," *International Migration Review* 20 (1986): 4–20; Pedraza-Bailey, "Cuba's Exiles."

30 C. Hirschman and L. M. Falcón, "The Educational Attainment of Religio-ethnic Groups in the United States," Research in Sociology of Education and Socialization 5 (1985): 83–120.

31 C. W. Reimers, "A Comparative Analysis of the Wages of Hispanics, Blacks, and Non-Hispanic Whites," in *Hispanics in the U.S. Economy*, ed. G. J. Borjas and M. Tienda (Orlando, Fla.: Academic Press, 1985), pp. 27–75.

32 Nelson and Tienda, "The Structuring of Hispanic Ethnicity"; L. Perez, "Immigrant Economic Adjustment and Family Organization"; G. Jasso and M. R. Rosenzweig, "What's in a Name? Country-of-Origin Influences on the Earnings of Immigrants in the United States," Bulletin 85–4 (Minneapolis: University of Minnesota, Economic Development Center, 1985, Mimeographed), table 4.

33 Jasso and Rosenzweig, "What's in a Name?"; Pedraza-Bailey, "Cuba's Exiles."

34 M. Tienda and L. Jensen, "Immigration and Public Assistance Participation: Dispelling the Myth of Dependency," Discussion Paper 777–85 (Madison: University of Wisconsin-Madison, Institute for Research on Poverty, 1985, Mimeographed); R. L. Bach, L. W. Gordon, D. W. Haines, and D. R. Howell, "The Economic Adjustment of Southeast Asian Refugees in the U.S.," in U.N. Commission for Refugees, *World Refugee Survey* (Geneva: United Nations, 1984), pp. 51–6.

35 Barrera, *Race and Class*; Nelson and Tienda, "The Structuring of Hispanic Ethnicity"; J. S. Passel, "Undocumented Immigrants: How Many?" (Paper presented at the annual meeting of the American Statistical Association,

Las Vegas, 1985); F. D. Bean, A. G. King, and J. S. Passel, "The Number of Illegal Migrants of Mexican Origin in the United States: Sex Ratio Based Estimates for 1980," *Demography* 20 (1983): 99–109; F. D. Bean, A. G. King, and J. S. Passel, "Estimates of the Size of the Illegal Migrant Population of Mexican Origin in the United States: An Assessment, Review, and Proposal," in *Mexican Immigrants and Mexican Americans: An Evolving Relation*, ed. H. L. Browning and R. de la Garza (Austin: University of Texas, Center for Mexican-American Studies, 1986), pp. 13–26; H. L. Browning and N. Rodriguez, "The Migration of Mexican Indocumentados as a Settlement Process: Implications for Work," in *Hispanics in the U.S. Economy*, ed. G. J. Borjas and M. Tienda (Orlando, Fla.: Academic Press, 1985), pp. 277–97.

36 J. De Wind, T. Seidl, and J. Shenk, "Contract Labor in U.S. Agriculture," *NACLA Report on the Americas* 11 (1977): 4–37; C. H. Wood, "Caribbean Cane Cutters in Florida: A Study of the Relative Cost of Foreign and Domestic Labor," (Paper presented at the annual meetings of the American Sociological Association, San Antonio, 1984); S. Sassen-Koob, "Formal and Informal Associations: Dominicans and Colombians in New York," *International Migration Review* 13 (1979): 314–32; S. Sassen-Koob, "Immigrant and Minority Workers in the Organization of the Labor Process," *Journal of Ethnic Studies* 1 (1980): 1–34; E. Glaessel-Brown, *Colombian Immigrants in the Industries of the Northeast* (Ph.D. diss., Massachusetts Institute of Technology, 1985); R. Waldinger, "Immigration and Industrial Change in the New York City Apparel Industry," in *Hispanics in the U.S. Economy*, ed. G. J. Borjas and M. Tienda (Orlando, Fla.: Academic Press, 1985), pp. 323–49.

37 F. D. Bean and M. Tienda, *The Hispanic Population of the United States* (New York: Russell Sage Foundation, 1987), chap. 1; Centro de Estudios Puertorriqueños, *Labor Migration under Capitalism* (New York: Monthly Review Press, 1979).

38 The characteristics of the Cuban enclave have been described at length in the research literature: K. L. Wilson and A. Portes, "Immigrant Enclaves: An Analysis of the Labor Market Experiences of Cubans in Miami," *American Journal of Sociology* 86 (1980): 295–319; A. Portes and R. D. Manning, "The Immigrant Enclave: Theory and Empirical Examples," in *Competitive Ethnic Relations*, ed. J. Nagel and S. Olzak (Orlando, Fla.: Academic Press, 1986), pp. 47–64; Wilson and Martin, "Ethnic Enclaves."

39 A. Portes and R. L. Bach, *Latin Journey: Cuban and Mexican Immigrants in the United States* (Berkeley: University of California Press, 1985).

40 De Wind et al., "Contract Labor in U.S. Agriculture"; Glaessel-Brown, *Colombian Immigrants*.

41 J. A. Garcia, "Political Integration of Mexican Immigrants: Explorations into the Naturalization Process," *International Migration Review* 15 (1981): 608–25.

42 Moore and Pachón, *Hispanics in the United States*, pp. 176–86.

43 E. R. Roybal, "Welcome Statement," in *Proceedings of the First National Conference on Citizenship and the Hispanic Community* (Washington, D.C.: National Association of Latin Elected Officials, 1984), p. 7.

44 A. Falcón, "Puerto Rican Politics in Urban America: An Introduction to the Literature," *La Red* (1983): 2–9; J. Jennings, *Puerto Rican Politics in New York City* (Washington, D.C.: University Press, 1977).

45 ***

46 L. J. Botifoll, "How Miami's New Image Was Created," Occasional Paper 1985–1 (Coral Gables: University of Miami, Institute of Interamerican Studies, 1984); Boswell and Curtis, *The Cuban-American Experience*, chap. 10; M. F. Petersen and M. A. Maidique, "Success Patterns of the Leading Cuban-American Entrepreneurs" (Coral Gables: University of Miami, Innovation and Entrepreneurship Institute, 1986, Mimeographed).

47 S. Nazario, "After a Long Holdout, Cubans in Miami Take a Role in Politics," *Wall Street Journal*, June 7, 1983.

48 Moore and Pachón, *Hispanics in the United States*, pp. 194–8.

49 R. Warren, "Status Report on Naturalization Rates," Working Paper CO 1326, 6C (Washington, D.C.: Bureau of the Census, 1979, Mimeographed); A. Portes and R. Mozo, "The Political Adaptation Process of Cubans and Other Ethnic Minorities in the United States," *International Migration Review* 19 (1985): 35–63.

50 W. S. Bernard, "Cultural Determinants of Naturalization," *American Sociological Review* 1 (1936): 943–53.

51 Jasso and Rosenzweig, "What's in a Name?"; Portes and Mozo, "The Political Adaptation Process of Cubans."

52 Garcia, "Political Integration of Mexican Immigrants"; L. Grebler, "The Naturalization of the Mexican Immigrant in the U.S.," *International Migration Review* 1 (1966): 17–32; R. R. Alvarez, "A Profile of the Citizenship Process among Hispanics in the United States: An Anthropological Perspective," Special Report to the National Association of Latin Elected Officials (1985, Mimeographed; 34 pp.); C. Fernandez, "The Causes of Naturalization and Non-naturalization for Mexican Immigrants: An Empirical Study Based on Case Studies," Report to Project Participar (1984, Mimeographed); D. S. North, *The Long Gray Welcome: A Study of the American Naturalization Program*, Monograph report to the National Association of Latin Elected Officials (1985, Mimeographed); W. A. Cornelius, "The Future of Mexican Immigrants in California: A New Perspective for Public Policy," Working Paper on Public Policy 6 (La Jolla: Center for U.S.-Mexico Studies of the University of California-San Diego, 1981).

53 Alvarez, "A Profile of the Citizenship Process among Hispanics in the United States"; A. Portes and J. Curtis, "Changing Flags, Naturalization and Its Determinants among Mexican Immigrants," *International Migration Review* 21 (1987): 352–71.

54 Garcia, "Political Integration of Mexican Immigrants"; Fernandez, "The Causes of Naturalization and Non-naturalization for Mexican Immigrants."

55 Alvarez, "A Profile of the Citizenship Process among Hispanics in the United States"; North, *The Long Gray Welcome*.

56 Garcia, "Political Integration of Mexican Immigrants"; D. S. Massey, "Understanding Mexican Migration to the United States," *American Journal of Sociology* 92 (1987): 1372–1403.

57 Sassen-Koob, "Immigrant and Minority Workers"; Glaessel-Brown, *Colombian Immigrants*; C. H. Wood, "Caribbean Cane Cutters in Florida: A Study of the Relative Cost of Foreign and Domestic Labor" (Paper presented at the annual meetings of the American Sociological Association, San Antonio, 1984).

7 Asian Immigrants: Social Forces Unleashed After 1965

Bill Ong Hing

In 1965, driven by its desire to be seen as the egalitarian champion of the "free world" and by a Kennedy-inspired sense of a single world, the United States changed the basic scheme of immigration law. Congress abolished the 1920s system that favored immigrants of Western European origins and established an open system premised on family reunification and designed to ensure that no country would have special preferences or quotas.

In considering and ultimately passing these reforms, policymakers did not pay careful attention to those Asian American and Asian social forces that Congress and state governments had previously endeavored to hold in check – Asian American family needs, economic ambitions, and residential patterns. Most policymakers did not understand how the political, economic, and social dynamics in Asian countries would influence immigration. They knew little about Asian American communities, Asian countries, and their relationship, and their analyses by and large were cursory and highly inaccurate. Asian immigration after 1965 took the United States by surprise.

The 1965 laws unleashed many of those social forces that national and local governments had effectively – and often cruelly – controlled but had never taken the time to understand. Families moved to "make themselves whole," and women joined their spouses. Workers, particularly in the secondary but also in the primary labor markets, immigrated to take advantage of new opportunities. Asian Americans multiplied, most often in regions and neighborhoods with the cultural and economic capacity to absorb newcomers.

All this activity might not have surprised anyone who had paid close attention before 1965 to the history and patterns of Asian

American life. Certain possibilities created in 1965 had already been available in less generous and systematic terms, particularly after World War II. And Asian American and Asian dynamics already had begun to respond to the new possibilities. Patterns that were recognized for the first time in the late 1970s and early 1980s often found their origins in the years immediately preceding 1965.

Asian American gender ratios, labor markets, resettlement patterns, occupations, and income all responded rapidly and extensively to the newly possible. Communities that were already undergoing important changes as a result of post-World War II reforms were remade even more dramatically after the 1965 amendments. The character of each community reflected both the conditions in its home country and the constricted possibilities of resettlement before 1965. As a result, each community's political, social, and economic power varied considerably.

Chinese Americans

The repeal of the Chinese exclusion laws in the 1940's had an immediate if limited impact on this community's profile. The entry of Chinese women and the forming of families, the reduction of the imbalanced gender ratio, the genesis of a professional class, and the shift in residential patterns all resulted in part from the liberation of social forces that policymakers had tried for decades to control. The overall size of the community, though, remained small, and demographic changes remained largely unappreciated in the debate over President Kennedy's global scheme of migration.

Population

From 1965 to 1990 the Chinese American population increased from about 360,000 to 1,645,000.[1] Chinese Americans surpassed Japanese Americans, who had been the most populous group from 1910 to 1970.[2] The huge increase can be attributed to the 1965 amendments.

After the Chinese Repealer in 1943 and the establishment of the Asia-Pacific triangle in 1952, the Chinese increased annually by fewer than 2,000 until 1965. But after 1965 Chinese admissions grew dramatically, and today more than 40,000 immigrate each year from China, Taiwan, and Hong Kong.[3] Between 1965 and 1990 approximately 711,000 Chinese immigrants entered the United States.[4]

In 1965 Congress did not foresee this increase, although the conditions for it were in place. Immigrants came through Chinese American family networks whose gradual development might have been apparent. The entry of more than 14,000 refugees prior to 1978 under the category created for persons fleeing Communist countries was no less predictable.[5] Political instability in Taiwan and the development of a substantial professional class in Hong Kong were both apparent before 1965.

These developments, both in the United States and in Asia, enabled the Chinese American community to take advantage of the more open immigration scheme. Chinese American family networks formed by 1965 began using the new family-oriented system. Almost 61 percent in 1969 entered in the family categories, and 21 percent entered in the categories for professionals (see table 7.1). Professionals could use the family categories to petition for

Table 7.1 [*orig. table 9*]Comparison of entrants in family reunification categories with those in occupational and investor categories, 1969, 1985, and 1989

Place of birth	Relatives 1969 (%)	Relatives 1985 (%)	Occupational 1969 (%)	Occupational 1985 (%)	Investors 1969[a] (%)
China[b]	60.9	80.9	20.8	15.8	4.5
India	27.0	85.9	45.0	12.6	26.8
Japan	74.5	59.4	17.6	33.1	6.1
Korea	64.0	89.2	23.2	7.6	11.6
Philippines	55.0	86.9	42.3	7.6	0.08
Vietnam	82.7	15.7	8.0	0.18	6.4

	1989[c] Relatives (%)	1989 Occupational (%)
China, Mainland	92.6	5.2
Taiwan	30.4	32.2
Hong Kong	90.3	1.1
India	85.1	1.4
Japan	64.1	28.9
Korea	88.9	9.5
Philippines	87.8	8.1
Vietnam[d]	98.8	1.1

[a] By 1985 no nonpreference visas were available, but some Asians were able to enter as nonimmigrant investors.
[b] Includes mainland China, Taiwan, and Hong Kong.
[c] Not including immigrants through legalization (amnesty).
[d] Not including refugee and Amerasian adjustments.

Sources: 1969 *INS Annual Report*, tables 6, 6B, 7A, pp. 40–8; 1985 *INS Statistical Yearbook*, tables IMM 2.6, 3.1, pp. 33–7; 1989 *INS Advance Reports*, table 4.

spouses, children, parents, and siblings. By 1985, 81 percent of Chinese immigrants were entering in the family categories and only about 16 percent as professionals.[6]

Most strikingly, by 1980 the Chinese American population was once again mostly foreign-born (63.3 percent),[7] ending the predominance of the American-born that had lasted from 1940 to 1970.[8] A large proportion of foreign-born Chinese may be present for some time because as the population increased 104 percent between 1980 and 1990 (from 812,178 to 1,650,000), almost 446,000 Chinese immigrated.[9]

These numbers reflect basic changes in immigration law and international relations, such as the normalization of the relationship between the United States and the People's Republic of China in 1978, which eased emigration of Chinese from mainland China. Taiwan and China had been counted as a single country for quota purposes, but Taiwan was given a separate quota of 20,000 in 1981.[10] Total immigration from Taiwan and mainland China increased from 25,000 in 1981 to 39,732 in 1985.[11] The increase of the colonial quota for Hong Kong from 600 to 5,000 in the 1986 Immigration Reform and Control Act has begun to add several thousand immigrants each year as well. Under 1990 amendments, the Hong Kong quota has been enlarged to 10,000 and will reach 20,000 in 1995.

Careers and Socioeconomic Status

Careers

Within five years of the 1965 reforms, it became evident that the numbers of professionals and technicians from all countries had increased largely because of the new professional and occupational categories.[12] Between 1953 and 1966 an annual average of about 22,000 immigrants worldwide (about 8 percent) indicated a prior professional or technical occupation. By 1969 the number was more than 40,000 (more than 11 percent of all immigrants).[13]

The shift was more dramatic among Chinese immigrants. Prior to 1965 about 12 percent from mainland China and Taiwan identified themselves as professionals or managers.[14] By 1977 the figure had increased to 25.1 percent, even though more were entering in family reunification categories.[15] It doubled because of the new categories and because of rapid modernization in Taiwan and Hong Kong.[16]

Some observers, who note fewer professionals among Chinese immigrants, contend that after the initial influx of professionals in the late 1960's and early 1970's, poorer, working-class Chinese began entering.[17] But this is only part of the story. The proportion who enter in professional and occupational categories decreased between 1969 and 1989 (see Table 7.1) in part because a 1976 law required all professionals to first secure a job offer from an employer.[18] The absolute number of professionals and executives, however, has increased. In 1969, for example, a total of 3,499 immigrated from mainland China, Taiwan, and Hong Kong.[19] In 1983 the total had jumped to 8,524.[20] Thus, the smaller percentage merely reflects the increase in other categories. The proportion of those who enter in professional and occupational categories from Taiwan is also much higher than for those from mainland China (28 percent to 5 percent in 1989). And though more than twice as many born in mainland China entered in 1989 (32,272 to 13,974), Taiwan had more occupational immigrants (3,842 to 1,599).[21]

Interest in emigration remains high among Chinese professionals. Taiwan's politically volatile environment has contributed to the desire of the educated class to look for residential options elsewhere, and the stability of the United States and its long-standing anti-Communist philosophy appeals to them. Similarly, the impending return of Hong Kong to mainland China's jurisdiction in 1997 has provided a strong impetus for its elite to look to the United States. And the Tiananmen Square massacre in June 1989 significantly accelerated emigration from Hong Kong.[22]

While the 1965 reforms have facilitated the entry of some professionals and executives, the family reunification provisions have also spurred the immigration of a large pool of service workers. After 1965 immigrants entering under family reunification provisions were required to prove that they were not likely to need public assistance.[23] Since this requirement could be fulfilled through a job offer or affidavit of support from a relative, it has not been difficult for service workers to gain admittance in the family reunification categories. Consequently, a large majority of Chinese immigrants have indicated that they are housewives or service workers or that they have had no occupation.[24]

The lack of English skills among new arrivals plays a part in the high proportions of service workers in Chinese American communities. In fact, because of racial discrimination and their own lack of skills, many immigrants are able to find work only in Chinatowns, but the jobs are low-paying, unstable, and seldom provide promotional opportunities.[25]

Opening categories for professionals and investors after 1965 greatly increased the percentage of professionals among Chinese Americans, as did the educational achievements of some American-born Chinese.[26] A higher percentage of Chinese immigrants (31 percent) than of white Americans (24 percent) are professionals or executives. At the same time, however, the percentage of foreign-born Chinese Americans who work in service occupations (22 percent) is twice that of white workers and is the highest for any group of foreign-born Asian Americans.[27] The simultaneous growth of the professional and the service-worker classes has created a divided community that bears little resemblance to the one before 1965.[28] By the early 1980's, 32.5 percent of all Chinese in the United States were professionals, managers, or executives, while 18.5 percent were in service work.[29]

Still, the proportion of Chinese classified as professionals and managers is misleading because it includes the scientific and technical fields into which they are often channeled.[30] Management statistics are also misleading because they include small-business owners. Chinese Americans have a slightly higher than average rate of small-business ownership (65.1 per thousand compared to 64 for the general population), especially in metropolitan areas where general economic expansion has occurred.[31] For example in 1987, Chinese-owned businesses in Los Angeles and San Francisco exceeded all other Asian American groups.[32] Management statistics also obscure the often unpublicized discrimination against Chinese Americans in promotions to management level or partnership positions in the professions.[33]

Income and poverty

The popular media have underscored the fact that the median family income for Chinese Americans is higher than that of the general population.[34] But this reporting has been misleading. Certainly, the postwar easing of controls has been reflected in Chinese American income, especially since 1965. However, they have more workers per family (1.9) than the general population (1.6).[35] And recent immigrants, who make up a large part of the community, earn less than American-born Chinese or those immigrants who came before them.[36]

The attention paid to successful Chinese Americans has often conveyed the false impression of a uniformly upper-income community.[37] The media and even some scholars tend to ignore the fact that more Chinese American families (10.5 percent) fall below the poverty level than white American families (7 percent).[38] Of those immigrants who entered between 1975 and 1980, 22.8 percent were below the poverty line in 1980.[39] Only 2.8 percent of those who immigrated before 1970 fell below it.[40]

Compounding the new immigrants' problems is their ineligibility for most government benefits. Under current rules for Supplemental Security Income, the income of the citizen or lawful permanent resident petitioning for an alien is included in the immigrant's income for three years in determining financial need.[41] This formula is followed even if the sponsor fails to provide financial support.

Filipino Americans

Population

The expansion of the Filipino American community, which was impeded by the 1934 Philippine Independence Act's yearly quota of 50, slowly increased after World War II. The 1965 reforms allowed the community to flourish. By 1990 the modest 1965 community of about 200,000 had grown to over 1,400,000.[42] Almost 982,000 Filipinos immigrated during that 25-year period, and today over two-thirds of the community is foreign-born, compared to about 40 percent in 1965.[43] Because of almost 60,000 immigrants each year, Filipino Americans are now the nation's second largest Asian community after the Chinese. Immigration from the Philippines, which is greater than that from China, Taiwan, and Hong Kong combined, is second only to Mexico.[44]

As with the Chinese, Koreans, and Indians, the surge in Filipino immigration after 1965 was not anticipated, even though strong evidence of what might happen was provided by patterns of entry before 1965 and by events in the Philippines. For example, the increase in the number of their professionals who entered after 1952 should have provided notice that Filipino immigrants would take advantage of the 1965 law's professional categories.

Filipinos entered in the family categories, but since their population was relatively small in the early 1960's, just after the 1965 amendments it was generally professionals who took advantage of the new occupational preference categories (e.g., accountants, doctors, nurses). As more arrived and became naturalized, they began to use the immigration categories for close relatives. Family reunification categories offered many more visas (80 percent of all preference and 100 percent of immediate-relative, nonquota, visas were designated for family reunification until the 1990 amendments) and less stringent visa requirements. A relationship as spouse, parent, child, or sibling is all that was necessary. In the occupational categories, on the other hand, a certification from the Department of Labor was needed to show that no qualified American worker could fill the position an immigrant was offered.[45]

The family-oriented culture of Filipinos helps to explain the surge in family reunification that could not have happened earlier because of the 1934 Independence Act. In 1969 and 1970 about 45 percent entered in the professional and 55 percent in the family unity categories (see tables 7.1 and 7.2). Within a few years, however, family networks developed that enabled naturalized citizens to take advantage of reunification categories. By 1976 Filipino immigration in the occupational categories dropped to about 21 percent.[46] By 1989, just over 8 percent came from the occupational categories compared to 88 percent in the family categories[47] (see table 7.1).

Political instability and economic problems in the Philippines convinced many people in the educated and the working classes that they would have better economic opportunities in the United States. After independence in 1946 the Philippine Islands experienced a succession of one-term presidents until 1965. Elections, which were called a "showcase of democracy in Asia," were commonly accompanied by violence and corruption.[48] The pattern of single-term presidencies ended when Ferdinand Marcos was elected in 1965 and re-elected in 1969, but violence and corruption did not cease.[49]

After someone tried to assassinate the secretary of national defense in 1972, Marcos declared martial law and began an era of repression.[50] The military immediately arrested dozens of oppositionists, including senators, congressmen, provincial governors, and prominent reporters, and detained several thousand others.[51] Many newspapers and radio and television stations were shut down, schools were temporarily closed, public rallies and demonstrations were forbidden, and a curfew was established and

Table 7.2 [*orig. table 10*] Proportions of entries in immediate relative and preference categories, 1970, 1979, and 1988

			Preference (%)							
Country and Year	*Total*	*Immediate Relatives*	*1st*	*2nd*	*3rd*	*4th*	*5th*	*6th*	*7th*	*Nonpreference (Including Investors)*
M. China/Taiwan										
1970	14,093	17.1	0.86	18.3	13.4	6.0	22.3	11.7	1.3	2.6
1979	28,600	28.5	2.5	46.0	7.6	14.9	36.3	10.4	5.9	0.03
1988	28,717	26.9	0.5	29.2	10.3	11.7	44.4	2.7		
India										
1970	10,114	4.5	0.06	13.4	19.7	0.2	4.0	7.9		54.7
1979	22,400	12.4	0.1	38.6	12.0	0.45	60.7	9.2		0.45
1988	26,268	29.2	0.16	31.0	12.0	3.2	50.4	3.1		
Korea										
1970	9,314	44.3	0.3	16.1	9.3	0.65	26.2	13.5		33.9
1979	31,800	37.8	0.17	35.6	4.2	1.3	62.8	5.0		0.76
1988	34,703	40.4	0.3	34.5	5.1	3.7	46.4	9.9		
Philippines										
1970	31,203	23.9	1.3	24.6	47.8	7.1	19.2	0.05		0.07
1979	47,000	53.0	4.9	49.2	12.8	13.5	32.4	4.6		0.44
1988	50,697	56.7	19.7	24.8	9.6	10.9	24.1	10.6		

Sources: 1970 *INS Annual Report*, 1979 and 1980 *INS Statistical Yearbooks*.

enforced.[52] Increasingly, the military emerged as a principal source of power.[53] Threats of Muslim and Communist insurgencies contributed to the political and social instability.[54]

The overall economy, which became heavily dependent on foreign capital, suffered during the Marcos era, even though segments of the private sector flourished.[55] Real wages fell 5 percent a year, reflecting the abundance of labor, while inflation rose 20 percent a year.[56] Industrial development stressed capital and not labor, so there were relatively few opportunities for employment available to the rapidly growing labor force. Unemployment and underemployment created great inefficiency within the economy. Official reports of unemployment fluctuated between 5 and 10 per cent between 1950 and 1970. Underemployment, which accounts for the number of workers employed in marginal jobs, might have affected over a quarter of the population.[57]

What impact the ouster of Ferdinand Marcos and the shift to democracy has had on emigration remains unresolved. Filipino immigration remains high, as backlogs in preference categories continue to grow. If political and economic instability persist, the demand for visas is likely to continue.[58]

Careers and Income

Careers

The 1965 amendments contributed to a distinct shift toward large numbers of immigrants who were professionals. With the exception of Asian Indians, Filipinos have made the most of the new opportunities. Fully 42.3 percent entered in professional categories in 1969, almost double the proportion of any other Asian group except Asian Indians (see table 7.1). As a result, the relatively large number of farm laborers that first distinguished Filipino American communities recently has fallen more precipitously, in contrast with the gradual decline between 1946 and 1965.[59]

After the early 1970's, family reunification began to dominate Filipino immigration, but the absolute number of professionals entering remained high. In 1969, 36.3 percent had been employed at professional or managerial levels.[60] In 1978, however, the figure declined to 22.8 percent.[61] By 1985, even though only 7.6 percent entered in the occupational categories, a significant proportion

(16.2 percent) designated their occupations as professionals, executives, or managers[62] (see table 7.1). While not as many immigrants in the 1980's were entering in categories reserved for professionals as in the late 1960's, thousands were in the professional ranks each year.[63]

The employment profile of the Filipino American community is therefore quite diverse. Not surprisingly, the 1980 census reported that the proportion employed in the professions or as managers and executives (24.8 percent) was about the same as that of white Americans.[64] This high percentage reflects in part large numbers of nurses.[65] And in some areas such as San Francisco, Filipino-owned businesses have steadily increased.[66] The proportion of blue-collar workers in 1980 was about the same as it was in the general population, but the percentage of service workers (16.5 percent) was higher than in the white population (11.6 percent).[67] Though not insubstantial, the gap between upper-income professionals and lower-income service workers is not as great as that in the Chinese American community.

The impact of the foreign-born on these demographics merits emphasis. A sizable 27 percent of foreign-born Filipino Americans in contrast to only 15 percent of those born in America were employed in 1980 as managers, professionals, and executives.[68] At the same time, 20 percent of immigrants between 1975 and 1980 held service-oriented jobs, helping to account for the high proportion of Filipinos in that sector.[69] Indeed, an increase in the proportion of service workers seems likely given the steady immigration of large percentages of Filipinos who indicate either employment as service workers or no occupation. The income disparity between foreign-born Filipino professionals and service workers is greater than between those born in America, auguring perhaps for a social and economic bifurcation like that of the Chinese American community.

Income

The median family income for Filipino Americans, particularly those who are foreign-born, is higher than that of the general population, but there are more workers per family among Filipinos. In fact, the median income for individual white American workers in 1980 was almost 14 percent higher than for Filipino Americans. Because so many professionals arrived after 1965, Filipino immigrants earn more than American-born Filipinos, particularly women, whose unemployment rate is the lowest among all Asian immigrant women.[70] A relatively large portion of Filipino women are in the professions, especially nursing, and fewer Filipino American families (6.2 percent) fall below the poverty level than white American families (7 percent), implying that the vast majority of Filipino immigrants are not poor.[71] Like the Chinese, however, a Filipino's income is lower if he is a recent immigrant.[72]

Korean Americans

Population

The expansion of the Korean American community has been remarkable. Families had begun reuniting and growing before 1965; still growth came slowly, and in 1965 the population totaled only about 45,000. By 1990, however, it was almost 800,000 – nearly a staggering eighteenfold increase in 25 years.[73] The 1965 reforms and deteriorating economic and social conditions in Korea set the stage for emigration.

After 1965, there was virtually no emigration from the closed Communist dictatorship in North Korea. In the 1960's and 1970's, South Koreans' right to dissent or to criticize the government was sharply restricted, and the government maintained complete control over the media. The Korean Central Intelligence Agency became infamous for its unlimited authority to investigate or detain political dissidents.[74] The Korean War had crippled the economy, and a dubious reconstruction plan made the country depend on foreign exports, raw materials, and capital investment. The economy was left vulnerable to recessions in the Japanese and American markets, even though it has performed well compared with other industrialized nations.[75]

Between 1969 and 1971 Korean immigration more than doubled from 6,045 to 14,297,[76] and in 1987 it topped 35,000.[77] More than 620,000 entered between 1966 and 1990.[78] In fact, Koreans have since 1973 been the third largest Asian immigrant group behind Filipinos and Chinese.[79] By 1980 an incredible 81.9 percent of the community was foreign-born,[80] second only to that of the newly developing refugee Vietnamese American community. Since 35,000 Koreans immigrate each year, the proportion of foreign-born will remain high for some time.

After the 1965 reforms a noteworthy share of Koreans (though not as many as Filipinos and Indians) came as occupational migrants, but eventually the use of family categories dominated (see table 7.1 and 7.2). In 1969, for example, 23.2 percent of Koreans entered in the occupational categories, and an additional 11.6 percent took advantage of the newly created investor category. Immigrants who entered through these occupational categories were able, in time, to petition for their relatives under the family categories, so more began to come as family members. In 1969, for example, 64 percent of Korean immigration came through family categories, and that figure rose to 91 percent by 1988, when those entering through occupational categories declined to less than 9 percent.

Careers

The professional and nonpreference investor categories established by the 1965 amendments facilitated the entry of a substantial number of wealthy and professional Koreans. As noted above, in 1969, 23.2 percent of Korean immigrants entered in occupational categories (which include professionals), and 11.6 percent entered on nonpreference visas, which were primarily used by investors (see table 7.1). Between these two categories, then, over a third in 1969 had professional job skills or sufficient funds to start a business.

Like Asian Indians and Filipinos, many potential immigrants began tailoring their training to meet the technical requirements of occupational categories.[81] The demand for specialized training was so strong that schools and companies in Korea were established solely to teach skills that would qualify.[82] Doctors, nurses, and pharmacists entered these training programs in large numbers. By 1977 thirteen thousand Korean medical professionals were working in the United States.[83]

Once Koreans had developed family ties in the United States, they were able to immigrate more easily through the family unity categories. Since those immigrants are not required to demonstrate that no qualified workers are available for particular jobs, they are able to obtain visas much more quickly.[84] By the 1970's, moreover, many Korean war brides became naturalized.[85] Naturalization created new ways of requesting the admission of relatives, since citizens under the 1965 amendments could petition for parents, married sons and daughters, and siblings.[86] At the same time, the practice of bringing in wives for native citizens that had started before 1965 continued through the next decade.[87]

Some commentators attribute the late 1970's decline in the Korean use of occupational categories to the decade-long recession that plagued the United States.[88] The greater demand for family reunification visas, however, probably was more significant. Immigration law changes in the 1970's also contributed. In response to intense lobbying from the American Medical Association, which feared competition by specially trained Koreans, the laws were amended in 1976 to limit the number of foreign-trained physicians and surgeons entering the United States.[89] Most of these doctors could not enter to practice medicine unless they passed an American national examination and were competent in English. As a result, the number of Korean-trained doctors who could enter was substantially reduced. A 1977 change in the procedures for professionals that imposed more requirements on employers also made the professional entry route more onerous.[90]

Although 90 percent of all Korean immigrants enter through family categories today, many are of the same class as the professionals and investors who first immigrated through the occupational and nonpreference categories. So while the proportion of Koreans who have entered in the occupational categories has decreased in the last fifteen years, the absolute number of professionals has not. In 1969, 1,164 immigrants indicated that they were professionals or managers prior to entry. This figure rose to 3,955 in 1972, 2,782 in 1985, and 3,109 in 1989.[91]

Since the community is over 80 percent foreign-born and 35,000 immigrants are added annually, its career and economic profile reflects the characteristics of Korean immigrants. Again, the numbers alone tell much of the story. For example, 25 percent of foreign-born Korean Americans are employed as professionals or managers, and 24.8 percent overall. A high percentage of Koreans are employed in service jobs (16.5 percent) because 19 percent of recent Korean immigrants report holding that sort of job.[92] The share of Koreans employed in blue-collar service, farming, factory, and laborer occupations (47.7 percent) is comparable to that of the general population (45 percent).[93]

The proportion categorized as professionals, managers, and executives is also comparable to the proportion for the general population.[94] This figure, though, includes a high percentage of small-business owners. In 1980, there were 90 Korean-owned businesses for every thousand Korean Americans. In the general population those figures were 64 per thousand.[95] Between 1982

158 Immigration and Contemporary Ethnicity

and 1987, the number of Korean-owned businesses in the United States more than doubled from 30,919 to 69,304.[96] In Los Angeles alone, Korean Americans operated 5,701 small businesses in 1987,[97] and 40 percent of Korean household heads and 34 percent of their spouses described themselves as proprietors.[98] In New York, where Korean Americans dominate the greengrocer business, 34 percent of the men run small retail businesses.[99] In the metropolitan areas with the most business-intensive Asian American communities (Dallas-Fort Worth, Houston, and Atlanta), Koreans have business rates of 130 or more per thousand.[100] These high rates of small-business ownership are more noteworthy when one considers that few of these immigrants had pursued merchant vocations before coming to the United States.[101]

From 1969 though the mid-1970's, the high percentage of Koreans operating small businesses stemmed partly from use of the nonpreference investor category available to those buying or starting American businesses.[102] Confronting strong barriers in the job market, lacking English fluency and knowledge of American customs, facing persistent discrimination, and refused a foothold in white-collar occupations, other Koreans turned to small business almost by default.[103]

Newly arriving immigrants, in turn, perceived their predecessors as successful in small businesses and were encouraged to try their hand. And, as more and more Koreans opened small businesses – such as the greengrocers in New York City – they established business and supply networks that made it easier for later arrivals to set up their own shops. The Korean small-business community has in fact become its own ethnic labor market.

Income figures reveal that family income is comparable to that of the general population, though there are more workers in Korean families.[104] The median income for Korean American full-time workers ($14,230) is lower than that of white Americans ($15,570). Recent arrivals are earning less still.[105] Not surprisingly, a wide discrepancy exists between men and women ($17,360 for men versus $10,260 for women).[106] And foreign-born women earn less than if they were born in America ($10,070 versus $12,760).[107] A higher proportion of Korean American families (13.1 percent) than white American families (7 percent) fall below the poverty level.[108] Most of the poor are American-born who hold service jobs. Of recent immigrants, 11 percent fall below the poverty level,[109] compared to only 6 percent of those who immigrated between 1970 and 1974.[110]

Asian Indian

Population

The Asian Indian American community increased from perhaps 50,000 before the 1965 reforms to 815,500 by 1990. During this period over 446,000 immigrated to the United States.[111] Not surprisingly, the population was over 80 percent foreign-born in 1980.[112] Since 1983 an average of more than 25,000 have entered annually.[113]

Immigration reform occurred when India had the highest rate of enrollment in postsecondary education of any low-income industrializaing nation.[114] The Indian economy is divided between a small, relatively high-salaried modern sector and a large, impoverished traditional agricultural sector.[115] Demand for better wages created a great demand for higher levels of education.

Political and economic uncertainty engendered by the failure to meet economic expectations since Indian independence contributed to a willingness by many to leave. The economy has not been able to keep pace with the demand for modern-sector jobs, leaving many highly educated persons who cannot be absorbed.[116] Unemployment, frustration, and resentment have created conditions favoring emigration.

Throughout this period relations between the United States and India modulated. Immediately after the 1965 reforms India suffered a food shortage and sought U.S. aid. The United States delayed its response to survey the extent of the shortage and was severely criticized for its inaction. Then in 1971 it intervened on the side of Pakistan in the Indo-Pakistani War, and India's victory forced better relations.[117]

But even initially strained relations during this period could not stifle the interest in the United States among Indians who could take advantage of new immigration possibilities. More than any other group of Asian immigrants, Indians used the occupational and investor categories of the 1965 reforms to develop family networks in the United States. Few lived in the United States in 1965 and the occupational categories were the only ones available. In 1969, for example, 45 percent entered in the occupational categories, 26.8 percent as investors, and only 27 percent under family reunification (see table 7.1). As family networks developed, the family reunification categories were used to petition for other relatives. This happened in the Chinese, Filipino, and Korean American communities as well, but the pattern was most evident in Indian immigration. By 1988 approximately 89 percent entered in the family categories, and less than 11 percent under occupational groupings.

Careers

In 1969, over 70 percent of Indian immigrants entered through the occupational and investor categories, and almost 50 percent were professionals and managers[118] (see table 7.1). As family immigration increased and investor visas became unavailable in the late 1970's, only one-fourth were professionals and managers.[119] By 1985 the share was under 20 percent.[120]

Yet while the proportion of professionals has decreased, their absolute number remains quite high. The number who designated their prior occupation as professionals or managers was 2,949 in 1969, 6,630 in 1977, 5,081 in 1983, and 6,681 in 1989.[121] The community includes an incredible 48.5 percent professionals, managers, or executives.[122] Indian Americans are the only Asian American group with a smaller proportion of service workers than the general population.

The post-1965 surge in professionals has created a relatively wealthy class with substantial capital.[123] The increase in family-based immigration, however, and the corresponding decrease in professionals will eventually affect the community's overall profile. Changes in the profile were already evident in 1989 as about 64 percent of new immigrants listed no occupation, and almost 12 percent listed blue-collar and service work occupations.[124] In 1970, by contrast, 42 percent listed no occupation and only 5 percent were blue-collar or service workers.[125]

Many who have been classified as managers, executives, and professionals own small businesses. In 1980 there were 70 Indian-owned businesses for every thousand Indian Americans, and even more in metropolitan areas that grew in the early 1980s.[126] The propensity to own small businesses is particularly evident in the motel and hotel industry where as many as fifteen thousand are owned by Asian Indians or about 20 percent of the U.S. total.[127] Indian Americans also own one-fourth of the trucking business in California.[128]

Small businesses are common among Indian Americans largely because after the 1965 amendments many immigrated under the nonpreference investors category.[129] Purchasing a motel or restaurant qualified prospective immigrants for this classification. In 1969, 1,456 (over 26 percent) entered in this manner.[130] In 1972, the number was 8,753 (a staggering 53.7 percent of all Indian immigrants).[131] From 1978 to October 1991, however, no immigrant visas were available in the nonpreference investors category.[132] Even though a nonimmigrant investor category was available to nationals of many countries under current law, the necessary treaty has not existed between the United States and India.[133] A new investor's category implemented in October 1991 may, however, renew that option.

At $24,990 per year the 1980 median family income for Indian Americans was 25.5 percent higher than that of the general population.[134] This figure owes largely to the high salaries of foreign-born Indians, whose median income is significantly higher than those born in America.[135] Japanese Americans and Indian Americans are the only groups to have median incomes per worker higher than the general population's. As among other Asian American groups, more recent immigrants earn less than earlier arrivals, probably because of the ascendance of family immigration.[136]

To no one's great surprise, the median wage of the men is greater than that of the women.[137] Yet this disparity is not simply the result of low earnings among the women. In fact, immigrant women earn a bit more than their American-born counterparts. And Indian immigrant men earn 22.6 percent more than those born in America.

Unemployment and poverty are not insignificant among Asian Indians. The unemployment rate among immigrant Indian women (9.8 percent) is the highest among all immigrant Asian women and is higher than that among American-born Indian women.[138] Slightly more of their families (7.4 percent) fall below the poverty level than white American families (7 percent), reflecting the profile of recent immigrants. Of those who immigrated between 1975 and 1980, 10.7 percent were below the poverty line in 1980, compared to only 3.2 percent of those who immigrated between 1970 and 1974.[139]

Conclusion on Group Characteristics

The 1965 amendments greatly expanded the possibilities for Asian American communities to develop and for Asian Americans to pursue their aspirations. Increases in population, shifts in demographics, and changes in gender balance and geographic preferences have been dramatic since 1965. Yet, because earlier efforts to control the social forces within each community differed, each group had developed differently. The social, economic, and political conditions in each Asian country have also strongly influenced patterns of immigration. Accordingly, population size, gender ratios, occupational profiles, ghettoization, residential preferences, and the like vary sharply.

Consider population. Roughly speaking, Chinese and Japanese communities had at least one thing in common when the 1965 reforms were instituted – each had a population in the hundreds of thousands. But while growth of the Japanese American community has been moderate since, the Chinese American community grew substantially, much more like the Filipinos, Koreans, and Asian Indians, which were not large in 1965. Political and economic stability in Japan in the past 25 years has reduced the desire of its nationals to emigrate, but the treatment of immigrants under U.S. laws is also important. Japanese were better able to form and maintain families in the United States before 1965 and did not take advantage of the family reunification provisions as other groups did.

Since Chinese and Filipino Americans substantially outnumbered Koreans and Asian Indians in 1965, they had a greater base from which to take advantage of the family-oriented admissions system of the reforms. Thus, as early as 1970, fairly large numbers of immigrants from mainland China, Taiwan, and the Philippines entered in the categories for immediate relatives, and for second (relatives of permanent residents) and fifth preference (siblings) (see table 7.2). Filipinos also often used the category for professionals (third preference) in 1970, helping to build a base for family immigration in subsequent years. Asian Indians used the investor and professional categories to establish a family base. Koreans also immigrated as investors soon after the 1965 reforms, and as immediate relatives and as preference siblings in 1970 (see table 7.2). For a group with a seeming small family base, this statistical oddity is attributable to the many Korean war brides and adopted orphans that continued to enter after the 1965 amendments.

To the surprise of U.S. policymakers, Asian American communities (except Japanese) grew dramatically between 1965 and the present. The small but substantial Filipino American population grew seven times by 1990 to become the second largest. The smaller Korean American and Asian Indian communities increased eighteen and sixteen times respectively in 25 years, approaching the size of the Japanese American community, which had been the largest group through the early 1970s. Chinese America, already relatively substantial in 1965, increased by four and a half times by 1990 to remain the largest group since 1980, just ahead of Filipinos. Overall, Asian America has increased from under 1.2 million in 1965 to almost 7.3 million in 1990. In the 1980's alone the Asian and Pacific Islander population grew 107.8 percent compared to only 9.8 percent for the entire nation.[140]

Filipinos, South Koreans, and Chinese are leaving behind political instability for a better economic environment. Many Indian nationals have pursued training abroad in specialties that cannot be absorbed by the Indian economy. Many Koreans and Filipinos have pursued careers, such as those in the medical field, that can be used both at home and in the United States. They have contributed to the higher proportion of female immigration from Korea and the Philippines since 1965. For many, economic independence, occupational opportunities, and progressive social attitudes (in short, greater gender equality) in the United States were influential. As a result, Korean and Filipino women out-number men, as Japanese American women outnumber Japanese American men. Chinese Americans are evenly divided because of 25 years of female-dominated immigration and the passing of the older male-dominated community. The sexes in the Asian Indian community appear fairly balanced, but most of its working-age immigrants are men, while more of its elderly are women.

Except for Asian Indians and Koreans, Asian Americans prefer living in the West. Since 1965 a huge number of Asian Indians have settled in the Northeast, as have many Chinese. Filipinos and Japanese continue to have an affinity for Hawaii and California. Many Korean immigrants are attracted to California, but their settlement pattern has been more widespread, even stretching into the South.

Asian Americans generally prefer living in urban areas; the extent and types of enclaves each group establishes vary. Chinatowns, established historically as the result of harsh laws, racism, and family separation, have provided places to live and work to new immigrants, many working-class relatives, and refugees who arrived after 1965. Some urban Chinatowns have flourished. Filipino American enclaves have blossomed as well after 1965, but they are more in suburban areas. Because of fewer Japanese immigrants, Japantowns, while still visible, are much smaller, but do provide a social and political network.

The immigrant-driven profiles of the newer Asian Indian and Korean American communities have resulted in different enclaves. Before and just after 1965, when most Asian Indian immigrants were professionals or owned small businesses, enclaves were not prevalent. Recent arrivals from family categories and working-class backgrounds require social and economic networks, so residential enclaves are now quickly developing. Until recently, most Korean immigrants have had the means to reside in suburban areas and entered through occupational and investor categories. Their propensity for small business resulted in business blocks, rather than in residential enclaves. But some recent immigrants also live in Korea-towns.

The income in Asian American families has generally been higher than in the general population, mostly because more members work. Preliminary reports from the 1990 census show that in California Asian American household income now lags behind white households.[141] Individual Chinese, Filipino, and Korean Americans make less than their white counterparts, but Asian Indian and Japanese American workers generally earn more.[142] Although a significant proportion of Asian Americans hold professional jobs, particularly Asian Indians, many immigrants – especially Chinese and Filipinos – are service workers or live below the poverty line. Professional and management proportions also reflect the prevalence of small businesses in Asian America. The number of businesses owned by Asian Americans increased six times faster than the national rate between 1982 and 1987.[143]

Demographic profiles of the Chinese, Japanese, Asian Indian, and Filipino American communities strongly reflect the 1965 reforms and will continue to even after recent changes. Size, gender ratios, residential patterns, and employment profiles manifest the presence of expanded opportunities after 1965. Immigration reforms enacted in 1990 will continue to facilitate Asian immigration in the family preferences, though perhaps not in the same proportions. Increases in the Hong Kong quota will allow thousands more Chinese each year. More visas for professionals and a new investor category are also accessible to Asians.[144]

Asian Americans and Political Participation

The work of some scholars who have begun to take stock of how Asian Americans act in and regard electoral politics parallels what we have learned about the force of immigration laws. For the first time some researchers have attempted to aggregate and carefully analyze data on electoral involvement. They seem to be reacting against the inattention to detail shown by earlier scholars. To their credit they appreciate both the need to explore the distinctions between groups and the importance of activities besides registering, voting, and running for office.

Other scholars have begun to question cultural explanations of putative Asian apathy. They have focused upon the pervasive discrimination Asians have encountered and their marginalization in electoral politics. Others have begun to explore the relationship between economic status and the propensity to participate. They examine the question of whether economic success leads to greater or lesser participation, and they also address the belief that Asian Americans uniformly hold high economic status. Together, these researchers have captured a degree of media attention.[145] This nascent challenge to the popular image may well be on its way to informing a newly critical view of Asian American electoral activity.

Yet these researchers cannot escape the logic of the same popular image they aim to question. For example, investigators who attempt to identify differences between Asian American groups unwittingly share with those who continue to promote the popular image the tendency to treat Asian Americans generically in certain important respects, a tendency no doubt reinforced by positivist social science.

The myth of the apolitical character of Asian Americans

In recognizing the problems inherent in relying exclusively on anecdotal accounts and popular histories for conclusions about political participation, a handful of researchers have begun to measure data regarding Asian Americans and electoral politics. Their effort is particularly noteworthy because scholars had developed a substantial literature on the differences between African American and white participation and now pay increased attention to Latino electoral activity, but they had until recently entirely ignored Asian Americans.[146] This newly focused attention has so far produced a 1984 study in San Francisco,[147] a 1986 study in Los Angeles County,[148] and a 1984 survey of California.[149]

The San Francisco and Los Angeles County studies reported findings that seem startling. While the voter registration rate for the general population in California was about 73 percent in 1986,[150] at about the same time in San Francisco the rate for Japanese Americans was only 36.8 percent and for Chinese Americans it was 30.9 percent.[151] Similarly, in Los Angeles County Japanese had a registration rate of 43 percent, while Chinese registered at 35.5 percent. Other groups had even lower rates: 27 percent for Filipinos, 16.7 percent for Indians, 13 percent rate for Koreans, and 4.1 percent rate for Vietnamese.[152] These findings caught the attention of the popular media, no doubt because they seemed to support the popular notion that many Asian Americans able to register did not.[153]

But anyone familiar with the makeup of Asian American communities would have been skeptical about what these numbers might mean. Should it not have been suspicious that the groups reported to have the lowest voter registration rates just happen to have the highest proportion of foreign-born members? As it happens, such a suspicion would have been reasonable because neither survey distinguished between those who qualified by law to register and those who did not – they failed, in other words, to "adjust for noncitizens." This failure may not explain the low rate for the predominantly American-born Japanese Americans, but it certainly helps to account for the low registration rates for the other groups, which include high proportions of foreign-born noncitizens. And it is yet another example of studies that perpetuate traditional misconceptions by failing to factor in immigration patterns determined by law and policy.

One study that does adjust for noncitizens makes plain how important such sensitivity is to understanding Asian American participation in electoral politics. Drawing on 1984 interviews of California Latinos, African Americans, Asian Americans, and whites, it revealed registration rates that contradict both the popular image and the media's loose interpretation of the San Francisco and Los Angeles County studies. In this study, registration statistics for Asian Americans were much higher: 77 percent of California Asian American citizens were registered compared to 87 percent of the whites.[154]

This same statewide study revealed voting patterns suggesting that registered Asian Americans are as likely to vote as some registered whites. Only 69 percent of the Asians who registered voted compared to 80 percent of whites and 81 percent of African Americans.[155] When groups were viewed separately, however, Chinese were more similar to whites in their voting pattern, while Vietnamese and Koreans had the lowest voter turnouts among Asians.[156] This lends some credence to, or at least renders less implausible, unpublished surveys in San Francisco that report that on certain issues, Chinese Americans actually vote at a rate 5 to 10 percentage points above the general electorate.[157]

What we know about Asian American communities strongly suggests that economic status and income likely figure prominently in registration and voting. The San Francisco and Los Angeles County studies suggest that those areas commonly believed to have higher concentrations of middle-as opposed to lower-income residents have higher registration rates. In San Francisco, for example, the Chinese registration rate in Chinatown was 23.1 percent compared to 39.9 percent in the more middle-income Richmond district. Yet because these studies fail to distinguish between citizens and noncitizens, they leave us to wonder whether lower rates in presumably less affluent areas are the result of the proportion of foreign-born residents, economic status, or something else.

Even more careful attention to noncitizenship and economic status may not provide the explanations one would expect, however. Among whites, African Americans, and Latinos, higher socioeconomic status characteristically implies higher voter participation. But those who simply presume that the same is true of Asian Americans might be puzzled to learn, as were the scholars of the statewide survey investigating this relationship for the first time, that at least in California the generally expected correlation between economic status and electoral participation is not there.[158] Asian American political participation, unlike that of whites, African Americans, and Latinos, is not predictably influenced by levels of employment, educational attainment, and home ownership. These findings do seem to resist facile explanations, but perhaps they should not be regarded as altogether puzzling. They appear simply to reflect a possibility that is too often either never entertained or stubbornly resisted: economic circumstance may have different consequences within different ethnic communities.

If ethnic diversity makes a sensible appreciation of Asian American politics difficult, so does the fact that electoral affairs involve more than registering and voting. Understanding this, those who conducted the statewide survey considered other forms of political activity. In particular, they also inquired about contributing money, exhibiting a campaign poster or sticker, working for a party or candidate, and attending a political meeting or rally. And they asked about nonelectoral activities like contacting the media or officials and working with groups. What these scholars learned supports the notion that there is no simple or easily intuited pattern to the political behavior of African Americans, whites, Latinos, or Asian Americans.

Contrary to the popular image of Asian Americans as uniformly inactive, this research reveals that involvement varies according to the type of political activity. While it is true that Asians and Latinos seemed to be less inclined than whites to work on campaigns, attend political rallies, and exhibit political signs and bumper stickers, Asian Americans are more likely than other groups to contribute money to candidates.[159] Latinos are less likely than African Americans or whites to work in groups, but they contact news media at about the same rates. Asian Americans are as likely as whites to work in groups and more likely than anyone to convey opinions to news media. Filipinos and Koreans were more likely to convey their opinions to the news media than Vietnamese, Japanese, and Chinese, but Japanese were more likely to work in groups than Filipinos, Vietnamese, Chinese, and Koreans.[160]

Asian Americans are not only more active along certain electoral and nonelectoral dimensions than is typically believed; their affiliations and attitudes belie the popular image. Rather than having no (or "only" weak) allegiances or viewpoints, they show about the same rates of party loyalty and commitment as the general population. For example, the statewide study indicated that of those Asian Americans surveyed in 1984, 42 percent were registered Democrats, 41 percent were registered Republicans, and 16 percent declined to choose either party.[161] The Los Angeles study indicated that of the 1983 list of registered voters for certain tracts, 52.4 percent of Asian Americans registered as Democrats, 31 percent as Republicans, and 15 percent were independent.[162] And the 1984 survey in sample districts of San Francisco revealed that 51.5 percent were registered Democrats, 21.3 percent were registered Republicans, and more than a quarter declined to state a party.

For many Asian Americans party loyalties are strong. In the statewide survey 19 percent said they were "strong Republicans" and another 10 percent said they were "strong Democrats." To be sure, strength of party affiliation is a complicated matter. A strong Republican may not think much about either candidates or issues. A "weak" or "leaning Republican" may both know and care deeply about every candidate and issue. In any case, the figures for Asian Americans are similar to those obtained for whites (38 percent either strong Democrat or Republican) and for Latinos (34 percent either strong Democrat or Republican). Only the findings for African Americans (56 percent strong Democrats, 2 percent strong Republicans) differed significantly, no doubt reflecting their well-documented and historically grounded ties to the Democratic party. These statistics seem at least to rebut the popular image of Asian Americans who have allegiances that are weaker than most.

Careful examination would ultimately reveal the differences in the loyalties and commitments within Asian American groups that the limited information gathered to date points to. Of those included in the Los Angeles study, for instance, Filipinos had the highest percentage affiliated with the Democratic party at 63.3 percent compared with 22.8 percent Republican. Asian Indians were 59.1 percent Democrat and 23.6 percent Republican. Japanese followed at 54.9 percent Democrat and 32.3 percent Republican. Koreans were 48.5 percent Democrat and 29.4 percent Republican. Chinese (41.9 percent) and Vietnamese (40 percent) had the lowest proportions of Democrats, and the highest proportions of Republicans (36.4 percent and 35.9 percent, respectively).[163]

Likewise, in the San Francisco study of Chinese and Japanese, 48.6 percent of the Chinese were Democrats and 21.4 percent were Republicans; 66.7 percent of the Japanese were Democrats and 20.2 percent Republicans.[164] It would be unwise to draw any definitive conclusions from the patterns found in either the Los Angeles or San Francisco studies about the allegiances of particular groups, their intensity, or their relationship to other aspects of political life. The patterns do, however, begin to unmask a people far more interestingly affiliated than the popular image has ever contemplated. And they would seem obviously to suggest the need for more scholars who are inclined to inquire rather than presume.

The limitations of the popular image and the need for more careful scholarly attention are more striking when one takes into account what we now know about how Asian Americans think about particular issues. The California survey indicates that attitudes are not easily categorized. Like whites, Asian Americans are less likely than African Americans and Latinos to favor increased spending on welfare and more likely to favor the death penalty. Like whites and African Americans and unlike Latinos, a majority of Asian Americans do not favor amnesty for undocumented aliens. Like Latinos and African Americans and unlike whites, most favor bilingual education programs. And unlike whites, African Americans, and Latinos, most favor a ban on handguns but not prayer in public schools.[165]

As with party affiliation, the little data we have suggest that attitudinal differences between groups may be at least as great as those between Asians and other ethnic groups. In the California study Koreans were more likely than Japanese to favor bilingual ballots, bilingual education, and amnesty for undocumented aliens. Filipinos were the strongest supporters of prayer in public schools and increased military spending. Japanese political attitudes resembled those of whites more than of other Asian groups. And in the view of the authors, "There was no distinguishing pattern to Chinese American attitudes other than being generally conservative."[166]

Voting patterns, which seem to defy party affiliation, may provide further evidence about Asian American attitudes toward particular issues. In the 1984 presidential election, for example, California Asian Americans, though predominantly registered Democrats, favored Ronald Reagan over Walter Mondale by 67 to 32 percent. Then in 1992 they voted 39 percent for Bill Clinton, 33 percent for George Bush, and 25 percent for Ross Perot (although differences were measured between Chinese, Japanese, and Filipinos).[167] Nationwide Asians favored Bush (52 percent to 32 percent for Clinton and 17 percent for Perot). In 1986 California Asian Americans favored Republican Governor George Deukmejian over Tom Bradley by 53 to 47 percent, and Deukmejian won, 62 to 38 percent. In the same election controversial Proposition 63, the "English only" initiative, passed by 77 to 23 percent but received only 52 percent of the Asian vote. And while the state rejected Supreme Court Justice Cruz Reynoso, a self-proclaimed liberal opponent of the death penalty and the court's only Latino judge, 60 to 40 percent, Asians favored him 54 to 46 percent.[168]

Perhaps this contrast confirms, as some believe, that Asian Americans are more inclined than others to cross party lines.[169] After all, African Americans and Latinos preferred Clinton and Mondale by margins that roughly paralleled formal party affiliations.[170] Yet party labels may simply be a poorer proxy for what Asian Americans care about and how strongly they care. And formal party affiliation may not reveal at all how responsive particular candidates are to their concerns or at least how responsive Asian Americans perceive them to be. In any case voting patterns raise far more questions than they answer. Like the other forms of electoral and nonelectoral activity we are finally beginning to learn more about, they expose the myth of the Asian apolitical character.

The distinctions between Asian American groups are undoubtedly reflected in other subcategories affected by immigration policies. More research is needed into patterns of electoral participation
between generations, between urban and rural groups, between
residents of enclaves and dispersed communities, and between pre-
and post-1965 immigrants, to name just a few.

Notes

1 See table 3 in Hing 1993.
2 Gardner et al. 1985: 8, table 2.
3 A total of 42,478 immigrated in 1987, *Immigration Statistics: Fiscal Year
  1987, Advance Report*, table 4, Immigration and Naturalization Service,
  June 1988.
4 From *1970 INS Annual Report*, table 13; *1988 and 1989 INS Statistical Yearbooks*, table 2. INS Statistical Branch, Detail Run 401 – Total FY 1990.
5 *1972–78 INS Annual Reports*, table 7A; *1977 INS Annual Report*, table 6E.
  Although this provision did not apply to aliens who had firmly resettled in a
  third country – Rosenberg v. Woo, 402 U.S. 49 (1971) – many of the
  Chinese who were admitted under seventh preference had resided in
  Hong Kong for many years. See, e.g., Matter of Ng, 12 I. & N. Dec. 411
  (Reg. Comm'r 1967); Matter of Chai, 12 I. & N. Dec. 81 (Reg. Comm'r
  1967).
6 There is, however, a noticeable variation in these proportions between
  immigrants from Taiwan and those from mainland China. In 1987, 93
  percent entered in the family categories and 4.2 percent in the occupational
  categories from mainland China. But for Taiwan, it was 64.3 percent family
  and 34.5 percent occupational (based on *Immigration Statistics Fiscal Year
  1987, Advance Report*, table 4).
7 Based on Dept. of Commerce 1988a: table 1.
8 The Immigration and Naturalization Systems of the United States, *Rept. of
  the Committee on the Judiciary Pursuant to S. Res. 137*, Apr. 20, 1950, p. 141;
  Takaki 1989: 254; Lee 1960: 42, 117.
9 Tabulations from *1985 INS Statistical Yearbook*, table IMM 1.2; *1988 and 1989
  INS Statistical Yearbooks*, table 2; 1990 data supplied by Blanche V. Shanks,
  Statistical Assistant, Immigration and Naturalization Service, Washington,
  D.C., June 13, 1991.
10 A separate quota for Taiwan was established as a rider to a defense bill to
   aid the Republic of China. *International Security and Development Cooperation
   Act of 1981*, Public Law 97–113, *United States Statutes at Large* 95: 1519.
11 Gardner et al. 1985: 37. L. Harrison, "Asians 40 Percent of 1985's Legal
   Immigrants," *Asian Week*, May 23, 1986, p. 24.
12 See generally Wong 1980: 511; Keely 1975: 179; Keely 1974: 89; Keely
   1971: 157.
13 Based on table 8 of *1953–1966, 1969 INS Annual Reports*.
14 From *1961 and 1966 INS Annual Reports*, table 8.

15 Based on *1969 and 1977 INS Annual Reports*, table 8. This is consistent with general findings today that family reunification categories provide most of the new immigrant professionals (Bach and Meissner 1989: 11–12).

16 Since immigrants are charged to their country of birth, many immigrants from Hong Kong were born in China and are regarded as coming from China. *United States Code*, 1152(*b*)(1990*ed.*).

17 Consider, for example, the statements of Barry Chiswick, the dean of Economics and Business Administration at the University of Illinois in Chicago, cited in the Introduction.

18 Visas were set aside for "qualified immigrants who are members of the professions or who [have] exceptional ability in the sciences or the arts." To qualify the applicant had to obtain a labor certification, which required a job offer from an employer. See *U.S. Code* 8: 1153(a)(3), 1182(a)(14) (1982 ed); Hing 1985: chap. 5.

19 From *1969 INS Annual Report*, table 8.

20 From *1983 INS Statistical Yearbook*, table IMM 6.1.

21 Based on *1989 INS Statistical Yearbook*, tables 5 and 6, pp. 12, 14.

22 Waller and Hoffman 1989: 313; "Beijing Death Toll at Least 200; Army Tightens Control of City But Angry Resistance Goes On," *New York Times*, June 5, 1989, p. 1; conversation with Eugene Chow, Aug. 15, 1989, private attorney in Hong Kong.

23 The statute requires every applicant for admission to demonstrate that he or she is "not likely to become a public charge" [*U.S. Code*, 1182(a)(4) (1992 ed); see also Hing 1985: 4.46–4.47].

24 In 1961, 8.5 percent were service or household workers and 69.4 percent were housewives or had no prior occupation; in 1966, 14.7 percent were service or household workers and 54 percent were housewives or had no prior occupation (based on *1961 and 1966 INS Annual Reports*, table 8). This occupational breakdown held until 1969, when 11.5 percent were household or service workers, and 52 percent were housewives or had no prior occupation (based on *1969 INS Annual Report*, table 8). By 1977, the proportion who designated household or service work jobs dropped to 5.4 percent, but 53 percent were housewives or had no prior occupation (*1977 INS Annual Report*, table 8). As recently as 1985, 57.5 percent continued to indicate no prior occupation (with 4.6 percent indicating service work) (*1985 INS Statistical Yearbook*, table IMM 6.1).

25 Mar 1985: 10–11, 83–7, 106.

26 See generally Wong 1980: 518, 522; Ng 1977: 106; Sung 1976: 69.

27 Gardner et al. 1985: 31 (corrected data based on telephone conversation with authors).

28 The bifurcation of labor in the Chinese American community is not uncommon. Sociological and economic literature often accounts for the labor experience of immigrants through a "split market theory" (higher-paid labor deals with the undercutting potential of cheaper labor by excluding them from certain types of work) or the "human capital model" (the labor market contains at least two groups of workers whose price differs for the same work, or would differ if they did the same work). For a discussion

of the split market theory, see Piore 1979; Bonacich 1972. For a discussion of the human capital theory, see Chiswick 1980; Ng 1977: 101; Chiswick 1978: 897.

29 Dept. of Commerce 1988a: table 21.

30 Discussed more fully in Chap. 5, Hing 1993.

31 Even in Minneapolis, which is the second lowest ranking metropolitan area, the rate is 74.9 per 1,000 for Chinese (Manning and O'Hare 1988: 35–7).

32 In Los Angeles, Chinese owned 7,664 businesses, Japanese 5,853, and Koreans 5,701 (Pei 1987). In the San Francisco Bay Area, the figures were Chinese 13,784, Filipinos 4,261, Japanese 4,075, Koreans 2,286, Asian Indians 1,707, and Vietnamese 1,339 (D. Waugh, "Asian American Businesses See Explosive Growth in State," *San Francisco Examiner*, Aug. 2, 1991, p. A-16).

33 Yu, "Asian-Americans Charge Prejudice Slows Climb to Management Ranks," *Wall Street Journal*, Sept. 11, 1985, p. 35; Chinese for Affirmative Action 1989: 20–2, 26–7; McLeod 1986: 51.

34 See, e.g., A. Ramirez, "America's Super Minority," *Fortune*, Nov. 24, 1986, p. 149; M. Kasindorf, "Asian-Americans: A 'Model Minority,'" *Newsweek*, Dec. 6, 1982, p. 39.

35 From Dept. of Commerce 1988b: table 7, p. 13.

36 Gardner et al. 1985: 34, table 14. Some scholars who note the higher earnings of older immigrants argue that immigrants assimilate quite well and over time their earnings overtake even native workers. But more thoughtful observers warn that the use of cross section data is misleading, because many immigrants eventually return to their country of origin – quite possibly those who have failed economically – and the average quality of the immigrant pool (in terms of education and job preparedness) may have been declining recently (Borjas 1986: 13–14).

37 Ignoring the existence of low-income Chinese Americans, Philip Martin of the University of California at Davis, who served on the staff of the Select Commission on Immigration and Refugee Policy, told a congressional committee, "In California it's hard to tell exactly what the [impact of the new wave of immigration has] been, but it seems as if Anglos and Asians tend to dominate the top of the income or wealth pyramid, while blacks and Hispanics tend to be over-represented at the bottom" (testimony before the Subcommittee on Economic Resources, Competitiveness, and Security Economics, May 29, 1986, p. 607).

38 Gardner et al. 1985: 34.

39 Ibid., table 14.

40 Ibid.

41 *U.S. Code* 42: 1381, 1382 (1990 ed.).

42 Based on Dept. of Commerce 1991: table 1.

43 Dept. of Commerce 1988b: 3; 1965 figure estimated from Smith 1976: 325; *1989 INS Statistical Yearbook*, table 2; INS Statistical Branch, Detail Run 401–Total FY 1990.

44 Based on Immigration and Naturalization Service, *Immigration Statistics: Fiscal Year 1987, Advance Report*, table 4. The total for Hong Kong, Taiwan,

and mainland China was 42,478 in 1987. So even with the territorial quota increase for Hong Kong provided in 1986 (from 600 to 5,000), the annual total immigration for those three areas will still be less than the Philippines. By 1995 the Hong Kong quota will be increased to 20,000.

45 *U.S. Code* 8: 1182 (a)(5) (1992); see generally Hing 1985: chaps. 4 and 5.

46 Based on *1976 INS Annual Report*, tables 6, 6B, 7A.

47 The availability of nonpreference visas for investors was never significant for Filipinos. As Table 8 shows, less than 1 percent entered as investors in 1969, compared to 26.8 percent of Asian Indians and 11.6 percent of Koreans. Although during the Marcos era, Filipino asylum applicants were approved at the relatively high rate of up to 25 percent in 1984, that only amounted to about 30 per year. Polish nationals were granted asylum at a rate of 30 percent, Nicaraguans at 17 percent, El Salvadorans at 1 percent, Guatemalans at 0.3 percent, Iranians at 63 percent (Hing 1985: 196–7).

48 Vreeland 1976: 67; Bunge 1984: 197.

49 Vreeland 1976: 67, 218; Bunge 1984: 49.

50 Bunge 1984: 49; Vreeland 1976: 191.

51 Vreeland 1976: 221; Bunge 1984: 49. Senator Benigno Aquino was among the arrested group, as he was considered by many to be Marcos's key rival. He was sentenced to eight years in solitary confinement (Steinberg 1982: 102). The assassination of Aquino on his return from exile in 1983 helped stir the public's outrage against Marcos, and resulted in the installation of Aquino's widow, Corazon, to the presidency ("Anatomy of a Revolution," *Time*, Mar. 10, 1986, 28–9).

52 Vreeland 1976: 221.

53 Bunge 1984: 52, 92.

54 Steinberg 1982: 104–6; Bunge: 1984: 50, 231.

55 Steinberg 1982: 122; Bunge: 1984: 120.

56 Steinberg 1982: 106; Bunge: 1984: 120.

57 Bunge 1984: 116; Vreeland 1976: 36; Steinberg 1982: 111.

58 See, e.g., T. Abate, "Money Woes Driving Many Filipinos to the U.S.," *San Francisco Examiner*, Dec. 24, 1991, p. A-3; Berlow, "U.S. Immigration Bill Seen as a Way Out of Philippines," *San Francisco Chronicle*, Nov. 23, 1990, p. B-18.

59 Filipino farm workers held the first modern agricultural strike in California, walking out of ranches on Sept. 8, 1965. A week later they were joined by Mexican farm workers in the grape strike that started the United Farm Workers (interview with Susan Bowyer, former UFW organizer, Mar. 18, 1991).

60 *1969 INS Annual Report*, table 8.

61 Based on *1975 and 1978 INS Annual Reports*, table 8.

62 Based on *1985 INS Statistical Yearbook*, table IMM 6.1, p. 63.

63 In 1969, 7,530 Filipino professionals or managers entered, 9,584 in 1970, 6,649 in 1983, and 8,127 in 1988 (*1969 and 1970 INS Annual Report, 1983 and 1988 INS Statistical Yearbook*).

64 Xenos et al. 1987: table 11.25.

65 "Emigration from Philippines Soars as Thousands Come to U.S.," *San Jose Mercury News*, June 24, 1985: "The Philippines graduates thousands of health workers every year, often more than the economy can absorb, and then routinely loses a large portion of these to the United States, Canada, and the Mideast."

66 In the San Francisco Bay Area in 1987, Filipinos owned more businesses (4,261) than Japanese (4,075) and Koreans (2,386), but not more than Chinese (13,784) (D. Waugh, "Asian American Businesses See Explosive Growth in State," *San Francisco Examiner*, Aug. 2, 1991, p. A-16).

67 Xenos et al. 1987: 31.

68 Gardner et al. 1985: 31, fig. 6 (corrected figures based on telephone conversation with authors).

69 Ibid.

70 Dept. of Commerce 1988a: table 29.

71 Gardner et al. 1985: 34.

72 While the proportion of families under the poverty line is only 4.6 percent for Filipino Americans who immigrated prior to 1970, a higher proportion (8.8 percent) of more recent (1975–80) immigrant families is below the line (Gardner et al. 1985: 34, table 14).

73 Based on Dept. of Commerce 1991: table 1.

74 Choy 1979: 196–8.

75 Ibid., 205–7.

76 *1971 INS Annual Report*, table 14. Over 25,000 Koreans immigrated from 1966 to 1970 (*1969 and 1971 INS Annual Reports*, table 14).

77 *1979 and 1987 INS Statistical Yearbook*, table 14.

78 *1989 INS Statistical Yearbook*, table 2; INS Statistical Branch, Detail Run 401– Total FY 1990.

79 INS Statistical Branch, Detail Run 401–Total FY 1990; *1973–1989 INS Annual Reports and INS Statistical Yearbooks*.

80 Dept. of Commerce 1983a: table B. In 1965 most Koreans in the United States were American-born. By 1970, 54 percent were foreign-born (Kim 1974: 24,36).

81 Kim 1981: 42–4. With some exceptions, occupational preference categories require a labor certification issued by the Dept. of Labor (see Hing 1985: chap. 5).

82 Kim 1981: 57.

83 Kim 1981: 42–4, 148.

84 See generally Hing 1985: chaps. 4 and 5. The immediate relative category for citizens is unlimited [*U.S. Code* 8: 1151 (b) (1990 ed.)]. In 1990 amendments more visas were added for occupational and professional immigrants.

85 Kim 1981: 32–3, 35. A large number of adopted Korean children also became citizens (Kim 1974: 35).

86 Those holding only lawful permanent resident alien status cannot petition for those relatives [*U.S. Code* 8: 1151(b), 1153(a) (1982 ed.)].

87 Kim 1981: 32–3.

88 See, e.g., Kim 1981: 32–3.

89　*U.S. Code* 8: 1182(a) (32) (1990 ed.), added by Act of Oct. 12, 1986, Public Law 94–484, *Statutes at Large* 90: 2301, and amended by sec. 302(q)(j), Act of Aug. 1, 1977, Public Law 95–83, *Statutes at Large* 91: 383; Kim 1981: 153–5. However, until Dec. 31, 1986, graduates of foreign medical schools who were going to be employed in areas Health and Human Services had designated as "manpower shortage" areas were actually given preferential treatment [*Code of Federal Regulations* 8: 656.22(c) 1986], so long as they had passed the National Board of Medical Examiners examination [*U.S. Code* 8: 1182(a)(32) (1982 ed.)]. Although this preferential treatment was deleted, general labor certification under occupational preferences is still available (see Hing 1985: 5.17, chap. 5). Under certain conditions foreign medical students may enter for graduate medical education or for training in residency or fellowship programs [*U.S. Code* 8: 1101(a)(15)(J), 1182(j) (1990 ed.); *Code of Federal Regulations* 22: 514.1 (1990)]. South Korea trained doctors have also had a difficult time passing a visa-qualifying examination implemented in 1977 (Kim 1981: 172–3).

90　Chan 1991a: 147–9.

91　Based on *1969 and 1972 INS Annual Report*, table 8; *1985 INS Statistical Yearbook*, table 6.1, p. 62; *1989 INS Statistical Yearbook*, table 20, p. 40.

92　Dept. of Commerce 1988a: table 45. Gardner et al. 1985: 31, fig. 6 (corrected data based on telephone conversation with authors).

93　Dept. of Commerce 1988a: tables 21, 45. This significantly exceeds that of the Chinese American population (37.3 percent).

94　Dept. of Commerce 1988a: table 45.

95　Manning and O'Hare 1988: 35.

96　D. Waugh, "Asian American Businesses See Explosive Growth in State," *San Francisco Examiner*, Aug. 2, 1991, p. A-16.

97　Pei 1987: 2.

98　Cariño 1987: 419; see also Gardner et al. 1985: 10.

99　Kim 1981: 38.

100　Manning and O'Hare 1988: 36–7.

101　See generally Min 1984: 333–52; Kim 1981: 102.

102　Wasserman 1979: 138–50.

103　See generally Min 1984: 333–52.

104　Dept. of Commerce 1988b: 9.

105　Gardner et al. 1985: 34, table 14, p. 34.

106　Dept. of Commerce 1988a: table 47.

107　Xenos et al. 1987: table 11.25.

108　Similar figures apply to Chinese, but not to Filipinos and Asian Indians (Gardner et al. 1985: 34).

109　Ibid., table 14.

110　Ibid.

111　Based on *1970 INS Annual Report*, table 13 and *1976 INS Annual Report*, table 14, p. 89; *1989 INS Statistical Yearbook*, table 2; INS Statistical Branch, Detail Run 401–Total FY 1990.

112　Based on Dept. of Commerce 1988a: table 1.

113 Based on *1983 INS Statistical Yearbook*, table IMM 1.2, and *1988 INS Statistical Yearbook*, table 2.
114 *World Development Report*, 1984, annex table 25 (New York: Oxford University Press).
115 *India to 1990, How Far Will Reform Go?*, Economist Intelligence Unit Special Report no. 1954, prospect series, p. 24.
116 Dandekar 1968: 121.
117 Tewari 1977: 132–7.
118 Based on *1969 INS Annual Report*, table 8, p. 49.
119 Based on *1978 and 1979 INS Annual Reports*, table 8.
120 Based on *1984 and 1985 INS Statistical Yearbooks*, table IMM 6.1.
121 From *1969 and 1977 INS Annual Reports*, table 8; *1983 INS Statistical Yearbook*, table IMM 6.1; *1989 INS Statistical Yearbook*, table 20, p. 40.
122 Based on Dept. of Commerce 1988a: table 39.
123 In Dec. 1986, the nation's first publicly held bank with shareholders exclusively of Asian Indian origin, First Indo, opened. The initial capitalization of the bank was $7.5 million, which was above the average ($3 million) for most newly organized California banks. Although the trend is changing, most minority-owned banks, except for Chinese American institutions, historically have had poor performance records in California despite the state's ethnic diversity (P. Ragsdale, "Bank Hopes to Capitalize on Its Origin," *San Francisco Examiner*, Jan. 30, 1987, C-1).
124 Based on *1989 INS Statistical Yearbook*, table 20, p. 40. The "no occupation" category included spouses and children.
125 Based on *1970 INS Annual Report*, table 8, p. 49. Many from the poorer working class in India continue to migrate to Great Britain instead of the United States where a majority may obtain unskilled jobs (Kitano and Daniels 1988: 101–2).
126 Among Asian Americans, this rate was second only to Koreans, and ranked above Japanese (68.5 per 1,000) and Chinese (65.1 per 1,000). Comparable figures for the general population were 64 per 1,000 (Manning and O'Hare 1988: 35–6).
127 "Surge in Indian Immigration," *Asian Week*, May 22, 1987, p. 5. Forty percent of the motels on Interstate 75 (between Detroit and Atlanta) are operated by Indians (Kitano and Daniels 1988: 101).
128 *India West*, Apr. 1, 1988, p. 47.
129 In fact, many reported cases involving legal interpretations of the investor category involve Asian Indians. See, e.g., Patel v. INS, 638 F.2d 1199 (9th Cir. 1980) (motel); Mawji v. INS, 671 F.2d 342 (9th Cir. 1982) (fast-food restaurant, then grocery store); Matter of Kumar, 11 I.&N. Dec. 315 (BIA 1980) (clothing store, then motel).
130 Based on *1969 INS Annual Report*, table 7A, p. 48.
131 Based on *1972 INS Annual Report*, table 7A, p. 35.
132 See Hing 1985: 4.13.
133 A commerce treaty is required under the law [*U.S. Code* 8: 1101(a)(15)(E) (1992 ed.)].

134 Dept. of Commerce 1988b: 9; Dept. of Commerce 1988a: table 38.

135 Dept. of Commerce 1988a: table 38.

136 Gardner et al. 1985: 34, table 14.

137 Dept. of Commerce 1988a: table 38.

138 Ibid., table 41.

139 Gardner et al. 1985: 34.

140 Dept. of Commerce 1991: table 1.

141 Bennett 1992: 10–11. Early calculations for the 1990 census showed that Asian American households in California had a lower income ($47,974) than that of white households ($49,103). S. Johnson, "Minorities" Income Higher in South Bay, *San Jose Mercury News*, May 13, 1992, p. 1A.

142 The 1990 census will likely reveal this same pattern found in 1980. Initial reports on the 1990 data show that in California per capita Asian American income ($13,733) is lower than that of whites ($19,028) (S. Johnson, "Minorities' Income Higher in South Bay," *San Jose Mercury News*, May 13, 1992, p. 1A). Nationwide per capita Asian American income ($13,420) is also lower than for whites ($15,560) (Bennett 1992: 11).

143 D. Waugh, "Asian American Businesses See Explosive Growth in State," *San Francisco Examiner*, Aug. 2, 1991, p. A-16.

144 Although 10,000 visas have been set aside for the new investor (employment creation) category, in its first year of operation (1992) fewer than 200 applications will be field, in part because of rigorous application requirements.

145 See, e.g., "Group Seeks to Reverse Voter Apathy by Asians," *Los Angeles Times*, Mar. 3, 1986, Metro, p. 1; J. Matthews, "Ethnic Asians Favor GOP in Poll," *Washington Post*, Nov. 10, 1985, p. A4.

146 The literature on differences in black and white participation include: R. Bush, "Black Enfranchisement, Jesse Jackson and Beyond," in R. Bush, ed. *The New Black Vote* (San Francisco: Synthesis Publishing, 1984) and M. B. Preston et al., *The New Black Politics: The Search for Political Power*, 2d ed. (New York: Longman, 1987).

147 Din 1984: 41.

148 Nakanishi 1986; see also Nakanishi 1985–86.

149 Uhlaner et al. 1989; Cain et al. 1986.

150 California Dept. of Finance, "California Statistical Abstract," 1987, pp. 228–29.

151 Din 1984: 79, 85.

152 Nakanishi 1986: 21.

153 See, e.g., M. Arax, "Group Seeks to Reverse Voter Apathy by Asians," *Los Angeles Times*, Mar. 3, 1986, Metro, p. 1.

154 Uhlaner et al. 1989: 199.

155 Uhlaner et al. 1989: table 1, p. 38.

156 Unpublished data supplied by Carole Uhlaner, University of California at Irvine.

157 Interview with Harold Yee, executive director, Asian Inc., San Francisco, Dec. 14, 1989.

158 Uhlaner et al. 1989: 203–4.

159 Cain et al. 1986: 34 (table I–4). African Americans had a level of participation in these activities that was quite comparable to whites.

160 Unpublished data supplied by Carole Uhlaner, University of California at Irvine.

161 Cain et al. 1986: 19–20. In 1986 in California 50.8 percent were registered Democratic, 38.3 percent Republican, and only 8.7 percent declined to state a party (California Dept. of Finance 1987: 226–27). The comparative figures for African Americans were 89 percent Democrats, 6 percent Republicans, and 6 percent who declined to state. As for Latinos 75 percent were Democrats, 17 percent Republicans, and 9 percent declined to state (Cain et al., 1986: 18–19).

162 Nakanishi 1985–86: table 2b, p. 15.

163 Nakanishi 1987: 42–52. In an informal survey conducted by the *San Jose Mercury News* in 1987, 53 percent of the Vietnamese Americans in Santa Clara County were registered Republicans and 21 percent Democrats (Trounstine, "Most Vietnamese Voters in County are Republican," *San Jose Mercury News*, Aug. 17, 1987, p. 1A; L. Harrison, "No One Dares to Disagree," *Asian Week*, Aug. 21, 1987, p. 5).

164 Din 1984: tables 3–11, 3–8, and 3–9 (Japanese figure is based on weighted average), pp. 8–9.

165 Cain et al. 1986: table I–1.

166 Ibid., p. 14. There is little beyond the California study from which to draw on regarding attitudinal differences between groups. A separate study on a group of "highly educated" Asian Indians from New York showed that 43.5 percent regarded themselves as liberal, 1 in 6 as highly conservative, and one-third as independent or middle-of-the-road ("Center for Management at Baruch College of CUNY," *India West*, Apr. 15, 1988, p. 30).

167 In Northern California, Chinese were split between Clinton and Bush 47–46 percent. Filipinos leaned heavily to Clinton (61–34 percent), as did Japanese (74–25 percent) (S. A. Chin, "Bay Area Asians Backed Clinton by Big Margin," *San Francisco Examiner*, Nov. 6, 1992, p. A-20; L. I. Barrett, "A New Coalition for the 1990s," *Time*, Nov. 16, 1992, p. 47). In 1984 Californians favored Reagan over Mondale 57.5 to 41.3 percent (James Fay, Sr., ed., *California Almanac*, 3d ed. [1987], p. 265). In 1992 they voted 47 percent for Clinton, 32 percent for Bush, and 21 percent for Perot ("How Californians Voted in the Presidential Race," *San Francisco Examiner*, Nov. 4, 1992, p. A-11).

168 "Polls: Asians Sensitive on Ethnic Issues," *Asian Week*, Nov. 14, 1986, pp. 1, 11.

169 Cain et al. 1986: 19–20; Tachibana 1986: 536; Aoki 1986: 546.

170 Cain et al. 1986: 18–19. In 1992 California African Americans voted 83 percent Clinton, 9 percent Perot, and 8 percent Bush. Latinos voted 65 percent Clinton, 21 percent Bush, and 14 percent Perot ("How Californians Voted in the Presidential Race," *San Francisco Examiner*, Nov. 4, 1992, p. A-11). The figures were similar nationwide (L. I. Barrett, "A New Coalition for the 1990s," *Time*, Nov. 16, 1992, p. 47).

References

Aoki, E. 1986. "Which Party Will Harvest the New Asian Votes?" *California Journal* (Nov.): 545–46.

Bach, R., and D. Meissner. 1989. *America's Economy in the 1990's: What Role Should Immigration Play?* Carnegie Endowment for International Peace.

Bonacich, E. 1972. "A Theory of Ethnic Antagonism: The Split Labor Market." *American Sociological Review* 37: 547–49.

Borjas, G. 1986. "Immigrants and the U.S. Labor Market." In S. Pozo, ed., *Essays on Legal and Illegal Immigration*, pp. 7–20. Kalamazoo, Mich.: Upjohn Institute for Employment Research.

Bunge, F. 1984. *The Philippines: A Country Study.* Washington D.C.: American University.

Cain, B. E., D. R. Kiewiet, and C. Uhlaner. 1986. "The Political Impact of California's Minorities." Paper prepared for the Western Political Science Association, Eugene, Ore., March 22.

Carino, B. V. 1987. "The Philippines and Southeast Asia: Historical and Contemporary Linkages." In J. T. Fawcett and B. V. Carino, eds, *Pacific Bridges*, pp. 305–25.

Chan, Sucheng. 1991a. *Asian Americans: An Interpretive History.* Boston: Twayne.

Chinese for Affirmative Action. 1989. "The Broken Ladder'89." San Francisco: Chinese for Affirmative Action.

Chiswick, B. 1978. "The Effects of Americanization on the Earnings of Foreign-Born Men." *Journal of Political Economy* 86: 897–921.

——. 1980. "Immigrant Earnings: Patterns by Sex, Race, and Ethnic Grouping." *Monthly Labor Review* 22 (Oct.): 22–25.

Choy, B. 1979. *Koreans in America.* Chicago: Nelson Hall.

Dandekar, V. M. 1968. "India." In W. Adams, ed., *The Brain Drain.* New York: Macmillan.

Din, G. 1984. "An Analysis of Asian/Pacific American Registration and Voting Patterns in San Francisco." Master's thesis, Claremont Graduate School, Los Angeles.

Gardner, R., B. Robey, and P. Smith. 1985. "Asian Americans: Growth, Change, and Diversity." *Population Bulletin* 40: no. 4 (Oct.).

Hing, B. 1985 [1992 supp.]. *Handling Immigration Cases.* New York: Wiley.

——. 1993. *Making and Remaking Asian America.* Stanford: Stanford University Press.

Keely, C. B. 1971. "Effects of the Immigration Act of 1965 on Selected Population Characteristics of Immigrants to the United States." *Demography* 8, 2: 157–69.

——.1974. "The Demographic Effects of Immigration Legislation and Procedures." *Interpreter Releases* 51 (Apr. 8): 89–93.

——. 1975. "Effects of U.S. Immigration Law on Manpower Characteristics of Immigrants." *Demography* 12, no. 2 (May): 179–91.

Kim, H. 1974. "Some Aspects of Social Demography of Korean Americans." *International Migration Review* 8, no. 1 (Spring): 23–42.

Kim, I. 1981. *Urban Immigrants: The Korean Community in New York.* Princeton, N. J.: Princeton University Press.

Kitano, H., and R. Daniels. 1988. *Asian Americans: Emerging Minorities.* Englewood Cliffs, N. J.: Prentice Hall.

Lee, R. H. 1960. *The Chinese in the United States of America.* Hong Kong: Hong Kong University Press.

McLeod, B. 1986. "The Oriental Express." *Psychology Today* 20, 7: 48–52.

Manning, W., and W. O'Hare. 1988. 'The Best Metros for Asian-American Businesses.' *American Demographics* 10, 8: 35–36.

Mar, D. 1985. 'Chinese Immigrants and the Ethnic Labor Market.' Unpublished diss., Dept. of Economics, University of California, Berkeley.

Min, P. G. 1984. "From White-Collar Occupations to Small Business: Korean Immigrants' Occupational Adjustment." *Sociological Quarterly* 25: 333–52.

Nakanishi, D. 1986. *The UCLA Asian Pacific American Voter Registration Study.* Report sponsored by the Asian Pacific American Legal Center of Los Angeles, UCLA Graduate School of Education.

———. 1985–86. "Asian American Politics: An Agenda for Research." *Amerasia Journal* 12, no. 2: 1–27.

Ng, W. 1977. 'An Evaluation of the Labor Market Status of Chinese Americans.' *Amerasia Journal* 4, no. 2: 101–22.

Pei, C. H. 1987. "Research Report." Study funded by the United Chinese Restaurants Association (Dec.).

Piore, M. 1979. *Birds of Passage, Migrant Labor and Industrial Societies.* Cambridge, Eng.: Cambridge University Press.

Steinberg, D. 1982. *The Philippines: A Singular and a Plural Place.* Boulder, Col.: Westview Press.

Sung, B. L. 1976. *A Survey of Chinese-American Manpower and Employment.* New York: Praeger.

Tachibana, J. 1986. "California's Asians: Power from a Growing Population." *California Journal* (Nov.): 535–43.

Takaki, R. 1989. *Strangers from a Different Shore.* Boston: Little, Brown.

Tewari, S. C. 1977. *Indo-U.S. Relations: 1947–76.* New Delhi, India: Radiant.

Uhlaner, C., B. E. Cain, and D. R. Kiewiet, 1989. "Political Participation of Ethnic Minorities in the 1980's." *Political Behavior* 11: 195–231.

U. S. Department of Commerce. 1988a. *Asian and Pacific Islander Population in the United States, 1980.* PC80-2-1E. Washington, D. C.: Bureau of the Census (Jan.)

———. 1988b. *We, the Asian and Pacific Islander Americans.* Washington, D.C.: Bureau of the Census (Sept.)

———. 1991. "Release CB91-215." *U.S. Department of Commerce News.* Washington, D. C.: Bureau of the Census (June 12).

Vreeland, N. 1976. *Area Handbook For the Philippines.* Washington, D.C.: Government Printing Office.

Waller, C., and L. M. Hoffman. 1989. "United States Immigration Law as a Foreign Policy Tool: The Beijing Crisis and the United States Response." *Georgetown Immigration Law Journal* 3, no. 3 (Fall): 313–59.

Wasserman, J. 1979. *Immigration Law and Practice.* Philadelphia: Joint Committee on Continuing Legal Education of the American Law Institute and the American Bar Association.

Wong, M. G. 1980. "Changes in Socioeconomic Status of Chinese Male Population in the United States from 1960 to 1970." *International Migration Review* 14:511–24.

Xenos, P., R. Gardner, H. Barringer, and M. Levin. 1987. "Asian Americans: Growth and Change in the 1970's." In J. Fawcett and B. Carino, eds, *Pacific Bridges*, pp. 249–84.

8 Voluntary Immigration and Continuing Encounters between Blacks

Roy Simón Bryce-Laporte

Voluntary Immigration

All the peoples of this hemisphere have experienced or been the products of one or more literal crossings from old worlds. While this includes even the indigenous peoples of this country, the Amerindians, who inhabited this land for thousands of years before Columbus ever set foot on their territory, in this article the term and concept of crossing-over are to be applied to one cohort of migrants: people of African descent. Black people have usually been portrayed and treated differently in conventional American sociology and history. Pertinent to the discussion to be pursued in this article is the invisibility, nonparticipation, passiveness, immobility, and homogeneity often attributed to them in the literature. The fact is that crossing-over has been and is as much an experience for blacks as for other Americans; as a concept it is familiar, and as a term it is multiple in its meaning.[1] One meaning is the voluntariness of black immigration – the historicity and continuity of which have been downplayed for a long time in the literature, policy, scholarship, media, and art of the establishment – and the new levels of intragroup encounters and interactions that accompany such movements.

Columbus's Quincentenary: A Challenge to Observance and Observation

In anticipation of the observance of the Columbus quincentenary, which was to take place in 1992, a short but truly stirring statement by the president of the Federation of State Councils for the

Humanities was published, entitled "The Scholarly Benefits of the Columbus Quincentenary Will Reach beyond 1992."[2] Its author laid out an optimistic prediction, really a critical challenge to his colleagues in the humanities, that the then-forthcoming quincentenary would be recognized and treated as an opportunity for more than the customary relaxation and ritualistic reconstructions of the past. He posited the existence of a quiet revolution in America's celebratory culture that would result in the introduction of a new style, level, and direction in engagement and observance beyond the pageantry and filiopietism that usually mark such moments. He implored that the quincentenary be characterized by the co-operative engagement of the American public and its academy in serious thought and scholarly reflections on its nature, effects, and meanings.

His statement directs our focus toward reconsidering (1) the powerful forces that were put in motion and have resulted in crucial changes in life and relations on both sides of the Atlantic since the end of the fifteenth century and (2) the differing meanings that the October event of 500 years ago has evoked from different peoples and nations of the world. Whatever may have been its motive, preconditions, or causes, it was a singular watershed that gave birth and breadth to the formation of a modern world community: one to be characterized more by international competition and conflict than by cooperation and consensus; by differences in historical trajectories, shifting alliances, political economic structures, and sociocultural formations between its member states; and by the promotion of newer levels and types of relationship within and across nations and their peoples.

Among the most persistent of the dynamics put into motion by the 1492 encounter is the continual and extensive human crossings from old to new worlds and the varied changes brought about and undergone by these immigrants in their conditions and ways of living. Generally true of the Americas, such crossings, whether over land, ocean, sea, or river, hold particular pertinence for the United States as a leading target of world immigration even through the present.

Having taken place at a moment of heightened postmodern ferment, the quincentenary of Columbus's celebrated crossing from Europe to the Americas did, indeed, elicit reactions of a wide sort, from familiar as well as strange and unexpected quarters. Many of the reactions were characterized by challenges to once axiomatically held historical claims and their subjection to intense reexamination and varied revision, to literary deconstructions and historical reconstructions, and to many public demonstrations and political protests. As for the various "discovered" peoples, their sentiments and voices reflect the deep bitterness and cynicism of people whose historical presence and critical roles in the shaping of early America have been denied, despised, and distorted, whose experience and treatment from the Age of Exploration onward have been characterized by dehumanization, discrimination, and disdain.[3] Even when professional sociology seemed to have been noticeably underrepresented in these debates, much of the discussion bordered on and reflected material of importance to critical and comparative historical sociology, to the sociology of culture, knowledge, and world systems, and to the study of race, ethnic relations, and human migration.

Overlooked Aspects of Black American History

Broadly defined, voluntary immigration has been a principal mode of peopling this hemisphere and has become a prominent aspect of its ideology and self-image – and projection to the world. Yet, as a term and concept, it has rarely been associated with people of African descent. Perhaps this is so because it has been overshadowed by the uniqueness, magnitude, and meaning of the African slave trade and American slavery itself and by the subsequent institutionalizing of segregation and stagnation as the prevailing conditions of black life even up to the present. Neither the works of Melville Herskovits, Alex Haley, and George Fredrickson, with all their powerful consciousness-raising influences in linking America's black population to its African past, nor the instructive volumes of Marvin Lee Hensen, Oscar Handlin, John Higham, and others on the centrality of immigrants to American history have successfully penetrated the American mind in this regard. The first three of these scholars stressed slavery and most others minimized blacks – if they mentioned them at all. Thus the migratory aspects of African American life and history have escaped deserving notice and have gained recognition only as occasional phenomena and isolated events rather than consistent constituents of the historical repertoire and record of blacks' effort to survive and escape bondage and inequality.

In fact, not only American but also African American history would be rendered incomplete and unconnected without the fuller recognition of the abstract tie between the various modes of black flight, migration, crossing-over, and encounter: from the plantations to the swamps and city outskirts; from the South to the North as far as Canada via the Underground Railroad and other surreptitious means, and also to the western and Floridian territories as accomplished by Dred Scott and the Black Seminoles, respectively; and even through spirituals or by ship to foreign lands; to Africa and the Caribbean on missions and to Europe and the Soviet Union for self-exile; and to Central and South America on work-and-fortune-seeking adventures.

Once we enter this domain of black history, we discover informative revelations about what the United States of America owes not only to white European pioneers and black slaves but also to foreign-born free blacks in its midst. There in the distant past were Melendez and other black militiamen and maroons who guarded the borders of St. Augustine; the founding of the Mission of Los Angeles by a commissioned party that included blacks and mulattoes among its members; the questionable identity of the black-amoor who appeared on the muster list of Plymouth village freeholders; and the black West Indian-born patriots and French Caribbean contingents who participated in the Revolutionary War and the War of 1812.

We also begin to appreciate the early encounters and key cooperation of black immigrants with native-born African Americans in the shaping of the latter's history and culture; the fear of their presence as captains and catalysts of slave rebellion in the antebellum South; the prevalence of free Africans, West Indians, and Pacific Islanders side by side with African American slaves and freemen in the whaling fleets on both American coasts; the black workers from the Hispanic Caribbean islands who accompanied the cigar-making industry as it was transplanted to Tampa and various east coast cities; the large contingents of black emigrants from the English-speaking and French creole-speaking Caribbean who, with some African American companions, provided labor to build and maintain several North American projects in the Middle American mainland, which, in turn, resulted not only in the developing of the U.S. West but also in developing the United States' leadership of the Western world; and the later migrations of these and other West Indians and Latin American blacks to the United States itself to pursue, alongside black southerners, the great migration to northern and midwestern cities.

Together with their northern-born peers, these various groups of migrants would give new vigor, complexity, and a cosmopolitan quality to the black community and to black culture. For them, too, Harlem was in vogue; Harlem was mecca. The Harlem Renaissance, the Garvey movement, the Schomburg Center, the Hispano Theater, and the West Indian carnival all emanated from there. They were by-products of the encounters and cross-fertilization that took place in New York City between black hosts and black strangers in the earlier decades of this century. But so, too, would be discovered culture shocks and tensions between them and the derisive sentiments, stereotypes, statements, and counterstatements that arose among them as they competed for jobs and housing and jostled for status and style of living in the confines of the black ghettos.

Out of this comingling emerged a litany of leaders and a variety of talented personalities such as Marcus Garvey, Claude McKay, Asadata Dafora, Bert Williams, Hazel Scott, Machito and Graciela, Hugh Mulzac, Hubert Julian, Juano Hernández, J. A. Rogers, P. M. Savory, Maida Springer-Kemp, Kid Chocolate, Mabel Saupers, Ashley Totten, Jesús Colón, Charles Petioni, and J. Raymond Jones ('The Harlem Fox'). Like the famed social psychologist Kenneth B. Clark, who gave critical testimony in *Brown v. Kansas*, which led to the integration of schools and resulted in subsequent civil rights victories, these black immigrants and their progeny worked alongside their native-born peers in shaping culture, steering politics, and providing professional services to the local black communities. At the same time, they exemplified models of struggle and success for humbler black immigrants among them, who worked double time in the war industries, clothing factories, public health institutions, and private homes to raise and educate their children in emulation of their ethnic and racial heroes. They also showed unflinching concern for the political developments and welfare needs of their home countries.[4]

The New Black Immigrants: From Invisibility to Visibility

With the passing of the Immigration Act of 1924 and the protraction of the Great Depression, the black immigrant stream subsided; it even reversed itself, although it never fully came to an end. The movement would not gather full momentum and magnitude again until the passing of the Immigration Act of 1965, which eliminated the quota system with its racial and geographical biases, facilitated family reunification, and identified work preferences in a manner that was compatible with labor needs of the new Western industrial power that the United States had become and also with the corpus of skills and kind of will that blacks and other immigrants of color from Third World countries could offer.

Since the historic 1965 act, there have been several other executive orders, pieces of legislation, federal policies, and court rulings that have so affected the flow and fate of foreign-born blacks in the United States. The most important of these were the Refugee Act of 1980, the Immigration Reform and Control Act of 1986, and the Immigration Act of 1990. Of these, only the act of 1986 specifically targeted a predominantly black population – undocumented Haitians and Cubans who constituted two groups of boat people who had sought asylum in Miami, escaping the duress or danger of their lives. Generally, however, while not specifying race, these immigration laws served more inadvertently to increase the number of black immigrants entering the United States and to ease their adjustment, and, despite increasing deportation and recent interdictions of black refugees, such legislation by itself has not convincingly deterred illegal entry or fraudulent extensions of residence by them. Undoubtedly, then, such flows have their impact on the size, composition, and distribution of blacks of foreign birth as well as of recent foreign ancestry in the United States, and more particularly on its large black population that traces to the slave trade its arrival in the United States. But generalizations are risky due to statistical incomparability, undercounting, and the ill fit between the categorization of race and ethnicity. They are further complicated by the difference in definitions of race or color held by the United States versus the home societies of these black immigrants.

The latest cumulative immigration statistics show that a total of about 59 million people came to the United States as legal residents between 1920 and 1990. During the decade of 1881–90 – one hundred years or so ago – the United States reportedly admitted some 5.25 million persons. Of these, Europe, as region of last residence, provided a little less than 5 million people; Asia, approximately 70,000; the Americas, some 420,000 (with Canada providing 390,000 and Mexico, only 1913; the Caribbean, 29,000; Central America, 404; and South America, 2304); Africa, 857; and Oceania, 12,500. One hundred years later, in the decade of 1981–90, the United States accepted for permanent residence slightly over 7 million legal immigrants, with Europe, as region of last residence, providing 700,000; Asia, almost 3 million; the other American states, approximately 4 million (160,000 from Canada; 2 million from Mexico; 900,000 from the Caribbean; 500,000 from Central America; and 500,000 from South America); Africa, 200,000; and Oceania, 45,000 persons. That decade also boasts the second-highest inflow of legal immigrants into the United States over the last 170 years. The numbers were surpassed only in 1901–10, the peak years of the Great Immigration, during which almost 9 million persons entered the United States, overwhelmingly from Europe.[5]

It is noteworthy that, in recent years, there have been significant increases and shifts in the sources and the people who have come to this country since 1960. There are shifts in the continents and countries of origin and in the proportion of the immigrant stream that they contribute; there are shifts also in the cultures and colors of the immigrants and consequently in the nature of their encounters, experiences, and expressions. On other occasions, I have called this post-1960 shift the New Immigration, meaning by that term the newest waves of immigrants to enter the United States.[6] But, historically speaking, the entry of Latin Americans, Caribbeans, Asians, and even free Africans into the United States is not new. Rather, as of the 1960s, it is their volume, visibility, and variety that are new.

Black, of Panamanian birth, and of Caribbean ancestry, I came to this country in 1959. I recall visiting New York City and Washington, D.C., with some frequency in those early years of residence and study and increasingly hearing strange languages and different accents from people of color who seemed to look very much like me and sometimes lived and worked in the same localities as their U.S.-born peers. Hence, in my earlier writings, I referred to the multiple levels of invisibility, characteristic of black immigrants as blacks and as foreigners.[7] Curiously enough, this invisibility was due in part to the resemblance they shared with native-born African Americans and therefore the disregard they suffered with respect to their presence, problems, or potential, as was the fate of most people of color in the society at that point in time. Not even their particularities were noticed by the larger society, its policymakers, public institutions, media, or social-scientific disciplines. Only their fellow blacks and the less naive observers among the few whites who daily engaged them perceived and sometimes reacted to those differences.

The invisibility to which black immigrants were relegated is strikingly reflected even in the literature of the social sciences.

Until the present, the only book-size comprehensive treatment of this population was published in 1939 by sociologist Ira de Augustine Reid, himself of Jamaican parentage. His classic, *The Negro Immigrant*,[8] deals primarily with the early waves of immigrants who arrived through the middle of the twentieth century. Scholarly attention to the post-1960 immigrants, whom we may want to call here the new black immigrants, was initiated with what are now regarded as two seminal pieces of mine, the article "Black Immigrants: The Experience of Inequality and Invisibility" in a special issue of the *Journal of Black Studies* dedicated to the theme of international dimensions of black inequality, and a chapter in *Through Different Eyes* entitled "Black Immigrants."[9] More recently, new scholarly treatments of these immigrants and their movements to the United States have been appearing with increasing rapidity.[10] The photographic exhibit "Give Me Your Tired, Your Poor...?" by the Schomburg Center for Research in Black Culture of the New York Public Library, on the occasion of the centennial of the Statue of Liberty, represents another level of academic visibility.[11]

With time, as these black immigrant groups became larger, their concentrations become more localized and their presence more pronounced. Their newly gained visibility is due not only to their problems and problematicalness as often may be reflected in policy-oriented studies and xenophobic anti-immigration politics – with respect to, for example, the Haitians' plight – but also to their large number and their contributions to the civic, cultural, and even economic activities of their host communities and to linkages and developments in their home countries or regions via the United States. It is also indicated by the attention they now obtain from the media, the market, and the academy.

Of late, the critical masses developed among these immigrants have been made particularly visible in North American cities, where their impact on urban culture can be readily felt and discerned. In the process, they have begun to participate and contribute as other earlier immigrants have and as present citizens do in the continuing Americanization of America. There are festivals, cultural and athletic clubs, radio programs, cultural programs, stores, restaurants, and churches, which constitute manifestations of successful crossing-over and continuing encounters in urban America. In our cities and suburbs everywhere, we now find ourselves confronting new black strangers with multiple experiences and different ways of expressing themselves. Among them there is an accumulating repertoire of talents and tales, which will obligate us as students in the humanities and social sciences to revisit and reevaluate the basic questions posed by our respective disciplines. As we acknowledge the differences between them, we must also realize that there are many, often considerable differences within each of their clusters. Thus the experiencing of different encounters, inequalities, and invisibilities still exists, particularly for the smaller, marginalized, and mixed minorities among them.

The 1991 immigration statistics show, for example, a total of 36,169 legal immigrants of African birth representing at least 20 countries of origin and 154,132 persons of Caribbean birth from at least 15 countries of origin, including Belize, Guyana, and various islands. While all these persons may not be black by even stringent U.S. terms, many of them would be so classified, as is true of some people from Oceania and Latin America. Of the countries with predominantly black populations, there are a few that provided 6000 or more of their nationals as legal immigrants in 1991; from largest to smallest contributor, they are the Dominican Republic, Jamaica, Haiti, Guyana, Nigeria, and Trinidad and Tobago. In addition to the countries that the immigration statistics specified, each producing more than 300 legal immigrants bound for the United States, there were also unspecified countries that provided even fewer.[12] It is particularly true among continental Africans that these populations often represent various ethnic groups that live within and across the boundaries of the sending countries, a circumstance that further complicates the level of diversity among the foreign-born black population in the United States.

Additionally, the detailed 1980 census provides information on ancestries declared by the U.S. population and thereby offers another level of appreciation of the wider diversity now characteristic of the nation's black population: 435,000 persons declared themselves to be of Jamaican ancestry; 290,000 of Haitian; 82,000 of Guyanese; 76,000 of Trinidadian and Tobagonian; and 159,000 of West Indian ancestry. An additional 92,000 declared themselves Nigerian, and 244,000 as African.

Like the latter, varying proportions of the persons declaring Latin American, Hispanic, or Spanish (not Spaniard) ancestry may also have been classifiable as black or of African descent in U.S. terms. There were 11 million of them declaring Mexican, 2 million of them declaring Spanish, 2 million more declaring Puerto Rican, and 1.1 million declaring Hispanic ancestry. Of those Latin American countries with a noticeable black or mixed population, each of the following is represented by 75,000 or more persons who claimed its ancestry: Cuba, the Dominican Republic, Colombia, Guatemala, Ecuador, Peru, Honduras, and Panama. Brazil fell just below the 75,000 range, and there may be a classifiable black segment among persons claiming a Pacific Island ancestry.

Even together, blacks claiming a foreign heritage are vastly outnumbered by the 24 million persons declaring themselves Afro-Americans and constituting the fourth-largest ancestry group in the United States. Nevertheless, even among the latter, there was noticeable variation in the terms used for self-classification: African American, Afro, black, Negro, colored, Creole, and so on.[13] In other words, the tendency to characterize the black population in the United States, whether native-born or foreign-born, as if it were a monolith cannot be supported in either external objective or internal subjective terms. Therefore, if a shift in parlance may be permitted here, all black people are not the same; they do not look alike, nor do they see themselves as all alike. Because of the new immigration, ancestry, ethnicity, and nationality now play an important part in the diversification of the U.S. black population, in addition to class, color, residential distribution and identity, as much of the current sociological literature has begun to suggest.[14]

Ethnic Diversification: Afro-Latinos and Other Black Americans

For reasons of focus, brevity, and familiarity, I call the reader's attention to blacks residing in the United States who are of Latin American birth or ancestry and some among them who have an intervening Caribbean rather than direct African heritage. Currently, some of us refer to ourselves as Afro-Latinos, a broad term which in itself connotes a motley collection of Spanish-speaking, Portuguese-speaking, and maybe French-speaking blacks of different national combinations and multiple cultural or ethnic permutations. The group stretches across the two largest segments of people of color in the United States, African Americans and Latinos. Their coming to this country with cognizance and volition qualifies them as part of its black voluntary immigrant population. While they share the stigma of their slave background and suffer no more happily the status of discrimination than do other blacks and Latinos born in the U.S. society, they often fail to gain full and unques-

tioned embrace from either of these two larger native-born reference groups. Thus these varied and smaller hyphenated subgroups
may not only be relatively lost in the larger black population, but
their specific visibilities tend to be veiled and their identities confused in the local arena, despite the serious contributions of individuals or small groups among them to popular culture, civic politics,
and professional life.

The Afro-Latinos as a particular sub-group remain largely unrecognized, unheard, unattended as such, as the following literary
excerpts certify:

Silently

In silence
and yet not so silently
We . . . expatriates
　　from behind a veil of laughter
　　we hide our pain . . .
Who are we?
Who are we?
　We sigh
Uniting two worlds
　　maybe three
A bit of everything
　　a lot of nothing.
We sing
We cry . . . in silence
We hide ourselves behind a mask
　　but not so silently.[15]

For Ana Velford

. . . and despite it all, New York is my home.
I feel fiercely loyal to this acquired homeland.
Because of New York, I am a foreigner in
　　whatever other place, . . .

But New York City is not the city of
　　my infancy . . .

Because of that I will always remain on the
　　margin,
a stranger between these rocks, . . .

Then, now and forever, I will always remain
a foreigner,
even when I return to the city of my infancy.
I will always carry this marginality...
too *habanera* to be a New Yorker
too New Yorker to be
– ever to become again –
anything else.[16]

Whatever the level, it seems that unsettling encounters, feelings of marginality, sometimes of futility, other times of dogged determination, and cries for human attention and civic recognition, are all part of the day-to-day cultural load and communicational effort of new – and old – black immigrants among us.[17] These are realities, processes, ongoing experiences that merit our attention and certainly must benefit from our greater appreciation as we reflect upon the aftermath of the Columbus visit of 1492. After all, the same holds for the entire hemisphere, including the United States, as Gordon Lewis noted with respect to the Caribbean, to which Old World immigrants began to flow at full force at least 100 years before extending to the U.S. mainland:

> Migration – as the vast, restless, circulatory movement of whole peoples – has its roots, historically, in the immediate post-Discovery period. For the first century of European colonization, migration meant the influx to the colonies of European peasants and the workers of the European seaports including the riff-raff of London, Paris and Madrid. After that came the African influx, organized by the African slave trade, which did not really cease in the islands until slavery abolition in Cuba in 1886. Following that, again, was the influx of Indian indentured labor, lasting for the period 1845–1917. Every person in the Caribbean has been a newcomer; and certainly by 1700, the region's identity had been established as a series of rich, picaroon, and polyglot societies.[18]

The Sociological Future of Ethnic Differentiation and Group Relations

But the pertinent question is, Where are we going here in the United States? Where will such reflections and projections take us – as scholars, policymakers, activists, and citizens of the larger human world community? What will it say about the character, composition, and conditions of the U.S. black population and about inter-and intragroup relations in this society?

By the year 2020, the African American population will have been numerically eclipsed by the Latino population. Much of this growth will have resulted directly and indirectly from immigration because, among other things, immigration from contemporary Africa and the Caribbean will be outnumbered significantly by the flow from Latin America – and also from Asia-Pacific regions – even though a certain percentage of the immigrants from these latter regions will also be black in U.S. terms. This motley group of black immigrants could add volume and diversity to an already diverse black population. And against the backdrop of the U.S. rule that one drop of black blood makes one black, some questions will rise concerning the location and identification of these groups of recent immigrants and their offspring, since in many of their countries of origin and ancestry the rule works quite to the inverse: there, one drop of white blood makes one white. In fact, in many of these countries, racial categorization is characterized with greater subtlety and fluidity and comprises several intermediate statuses, as opposed to the basic binary arrangements typical of U.S. society. Furthermore, often color or class, not race, becomes the salient base of social classification and mobility in many of the sending societies and in the thinking of their people, since wealth whitens and light coloring catapults one to a higher social position.

For one who struggled in obscurity and solitude for many years for the rekindling of social scientific interest in the study of immigration as an ongoing process, and more particularly for the pursuit of a fuller understanding of the intricacies and implications of black immigration to the United States, it is with an encouraging sense of fulfillment to read a recent article by Ellen Coughlin, which reviews several new and forthcoming social science publications on the growing complexities of ethnicity and race in American society. The article points out that much of the earlier research on race and ethnicity was modeled on the white European immigration experience. The shift in the racial composition of post-1960 immigration has resulted in a shift in definition so that being black does not necessarily mean being African American, narrowly defined, and therefore it no longer holds that "a black person is a black person is a black person."[19]

At present, it is more likely that new black immigrants – and native-born blacks, too – often find ethnicity to be more crucial in certain circumstances than race, although in other situations the opposite may be true. In fact, many black immigrants arrive with an acute sense of nationality while taking race for granted and placing less importance on regional or ethnic identity than is anticipated of them by others. But often they will soon find themselves branded and bonding along racial, regional, or pan-ethnic lines. Hence the pan-Caribbean dreams that have escaped the governments and political leaders of that region now find opportunities for intimate and dramatic expression in cities of the United States and other parts of the diaspora. If the same process is occurring with pan-Africanism, pan-Latinoism, pan-Asianism, and the like, what then will be the nature of politics – coalition, conflict, or competition – among the various hyphenated groups of African descent? Who is or will be considered an African American, strictly speaking, among them? When does a black person of foreign birth or ancestry become African American? What will be the character of immigration, particularly black immigration, as the world experiences further restructuring, realignment, and reduction in space and time and as its people's redefinition of "home" comes to reflect multiple or linking places of abode, operation, and identity? Will multiethnicism become the norm or remain at the margins? Will black multiethnics become lonesome isolates or serve as critical liaisons?

We can hardly imagine what new categories and systems of human differentiation or homogenization or whether new definitions of intra-or intergroup relations will emerge in the distant future. For the foreseeable future, however, as much as we may wish to condemn racism and ethnocentrism and try to obliterate them as legitimate modes of social or political behavior, we must also realize that race and ethnicity, like class and status, are dynamic and sometimes interrelated social realities that cannot be written off or washed away by even a well-wishing but naive sociology. Events of the 1990s like those of Bosnia, Los Angeles, Crown Heights, and South Africa, call for a new sociology, new social policies, and new standards of commitment that will enable us to more fully comprehend the nature of, and to more effectively act upon the consequences and causes of, continuing human crossings-over and expanding ethnic encounters.

A true reflection on the Columbus quincentenary, then, should leave us hoping that we could and would better know our world, govern the use of our social inventions, steer the results of our discoveries, and be prepared to assume responsibility for our claims and the developments deriving from them.

Notes

1 For fuller discussion of the meaning of the term, see Roy Simón Bryce-Laporte, *Crossing Over: Continuing Encounters/Encuentros Continuous* (Washington, DC: D.C. Community Humanities Council, forthcoming).

2 Jamal S. Zaimalden, "The Scholarly Benefits of the Columbus Quincentenary Will Reach beyond 1992," *Chronicle of Higher Education*, 12 Apr. 1989, p. B3.

3 For fuller discussion and examples of foreign-born black literature and artistic reaction, see Bryce-Laporte, *Crossing Over*, which quotes or cites the following: Winston ('Mighty Shadow') Bailey, *Columbus Lie* (Port-of-Spain, Trinidad and Tobago: Copyright Organization of Trinidad and Tobago, 1988); Jan Carew, *Fulcrums of Change* (Trenton, NJ: Africa World Press, 1988), pp. 3–4; Cubena (Carlos Guillermo Wilson), "Las Americas," *Pensamientos del Negro Cubena* (Los Angeles: Cubena, 1977), p. 12; Ivan Van Sertima, *They Came before Columbus* (New York: Random House, 1976).

4 For a fuller discussion of these migrations and encounters, see Roy Simón Bryce-Laporte, *Give Me Your Tired, Your Poor...?* (New York: New York Public Library, Schomburg Center for Research in Black Culture, 1986), pp. 9–19.

5 U.S., Department of Justice, *Statistical Yearbook* (Washington, DC: Department of Justice, Immigration and Naturalization Service, 1990), tab. 2, pp. 48–50. These figures refer only to the legal immigrants and not to the legal nonimmigrants or the so-called illegal immigrants who have entered and now reside in the United States.

6 Roy Simón Bryce-Laporte, "The New Immigration: A Challenge to Our Sociological Imagination," in *Sourcebook on the New Immigration*, ed. Roy Simón Bryce-Laporte et al. (New Brunswick, NJ: Transaction, 1979), pp. 459–72.

7 Roy Simón Bryce-Laporte, "Black Immigrants: The Experience of Invisibility and Inequality," *Journal of Black Studies*, 4(1): 29–56 (Sept. 1972); idem, "Black Immigrants," in *Through Different Eyes*, ed. Peter Rose, Stanley Rothman, and William J. Wilson (New York: Oxford University Press, 1973), p. 44.

8 Ira de Augustine Reid, *The Negro Immigrant* (New York: Columbia University Press, 1939). See also Arthur Paris, "Ira de Augustine Reid: An Alternative Approach to Immigrant Studies in Sociology" (Paper delivered at the Meeting of the Eastern Sociological Society, Boston, 25–28 Mar. 1993).

9 Bryce-Laporte, "Black Immigrants: The Experience of Invisibility"; idem, "Black Immigrants" (1973).

10 See, for example, Marcia Bayne-Smith, "Health Problems of Caribbean Immigrants in New York City: The Case for Ethnic Organizations" (Paper delivered at the annual meeting of the Eastern Sociological Society, Arlington, VA, 3–5 Apr. 1992); Christine Ho, *Salt Water Trinnies* (New York: AMS Press, 1991); Philip Kasinitz, *Caribbean New York* (Ithaca, NY: Cornell University Press, 1992); Michel Laguerre, *American Odyssey: Haitians in New*

York City (Ithaca, NY: Cornell University Press, 1984); Delores Mortimer and Roy S. Bryce-Laporte, eds., *Female Immigrants to the United States: Caribbean, Latin American and African Experiences*, Research Institute on Immigration and Ethnic Studies Occasional Papers, no. 2 (Washington, DC: Smithsonian Institution, Research Institute on Immigration and Ethnic Studies, 1982); Constance R. Sutton and Elsa M. Chaney, eds., *Caribbean Life in New York City* (New York: Center for Migration Studies of New York, 1987); W. Burghardt Turner and Joyce Moore Turner, *Richard B. Moore: Caribbean Militant in Harlem* (Bloomington: Indiana University Press, 1992); John C. Walter, *The Harlem Fox* (Albany: State University of New York Press, 1989); Mary C. Waters, "From Majority to Minority Status: Expectations and Perceptions of Racism among Caribbean Immigrants and Their Children in New York City" (Paper delivered at the American Studies Association Conference, Boston, 4–7 Nov. 1993); Tekle Woldemikael, *Becoming Black American: Haitians and American Institutions in Evanston, Illinois* (New York: AMS Press, 1989).

11   Bryce-Laporte, *Give Me Your Tired, Your Poor...?*

12   U.S., Department of Justice, *Statistical Yearbook* (Washington, DC: Department of Justice, Immigration and Naturalization Service, 1991), tab. 3, pp. 32–3.

13   U.S., Department of Commerce, *1990 Census of Population, Supplementary Reports: Detailed Ancestry Groups for States* (Washington, DC: Department of Commerce, Bureau of the Census, Oct. 1992), tab. D, pp. III 5–6; tab. 2, pp. 4–5.

14   See for example, William E. Cross, *Shades of Black* (Philadelphia: Temple University Press, 1991); F. James Davis, *Who Is Black: One Nation's Definition* (University Park: Pennsylvania State University Press, 1991); James Jackson, ed., *Life in Black America* (Newbury Park, CA: Sage, 1991); Bart Landry, *The New Black Middle Class* (Berkeley: University of California Press, 1987); National Urban League, *The State of Black America* (New Brunswick, NJ: Transaction, 1991); William O'Hare et al., *African Americans in the 1990's*, Population Bulletins, vol. 46 (Washington, DC: Population Reference Bureau, 1991); Kathy Russell, *The Color Complex: The Politics of Skin Colors among African Americans* (University Park: Pennsylvania State University Press, 1991); William Julius Wilson, *The Declining Significance of Race* (Chicago: University of Chicago Press, 1978); idem, *The Truly Disadvantaged* (Chicago: University of Chicago Press, 1987).

15   Carlos C. Russell E., "Silenciosamente," *Revista nacional de cultura*, pp. 1–5 (Oct.–Dec. 1976); English translation by R. S. Bryce-Laporte.

16   Lourdes Casals, "Para Ana Velford," *Areíto*, 3(1): 52 (Summer 1976); English translation by R. S. Bryce-Laporte.

17   See, for example, Piri Thomas, *Down These Mean Streets* (New York: Vintage Books, 1974), pp. xi–xii.

18   Gordon K. Lewis, "Foreword," in *In Search of a Better Life: Perspectives on Migration from the Caribbean*, ed. Ransford W. Palmer (New York: Praeger, 1990), p. xiii.

19 Ellen K. Coughlin, "Sociologists Examine the Complexities of Racial and Ethnic Identity in America," *Chronicle of Higher Education*, 24 Mar. 1993, p. A7. See also *Challenges of Measuring an Ethnic World: Science, Politics, and Reality*, preliminary version (Ottawa: Statistics Canada; Washington, DC: Department of Commerce, Bureau of the Census, 1992); Lelia De Andrade, "The Discourse of Racial-Ethnic Identity: The Social Construction of Race and Ethnicity among Cape Verdian Americans" (Paper delivered at the annual meeting of the Eastern Sociological Society, Arlington, VA, 3–5 Apr. 1992); Michael Omi and Howard Winant, *Racial Formation in the United States* (New York: Routledge & Kegan Paul, 1986).

9 The Social Organization of Mexican Migration to the United States

Douglas S. Massey

During the 1970s, Mexican immigration to the United States became a mass phenomenon involving millions of people on both sides of the border. Annual legal immigration rose from just over 44,000 in 1970 to more than 100,000 in 1981, while the number of undocumented Mexicans annually apprehended increased from about 277,000 to nearly 900,000. It has been estimated that some 931,000 undocumented Mexicans were counted in the 1980 U.S. census, 81 percent of whom entered during the prior decade. Overall, the population of the United States that is of Mexican origin increased by 93 percent during the 1970s, and about one-third of this increase was attributable to immigration.

Whatever figures one considers, it is obvious that there was a sharp upswing in Mexican immigration during the 1970s, one not adequately explained by economic conditions alone. In the United States, the 1970s brought rising unemployment and falling real wages for American workers, while in Mexico an oil-driven economic boom increased wages and lowered unemployment. If anything, economic conditions predicted a dampening of migration during the late 1970s. The large upsurge in migration between Mexico and the United States reflects the inevitable culmination of a long social process, one intrinsic to the migration enterprise itself.

Massive Mexican migration today reflects the prior development of social networks that support and sustain it. These networks consist of kin and friendship relations that link Mexican sending communities to particular destinations in the United States. People from the same family or town are enmeshed in a web of reciprocal obligations. New migrants draw upon these obligations in order to enter and find work in the United States. As these networks develop and mature, they dramatically reduce the costs of migration, inducing others to enter the migrant work force. The entry of additional migrants, in turn, leads to more extensive networks, which encourages still more migration. Over time, therefore, international migration tends to become a self-perpetuating social phenomenon.

Mature migrant networks provide a social infrastructure capable of supporting mass migration. They have put a U.S. job within reach of nearly all people in western Mexico, the traditional source region for migration to the United States. Temporary migration to the United States is now an integral part of economic strategies in households throughout the region and has become a common event in the family life cycle.

This article examines the structure and development of migrant networks using ethnographic and survey data collected in four Mexican communities between November 1982 and February 1983 and in California between August and September of 1983. A random sample of 200 households was gathered in each of two rural and two urban Mexican communities located in the states of Michoacán and Jalisco. These data were supplemented by nonrandom samples of 60 households that had settled permanently in California. In both the United States and in Mexico, the surveys were administered by Mexican anthropologists, who also conducted extensive ethnographic fieldwork.

The Social Bases of Network Migration

Migration from Mexico to the United States is an inherently social enterprise. Migrants do not go north alone, but travel in groups composed of relatives, neighbors, and friends. In moving to a strange and often hostile land, these people naturally draw upon the existing ties of kinship and friendship to share the problems of life abroad. Over time, these basic human relationships acquire new meanings and social functions. They are transformed into a set of social relations the meaning of which is defined within the migrant context. Shared understandings develop about what it means to be a friend, relative, or neighbor within a community of migrants, and eventually these understandings crystallize into a web of interrelationships that constitute a migrant network. Migrant networks grow out of universal human relations that are adapted to the special circumstances of international migration. The relations are not created by the migratory process, but molded to it, and over time they are strengthened by the common bond of the migrant experience itself.

Kinship is the most important base of migrant social organization, and family connections provide the most secure network connections. Male relatives, in particular, have evolved well-established expectations of mutual aid and cooperation in the United States. The strongest relationship is between migrant fathers and sons. Long after they have grown up to form their own families, fathers and sons migrate together. Out of this common experience, the paternal bond is strengthened, and a new relationship between migrant fathers and sons develops. Throughout their lives, migrant fathers and sons are more likely to offer help, information, and services to one another, both at home and abroad.

Between brothers there is also a continual exchange of favors. Facing many demands for assistance from friends and relatives while abroad, migrants favor brothers. To a brother arriving in the United States without money, job, or documents, there is a series of obligations. A place to stay, help in finding work, a loan of money, and the payment of trip expenses are common ways that fraternal ties are strengthened in the migrant context. This relationship between migrant brothers carries over to their sons, with nephews similarly being given preferred treatment over other relatives. A new migrant arriving in the United States can generally count on the help of his father's brother, and many uncles take it upon themselves to initiate their nephews into the migratory process. The strength of the brotherly tie also extends to cousins linked by common male relatives. When young men strike out together for the United States, they are often parallel cousins.

Because of its explosive growth, migration has outgrown a social organization based solely on kinship, and networks have increasingly incorporated other close social relations. The closest bonds outside of the family are those formed by people as they grow up together. These are typically friendships between people of roughly the same age who shared formative experiences as children. A lifetime of shared experiences creates a disposition to exchange favors and to provide mutual assistance, and friends who find themselves sharing another formative experience – international migration – assist one another in a variety of ways: finding an apartment in the United States, sharing information about jobs, pooling resources, borrowing or loaning money.

Although a migrant's friendship connections are initially concentrated among those of the same age, ties gradually extend to other generations as migrants of all ages are drawn together in the United States. If friends from the same town migrate repeatedly, their relations eventually overlap with circles of friends from other communities, greatly expanding the range of the community's network.

The most diffuse type of social relations in the networks is that of *paisanaje*, the sharing of a community of origin, and it has become an increasingly important base of migrant social organization. As with friends and relatives, migrant *paisanos* call upon one another for mutual assistance during their time abroad. *Paisanos* have an obligation to one another not shared with acquaintances from other communities.

Moreover, *paisanaje* reinforces the network in another way. The most important representation of *paisanaje* is the patron saint. Every Mexican town holds an annual fiesta in honor of its benefactor. This celebration represents a reaffirmation of the community and its people, and it has traditionally been an important integrative mechanism in rural Mexico. With the advent of U.S. migration, however, the symbolic value of the patron saint has been shaped to the new reality of a migrant community, and the traditional importance of the fiesta has been greatly augmented.

The saint's fiesta provides a very practical framework within which to reunite families and friends. It is now more a celebration of the return of *los ausentes*, the absent ones, than a ceremony in honor of a saint. By sponsoring the periodic reunion of *los ausentes* and nonmigrant *paisanos*, the fiesta facilitates the reintegration of the former into the community and reaffirms their continuing place in social life by providing a very public demonstration of the community's commitment to them as true *paisanos*.

In the two rural towns under study, a special day in the fiesta has been set aside to honor *los ausentes*. On this day, migrants pay the costs of music, church decorations, fireworks displays, and other diversions. Those who have been able to return are featured in the processions and liturgic acts, and in his sermon for that day, the town priest reaffirms the collective sentiment of unity, speaking of a single community and of a great family with a patron saint that looks over them. In this way, a concrete cultural manifestation of *paisanaje*, the saint's fiesta, has become a very important social institution supporting migration. Symbolically, it reaffirms the existence of an international network of *paisanos* linked together by a common heritage, and, practically, it strengthens the network by facilitating contact between active migrants and prospective migrants at home.

Other institutional mechanisms besides the saint's fiesta have evolved to enable migrants to use the social connections of the network. Although migrants belong to a variety of voluntary organizations in the United States, the most important is the soccer club. One of the two urban communities under study provides a particularly good example of how an organization apparently unrelated to the migrant process, a soccer club, has been adapted to serve the needs of a binational migrant community. Although its manifest functions are recreational, its latent functions are to strengthen and expand the social connections within the network, thereby supporting the migrant enterprise.

The vast majority of migrants from this community go to Los Angeles, a large and sprawling city, where it is not easy to maintain regular contact with friends, relatives, and *paisanos*. Migrants from the community under consideration have resolved this problem through their soccer club, to which all *paisanos* belong as a right. The club was formed to support a team of hometown players competing in a California soccer league. The team trains every Sunday in a public park and has won its league championship for five consecutive years.

The team's success on the playing field has made the club so popular that nearly all *paisanos* in the Los Angeles are involved. Indeed, the practice field has become an obligatory place of reunion for all out-migrant *paisanos*. It is the place where dates are made, work obtained, friends located, new arrivals welcomed, and news of the town exchanged. Sunday after Sunday, townspeople meet to watch soccer and to socialize. This weekly reunion not only breaks up the routine of work, but it also provides a regular forum for communication and exchange. By sponsoring the regular interaction of townspeople, the soccer club serves as a clearinghouse for jobs, housing, and other information.

These encounters also facilitate the formation of friendly relations with people from other communities in Mexico, who also frequent the athletic fields. On some occasions, when there is a scarcity of hometown players, these people join the team and share in the party mood that prevails after each game, permitting them to take advantage of the information and offers of assistance that spring from these reunions. Their incorporation into the circle of friends, relatives, and *paisanos* from another home community further extends the range of the migrant network.

A Qualitative Study of Network Development

One of the two rural communities under study provides a good case study of network development. The first migrants went north at the turn of the century through the efforts of U.S. labor recruiters, who put them in touch with railroad track crews in the southwestern United States. Toward the end of the 1920s, migrants began entering the steel mills around Chicago. These migrants, in turn, got jobs for their friends and relatives, and the flow of migrants shifted primarily to the upper Midwest. Recent arrivals were informed of opportunities for work and housing and were incorporated into the social life of migrants in Chicago. By 1929, a large daughter community of permanent out-migrants had emerged in that city. However, with the onset of the depression, and the subsequent repatriation and return of many families, the social network into Chicago was ruptured. Between 1930 and 1942, this network withered away and died.

With the advent of the *bracero* program in 1942, new contacts were established with agricultural work sites in California, and the flow of migrants was redirected there. These California-directed networks were different from the earlier ones going into Chicago. The *bracero* program permitted the immediate resumption of large-scale international migration because it did not require an extensive social infrastructure of contacts and previous experience. The socioeconomic organization of migrants was accomplished through institutional channels sponsored by the U.S. and Mexican governments.

Within a few years, the demand for *bracero* permits greatly exceeded their supply, and undocumented migration began to grow. While U.S. employment was initially arranged through government channels, these soon became irrelevant to migrant recruitment. Government-regulated contracts were replaced by personal relationships between migrants and employers. Information flowed back into the home communities from agricultural areas in California, bypassing the official *bracero* recruitment centers.

Undocumented migration initially developed among men with prior *bracero* experience, whose knowledge, contacts, and experience enabled them to go north with some assurance of finding work. These contacts were encouraged by the growers themselves, who preferred dealing directly with undocumented workers to arranging contracts through the government. By establishing personal relationships with particular migrants, the growers assured themselves of a stable and reliable labor force, without incurring any legal obligations to the workers and above all without having to pay the transportation costs that were stipulated in the *bracero* treaty.

In these direct relations between migrants and growers, intermediaries such as foremen or labor contractors played a key role. They drew upon their kin and friendship connections with townspeople and recruited those people into U.S. agricultural work. These *contratistas*, the intermediaries, tended to settle in the United States and serve as permanent U.S. anchors for the emerging migrant networks. Many of them were former *braceros* who managed to arrange their legal papers before restrictive amendments to U.S. immigration law took effect in 1968. These settlers allowed the development of a pattern of migration typified by the predominance, in a particular place, of a core of settled migrants surrounded by a larger free-floating population of temporary *paisanos*.

Relations between the hometown and the various California communities gradually developed into a stable configuration, and by the end of the *bracero* program in 1964, several specific migrant networks were in place. The maturation of the networks after 1964 coincided with a wave of capital-intensive agricultural modernization in rural Mexico, giving rise to a massive upsurge in out-migration, most of it undocumented. Townspeople turned to international rather than internal migration because the networks put a U.S. job within easy reach. For a resident of this particular town, the networks meant that it was easier to go to California and find a job than to go to Mexico City or Guadalajara.

A Quantitative Study of Network Development

The development of the migrant networks is clearly indicated by quantitative survey data from the four sample communities. Table 9.1 examines a variety of social ties to the United States reported by migrants on their most recent U.S. trip. In order to show the development of the networks over time, the data are broken down by period of trip.

As networks matured over time, migrants reported a growing number of family connections in the United States. Those migrating before 1940 generally had the fewest family connections abroad, with rural-origin migrants reporting about 10 relatives in the

Table 9.1 [*orig. table 1*] Social ties to the United States by period of trip and rural/urban status: migrants from four Mexican communities

| Social Tie | Period of Trip | | | |
	Pre-1940	1940–64	1965–82	Pre-1940 to 1982
Rural communities				
Personal ties to the United States				
Mean number of relatives in the United States	9.9	10.3	15.9	14.3
Mean number of *paisanos* in the United States	29.9	19.9	25.6	24.1
Percentage with migrant parent	0.0%	25.7%	52.9%	43.9%
Percentage with migrant grandparent	0.0%	4.3%	11.2%	8.9%
Organizational ties to the United States				
Percentage in a U.S. social club	0.0%	4.1%	6.0%	5.4%
Percentage in a U.S. religious club	0.0%	5.7%	5.0%	5.1%
Percentage in a U.S. sports club	0.0%	4.1%	16.1%	12.7%
Number of migrants	(6)	(75)	(208)	(289)
Urban communities				
Personal ties to the United States				
Mean number of relatives in the United States	15.7	23.3	20.7	21.2
Mean number of *paisanos* in the United States	6.3	7.8	19.1	15.3
Percentage with migrant parent	14.3%	13.9%	27.6%	23.0%
Percentage with migrant grandparent	0.0%	2.8%	7.0%	5.4%
Organizational ties to the United States				
Percentage in a U.S. social club	0.0%	2.7%	3.8%	3.3%
Percentage in a U.S. religious club	0.0%	5.4%	5.7%	5.3%
Percentage in a U.S. sports club	0.0%	5.4%	40.6%	29.8%
Number of migrants	(8)	(37)	(106)	(151)

United States, and urban-origin migrants about 16. Prior to 1940 no one had a grandparent with prior migrant experience, and no rural dweller had a migrant parent. Only 14 percent of urban dwellers reported a parent with migrant experience.

During the *bracero* period from 1942 to 1964, however, the foundations for modern network migration were established and the number of family connections grew. After 1965, migrants could count on a much larger set of kinship ties to assist them in getting established and securing employment in the United States. In the most recent period, migrants of rural origin reported about 16 U.S. relatives and urban-origin migrants about 21. Similarly, those with migrant parents had risen to 53 percent in rural areas and to 28 percent in urban areas, and the percentage with migrant grandparents increased in both places as well.

Survey data also show that friendship connections increased over time. Before 1940 urban dwellers reported knowing only 6 *paisanos* on their latest trip to the United States, but after 1965 the number had increased to 19. Among rural dwellers, however, the number of U.S. *paisanos* started high at around 30 before 1940, fell to 20 during the 1940–64 period, and then rose to 26 after 1965. The high number before 1940 reflects the relatively well-developed Chicago network that flowered before the depression.

Ties to voluntary organizations based in the United States grew steadily over time, especially ties to sports clubs. Among urban-origin migrants, soccer clubs grew to become key organizational elements of the migrant network, with the share reporting membership in a sports club increasing from zero percent before 1940 to 41 percent after 1965, and among rural migrants the increase was from zero percent to 16 percent. In the urban community whose soccer club we described earlier, a majority of post-1965 migrants, 53 percent, reported membership in the sports club, compared to under 10 percent before 1965.

The maturation of the networks is also indicated by the emergence of daughter communities in the United States. Around these daughter communities, a social and economic organization grows, channeling migrants in ever increasing numbers to specific points of destination. This channeling occurs as the social networks focus increasingly on specific communities. As the daughter communities develop, the social infrastructure linking them to the parent community becomes ever more complex and reified, and the network becomes increasingly self-sustaining. More migrants move to a particular place because that is where the networks lead and because that is where social connections afford them the greatest chance for success. As more migrants arrive, the range of social connections expands, making subsequent migration to that place even more likely.

This channeling of migrants is evident in figures 9.1 and 9.2, which present the share of new migrants going to different areas of California at various points in time. One rural and one urban community were chosen to illustrate the process. In the rural town, destinations fluctuated considerably up through the 1950s. After 1960, however, the range of U.S. destinations steadily dwindled, when Los Angeles and the middle San Joaquin Valley emerged as the two predominant poles of attraction, capturing between 50 percent and 80 percent of all migrants. Data for the urban community also show the progressive channeling of migrants into Los

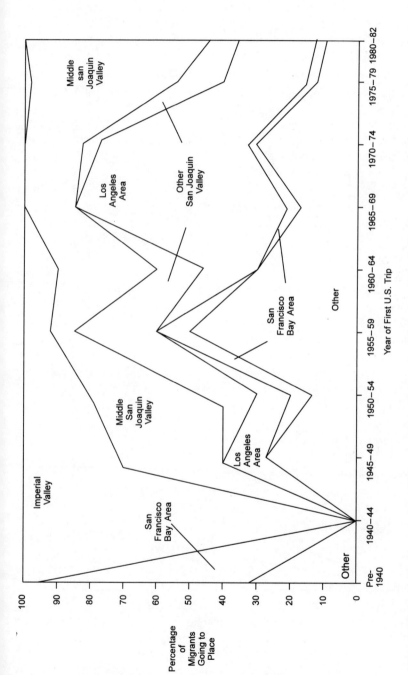

Figure 9.1 [*orig. figure 1*] California destination of migrants from a rural Mexican town, 1910–82.

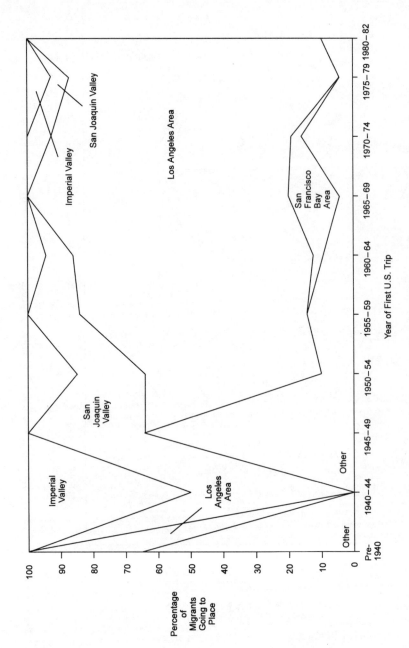

Figure 9.2 [*orig. figure 2*] California destination of migrants from a Mexican urban community, 1910–82.

Table 9.2   How migrants obtained their U.S. job and to whom they turned for financial assistance in the United States: migrants from four Mexican communities (percentage)

Source of Aid	Rural Communities	Urban Communities
How U.S. job was obtained		
Through migrant's own search	44.9	42.2
Through friend, relative, *paisano*	34.5	45.8
Through labor contractor	18.9	10.1
Through *coyote**	1.1	0.8
Other	0.6	1.1
Number of jobs	(740)	(353)
Where migrant turned for financial help on last trip		
Friend	63.1	28.9
Relative	15.4	23.7
Paisano	3.0	7.9
Employer	7.7	2.7
Bank	7.7	18.4
Other	3.1	18.4
Number needing financial help	(65)	(38)

* A *coyote* is a person who guides undocumented migrants across the border between Mexico and the United States.

Angeles. While the *bracero* program recruited townspeople into agricultural areas during the 1940s, after 1950 Los Angeles became the overwhelmingly favorite destination of new U.S. migrants. By the most recent period, about 90 percent of new urban-origin migrants went to work in the Los Angeles area.

The importance of network connections to the migrant enterprise is suggested by table 9.2, which shows how migrants got their U.S. jobs and to whom they turned for financial assistance while in the United States. Of the rural-origin migrants, 35 percent found a job in the United States through a friend, relative, or *paisano*, while 46 percent of urban-origin migrants did so. When rural migrants needed money while abroad, 82 percent fell back on one of these network connections, and 61 percent of the urban migrants did so.

Perhaps the best indication of the important role that networks have played in migration between Mexico and the United States is the effect they have had on the likelihood of out-migration, especially from rural areas. Figure 9.3 presents the lifetime probability of out-migration for males in the two rural communities under study, estimated for successive five-year periods from 1940 to 1982. These figures were derived from an age-period-cohort analysis of first migration to the United States. The lifetime probability of out-

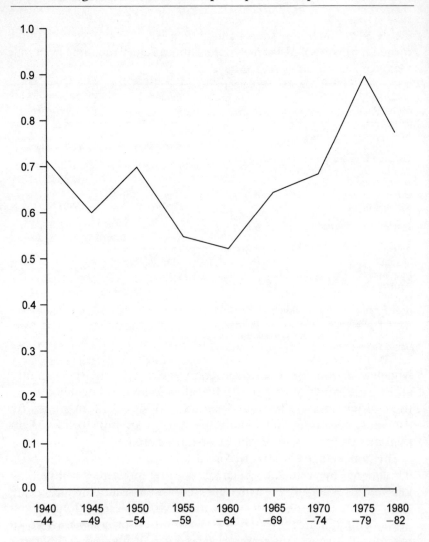

Figure 9.3 [*orig. figure 3*]   Life time probability of becoming a migrant by period: males from two rural Mexican town

migration represents the hypothetical probability of going to the United States at least once before age 60. It was estimated for successive five-year periods by asking what would happen if men born in that interval went through life subject to the out-migration rates prevailing at the time.

The end of the *bracero* program in 1964 coincided with two events of great importance to rural areas. First, the migrant networks matured and began to acquire increasing momentum. Second, a wave of agricultural modernization mechanized farm production and supplanted traditional crops, displacing farm workers from their traditional sources of sustenance. The result of these developments was a massive upswing in the likelihood of migration after 1965. Modernization spurred migration and the networks directed it northward. A man born in the period 1960–64 had a 56 percent chance of going to the United States at some point in his life, but in the ensuing years the probability of migration rose steadily, and by 1975–79 it reached nearly 90 percent. In other words, by the late 1970s, migration had become universal among men in the communities studied.

Conclusion

Prior sections have shown how migration is a social process in which basic human relationships are adapted to play new roles in the migratory enterprise. The familiar relations of kinship, friendship, and *paisanaje* are woven into a social fabric that provides migrants with a valuable adaptive resource in a strange new environment. Through networks of interpersonal relations, people and information circulate to create a social continuum linking communities in Mexico with daughter settlements in the United States. The networks are strengthened by a variety of institutional mechanisms, ranging from the fiesta of the patron saint to United States-based soccer clubs. Social networks provide aspiring migrants with food, housing, transport, work, and a social life in the United States. Their existence greatly reduces the cost of U.S. migration, permitting its regular and repeated use by Mexican families in a conscious economic strategy.

Thus, networks are key elements in understanding Mexican migration to the United States. While the displacement of farm labor by agricultural modernization may cause out-migration, networks direct it to the United States. Over time, the operation of networks tends to be self-perpetuating, so that international migration continues independently of the conditions that originally sparked it. Expansion of the networks leads to more migration, which leads to expansion of the networks. Thus, in the late 1970s, when economic conditions in Mexico dramatically improved and those in the United States deteriorated, the likelihood of U.S. migration continued to climb to the point where it became virtually universal among men.

The increasing probability of migration during the past decade occurred in spite of an increasingly restrictive U.S. immigration policy toward Mexico. American policies have not always been so inefectual, however. In the regeneration of migrant networks after the Great Depression, the *bracero* program sponsored by the United States was pivotal. It permitted the instantaneous resumption of mass migration without developed networks. The program's duration for 22 years, between 1942 and 1964, provided the time necessary for new networks to take hold and grow, so that by the time it ended, it was largely irrelevant to the ongoing migrant process. Migration to the United States had become a self-sustaining social enterprise. Perhaps the most important lesson of this study is that migration is much easier to start than to stop.

PART III

IMMIGRATION AND THE ECONOMY

10 The Impact of Immigrants on Employment Opportunities of Natives

George J. Borjas

Do immigrants have an adverse effect on natives' earnings and employment opportunities? If so, how large is the loss in the economic welfare of natives? Are all native groups equally affected by the entry of immigrants into the labour market?[1]

These questions address some of the most important and most emotional issues in the debate over immigration policy. The fear that "immigrant hordes" displace natives from their jobs and reduce the earnings of those lucky enough to keep their jobs has a long and not so honourable history in the U.S. immigration debate.[2] The presumption that immigrants have an adverse impact on the labour market continues to be used as a key justification for policies designed to restrict the size and composition of immigrant flows into the United States.

Remarkably, little was known about the impact that immigrants have on the native labour market until the last few years. Discussions of whether immigrants harmed the earnings and job opportunities of natives were typically conducted without any supporting evidence either confirming or rejecting the hypothesis. The situation changed rapidly in the 1980s. A large number of data sets became available to U.S. researchers, and econometric methodologies were discovered that allow a straightforward analysis of this important problem. Analysts quickly reached a consensus on the direction and magnitude of the labour market impact of immigration.

This paper clarifies the nature of the problem, poses the questions in a way that can be addressed by empirical research and summarises the answers provided by the recent studies. The conclusion reached by the empirical evidence is surprising and controversial: the methodological arsenal of modern econometrics cannot find a single shred of evidence that immigrants have a major adverse impact on the earnings and job opportunities of natives in the United States.

1   The Alternative Hypotheses

There are two opposing views about how immigrants affect the native labour market (Borjas and Tienda, 1987; Bean et al., 1987). One asserts that immigrants have a harmful effect on the employment and earnings opportunities of natives. Put succinctly, immigrants "take jobs away" from natives: as immigrants enter the labour market, natives are displaced. This hypothesis is sometimes stated even more extremely: immigrants displace natives on a one-to-one basis; for every immigrant admitted to the United States, an American native worker loses his/her job.

Such assertions are not based on any empirical evidence but follow from a set of assumptions about the kind of labour market that characterises the economy and the types of workers that migrate to the United States. Basically, three assumptions are required to reach the conclusion that immigrants displace workers from their jobs on a one-to-one basis.

The first is that the number of jobs in the labour market is fixed. New labour market entrants compete with the existing labour force for the same pool of jobs. Because no economic growth takes place as immigrants enter the labour market, this view implies that for every person taking a job, some other worker must be displaced.

The second assumption is that immigrants and natives are perfectly interchangeable in the labour market. For an immigrant to be able to take over a job formerly held by a native, the immigrant must be equally qualified for the job. In other words, immigrants and natives are perfect substitutes in production.

It is unclear why employers, given a choice between equally skilled immigrants or natives, would prefer to hire immigrants. That is, it is unclear why immigrants must displace natives, and why employers would not choose to keep the natives in their jobs and leave the immigrants unemployed. After all, firing old workers and hiring new workers is costly. Hence a third assumption is required: immigrants are willing to work for lower wages than equally productive natives. Because immigrants offer profit-maximising employers a given set of skills at a lower price, it necessarily follows that immigrants "take jobs away" from natives.

Viewed in terms of these three very restrictive assumptions, the proposition that immigrants displace native workers becomes less plausible. For example, the assumption that the number of jobs in the economy is fixed is patently false. Increases in population, whether they occur by immigration or by natural fertility, lead to increases in the demand for goods and services. Employers will typically expand their workplaces to satisfy the increased demand, and the number of persons employed will necessarily increase.

Similarly, the assumption that immigrants and natives are perfectly interchangeable is questionable. It is difficult to take seriously the proposition that the typical Mexican illegal alien in the United States is perfectly interchangeable with the typical native in the labour force.

Finally, there is no evidence suggesting that immigrant labour is cheaper than equally skilled native labour. Such a difference could arise if there were systematic labour market discrimination against some racial or national origin groups.[3] There is no evidence, however, supporting the assertion that immigrants in the United States are systematically discriminated against. Alternatively, it is sometimes argued that illegal aliens, afraid of being reported to the immigration officials, are an easy prey for exploitation and are paid less than the going wage. However, the evidence that illegal aliens in the United States are paid less than demographically comparable legal immigrants is extremely weak. There is therefore no reason to believe that employers would prefer to hire immigrants over equally qualified natives. The presumption that immigrants must displace natives rests on a rather peculiar, and erroneous, view of the way the labour market operates.

A second school of thought argues exactly the opposite. Piore (1979), for instance, believes that immigrants entering the U.S. labour market cause very little displacement of natives because immigrants "take on a distinct set of jobs, jobs that the native labour force refuses to accept."

In this view, the American labour market is segmented into two sectors: a primary sector, containing "good" jobs, and a secondary sector of "bad" jobs. By assumption, natives prefer the better jobs available in the primary sector. Because of labour market discrimination against immigrants, or because some immigrant groups tend to be less skilled and have little knowledge of the English language or the workings of the U.S. labour market, or because they simply do not know any better, immigrants are crowded into the secondary sector and hence hold jobs that natives refuse to take.

This view is flawed because it too depends on assumptions that are basically arbitrary, logically inconsistent and without empirical support. First, the breakdown of the economy into two sectors is an extremely simplistic view of the way labour markets operate and has been difficult to establish as empirically relevant.

Moreover, if natives did not wish to work in "secondary" jobs it seems natural that a shortage of these types of workers would soon develop. In a market economy, the labour shortage in the secondary sector would increase competition for the few workers willing to provide these services and create pressures for an increase in the wages paid to secondary sector workers. This would tend to equate the rewards between the primary and secondary sectors, and as wages for "bad" jobs rose, even natives would be willing to work in them.

Hence there is no compelling theoretical rationale or empirical evidence to support the view that natives refuse to work in certain types of jobs and that immigrants are somehow relegated to the "bad" jobs. The conclusion that natives and immigrants never interact in the labour market, like the assertion that immigrants displace natives from their jobs on a one-to-one basis, depends on assumptions that are at odds with the way the labour market actually operates. In fact, there is no theoretical reason to assume that immigrants are either "good" or "bad" for natives' opportunities in the labour market.

2   The Interaction of Immigrants and Natives in Production

A more instructive approach focuses on the following question: what happens to a company's demand for native workers when immigrants enter the labour market? This type of question is easily addressed in terms of basic principles of economic theory.

Profit-maximising enterprises combine inputs, such as different types of labour and capital, and use them to produce an output that they sell to consumers. Since companies want to maximise profits, they would like to hire the cheapest possible labour – for any given level of skill desired – and sell the output at the highest possible price. Of course, they cannot lower the wage below the going rate; otherwise workers would leave for companies that offer better opportunities. Similarly, the firm cannot sell the output at too high a price, or other businesses will sell at lower prices and steal all the consumers away.

What happens to the company's incentives to hire native labour when the supply of immigrants increases? It turns out that there is no definite answer to this question. It is possible that immigrants and native workers are substitutes in production; that is, that immigrants and natives tend to have similar skills and are suited for similar types of jobs. As immigrants enter the labour market, the supply of these skills to the market increases and there is more competition among the workers supplying these skills to employers. Companies can therefore attract workers – both immigrants and natives – at lower wages because these skills are now abundant in the marketplace.

Because of the lower wages now paid native workers, some natives find it worthwhile to withdraw from the labour force; the number of native workers employed declines. This "displacement" will not be on a one-to-one basis. The number of natives that leave their jobs depends on how many find it worthwhile to leave the labour market altogether, which in turn depends on the value of their alternatives (such as leisure or managing the household).

This conclusion assumes that natives and immigrants are interchangeable, or substitutes, in production. It is also possible, however, that instead immigrants and natives complement one another. For instance, some immigrant groups may have very low skill levels and a comparative advantage in agricultural production. This would free up the more skilled native workforce to perform tasks that require higher skills. The presence of immigrants increases native productivity because natives can now specialise in tasks where they too have a comparative advantage.

If the two groups are complements in production, an increase in immigrant supply increases the productivity of natives, making natives more valuable to companies and increasing companies' demand for native labour. Since employers are now competing for native labour, native wage rates are bid up. In addition, because of the wage increase in the native labour market, some natives who previously did not find it profitable to work will now see the higher wage rate as an additional incentive to enter the labour market, and native employment will increase.

An important insight from this approach is the possibility that immigrants do not harm the economic opportunities of natives but in fact may be quite beneficial. Whether immigrants and natives are complements or substitutes in production is entirely an empirical question. Conceptual discussions of the impact of immigrants on the native labour market typically make an assumption about the extent of substitutability or complementarity between the two groups.

An additional implication of this framework is that it need not be the case that all immigrants and all natives are related in the same way in the production process. Some immigrant groups, for instance, may be close substitutes in production with some native groups, but may be complements in production with other native groups. In other words, various combinations of complementarity or substitutability among the many immigrant and native groups are possible, and only a systematic analysis of the data can determine the impact that immigrants have on the native labour market.

3   Empirical Evidence

This conceptual framework suggests a simple way of establishing empirically whether immigrants and natives are complements or substitutes in production. If they are substitutes, the earnings of native workers should be lower in labour markets where immigrants are in abundant supply. If they are complements, native earnings should be lower in labour markets where the supply of immigrants is scarce.

Practically all recent U.S. research takes this implication of the theory as its departure point.[4] The methodological approach is to compare native earnings in Standard Metropolitan Statistical Areas (SMSAs) where immigrants are a substantial fraction of the labour force (for example, Los Angeles or New York) with native earnings in SMSAs where immigrants are a relatively trivial fraction of the labour force (for example, Pittsburgh or Nashville).

Of course, native wages would be likely to vary across labour markets even if immigration did not exist. The validity of the analysis, therefore, crucially depends on the extent to which the analyst can control for all the other factors that lead to variations in native wage rates across labour markets. These factors include geographic differences in the skill levels of natives, regional wage differentials and differences in levels of economic activity.

Table 10.1 summarises the findings of a large number of studies that use this basic approach. Overall, the comparison to the "standardised" earnings of natives across labour markets indicates that

Table 10.1   [*orig. table B.1*]   The impact of a 10 percent increase in
the number of selected immigrants on earnings of selected groups
of native workers

Study	A 10 percent increase in the number of:
1. Altonji-Card	– Immigrants workers reduces weekly earnings of unskilled black men by 0.1%; – and of unskilled white men by 0.2%; – increases weekly earnings of unskilled black women by 0.5%; – and of unskilled white women by 0.4%.
2. Borjas	– immigrant men reduces annual earnings of native white men by 0.1%; – increases annual earnings of native black men by 0.2%; – increases annual earnings of women by 0.2%.
3. Borjas	– white immigrant men increases annual earnings of black native men by 0.2%; – black immigrant men reduces annual earnings of black native men by 0.3%; – hispanic immigrant men reduces annual earnings of black native men by 0.04%; – asian immigrant men does not change the annual earnings of black native men.
4. Grossman	– immigrants reduces annual earnings of natives by 0.2%.
5. DeFreitas-Marshall	– immigrants employed in manufacturing reduces manufacturing wages by 0.04%.
6. King-Lowell-Bean	– hispanic immigrants does not change the annual earnings of natives.
7. LaLonde-Topel	– pre-1965 immigrants decreases annual earnings of young blacks by 0.1%, decreases annual earnings of young Hispanics by 0.3%; – post-1965 immigrants decreases annual earnings of young blacks by 0.1%, increases annual earnings of young Hispanics by 0.2%.
8. Muller-Espenshade	– mexican immigrants reduces black family income by 0.1%.
9. Stewart-Hyclak	– mexican immigrants does not change the black/white wage ratio; – cuban immigrants increases the black/white wage ratio by 0.003 points; – other immigrants decreases the black/white wage ratio by 0.02 points.

Source: 1 Altonji and Card (1991);
2 Borjas (1986);
3 Borjas (1987);
4 Grossman (1982);
5 DeFreitas and Marshall (1984);
6 King et al. (1986);
7 LaLonde and Topel (1991);
8 Muller and Espenshade (1985);
9 Stewart and Hyclak (1986).

the average native wage is slightly smaller in labour markets where immigrants tend to reside. That is, after controlling for geographic differences in age, schooling and other observable skills of natives and in levels of economic activity in local labour markets, native earnings are slightly lower in markets with large numbers of immigrants.

However, the decline in the native wage attributable to an increase in the supply of immigrants is numerically trivial. A 10 percent increase in the size of the immigrant labour force reduces the native wage by, at most, two- or three-tenths of one percentage point. Doubling the number of immigrants reduces the native wage rate by 2–3 per cent. The overwhelming consensus of the literature seems to be that native and immigrant workers are, on average, very weak substitutes in production. Despite all the concern about the presumed large adverse effects of immigration on the earnings opportunities available to natives, careful empirical research suggests that this concern is not justified. The earnings of the average native are barely affected by the entry of immigrants into the local labour market.

Table 10.1 also shows that this finding holds up even after the labour force is broken down by sex, age, race or ethnicity. Some native groups might be adversely affected by labour market competition from some immigrant groups, even if on average the native population is unaffected. For instance, some native groups are complements in production with immigrants, but other native groups may be substitutes. The aggregation across native groups would obscure this, the aggregate data revealing that, on average, immigrants have little effect on the earnings of natives, even though they may have large positive and negative effects on different native groups.

The empirical evidence suggests that this is not the case. Generally, some immigrant groups tend to be weak complements with some native groups and weak substitutes with others. Regardless of the combination of groups being analysed, the very detailed breakdown of the labour force by demographic group indicates that the impact of an increase in the supply of immigrants on the wage of any native group is numerically small.

It has been argued that blacks are the group whose economic progress is most likely to be hurt by the entry of immigrants in the United States. Perhaps the most surprising result provided by the recent econometric evidence is that no study finds any evidence that immigrants and blacks are strong substitutes. In fact, some studies report that blacks in SMSAs with relatively large numbers of immigrants actually have slightly higher earnings than blacks in SMSAs with relatively small immigrant populations. A 10 percent increase in the number of immigrants in the SMSA increases the average black wage, after controlling for regional differences in the observable labour market skills of employed blacks, by about two-tenths of 1 percent. Moreover, a 10 percent increase in the number of Hispanic immigrants, who are presumably the source of much of the concern, reduces the black wage by less than one-tenth of 1 percent. Finally, a 10 percent increase in the number of immigrants reduces the earnings of young black people, a group that presumably is particularly sensitive to changes in economic conditions, by only one-tenth of 1 percent.

Some studies in the literature move beyond the analysis of cross-section data and focus on the earnings and employment opportunities available to natives in the same labour market before the immigrant inflow and after. This longitudinal comparison holds constant all the factors that are labour market specific.

A few U.S. studies track the wage and employment opportunities of natives in a large number of labour markets between 1970 and 1980, a decade that witnessed a substantial increase in the size of the immigrant flow.[5] If immigrants adversely affect the earnings and employment opportunities of natives, the longitudinal analysis should indicate that native labour market conditions substantially worsened in markets that attracted large numbers of immigrants.

None of the longitudinal studies reveals this to be the case. The tracking of native earnings and employment levels over the decade reconfirms the general validity of the cross-section results. For instance, the longitudinal analysis suggests that a 10 percent increase in the number of immigrants decreases the earnings of white native men by three-tenths of 1 per cent, compared with the cross-section finding that it would lead to a decrease of one-tenth of 1 percent. The longitudinal analysis reveals that a 10 percent increase in the number of immigrants increases the earnings of black men by two-tenths of 1 percent, as did the cross-section analysis (Borjas, 1986). There is thus no evidence that native labour market conditions were adversely affected in labour markets that experienced large increases in the size of the immigrant population.

In what is perhaps the best study in the literature, Card (1990) analysed the impact of the Mariel flow on the Miami labour market. On 20 April 1980, Fidel Castro declared that Cuban nationals wishing to move to the United States could leave freely from the port of Mariel, Cuba. By 19 September 1980, about 125,000 Cubans, mostly unskilled workers, had chosen to undertake the journey. The numerical impact of the Mariel flow on Miami's population and labour force was sizeable. Almost overnight, Miami's labour force had unexpectedly grown by 7 percent.

Card's systematic analysis of the data demonstrates that the labour market experiences of Miami's native population, including unskilled blacks, were barely affected by the Mariel flow. Economic conditions in Miami between 1980 and 1985, in terms of wage levels and unemployment rates, were similar to those in such cities as Los Angeles, Houston and Atlanta, which did not experience the Mariel flow.

Recent econometric research has not been able to establish a single instance in which the earnings of U.S.-born workers have been strongly and adversely affected by the increase in the supply of immigrants over the last two decades. This unexpected finding raises an important question: why is the empirical evidence so at odds with the typical presumption in the public arena?

As noted earlier, economic theory provides little guidance as to what to expect from a careful, objective analysis. Immigrants are either substitutes or complements with natives, and production interactions between immigrants and natives are rarely observed. Many participants in the public debate have assumed, without justification, that immigrants and natives are strong substitutes in production. In the end, the nature of the technological relationship between immigrant and native labour depends on the type of sorting generated by the immigration market.

Another reason for the absence of any sizeable adverse effects is the fact that immigration to the United States, though large and increasing in size, is still a relatively small component of demographic change in the United States. This is particularly true in terms of the immigrant contribution to the growth of the labour force.

At the same time that immigrants were entering the labour force in increasing numbers, two other, much larger groups of natives were also entering the labour force: women and the baby boom cohorts. These demographic events dwarfed the increase in immigration. The labour force participation rate of women increased from 38 percent in 1960 to 52 percent in 1980. This increase alone meant the entry of an additional 8.5 million women into the labour force over the period (U.S. Department of Commerce, 1988).[6] Moreover, an average of more than 4 million people a year were born in the United States during the baby boom period of 1945 to 1960, and entered the labour market in the late 1960s and '70s (U.S. Department of Commerce, 1988).[7]

During the 1950s, before the significant increase in the size of the immigration flow, immigration accounted for 17 percent of the growth in the labour force. During the 1970s, it accounted for between 11 percent and 17 percent (depending on the size of the illegal alien population) despite the increase in the number of immigrants entering the country (Abowd and Freeman, 1991). The contribution of immigration to the growth of the labour force was overshadowed by the other major demographic changes. Given that immigration accounted for a relatively small, perhaps even declining component of labour force growth, it is not surprising that the labour market need hardly adjust to the entry of immigrants and that native earnings opportunities were not greatly affected.

Filer (1988) has raised the possibility that the impact of immigrants on native employment opportunities is dampened by the fact that natives respond to the economic pressures introduced by immigrants by not migrating to areas where immigrants reside. Filer's analysis of the 1980 U.S. Census documents a negative correlation between immigration rates into particular SMSAs and the in-migration rates of natives. In other words, voting with their feet, natives avoid areas where their labour market opportunities would be adversely affected by the presence of immigrants. Although Filer's study raises an interesting hypothesis, we do not yet know the extent to which the migration patterns of natives are responsible for the relatively small impact that immigrants have on the native wage structure in the United States.

4 Conclusion

Little was known about how immigrants affected the employment and earnings opportunities of natives until recently. Despite this almost complete lack of information, the debate over immigration policy continually used the presumption that immigrants have an adverse impact on the labour market to justify many of the restrictions in immigration law. In the last few years, the availability of a number of large data sets and advances in econometric methodology have led to the development of a growing literature that estimates the immigrant impact on the labour market. The empirical evidence indicates that immigrants do not have a major impact either on the earnings or on the employment levels of natives in the U.S. labour market. This result is all the more remarkable because practically every study in the literature finds essentially the same result despite differences in the data sets analysed and in the econometric methodologies.

Although most of the literature focuses on the U.S. labour market, it is evident that the policy concerns that motivate this literature exist in all countries that allow significant levels of immigration. The empirical documentation of international differences in the impact of immigrants on host countries, and the explanation of similarities or differences between countries, remains an important research agenda.

Notes

1 This paper summarises the discussion of labour market competition between immigrants and natives in chapter 5 of Borjas (1990).

2 Higham (1955) presents an interesting discussion of how economic fears of job displacement and unemployment interacted with nativist feelings and led to increasing restrictions on immigration.

3 See Borjas (1990) for an interpretation of wage differentials among national origin groups that is not based on a discrimination hypothesis.

4 Although this simple description of the empirical insight is correct, the actual methodological approach followed by most of the studies in the literature is far more complex. Immigrants affect the economic opportunities of natives through their effect on the demand for native labour. What is required, therefore, is an estimate of the company's demand for various inputs. To estimate the system of demand functions (which includes one demand function for each input used in the production process), the analyst must specify a functional form for the company's production technology. This technical assumption, combined with the behavioural assumption that businesses maximise profits, leads to a system of equations that can be estimated with data on the quantities and prices of the inputs. The econometric methodology estimates all the equations in this demand system jointly, and it is from these demand functions that the impact of immigrants on the native labour market is determined.

5 The studies include Altonji and Card (1991), Borjas (1986) and LaLonde and Topel (1991).

6 A classic study of the increase in the labour force participation rate of women is given by Mincer (1962).

7 See Welch (1979) for a study of the impact that the baby boom cohort had on its own earnings.

References

Abowd, J. M., and Freeman, R. B., (1991), "The Internationalization of the U.S. Labor Market," in John M. Abowd and Richard B. Freeman, editors, *Immigration, Trade, and the Labor Market* (Chicago: University of Chicago Press), table 1.

Altonji, J., and Card, D, (1991), "The Effects of Immigration on the Labour Market Outcomes of Natives," in John M. Abowd and Richard B. Freeman, editors, *Immigration, Trade, and the Labour Market* (Chicago: University of Chicago Press, 1991).

Bean, F. D., Telles, E.E. and Lowell, B.L. (1987), "Undocumented Migration to the United States: Perceptions and Evidence," *Population and Development Review*, 13, (December 1987).

Borjas, G. J., (1986), "The Sensitivity of Labor Demand Functions to Choice of Dependent Variable," *Review of Economics and Statistics* 68 (February 1986), pp. 58–66.

Borjas, G. J., (1987) "Immigrants, Minorities, and Labor Market Competition," *Industrial and Labor Relations Review*, 40, (April 1987), pp. 382–92.

Borjas, G. J. (1990), *Friends or Strangers: The Impact of Immigrants on the U.S. Economy* (New York: Basic Books).

Borjas, G. J., and Tienda, M. (1987), "The Economic Consequences of Immigration," *Science*, 235 (February 6, 1987).

Card, D. (1990), "The Impact of the Mariel Boatlift on the Miami Labor Market," *Industrial and Labor Relations Review*, 43 (January 1990), pp. 245–57.

Defreitas, G., and Marshall, A. (1984), "Immigration and Wage Growth in U.S. Manufacturing in the 1970s," in: Barbara D. Dennis, editor, *Proceedings of the Thirty-Sixth Annual Meeting* (Madison, Wisconsin: Industrial Relations Research Association, 1984), pp. 148–56.

Filer, R., (1988), "The Impact of Immigrant Arrivals on Migratory Patterns of U.S. Workers," mimeograph, October 1988.

Grossman, J. B., (1982), "The Substitutability of Natives and Immigrants in Production," *Review of Economics and Statistics, 64* (November 1982), pp. 596–603.

Higham, J. (1955), *Strangers in the Land: Patterns of American Nativism 1869–1925* (New York: Atheneum).

King, A. G., Lowell, L., and Bean, F.D. (1986), "The Effects of Hispanic Immigrants on the Earnings of Native Hispanic Americans," *Social Science Quarterly, 67* (December 1986), pp. 673–89.

Lalonde, R. J., and Topel, R.H., (1991), "Labor Market Adjustments to Increased Immigration," in John M. Abowd and Richard B. Freeman, editors, *Immigration, Trade, and the Labor Market* (Chicago: University of Chicago Press, 1991).

Mincer, J., (1962), "Labor Force Participation of Married Women: A Study of Labor Supply," in *Aspects of Labor Economics* (Princeton, N.J.: Princeton University Press for the National Bureau of Economic Research, 1962) p. 63–105.

Muller, T., and Espenshade, T. J. (1985), *The Fourth Wave* (Washington, D.C.: The Urban Institute, 1985).

Piore, M. J. (1979), *Birds of Passage: Migrant Labor and Industrial Societies* (New York: Cambridge University Press).

Stewart, J. B., and Hyclak, T. J. (1986), "The Effects of Immigrants, Women, and Teenagers on the Relative Earnings of Black Males," *Review of Black Political Economy*, 15 (Summer 1986), pp. 93–102.

U.S. Department of Commerce, *Statistical Abstract of the United States, 1988* (Washington, D.C.: Government Printing Office, 1988).

Welch, F. (1979), "Effects of Cohort Size on Earnings: The Baby Boom Babies' Financial Bust," *Journal of Political Economy*, 87 (October 1979), p. S65–S98.

11 U.S. Immigration and the New Welfare State

Thomas J. Espenshade

Introduction and Overview

Economic consequences of immigration are usually sorted into two categories. The one that has received the most attention from economists concerns the labor market impacts of immigrants. How do increased supplies of foreign workers in domestic labor markets affect the earnings and employment opportunities of native workers? Despite a widely shared view among the American public that immigrants take jobs away from U.S. workers, increase unemployment and depress wages (Espenshade and Hempstead, 1996), most research has failed to provide strong support for these beliefs. The literature has been ably summarized by Borjas (1994) and by Friedberg and Hunt (1995a, 1995b). The main conclusion, based largely on cross-sectional data, is that there are only "modest effects of immigrants on natives' labor market outcomes" (Friedberg and Hunt, 1995b: 35). A potentially important qualifier has been added by Manson, Espenshade, and Muller (1985), Filer (1992), Frey (1995), and White and Hunter (1993). It may indeed be the case that some natives are displaced by foreign workers, but if these native workers move away from high immigrant-impact areas to labor markets where they perceive better opportunities, then cross-sectional studies may fail to detect negative effects on wages or employment.

A second topic of economic consequence concerns the fiscal impacts of immigrants. How much do immigrants pay in taxes to federal, state and local governments, how large are the benefits immigrants receive in return, and how do the two amounts compare within various jurisdictions? These issues are of more recent origin than the labor market effects of immigrants and have received less attention, especially from economists. Satisfactory answers to even the most basic questions are hampered by inadequate data (for example, the inability to separate legal and undocumented migrants in census and administrative records), methodological differences (should estimates be calculated from an aggregate, top-down approach or should they be built up from household-level data), and conceptual inconsistencies (is the individual, the family, or the household the appropriate unit of analysis? is marginal cost or average cost the relevant concept?).

Despite these difficulties, numerous fiscal impact studies exist. Using census data, Borjas (1994) found that immigrants were slightly less likely than natives to receive cash welfare benefits in 1970, but that immigrant households were over-represented among the welfare population by 1990 (the fraction of immigrant households receiving welfare was 1.7 percentage points higher than the fraction of native households – 9.1 versus 7.4 percent). Moreover, tracking immigrant cohorts over time revealed that immigrants "assimilate into welfare" the longer they are in the United States. Data for 1984–91 from the Survey of Income and Program Participation show little difference between natives and immigrants in the probability of receiving cash welfare benefits, but a larger native-immigrant differential emerges when other programs are included (Borjas and Hilton, 1996). The fraction of immigrant households receiving some kind of public assistance is 50 percent larger than the native fraction (21 versus 14 percent).

Growth in the refugee population helps to explain the rising proportion of immigrant households receiving welfare. When refugees are excluded, working-age migrants are less likely than their native-born counterparts to receive welfare (Fix and Passel, 1994). This conclusion is consistent with Borjas' (1994) finding that households originating in Cambodia or Laos had a 1990 welfare participation rate of nearly 50 percent. The legal status of immigrant households matters in other ways as well. Vernez and McCarthy (1995) find that there is a progression in tax payments that rises steadily from contributions by current illegal migrants, to former undocumented migrants who received amnesty under the 1986 Immigration Reform and Control Act (IRCA), to legal immigrants, and finally to the native born. But they point out that these differentials may reflect differences in average income rather than immigration status *per se*.

Much less work has gone into examining the *net* fiscal costs of migrants. Fix and Passel (1994) assert that, "Contrary to the public's perception, when all levels of government are considered together, immigrants generate significantly more in taxes paid than they cost in services received" (p. 57). These effects are not uniformly distributed across all levels of government. Immigrant households appear to be a fiscal asset only for the Federal Government. Revenues and expenditures are more or less offsetting for state governments, and it is typically at the local level where immigrants are the greatest fiscal drain (Rothman and Espenshade, 1992). In some states, both immigrant and native households receive more benefits than they pay for with taxes, but immigrant households appear to generate larger negative impacts on local governments (Espenshade and King, 1994; Garvey and Espenshade, 1997).

Many unanswered questions remain in building estimates of immigrants' fiscal impacts. But this is not the place to attempt to break new empirical or methodological ground. Instead, with this brief review as background, we turn our attention to prospective changes in the fiscal consequences of U.S. immigrants, especially those embodied in recently enacted Congressional revisions to the legal rules for program use (otherwise known as welfare reform). These changes have the effect of reducing the public costs of immigration by eliminating or restricting immigrants' access to public benefits.

It is not by coincidence that welfare reform policies come at this moment. They arise out of a public sense of frustration and anxiety with growing economic insecurity fueled by stagnant wages, corporate downsizing and white-collar layoffs, the threat of additional jobs lost overseas, and a concern over high taxes. Most workers have seen their real wages either stagnate or decline over the past two decades. Between 1989 and 1991 real median household income also fell by 5 percent (Plotkin and Scheuerman, 1994). The announcement by AT&T that it plans to reduce its workforce by 13 percent or 40,000 employees over the next three years means that the telephone industry ranks alongside such Fortune 500 companies as General Electric, General Motors, and IBM in the extent of corporate restructuring (Andrews, 1996). As more manufacturing, low-wage service and, increasingly, higher skill computer-programming jobs are exported overseas, a growing fraction of the domestic workforce is engaged in part-time employment. Rising income inequality adds to the sense of relative deprivation among lower and middle-income families, and the weight of accumulating federal deficits means that roughly one in every seven federal dollars goes to pay interest on the national debt (Plotkin and Scheuerman, 1994).

Adding to this economic uncertainty is the demographic disequilibrium caused by rapid changes in the racial and ethnic composition of the U.S. population (Cornelius, 1996). Most of these stem from the volume of immigration, which is now the largest in U.S. history when measured in absolute terms (Fix and Passel, 1994). As of March 1994, 8.7 percent of the U.S. population, or 22.6 million persons, were foreign born (U.S. Bureau of the Census, 1995). This proportion is up from 4.8 percent in 1970 and is the highest since 1940, although it is surpassed by levels that approached 15 percent at the beginning of the twentieth century. Roughly 20 percent of the U.S. foreign-born population arrived in the last five years, which suggests an accelerating tempo to migration. Some areas of the country are affected more than others. California is home to one-third of U.S. immigrants, and nearly one-quarter of California's population is foreign born. Perhaps not surprisingly, because foreign-born individuals include both legal and undocumented migrants, the largest share of the foreign-born population (nearly 30 percent) originates in Mexico. These demographic changes are affecting the "look" of our population, the foods we eat, and the languages we hear spoken, and together are seen by many as having an unsettling effect on the status quo (Teitelbaum and Weiner, 1995).

Declining economic prospects and disquieting demographic change have produced in the United States a new form of isolationism, marked in part by a growing anti-immigrant tone and by mounting fiscal conservatism, exhibited most poignantly in the Republican Party's Contract With America – an attempt to shrink the size of the Federal Government and turn many traditional federal responsibilities over to states. Anti-immigrant sentiment and fiscal conservatism have in turn coalesced in a "new fiscal politics of immigration." Immigrants are viewed as part of the reason for the high cost of social services and are especially vulnerable to attempts to reduce government welfare expenditures. Congress has just extended to legal immigrants restrictions on their eligibility for major means-tested federal entitlement programs and other social services that have customarily applied only to illegal or undocumented migrants. A shrinking welfare state increases the likelihood that legal aliens will be a windfall gain to the federal treasury. There is also a state-level component to this activity marked by efforts to obtain reimbursement from the Federal Government for the costs of health and other services that states are required to provide to illegal aliens and by initiatives, such as California's Proposition 187, to withhold education and health benefits from undocumented individuals. Because resident aliens cannot vote and because they have no strong constituency apart from immigrant-rights groups, immigrants are an attractive fiscal target from the perspective of federal policymakers. Finally, Congressional welfare reforms raise important questions about the meaning of membership in U.S. society. They also create additional incentives for legal aliens to become naturalized citizens without simultaneously easing the constraints on citizenship acquisition.

The New Fiscal Politics of Immigration

The election of Ronald Reagan in 1980 signaled the public's acceptance of a redefinition of economic problems in the United States (Plotkin and Scheuerman, 1994). No longer was the issue mainly one of slow growth in the private sector; rather the problem was that government had become too big. The electorate liked the idea of a balanced budget and less government spending, but they resisted having fewer government services. Reagan's popular tax cuts were not followed by spending reductions, and the federal deficit ballooned as a result. Between 1981 and 1983 the deficit doubled as a proportion of total government spending (from 12 to 25 percent), and the sight of unprecedented $200 billion annual deficits soon gave rise to what Plotkin and Scheuerman (1994: 6) call balanced-budget conservatism, an "omnipresent political focus on deficits, spending cuts, and tax avoidance." Balanced-budget conservatism has gone through several reincarnations,[1] but Plotkin and Scheuerman (1994) argue that in the process it has had at least two implications. It has meant first that the size of the deficit, and not the health of the macroeconomy, has been the yardstick for measuring Congressional budgeting policy and, second, that groups have been pitted against each other, heightening tensions and leading to a fractured society along race, age, and class lines.

U.S. immigration policy is already tilted in the direction of selecting those immigrants who are expected to place few demands on the federal treasury. An application for permanent residence can be rejected if it is judged likely that a potential immigrant will become a public charge any time after settling in the United States. Each year, in fact, about 10 percent of visa applications are denied for this reason (Congressional Budget Office, 1995).[2] Immigrants must demonstrate that they have the financial means to support themselves by, for example, proving sufficient personal resources, having a job offer with an adequate salary, or posting a public charge bond. If they cannot show prospective self-sufficiency, immigrants may be still be admitted into the country under the financial sponsorship of a U.S. resident. Sponsors sign an affidavit of support on behalf of the immigrant, which signifies the sponsor's ability and willingness to provide financial assistance to the migrant.

A problem with this arrangement, however, is that several courts have ruled that support affidavits are not legally binding (U.S. General Accounting Office, 1995b). Consequently, because about half of all legal immigrants have sponsors (Fix and Zimmermann, 1995), there is the possibility that an important fraction of newly admitted permanent residents could eventually become public charges. Congress responded to this situation by instituting deeming provisions. If a sponsored immigrant applies for a federal means-tested benefits program within a certain period after arrival, part of the sponsor's income and assets are "deemed" or considered to be available to the migrant for the purpose of determining benefit eligibility and amount.[3] Deeming provisions have the clear effect of disqualifying from access to public benefits many immigrants who would otherwise be eligible (Fix and Zimmermann, 1995).

Despite the long-standing exclusion of immigrants who are likely to become a public charge and the institution of deeming provisions, the number of immigrants who receive public assistance has been rising. Participation rates in the Supplemental Security Income (SSI) or Aid to Families with Dependent Children (AFDC) programs are higher for immigrants than for citizens–6 percent versus 3.4 percent, respectively. Between 1983 and 1993 the number of immigrants receiving SSI more than quadrupled–from 151,000 to 683,000 – as immigrants increased their share of the SSI caseload from 4 to 11 percent. Growth was greatest among the elderly as opposed to poor disabled or blind recipients. Immigrants increased their share of all adult AFDC recipients from 5 to 8 percent during the same period. Altogether, immigrants in 1993 received a total of $4.5 billion in AFDC and SSI benefits (U.S. General Accounting Office, 1995b). If food stamps are included, the total rises to $5.3 billion in 1996 (Congressional Budget Office, 1995).

Escalating welfare costs for the foreign-born population generated pressures to do even more. Congress responded with welfare reforms that share a common feature of either further severely restricting or eliminating entirely the eligibility of *legal* immigrants for the major means-tested federal entitlement programs. These reforms not only have fiscal implications, but they also drastically reshape the meaning of permanent membership in U.S. society. Reflecting on the situation, Fix and Zimmermann (1995: 2) comment, "Imminent changes in welfare policy would dramatically reorder the relationship of immigrants to the social welfare state.... If enacted, they would move the nation closer to an explicit immigrant policy, but it would be a policy of exclusion rather than inclusion."

Authors of the Contract With America justify these new provisions as necessary to provide the additional education and training funds required to move poor Americans from welfare to work (Associated Press, 1994). An alternative interpretation, however, is that the measures embody the convergence of established anti-immigrant sentiment with the fiscal imperatives of balanced-budget conservatism. Within this new fiscal politics of immigration, legal aliens are viewed as part of the reason for the high cost of social services. Having little or no voice in the electorate and trapped by the forces of budgetary opportunism and political expediency, they represent to many policymakers an attractive and altogether vulnerable fiscal target.[4] Even more than in the past, the consequence of a shrinking welfare state is to metamorphose legal immigrants from public charges to windfall gains for the federal treasury.

Federal Welfare Reforms Affecting Immigrants

The set of federal benefits and services for which immigrants are eligible depends on their legal status.[5] Prior to the 1996 welfare reform bill, naturalized U.S. citizens had (and still retain) full eligibility on the same terms as native-born individuals. Likewise, with the exception of deeming provisions that extended to the receipt of SSI, AFDC and food stamps by sponsored immigrants, lawful permanent residents were treated on the same basis as citizens. Refugees and asylees also had access to the same range of benefits as citizens, although refugees were entitled to benefits from the date of their arrival in the United States, and intact (not just single-parent) poor refugee families were eligible for public assistance.

Applicants for asylum as well as persons in the country legally but required to depart by a certain date (that is, those in temporary protected status) were permitted to receive unemployment compensation, emergency health care, supplemented food coupons for mothers with small children under the Women, Infants and Children (WIC) program, public elementary and secondary school education including Head Start and school meal programs, college loans and federal housing (No Author, 1994). They were excluded, however, from AFDC, Medicaid, and food stamps.

Courts have considered certain classes of immigrants eligible for some social welfare benefits even though the migrants are not permanent U.S. residents. For example, immigrants whose deportation has been suspended fall into this category. Restrictions kept many of these so-called PRUCOL aliens (individuals "permanently residing under color of law") from receiving food stamps, but they were eligible for AFDC and SSI. Immigrants who legalized under IRCA's amnesty provisions were barred from most federal assistance programs for five years from the date of their legalization application, but the temporary exclusionary period has now lapsed. Finally, illegal aliens and legal nonimmigrants (persons such as tourists, students, or businesspeople who are legally in the country for a temporary period and a specific purpose) were ineligible for most public assistance programs. There were exceptions, however, including emergency medical assistance under Medicaid, the supplemental food program (WIC), and public schooling which is not means-tested. In general, therefore, prior law treated native-born persons, naturalized U.S. citizens, refugees, asylees, and legal permanent residents more or less on the same footing when determining eligibility for federal public assistance programs.

Vast new changes recently approved by the U.S. Congress have sharply curtailed or eliminated completely the eligibility of legal immigrants to most federal means-tested programs. In March 1995 the House of Representatives passed The Personal Responsibility Act of 1995 (H.R. 4, sponsored by E. Clay Shaw, R-FL). The Senate in September 1995 passed its own welfare reform bill (S. 1120) introduced by Robert Dole (R-KS). An earlier version of a compromise proposal was packaged with the omnibus budget reconciliation bill in November 1995. In late December 1995 both the House and Senate passed a stand-alone conference welfare reform measure that was sent to President Clinton who vetoed it in early January 1996. A modified comprehensive welfare reform bill was passed by Congress in a subsequent attempt and signed into law by the President in August 1996. In brief, the new legislation (known officially as the Personal Responsibility and Work Opportunity Reconciliation Act of 1996) creates a three-tier system for determining welfare eligibility for immigrants. Naturalized U.S. citizens retain their full eligibility; lawful permanent residents are demoted to second-class standing for most federal public assistance programs; and illegal immigrants continue to be ineligible for practically all public benefits and services.[6]

The new federal welfare reform law converts the existing welfare program into block grants to states, ends the AFDC program begun in 1935, and reduces food stamp program expenditures by more than $20 billion. It permanently bans legal aliens from receiving food stamps and SSI (a program serving the elderly, blind, and disabled). New immigrants who enter the country after the bill is enacted are denied access to most federal means-tested programs for the first five years following their arrival. After five years, deeming provisions which have been extended to all federal means-tested public benefits determine eligibility status for sponsored immigrants until they become citizens (but not beyond naturalization, as proposed in an earlier Senate version). The law makes affidavits of support legally enforceable against the sponsor, and sponsors are liable for up to ten years to federal, state, or local government agencies for benefits the immigrant receives prior to naturalizing. Mechanisms are to be implemented to verify the benefit eligibility status of all aliens, and some agencies that administer federal benefit programs are required to report to the Immigration and Naturalization Service (INS) the names and addresses of individuals they know to be in the United States without authorization.

Only "qualified" aliens may receive federal support. These include legal permanent residents, refugees, asylees, persons granted withholding of deportation, and parolees after their first year in the United States. Aliens not qualified for federal assistance (comprising legal nonimmigrants, parolees in their first year, persons in temporary protected status, and undocumented migrants) may receive support only from emergency Medicaid, short-term emergency disaster relief, public health immunizations and necessary testing and treatment for communicable diseases, programs needed to protect life or safety, and housing or community development funds if aliens currently receive them.

Some immigrants are exempted from the generalized ban on federal program assistance. They include (1) refugees, asylees and persons granted withholding of deportation, who are allowed a five-year grace period after arrival, (2) veterans and active-duty military personnel and their dependents, (3) legal immigrants who have worked 40 quarters that qualify for Social Security coverage and who have not received federal means-tested public assistance in the same period, and (4) current recipients of SSI and food stamps who are grandfathered until the date of their annual recertification of eligibility. The practical implication of these exceptions is that poorer lawful permanent residents who lack a lengthy work history in the United States are the hardest hit by the new reforms. This group includes the elderly parents of naturalized citizens.

Some programs are also excepted from the prospective five-year ban: child nutrition programs such as school lunches and food supplements through WIC, means-tested Elementary and Secondary Education Act programs, higher education grants and loans, foster care and adoption assistance, and other programs to which illegal immigrants are entitled. On the other hand, the ban extends to food stamps and SSI (two major welfare programs that, together with AFDC and nonemergency Medicaid, accounted for about 85 percent of total federal spending on needs-based entitlement programs in 1994; Congressional Budget Office, 1995) and encompasses a broad range of other programs affecting health, nutrition, child welfare, housing, job training and education, and legal services (Fix and Zimmermann, 1995).[7]

These reforms disqualify many current and future legal immigrants from public assistance. For example, total cost savings over six years for the comprehensive 1996 welfare reform bill are estimated at $54 billion, with nearly half of the savings ($24 billion) coming from denying services to legal immigrants. Moreover, the U.S. General Accounting Office (1995b) estimated that H.R. 4, which shares many features with the new welfare reform law, would have removed from the welfare rolls 522,000 SSI recipients and 492,000 AFDC recipients out of the 1.4 million immigrants receiving public assistance benefits in 1993, if it had been enacted as introduced in January 1995. Most of those losing eligibility are lawful permanent residents, but some of the approximately 230,000 refugee recipients would no longer be eligible if they have been in the United States more than five years. The total cost savings to the Federal Government from reduced outlays to immigrants were estimated at $20–25 billion for the four-year period between 1997 and 2000. Most of these reduced outlays arise from SSI, Medicaid, food stamps, and AFDC (Congressional Budget Office, 1995).

In the face of these cutbacks, legal permanent resident aliens have an incentive to become naturalized citizens as quickly as possible. Not surprisingly, a record one million immigrants applied for U.S. citizenship in FY 1995, double the number in FY 1994, and three times as large as the number of 1992 requests (Cohen, 1995; Jones, 1996). A Deputy INS Commissioner gave as one reason for the abrupt jump a fear among the foreign-born population that Congress will enact laws restricting the rights of legal immigrants.

State-led initiatives

Individual states are also expressing concern about the fiscal impacts of immigrants. Some have begun to look to the Federal Government for reimbursement for the costs of benefits and services that they are required to provide to undocumented immigrants (Clark et al., 1994; U.S. General Accounting Office, 1994, 1995a). During 1994 six states (Arizona, California, Florida, New Jersey, New York, and Texas) filed separate suits in federal district courts to recover costs they claim to have sustained because of the Federal Government's failure to enforce U.S. immigration policy, protect the nation's borders, and provide adequate resources for immigration emergencies (Dunlap and Morse, 1995). All lawsuits sought relief for the costs of incarcerating undocumented criminal aliens in state or local correctional facilities, and many included claims for public education, emergency health care and other social services that states are required by federal mandate to extend to illegal immigrants. The amounts range from $50.5 million in New Jersey for the FY 1993 costs of imprisoning 500 undocumented criminal felons and for future capital construction expenses to build new prisons to $33.6 billion in the New York case brought by state and local officials for reimbursement for all state and county costs (incarcerations, education, and social services) associated with undocumented immigration between 1988 and 1993 (State and Local Coalition on Immigration, 1994b). U.S. District Court judges have dismissed all six immigration lawsuits, arguing among other things that the suits are not subject to judicial review because the complaints revolve around political and not judicial questions. Some of the states are appealing the decisions.

In separate action, the Justice Department provided partial relief to key states that house more than 85 percent of all illegal aliens in state prisons. President Clinton's 1994 crime bill earmarked a total of $1.8 billion over six years to help reimburse states for these incarceration costs. The FY 1995 appropriation was $130 million, one-third of which was disbursed to the six states filing lawsuits, plus Illinois, in October 1994. California, with more undocumented immigrants than any other state, received nearly 80 percent of the initial disbursement, whereas shares for Arizona, Illinois, and New Jersey totaled less than $1 million (State and Local Coalition on Immigration, 1994a). These amounts are less than those requested in state lawsuits. On the other hand, the state-by-state suits fail to recognize that undocumented aliens also pay a variety of state and local taxes that partially offset their use of services. Moreover, the suits overlook the fact that the 1990 census included a portion of the U.S. undocumented migrant population in the enumerated state totals. Because some federal-to-state government funding formulas take into account population size, states with disproportionate numbers of undocumented aliens have over the years been receiving more federal funding (at the expense of states with few undocumented migrants) than they otherwise would (and, perhaps, should) have.[8]

In a dramatic move to take charge of their own fiscal destiny, California residents set out to establish standards for undocumented migrants' eligibility for public assistance and services. By a margin of 3 to 2 in November 1994, voters approved the ballot initiative known as Proposition 187. The initiative denies public education (including K-12, community colleges, and higher education), health care (except emergency medical services), and social services to undocumented immigrants. The measure requires publicly funded social and health service agencies, school districts, and law enforcement offices to verify the legal status of all applicants and to notify the California attorney general and INS officials of persons determined or suspected of being in the United States illegally. Finally, the proposition creates two new state felony offenses for manufacture or use of false documents to conceal immigration or citizenship status (State and Local Coalition on Immigration, 1995b).

Estimated annual savings of roughly $200 million would be realized from reduced expenditures by state and local governments for social services, health care, and higher education. Anticipated savings of $1.2 billion per year for public elementary and secondary education would not materialize, however, unless the U.S. Supreme Court overturns its decision in Plyler v. Doe.[9] At the same time Proposition 187 imposes heavy administrative costs on school districts and health service providers, and it could mean the loss of up to $15 billion in annual federal funds because of conflicts with federal reporting requirements and privacy protections (State and Local Coalition on Immigration, 1995b).

In November 1995 a federal judge ruled large sections of Proposition 187 unconstitutional, citing individual rights and the fact that "the state is powerless to enact its own scheme to regulate immigration" (Ayres, 1995: A10). Specific provisions that were held unconstitutional are those affecting the rights of illegal immigrant children to attend public elementary and secondary school, and the reporting requirements whenever someone is known or reasonably suspected to be illegal. On the other hand, the judge ruled that undocumented immigrants could be denied nonemergency medical aid as well as admission to California colleges and universities (Lively, 1995), but that federal officials (not state or local) would first have to determine the legal status of the applicants and then decide to share that information. The only section of Proposition 187 left standing relates to the manufacture, sale, and use of fraudulent documents.[10]

Interest in Proposition 187 has spilled over into other states. Groups in Arizona, Florida, New York, and Texas have expressed an interest in similar ballot initiatives in the 1996 elections. There has even been a flirtation of interest in Congress. In the summer of 1995, Rep. Frank Riggs (R-CA) withdrew an amendment that he had planned to attach to the Labor, Health and Human Services, and Education appropriations bill that would have implemented on a national scale a slightly less restrictive version of California's Proposition 187 (State and Local Coalition on Immigration, 1995a).

Discussion

The issues that welfare reform poses for the rights of lawful permanent resident aliens and their continued eligibility for public assistance are more philosophical than legal. The Congress can, if it wishes, deny welfare and other federal benefits to legal immigrants citing its plenary authority over immigration (Pear, 1994). Whether it should or not is another matter. At their root, recent welfare reforms raise questions about the meaning of membership in U.S. society. Robert Pear (1994: E5) puts the matter succinctly: "Despite the country's history as a nation of immigrants, popular opinion in the United States has continually vacillated on the question of whom the Government is meant to serve: its people, or just its citizens."

Opinion over the issue is clearly divided. The U.S. Commission on Immigration Reform (1994: 23) supports a broadly inclusive interpretation of the government's mandate and recommends "against any broad, categorical denial of public benefits to legal immigrants" on the grounds that legal immigrants whom we have affirmatively accepted for permanent residence in the United States should be protected by a social safety net afforded citizens. A similar stance is taken by Cornelius, Martin, and Hollifield (1994: 10) who ask, "How can a 'liberal' society tolerate the presence of individuals who are *members* but not *citizens* of that society? Should not all individuals who are members (i.e., permanent residents) of a liberal society be accorded the full panoply of rights (social and political as well as civil) enjoyed by those who are citizens?" (emphasis in the original). Legomsky (1994) raises fairness issues by asking whether it is equitable to remove accustomed rights from legal aliens while insisting that they are still responsible for obeying U.S. laws governing tax payments, conscription, and criminal activity.

Supporters of a liberal interpretation of civic inclusion are backed by Constitutional principles. Although the Federal Government can make citizenship a prerequisite for receiving public assistance, this step contravenes traditions that run deep in America's political culture. The Constitution speaks of "We the People of the United States," not "We the Citizens . . .," and the Bill of Rights is designed to protect the interests of people, not citizens (Pear, 1994). Other arguments against eliminating benefits have mentioned the potential adverse effects on the economic well-being of migrants and their children and the additional costs that federal actions may impose on states (Congressional Budget Office, 1995).

Nevertheless, a mood swing in Europe and the United States is promoting a far narrower interpretation of the Federal Government's responsibilities. In an effort to discourage immigration, France tightened citizenship requirements in 1993 by removing automatic citizenship from children born on French soil to foreign parents (Whitney, 1996), and similar initiatives are being considered in Congress to reduce illegal immigration (Lewis, 1995). In Germany, citizenship is defined primarily by blood line, making it almost impossible for a German-born child of a Turkish guest worker to become a German citizen. Despite the forward momentum of rights-based liberalism, recent judicial rulings in the United

States and Europe have "whittled away at some of the rights and protections previously accorded to immigrants," and many western industrialized democracies are grudgingly coming to recognize that "effective control of immigration requires a rollback of civil and human rights for noncitizens" (Cornelius, Martin, and Hollifield, 1994: 10).

Specific arguments that have been advanced in support of tighter restrictions on welfare eligibility for legal immigrants include the following. First, because legal aliens who choose not to become citizens are demonstrating a questionable commitment to the United States, it is appropriate to limit their access to benefits received by citizens. Second, immigrants' sponsors have been shirking their responsibility to provide financial support, and this trend would be reversed if the government did not provide assistance. Third, public assistance becomes a crutch that inhibits immigrants from adapting more quickly to the nation's culture and from seeking productive work. And, fourth, public benefits act as a welfare magnet that attracts to the United States poor immigrants who then end up competing with disadvantaged Americans in the labor market (Congressional Budget Office, 1995).[11]

In short, growing anti-immigrant sentiment has colluded with forces of fiscal conservatism to make immigrants an easy target of budget cuts. The latest round of welfare reforms directed at immigrants seems motivated not so much by a guiding philosophy of what it means to be a member of American society as by a desire to shrink the size of the Federal Government and produce a balanced budget.

The new reforms also reinforce existing incentives for legal aliens to become U.S. citizens. In addition to guaranteeing the right to vote, citizenship protects immigrants from threatened cuts in eligibility for public assistance and puts them in a privileged position vis-à-vis legal aliens to bring close family members to join them in the United States. The U.S. Commission on Immigration Reform (1995) has recommended a renewed emphasis on "Americanization" as part of a total package of legal immigration reforms. Such policies aim to cultivate a shared commitment to enduring American values of liberty, democracy, and equal opportunity. They also encourage naturalization as the path to full civic participation. It would be wholly consistent with the incentives created by proposed immigration reforms and new welfare practices if Congress eased the path to citizenship by reducing the number of probationary years legal immigrants must now serve. Under current law, in addition to satisfying other eligibility criteria having to do with age, character, English proficiency, and an understanding of U.S. civics, lawful permanent residents must usually reside in the United States continuously for five years before being permitted to apply for naturalization. Shortening this period to, say, two or three years would provide partial relief from the crescendo of measures that are pressing legal immigrants in the direction of full citizenship.

Notes

1 The Republicans' Contract With America is the latest rebirth of balanced-budget conservatism. An important element of this contract is the omnibus budget reconciliation bill, passed by Congress in November 1995. Although President Clinton vetoed the measure, this large budget bill lays out a blue-print for public programs for the next seven years that will scale back the size of Federal Government in American life, turn numerous traditionally federal responsibilities over to states, and balance the budget by the year 2002.
2 In addition, permanent resident aliens can be deported if, within five years after arrival, they receive public cash assistance and refuse a demand for repayment, and if the receipt of benefits is due to pre-existing conditions and not to causes that arose after entry (State and Local Coalition on Immigration, 1995d).
3 Prior to the 1996 welfare reform bill, the AFDC, Food Stamp, and Supplemental Security Income (SSI) programs were the only ones restricted by deeming provisions. The deeming period lasted for three years after a person migrated, but in 1993 the deeming period for SSI was temporarily extended from three to five years, beginning in January 1994 and extending until September 1996 when it reverted back to three years (U.S. General Accounting Office, 1995b).
4 A related interpretation is offered by Calavita (1996) for California's Proposition 187.
5 For additional details, see Fix and Zimmermann (1995: 15–17) from whom this discussion is adapted.
6 The following description of the 1996 welfare reform bill as it applies to immigrants is based on State and Local Coalition on Immigration (1996).
7 The welfare reform bill also places new rights and responsibilities on state and local governments, including state options to deny Medicaid benefits to immigrants, to limit eligibility for state-funded benefits, and to apply deeming to state programs. School breakfasts and lunches must be provided to all immigrants regardless of status, but states may provide public benefits to illegal immigrants only by enacting special state laws. This provision does not affect the current right of illegal immigrant children to receive a free public education. Finally, states are given the discretion to deny needs-based programs to qualified aliens beyond the prospective five-year ban until citizenship is attained.

8 Florida's Governor Chiles announced in August 1995 that the state is slated to receive $18 million from the U.S. Department of Justice Immigration Emergency Fund to assist with costs in helping with the resettlement of Cuban immigrants from the Guantanamo Bay military base. Although the Emergency Fund was created in 1986, this will be the first time that it has actually provided money to a state with an immigration emergency (State and Local Coalition on Immigration, 1995c).

9 In June 1982 by a 5–4 margin, the U.S. Supreme Court ruled that undocumented immigrant children cannot be denied access to public elementary and secondary education (*Plyler v. Doe*, 457 U.S. 202 [1982]). This decision overturned a 1975 Texas law that banned the use of state funds to educate illegal aliens (Heer, 1996: 121).

10 Acting just days after President Clinton signed the welfare reform bill, California's Governor Pete Wilson issued an executive order ending illegal immigrants' access to state benefits including public housing, prenatal care, child abuse prevention programs, long-term health care, all professional and commercial licenses, and state colleges and universities unless illegal migrants pay the full cost of tuition (Golden, 1996).

11 Available empirical evidence suggests that low-skill migrants are attracted to the United States by the prospect of employment and not welfare benefits (Cornelius, 1996; Massey and Espinosa, 1995).

References

Andrews, Edmund L. 1996. "Job Cuts at AT&T will Total 40,000, 13% of its Staff," *The New York Times*, January 3, p. A1.

Associated Press. 1994. "Republicans Expected to Propose Ban on Welfare for Legal Immigrants," *The Star-Ledger*, November 22, p. 9.

Ayres, Jr., B. Drummond. 1995. "California Immigration Law is Ruled to be Partly Illegal," *The New York Times*, November 21, p. A10.

Borjas, George J. 1994. "The Economics of Immigration," *Journal of Economic Literature*, December, 32(4): 1667–717.

——— and Lynette Hilton. 1996. "Immigration and the Welfare State: Immigrant Participation in Means-tested Entitlement Programs," *Quarterly Journal of Economics*, May, 111(2): 575–604.

Calavita, Kitty. 1996. "The New Politics of Immigration: 'Balanced Budget Conservatism' and the Symbolism of Prop. 187," *Social Problems*, August, 43(3): 284–305.

Clark, Rebecca L., Jeffrey Passel, Wendy Zimmermann, and Michael Fix. 1994. *Fiscal Impacts of Undocumented Aliens: Selected Estimates for Seven States*. Report to the Office of Management and Budget and the Department of Justice, September. Washington, D.C.: The Urban Institute.

Cohen, Robert. 1995. "Citizenship Applications Hit 1 Million," *The Star-Ledger*, December 9, p. 1.

Congressional Budget Office. 1995. *Immigration and Welfare Reform*. CBO Papers, February. Washington, D.C.

Cornelius, Wayne A. 1997. "Appearances and Realities: Controlling Illegal Immigration in the United States," in Myron Weiner and Tadashi Hanami, eds, *Temporary Works or Future Citizens: Japanese and U.S. Migration Policies.* London: Macmillan.

——, Philip L. Martin, and James F. Hollifield. 1994. "Introduction: The Ambivalent Quest for Immigration Control," in Wayne A. Cornelius, Philip L. Martin, and James F. Hollifield, eds, *Controlling Immigration: A Global Perspective.* Stanford, CA: Stanford University Press, pp. 3–41.

Dunlap, Jonathan C. and Ann Morse. 1995. "States Sue Feds to Recover Immigration Costs," *NCSL Legisbrief,* January, 3(1). Washington, D.C.: National Conference of State Legislatures.

Espenshade, Thomas J. and Katherine Hempstead. 1996. "Contemporary American Attitudes Toward U.S. Immigration," *International Migration Review,* Summer, 30(2): 535–70.

Espenshade, Thomas J. and Vanessa E. King. 1994. "State and Local Fiscal Impacts of U.S. Immigrants: Evidence from New Jersey," *Population Research and Policy Review* 13: 225–56.

Filer, Randall K. 1992. "The Effect of Immigrant Arrivals on Migratory Patterns of Native Workers," in George J. Borjas and Richard B. Freeman, eds, *Immigration and the Work Force: Economic Consequences for the United States and Source Areas.* Chicago: The University of Chicago Press, pp. 245–69.

Fix, Michael and Jeffrey S. Passel. 1994. *Immigration and Immigrants: Setting the Record Straight.* Washington, D.C.: The Urban Institute.

Fix, Michael and Wendy Zimmermann. 1995. "Immigrant Families and Public Policy: A Deepening Divide," Immigrant Policy Program, November, Washington, D.C.: The Urban Institute.

Frey William H. 1995. "The New Geography of Population Shifts: Trends Toward Balkanization," in Reynolds Farley, ed., *State of the Union – America in the 1990s, Volume II: Social Trends.* New York: Russell Sage, pp. 271–334.

Friedberg, Rachel and Jennifer Hunt. 1995a. "Immigration and the Receiving Economy," paper prepared for the SSRC Conference on America Becoming/ Becoming American, Sanibel Island, Florida, January 18–21, 1996.

——.1995b. "The Impact of Immigrants on Host Country Wages, Employment and Growth," *Journal of Economic Perspectives,* Spring, 9(2): 23–44.

Garvey, Deborah L. and Thomas J. Espenshade. 1997. "State and Local Fiscal Impacts of New Jersey's Immigrant and Native Households," in T. J. Espenshade, ed., *Keys to Successful Immigration: Implications of the New Jersey Experience.* Washington, D.C.: The Urban Institute Press, pp. 139–72.

Golden, Tim. 1996. "California Governor Acts to End State Aid for Illegal Immigrants," *The New York Times,* August 28, p. A1.

Heer, David M. 1996. *Immigration in America's Future: Social Science Findings and the Policy Debate.* Boulder, CO: Westview Press.

Jones, Charisse. 1996. "For New York's Newcomers, Anxiety Over Welfare Law," *The New York Times,* August 26, p. A1.

Legomsky, Stephen H. 1994. "Why Citizenship?" *Virginia Journal of International Law,* 35: 279–300.

Lewis, Neil A. 1995. "Bill Seeks to End Automatic Citizenship for All Born in the U.S.," *The New York Times*, December 14, p. A26.

Lively, Kit. 1995. "Judge Says Cal. Ban on Immigrants Is Not Unconstitutional," *Chronicle of Higher Education*, December 1, p. A40.

Manson, Donald M., Thomas J. Espenshade, and Thomas Muller. 1985. "Mexican Immigration to Southern California: Issues of Job Competition and Worker Mobility," *The Review of Regional Studies*, Spring, 15(2): 21–33.

Massey, Douglas S. and Kristin E. Espinosa. 1995. "What's Driving Mexico–U.S. Migration? A Theoretical, Empirical, and Policy Analysis," unpublished manuscript, September, Department of Sociology, University of Pennsylvania.

No Author. 1994. "Checklist: Who's Eligible?" *The New York Times*, June 8, p. B10.

Pear, Robert. 1994. "Deciding Who Gets What in America," *The New York Times*, November 27, p. E5.

Plotkin, Sidney and William E. Scheuerman. 1994. *Private Interest, Public Spending: Balanced-Budget Conservatism and the Fiscal Crisis*. Boston: South End Press.

Rothman, Eric S. and Thomas J. Espenshade. 1992. "Fiscal Impacts of Immigration to the United States," *Population Index*, Fall, 58(3): 381–415.

State and Local Coalition on Immigration. 1994a. "Justice Department Reimburses States for Imprisoning Illegal Criminal Felons," *Immigrant Policy News...(Inside the Beltway)*, 1(9), November 7, Washington, D.C.

——.1994b. "Three More States Sue Feds for Costs of Immigration," *Immigrant Policy News...The State-Local Report*, 1(2), November 9, Washington, D.C.

——.1995a. "Amendment to Create National Proposition 187 Withdrawn," *Immigrant Policy News...(Inside the Beltway)*, 2(7), August 31, Washington, D.C.

——.1995b. *California State Ballot Initiative on Undocumented Immigrants (Proposition 187)*. Immigrant Policy Project, February 28. Washington, D.C.

——.1995c. "Florida Receives Assistance From Federal Immigration Emergency Fund," *Immigrant Policy News...(Inside the Beltway)*, 2(7), August 31, Washington, D.C.

——.1995d. "Overview of Major Welfare/Immigration Bills and Current Law–104th Congress," *Immigrant Policy News...(Inside the Beltway)*, 2(6), July 12, Washington, D.C.

——.1996. "Welfare Reform Legislation Zooms to Completion," *Immigrant Policy News...(Inside the Beltway)*, 3(5), August 2, Washington, D.C.

Teitelbaum, Michael S. and Myron Weiner. 1995. "Introduction: Threatened Peoples, Threatened Borders: Migration and U.S. Foreign Policy," in Michael S. Teitelbaum and Myron Weiner, eds, *Threatened Peoples, Threatened Borders: World Migration and U.S. Policy*. New York: W. W. Norton and Company, pp. 13–38.

U.S. Bureau of the Census. 1995. "The Foreign-Born Population: 1994," *Current Population Reports*, August, P20–486. Washington, D.C.: U.S. Government Printing Office.

U.S. Commission on Immigration Reform. 1994. *U.S. Immigration Policy: Restoring Credibility*. 1994 Executive Summary, September. Washington, D.C.

———.1995. *Legal Immigration: Setting Priorities.* 1995 Executive Summary, June. Washington, D.C.

U.S. General Accounting Office. 1994. *Illegal Aliens: Assessing Estimates of Financial Burden on California.* November, GAO/HEHS-95-22. Washington, D.C.

———.1995a. *Illegal Aliens: National Net Cost Estimates Vary Widely.* July, GAO/HEHS-95-133. Washington, D.C.

———.1995b. *Welfare Reform: Implications of Proposals on Legal Immigrants'' Benefits.* February, GAO/HEHS-95-58. Washington, D.C.

Vernez, Georges and Kevin McCarthy. 1995. *The Fiscal Costs of Immigration: Analytical and Policy Issues.* Center for Research on Immigration Policy, DRU-958-1-IF, February. Santa Monica, CA: The Rand Corporation.

White, Michael J. and Lori M. Hunter. 1993. "The Migratory Response of Native-Born Workers to the Presence of Immigrants in the Labor Market," Working Paper Series 93–08, Population Studies and Training Center, Brown University.

Whitney, Craig R. 1996. "Europeans Redefine What Makes a Citizen," *The New York Times,* January 7, p. E6.

12 Foreign Investment: A Neglected Variable

Saskia Sassen

There is considerable evidence both on international labor migrations and on the internationalization of production. But they are mostly two separate bodies of scholarship. Analytically these two processes have been constructed into unrelated categories. As socioeconomic givens, there are certain locations where one can identify the presence of both. Our question then becomes whether there is an articulation between these two processes and, if so, how we can capture this analytically. Furthermore, the notion of the internationalization of production needs to be elaborated in order to incorporate more of its central components. Theoretical and empirical studies of this process have focused largely on one particular component: the massive shift of jobs to Third World countries through direct foreign investment, resulting in the development of an off-shore manufacturing sector.

The question about the articulation of these two processes stems from both a broader theoretical argument on the nature of the world economy and from the concrete details of the new migrations to the U.S. Similarly, the need to elaborate the notion of the internationalization of production stems from that broader theoretical argument as well as from the concrete details of the U.S. economy over the last twenty years. In this chapter I briefly review the main conceptual and empirical lines of analysis that bring these various concerns together.

The new Asian and Caribbean Basin immigration to the U.S. reveals patterns that escape prevailing explanations of why migrations occur. Two of these patterns are of interest here. One concerns the timing, magnitude and origins of the new immigration. Why did the new immigration take place at a time of high unemployment in the U.S., including major job losses in sectors traditionally employing immigrants, and of high growth rates in the major immigrant sending countries? There are two separate issues worth considering here, to with, the *initiation* of a new migration flow and its *continuation* at ever higher levels. Understanding why a migration began entails an examination of conditions promoting outmigration in countries of origin and the formation of objective and subjective linkages with receiving countries that make such migration feasible. Understanding why a migration flow continues and sustains high levels invites an examination of demand conditions in the receiving country. This brings up the second pattern, the continuing concentration of the new immigration in several major cities which are global centers for highly specialized service and headquarters activities, an economic base we do not usually associate with immigrant labor. The questions raised by these patterns in the new immigration become particularly acute when we consider that the major immigrant-sending countries are among the leading recipients of the jobs lost in the U.S. and of U.S. direct foreign investment in labor-intensive manufacturing and service activities. If anything, this combination of conditions should have been a deterrent to the emergence of new migrations or at least a disincentive to their continuation at growing levels. Why is it that the rapidly industrializing countries of South-East Asia, typically seen as the success stories of the Third World, are the leading senders of the new immigrants? I will briefly examine each of these patterns.

Immigrant entry levels since the late 1960s are among the highest in U.S. immigration history. Legally admitted immigrants numbered 265,000 in 1960. By 1970 such entries reached half a million, a level sustained since then with a gradual tendency to increase over the years. The overall estimate now is that the combination of all different types of entry had reached about 1 million a year by 1980 (see INS, 1978; 1985; Teitelbaum, 1985). The highest numbers of immigrants from 1970 to 1980 came from Mexico, the Philippines, and South Korea, followed by China (Taiwan and People's Republic), India, the Dominican Republic, Jamaica, Colombia, and several Caribbean Basin countries. New entries and natural growth resulted in the pronounced expansion of the Asian and Hispanic populations in the U.S. From 1970 to 1980, the Asian population increased by 100 percent and the Hispanic by 62 percent (U.S. Bureau of the Census, 1981b,c). These growth rates were surpassed by some nationalities, notably the 412 percent increase of South Koreans.

The new Caribbean Basin and South-East Asian immigration, by far the largest share in the current immigration, is heavily concentrated in cities with high job losses in older industries, and job growth in high-technology industries and specialized services. Asians have gone largely to Los Angeles, San Francisco, and New York City; these have the three largest concentrations of Asians. West Indians and the new Hispanics (excluding Mexicans and Cubans) have gone largely to New York City. What conditions in the economies of these cities have facilitated the absorption of such massive immigrant flows and induced their continuation at ever higher levels? The fact that these are traditional destinations and contain large immigrant communities goes a way towards answering the question. And so does the fact that declining sectors of the economy need cheap labor for survival. But the magnitude and new origins of the immigrant influx, its continuation at ever higher levels and the extent of job losses in sectors historically employing immigrants point to the need for additional explanations.

The increase in immigration took place at a time of rather high economic growth in most countries of origin. For example, annual GNP growth in the decade of the seventies hovered around 5 to 9 percent for most of these countries. Growth rates in manufacturing employment were even higher. Massive increases in direct foreign investment, mostly from the U.S. but also from Japan and Europe, contributed to these growth rates.

While U.S. direct foreign investment generally accelerated from 1965 to 1980 and continues to go to Europe and Canada, it quintupled in the less developed countries. This is a noteworthy trend, since much of it goes to a few select countries in the Caribbean Basin and South-East Asia. The average annual growth rate of U.S. direct foreign investment from 1950 to 1966 was 11.7 percent for developed countries and 6.2 percent for developing countries; from 1966 to 1973 these rates were, respectively, 10.7 percent and 9.7 percent, and, from 1973 to 1980, 11.8 percent and 14.2 percent (these figures exclude the petroleum industry). There has also been a massive increase of Western European direct foreign investment during the 1970s, mostly in these same countries. Given the particular conceptualization of the migration impact of such investment briefly described later in this chapter, this increase of European and Japanese investment in countries sending migrants to the U.S. is also significant. The average annual growth rates of direct foreign investment in developing countries by all major industrial countries were 7 percent from 1960 to 1968; 9.2 percent from 1968 to 1973, and 19.4 percent from 1973 to 1978.

Furthermore, a growing share of direct foreign investment in developing countries over the last two decades has gone into production for export, mostly to the U.S. As I will discuss later, export manufacturing and export-agriculture tend to be highly labor-intensive kinds of production which have mobilized new segments of the population into waged-labor and into regional migrations. The main migrant-sending countries to the U.S. over the last fifteen years all have received large export-oriented foreign investment. This would seem to go against a central proposition in the development literature, to wit, since foreign investment creates jobs it should act as a deterrent to emigration; this deterrent should be particularly strong in countries with high levels of export-oriented investment because of its labor-intensive nature.

Using Export Processing Zones (EPZs) as an indicator of export-oriented direct foreign investment, a distinct pattern emerges. These zones, all built in the last fifteen years, tend to be concentrated in a few countries, most of which represent the areas of origin of the overwhelming share of new immigrants. In Latin America, and the Caribbean, the three countries with the largest number of zones are Mexico, Colombia and the Dominican Republic. In 1975 they accounted for sixteen of the twenty-two zones. These are also countries with large export-agriculture sectors. And they account for a very large share of all Hispanic immigrants. We find a similar situation in South-East Asia. The question then is whether there is any connection between large increases in foreign investment and large-scale emigration.

While the change in U.S. immigration legislation can explain a good part of the increase in entries to the U.S. after 1965, it is insufficient to explain the magnitude of the increase and the disproportionate weight of certain countries of origin. Indeed, the family reunion emphasis in the 1965 legislation was expected to bring in largely Europeans because the main immigrant stock in the U.S. was European. It was not expected that Asian and Caribbean Basin nationalities would dominate the flow and would do so in such high numbers. This lack of correspondence between the expectations associated with the legislation changes and the ensuing reality has led one historian to call the 1965 Immigration and Naturalization Act the "unintended reform" (Reimers, 1983).

Though not necessarily addressed directly to these questions, the migration literature does contain partial explanations as to why migration would occur under the conditions described above. Elements of answers can be found in explanations that emphasize a combination of strong push factors such as high unemployment in the sending country; resources for mobility, i.e., it is not the poorest who migrate; and *perceived* opportunity in the country of destination (Reubens, 1981). Secondly, explanations that emphasize the importance of an already existing immigrant community as a pull factor and as a structure that facilitates access to employment and housing for newly arrived immigrants (Chaney, 1976; Wilson and Portes, 1980; Sassen-Koob, 1979). Thirdly, explanations that emphasize the internal differentiation of the labor market in industrialized countries to explain the co-existence of growing unemployment and relative labor scarcity in declining and/or backward industries in need of cheap labor for survival (Piore, 1979; Bailey and Freedman, 1981). Fourthly, an elaboration of this last type of explanation which emphasizes the different requirements for control over labor at the workplace that characterize different types of work organization; thus it is not primarily the low wages of immigrants but their willingness to work at certain kinds of jobs, which explains their obtaining employment in the face of growing unemployment (Sassen-Koob, 1980). Finally, analyses of immigration policies (Keely, 1979) and of the role of the state in regulating the labor supply (Bach, 1978). In sum, the push of unemployment, the pull of an existing immigrant community, and the need for cheap labor in declining and backward industries are elements for an explanation about high immigration in a period of high unemployment in the U.S.

But the developments of the last fifteen years in international and domestic aspects of the U.S. economy point to a need for refinement of existing explanations and specification of additional variables. Important contributions in this direction, and ones I will draw on, can be found in the studies on the relation between U.S. investment in Mexico and Mexican immigration (Cornelius, 1981; Fernandez Kelly, 1983); U.S. investment in Puerto Rico and emigration (Centro de Estudios Puertorriqueños, 1979); U.S. investment in the Caribean Basin and emigration (Ricketts, 1983); immigration and foreign policy (Keely, 1979) and characteristics of the international system as they affect migration (Portes and Walton, 1981). This body of scholarship brings to the fore the active participation of the U.S. through investment and other development programs in creating linkages that contributed, directly or indirectly, to emigration. The clearest historical example is Puerto

Rico where by the late 1940s the impact of U.S. investment and modernization of the economy had resulted in the formation of a vast supply of migrant workers (Centro de Estudios Puertorrique-ños, 1979). This study attempts to continue this theoretical and empirical work, but the focus is somewhat less on migration and somewhat more on economic restructuring processes in sending and receiving areas.

The foremost concern is not a full explanation of emigration. Nor is the focus one that can account for the various stages in international migrations. Rather, the concern is with capturing the particular moment in the process of labor migration that links it with fundamental processes in the contemporary phase of the world economy. The overall theoretical stance is that to specify the place of labor migration in a particular historical period, within the general history of capitalist development, we need to identify the modes of articulation with the leading economic dynamic of that period. This is not to deny the many general conditions at work in all migrations nor the different individual reasons for migrating. The specificity of labor migration in the current historical period lies not in these general conditions or individual motivations but in its articulation with the internationalization of production, a dynamic which assumes concrete forms in particular locations.

The Growth of Direct Foreign Investment and the Uprooting of People

The generalization of market relations and the development of modern forms of production have historically had a disruptive effect on traditional work structures. The argument, briefly, is as follows.

The expansion of export manufacturing and export agriculture, both inseparably related with direct foreign investment from the highly industrialized countries, has mobilized new segments of the population into regional and long-distance migrations. I am using the term "mobilize" somewhat freely to refer to a variety of processes. First, the transformation of subsistence workers into wage-labor, either directly, e.g., through large-scale employment in commercial agriculture, or indirectly, through rural to urban migration due to small farmers' displacement by commercial agriculture. Even if these rural migrants fail to find a job in the city, they have been mobilized into an urban reserve of wage-labor.

Second, the recruitment practices of foreign plants, notably world market factories and plants in Export Processing Zones, have led to a large-scale movement of young women into waged labor (UNIDO, 1980; Lim, 1980; Wong, 1980; Grossman, 1979). Electronics plants, especially semi-conductor assembly plants, require highly disciplined workers. Young women in patriarchal societies are probably among the more controllable workers (Safa, 1981; Grossman, 1979), at least initially.

One key process mediating between the introduction of these modern forms of production and the formation of labor migrations is the disruption of traditional work structures. The mechanisms involved are quite different in the case of export manufacturing from those in commercial agriculture. The development of commercial agriculture, which is almost completely for export, has directly displaced small farmers who are left without means of subsistence. This forces them to become wage-laborers in commercial agriculture or to migrate to cities. Sometimes the move from sharecropper or subsistence farmer to rural wage-laborer becomes a move to another country, e.g., Colombians in Venezuela agriculture or Mexicans in U.S. agriculture. Sometimes this move becomes a move to an urban job in another country, e.g., Dominicans to New York City.

In export manufacturing this disruption is mediated by a massive recruitment of young women into newly created jobs. The mobilization effect has been particularly strong due to the high degree of concentration of the employment effects of direct foreign investment in manufacturing in a few countries. The "new industrialization" has generated domestic and international migrations *within* the regions which eventually may overflow into long-distance migrations. These migrations have been found to contribute to the disruption of traditional, often unwaged, employment structures. This disruption reduces the possibility of returning if laid-off or unsuccessful in the job search. The available evidence shows a large mobilization of young women into waged labor, women who under other conditions would not have entered waged employment. This has an additional disruptive effect on traditional employment structures, notably household production for internal consumption or local markets. The feminization of the new proletariat has also been found to contribute to male unemployment and, in several cases, to male emigration. It does so both directly and indirectly. There is now a female labor supply competing for jobs with men, a supply that did not exist only a few years ago. An indirect emigration inducement among males results from the disruption of traditional work structures: with the massive departure of young women there is a reduction in the possibilities of making a living in many of these rural areas. Eventually this disruption of traditional work structures adds to the pool of unemployed. Finally, the widespread practice of firing the new, mostly female, workers after a few years also adds to a pool of potential emigrants. These women, left unemployed and westernized, may have few options but emigration.

Though these developments are not necessarily a function of foreign investment *per se*, it seems important to emphasize the presence of foreign investment. First, because in the absence of such investment the large-scale development of export manufacturing and export agriculture could not have occurred. Here I want to emphasize that foreign investment stands for a variety of arrangements, some involving direct ownership, others consisting of subcontracting with domestic producers, and yet others being simply foreign buying groups. The key is that these developing countries could not have penetrated the export market in the absence of these arrangements with foreign investors which *have* access to those markets. Second, because the presence of such investment creates cultural–ideological and objective links with the countries providing this capital. And these are of course largely the highly industrialized countries which have also been major recipients of immigration from the less developed countries. Besides the long recognized westernization effect of large-scale foreign investment in the less developed world, there is the more specific impact on workers employed in production for export or in services in the export sector. These workers are using their labor power in the production of goods and services demanded by people and firms in the U.S. or any other highly developed country. The distance between a job in the off-shore plant or office and in the *on*-shore plant or office is subjectively reduced. Under these conditions emigration may begin to emerge as an option actually felt by individuals.

Foreign plants are a factor establishing linkages with the U.S., especially cultural ones. The workers mobilized into wage-labor on plantations or world market factories probably are only a small share of those that make use of these linkages. But they are part of the linkage for potential emigrants. On the other hand, those employed in services and office work necessary for the export sector are more likely to become part of the pool of emigrants. The ideological effect is not to be underestimated: the presence of foreign plants not only brings the U.S. or any other "western" country closer, but it also "westernizes" the less developed country and its people. Emigration to the U.S. emerges as an option. In an "isolated" country, that is one lacking extensive direct foreign investment, emigration would be quite unlikely to emerge as such an option.

This is a highly mediated process, one wherein direct foreign investment is not a cause but a structure that creates certain conditions for emigration to emerge as an option. Furthermore, it is important to differentiate those workers actually employed in foreign plants, offices and plantations and those representing the supply of potential emigrants. They are often not the same individuals.

Under these conditions, the origin of the foreign capital may matter less than the types of production it goes into. Thus, the large increase in direct foreign investment by all major industrialized countries will tend to have similar effects. It is in this context that the 1965 Immigration Act and the continued image of the U.S. as a land of opportunity acquire their full impact. Whether West German, Dutch or U.S., foreign investment may well have the effect of promoting emigration to the U.S.

Continued vitality of the U.S. as an immigration country and the absence of alternatives acquire particular significance in the context of a continuing growth of direct foreign investment and its expansion to additional countries. The general trend is for all the major industrial countries to increase investment in less developed countries. Though most of this investment is concentrated in a few countries, there is also a trend towards significant levels of investment in "new" countries. Accepting my analysis of the effect of direct foreign investment on the formation of a pool of potential emigrants and on the emergence of emigration as an actual option, it could be argued that this expansion of direct foreign investment by the major industrial countries will contribute to additional emigration to the U.S. Proposed changes in U.S. immigration laws would hardly affect these countries which probably have underused entry quotas.

In brief, I examine how significant levels and concentrations of direct foreign investment are one factor promoting emigration through: (a) the incorporation of new segments of the population into wage-labor and the associated disruption of traditional work structures both of which create a supply of migrant workers; (b) the feminization of the new industrial workforce and its impact on the work opportunities of men, both in the new industrial zones and in the traditional work structures; (c) the consolidation of objective and ideological links with the highly industrialized countries where most foreign capital originates, links that involve both a generalized westernization effect and more specific work situations wherein workers find themselves making goods for people and firms in the highly industrialized countries.

What I posit is a generalized effect that contributes to the formation of a pool of potential emigrants and, at the same time, to the emergence of emigration as an actual option. This effect would seem to be present regardless of whether the direct foreign investment originates in the U.S. or in any of the other major advanced industrialized countries. The lasting image of the United States as a land of opportunity, which can only be reinforced by the current massive immigration, will tend to have the effect of making "emigration" identical with "emigration to the U.S."

The Rise of Global Cities and the New Labor Demand

Transformations in the world economy, including that discussed in the preceding section, generate a new or significantly expanded role for major urban centers, particularly in the highly developed countries. The technological transformation of the work process, the shift of manufacturing and routine office work to less developed areas domestically and abroad, in part made possible by the technological transformation of the work process, and the ascendance of the financial sector in management generally with the decline of production focused management, have all contributed to the consolidation of a new kind of economic center, global cities from which the world economy is managed and serviced. That is to say, these trends have intensified the role of major urban centers as producers and exporters of advanced services, including finance and management and control functions. Alongside the growing decentralization of manufacturing and office work we see the growing concentration of high-level servicing, control and management operations.

While the redeployment of manufacturing and office work to less developed countries has contributed to conditions that promote emigration from these countries, the concentration of servicing and management functions in global cities has contributed to conditions for the demand and absorption of the immigrant influx in cities like New York, Los Angeles and Houston. *The same set of basic processes that has promoted emigration from several rapidly industrializing countries has also promoted immigration into several booming global cities.* The growth conditions in both types of areas will, doubtlessly, become exhausted. But in the meantime they will have created major transformations in the economic and population dynamics of the areas involved.

The consolidation of such global centers generates a restructuring of labor demand. The job supply is shaped by several key trends, notably (a) the growth of the advanced service sector, including the financial system, and (b) the shrinking of traditional manufacturing industries and their replacement with a downgraded manufacturing sector and high technology industries, in both of which sweatshops are mushrooming. The evidence shows that the result is an expansion of very high-income professional and technical jobs, a shrinking of middle income blue-and white-collar jobs, and a vast expansion of low-wage jobs. The expansion of the low-wage job supply is in good part a function of growth sectors and only secondarily of declining industries in need of cheap labor for survival. It is in this expansion of the low-wage job supply that we find the conditions for the absorption of the immigrant influx.

Immigration can be seen as providing labor for (1) low-wage service jobs, including those that *service* (a) the expanding, highly specialized, export-oriented service sector and (b) the high-income lifestyles of the growing top level professional workforce employed in that sector; (2) the expanding downgraded manufacturing sector, including but not exclusively, declining industries in need of cheap labor for survival, as well as dynamic electronics sectors, some of which can actually be seen as part of the downgraded sector. A third source of jobs for immigrants, is the immigrant community itself (Light, 1972; Chaney, 1976; Portes and Bach, 1980). These jobs include not only those that are a temporary arrangement until a job in the mainstream society can be found. They include also a large array of professional and technical jobs that service the expanding and increasingly income-stratified immigrant communities in the city (Cohen and Sassen-Koob, 1982). And they include jobs that produce services and goods for the subsistence of members of the community, and therewith contribute to lower the costs of survival – both for themselves and, ultimately, for their employers.

The redeployment of manufacturing and the associated international trade in specialized services, contain new business opportunities for major urban centers. There has been a sharp rise in the national and international demand for specialized services, induced both by the dispersion of manufacturing and clerical work and by the technological transformation of work. Thus this growth rests in part on the crisis of traditional manufacturing. While a city like Detroit just loses factories, New York and Los Angeles find new business opportunities in their own *and* Detroit's factory losses. Furthermore, unlike what is the case with other kinds of services, production of specialized services does not tend to follow population patterns. On the contrary, they are subject to agglomeration economies and hence tend towards strong locational concentration and production for export nationally and internationally. Since the highly specialized service sector is the most dynamic in the U.S. economy, its concentration in major cities also entails that these come to contain a disproportionate component of national economic growth.

The timing, magnitude and destination of the new immigration become particularly noteworthy when juxtaposed with the pronounced changes in the job supply in major urban centers. I will be particularly interested in examining the generation of low-wage jobs in major growth sectors, the advanced services and the downgraded manufacturing sector. I use the term downgraded manufacturing sector to refer to both the downgrading of old industries, e.g., replacing unionized shops with sweatshops and industrial homework, and to the prevalence of low-wage, dead-end production jobs in new industries, particularly in the field of high technology. What is notable is that even the most dynamic and technologically developed sectors of the economy, such as the advanced services and high-technology industries generate a considerable supply of low-wage jobs with few skill and language proficiency requirements.

Two analytical distinctions important to my argument are (a) the distinction between job characteristics and sector characteristics, and (b) the distinction between sector characteristics and growth status. Thus, backward jobs can be part of the most modern sector of the economy and backward sectors can be part of major growth trends in the economy. Use of these two kinds of distinctions allows me to explain the presence of immigrants in technologically developed sectors of the economy and it allows me to posit that the downgraded manufacturing sector – also an important employer of immigrants – is part of major growth trends.

References

Bach, Robert L., 1978. "Mexican immigration and the American state," *International Migration Review* 12 (Winter): 536–58.

Bailey, Tom and Marcia Freedman, 1981. "The restaurant industry in New York City." New York: Conservation of Human Resources, Columbia University. Project on Newcomers to New York City (Conservation of Human Resources). Working Paper No. 2.

Centro de Estudios Puertorriqueños, 1979. *Labor Migration Under Capitalism: The Puerto Rican Experience.* History Task Force. New York: Monthly Review Press.

Chaney, Elsa, 1976. *Colombian Migration to the United States* (Part 2). Occasional Monograph Series, Smithsonian Institution, Interdisciplinary Communications Program, vol. 2, no. 5.

Cohen, S. and Saskia Sassen-Koob, 1982. "Survey of six immigrant groups in Queens." Department of Sociology, Queens College, City University of New York.

Cornelius, Wayne A. 1981. *Mexican Migration to the U.S.: The Limits of Governmental Intervention. Working Papers,* No. 5. Center for U.S.–Mexican Studies, University of California, San Diego.

Fernandez Kelly, Maria Patricia, 1983. *For We Are Sold, I and My People: Women and Industry in Mexico's Frontier.* Albany: SUNY Press.

Grossman, Rachael, 1979. "Women's place in the integrated circuit," *Southeast Asia Chronicle 66–Pacific Research 9* (Joint Issue): 2–17.

INS [Immigration and Naturalization Service], 1972. *Annual Report.* Washington, D.C.: U.S. Government Printing Office.

1978. *Annual Report.* U.S. Gov. P.O.

1985. *Annual Report,* U.S. Gov. P.O.

Keely, Charles B. 1979. *U.S. Immigration: A Policy Analysis.* New York: The Population Council.

Light, Ivan, 1972. *Ethnic Enterprise in America.* Berkeley: University of California Press.

Lim, L. Y. C., 1980. "Women workers in multinational corporations: the case of the electronics industry in Malaysia and Singapore," in Krishna Kumar, *Transational Enterprises: Their Impact on Third World Societies and Cultures.* Boulder, CO: Westview Press.

Piore, Michael P., 1979. *Birds of Passage: Migrant Labor and Industrial Societies.* Cambridge University Press.

Portes, Alejandro and R. L. Bach, 1980. "Immigrant earnings: Cuban and Mexican immigrants in the United States," *International Migration Review* 14: 315–41.

Portes, Alejandro and John Walton, 1981. *Labor, Class and the International System.* New York: Academic Press.

Reimers, David M., 1983. "An unintended reform: the 1965 Immigration Act and Third World Immigration to the U.S.," *Journal of American Ethnic History* 3 (Fall): 9–28.

Reubens, E. P., 1981. "Interpreting migration: current models and a new integration." Paper presented at the New York Research Program in Inter-American Affairs at New York University on Hispanic Migration to New York City: Global Trends and Neighborhood Change (December).

Ricketts, Erol R., 1983. "Periphery to Core Migration: Specifying a Model." Unpublished Ph.D. dissertation, University of Chicago, Department of Sociology.

Safa, Helen I., 1981. "Runaway shops and female employment: the search for cheap labor," *Signs* 7 (2; Winter): 418–33.

Sassen-Koob, Saskia, 1979. "Colombians and Dominicans in New York City," *International Migration Review* 13 (Summer): 314–31.

———. 1980. "Immigrant and minority workers in the organization of the labor process," *Journal of Ethnic Studies* 8 (Spring).

Teitelbaum, Michael S., 1985. *Latin Migration North: The Problem for U.S. Foreign Policy*. New York: Council on Foreign Relations.

UNIDO [United Nations Industrial Development Organization], 1980. *Export Processing Zones in Developing Countries*. Working Papers on Structural Change No. 19. New York: UNIDO.

United States Department of Commerce, Bureau of the Census, 1981b. *1980 Census of Population, Supplementary Report*. Washington D.C.: U.S. Government Printing Office.

———. 1981c. *1980 Census of Population and Housing: Advance Report*. Washington D.C.: U.S. Government Printing Office.

Wilson, Kenneth L. and Alejandro Portes, 1980. "Immigrant enclaves: an analysis of the labor market experiences of Cubans in Miami," *American Journal of Sociology* 86: 295–319 (Sept.).

Wong, A.K. 1980. *Economic Development and Women's Place: Women in Singapore. International Reports: Women and Society*. London: Change.

13 Immigrant Entrepreneurs in America: Koreans in Los Angeles

Ivan Light

In the mid-1970s, Los Angeles became aware that a large and rapidly growing Korean colony had formed along Olympic Boulevard about three miles west of the Civic Center. Anyone traveling down this boulevard would notice the many English/Hangul-lettered signs proclaiming the presence of Korean small businesses. The growing Korean colony was the more striking because in 1970 hardly any Koreans had resided in Los Angeles. In recognition of the new Korean enclave, and in response to repeated requests from the Koreatown Development Association, the City of Los Angeles proclaimed the Olympic Boulevard neighborhood "Koreatown" in 1980, and posted signs so stating on major streets and freeways. Representing, by 1980, about four-fifths of one percent of the total population of Los Angeles County, 60,618 Koreans were still a numerically small minority even after a decade of immigration. Nonetheless, the Korean minority was conspicuous among those "persevering Asians" whom the *Los Angeles Times* editorially identified as the city's "new middle class" chiefly on the basis of their visibility in small business.[1]

The extent of Korean entrepreneurship was, in fact, remarkable. In 1982, the yellow pages of the Korean telephone directory enumerated 4,266 Korean-owned business firms in Los Angeles County, approximately 2.6 percent of all county firms. In retail trade, Koreans operated nearly 5 percent of all firms in the county. Since Koreans numbered less than one percent of county population, their "overrepresentation" was appreciable in business, especially retail business. However, other measures discovered even higher "overrepresentation" in business. A Korean-American scholar found that 40 percent of Korean heads of household were self-employed in 1978 compared to only 7.6 percent of the Los Angeles County population. Moreover, these Korean entrepreneurs employed an additional 40 percent of coethnics in their firms so that fully 80 percent of employed Koreans in Los Angeles County actually worked in Korean-owned firms, mostly service and retail proprietorships.

As these figures suggest, Koreans did not achieve so large a small-business sector by reliance upon coethnic customers. Of course, some Korean-owned stores specialized exclusively in coethnic trade. However, taking all the Korean firms together, only about one-fourth of their customers were Korean, while three-quarters were non-Korean. Blacks, whites, and Hispanics each represented about one-quarter of the Koreans' customers, but, in view of their representation in county population, blacks were overrepresented twofold and whites appreciably underrepresented by their quarters. Hispanics were represented at approximately their expected number.

Korean entrepreneurship did not develop in what mainstream business corporations regarded as an attractive business climate. Despite its glittering reputation, Los Angeles suffered the blighted conditions common among big American cities. Crime, unemployment, residential crowding, time consumed in the journey to work, and housing prices all increased faster than national averages in the 1970s. *De facto* segregation of public schools was not reduced, and educational quality declined. These changes accompanied demographic trends generally indicating lower socioeconomic population characteristics in the urban core relative to the ring – and increased residential segregation of whites from blacks, Asians, and Hispanics. The percentage white in the city's population declined from 59.0 in 1970 to 44.4 in 1980. In the surrounding county of Los Angeles, the percentage white declined from 65.9 percent to 49.4 percent.

More to the point, the growth of retail business firms was negligible in both the city and the surrounding county, but the suburban ring registered a 23 percent increase. As measured by employees, the average size of retail firms increased in the ring, but decreased in the core. Service firms increased 59 percent in city and county, but in the outer ring service firms increased 118 percent. Average size of service firms increased in the core as well as in the ring, but it increased much faster in the ring. Although typically small "mom and pop" stores, Korean firms were not the smallest firms in the non-agricultural economy. True, Korean firms in Los Angeles were smaller than the average of all firms in terms of employees, legal form of organization, and invested capital. However, since this average of all firms includes large corporations, it diminishes by contrast the relative stature of Korean firms. Compared to proprietorships, Korean firms were larger than average in employees and invested capital.

Benefits of Korean Entrepreneurship

Korean-owned firms conferred obvious economic benefits upon Los Angeles in that they serviced low income, heavily non-white neighborhoods generally ignored and underserved by big retail corporations. As a result, wheels of commerce ground where they would otherwise have been still, and the City of Los Angeles took a percentage in sales tax. Additionally, the Koreans injected foreign capital into the Los Angeles economy, thus stimulating employment and earnings. Some Americans had jobs in Korean-owned firms established with Korean capital. When these Americans spent their paychecks, other Americans became indirect beneficiaries of Korean immigration and entrepreneurship.

Despite these economic benefits, Koreans experienced conflicts with some Americans as a result of their rapid influx and concentration in mercantile roles. The most serious tensions arose between Korean merchants and black customers in central Los Angeles. Some blacks complained about high prices in Korean stores, discourteous service, non-employment of blacks in Korean firms, and the tendency for Korean merchants to reside outside the black neighborhoods in which they located their markets. Indeed, Los Angeles' black newspaper, *The Sentinel*, complained that when Korean merchants replaced Jewish predecessors, blacks who had been working in the stores lost their jobs and prices increased. Nonetheless, black efforts to boycott Korean merchants fizzled because black leaders opposed a boycott that they regarded as extreme, unwarranted, and impolitic. In addition, black consumers had no realistic alternative to shopping in Korean markets. Finally, Los Angeles Koreans made intelligent efforts to reduce intergroup tensions having learned about earlier black–Korean conflict in Washington, D.C.; Philadelphia; and New York City. Therefore, Los Angeles' Korean organizations arranged a "treaty" of cooperation with black civic organizations. Korean and black leaders toasted this treaty at a festive banquet. Although this treaty did not prevent tensions, it greatly reduced black interest in a boycott.

Korean entrepreneurship conferred social as well as economic benefits upon Los Angeles. The Korean influx tended to restore and revive the neighborhoods in which Koreans settled. In addition to Koreatown, residential home of one-third of county Koreans, Koreans clustered in a handful of widely scattered locations, often associating with other Asians. Koreatown itself developed in a deteriorating, underutilized area on the northern boundary of the city's black ghetto. As Koreans moved in, this neighborhood's appearance and prosperity revived. Property values increased. As the *Los Angeles Times* editorially observed:

> Koreans have taken run-down structures, weedy lots, and neglected streets in the previously declining area, and turned them into thriving businesses interspersed with clean, landscaped areas.[2]

Further, residential and commercial interests compelled Koreans to take a stand against street crime. Unlike whites who fled to the suburbs, Koreans were tethered to inner-city businesses and to Koreatown. Crime rendered Koreatown stores and streets unprofitable as well as unsafe. Hard as it was for Koreatown residents to tolerate street crime, it was impossible for Koreatown merchants who required safe streets and parking lots in order to guarantee access to their business premises. Moreover, retail store and service proprietors lived in fear of armed robbers whose street culture had discovered the wisdom of routinely murdering victims and witnesses. Several Korean merchants died at the hands of gunmen. The Korean Chamber of Commerce accordingly undertook vigorous anti-crime campaigns in Koreatown. Koreans demanded additional police protection and, when politicians were insufficiently accommodating, Koreans conducted public subscriptions to pay for a bilingual police outpost in Koreatown, citizen patrols of Koreatown streets, anti-crime seminars, and even anti-crime billboard advertising in the Korean language.

Ambitious Koreans also raised the level of achievement in the public schools. Korean parents encouraged their children to excel in school. As a result, Korean students were outstanding academic achievers in the public schools, easily winning more than their share of honors, prizes, and college scholarships. In 1982 Koreans represented 2.9 percent of the undergraduate student body at the University of California, Los Angeles even though Koreans numbered less than one percent of Los Angeles County population. In a national context of deteriorating academic performance, the Koreans' academic achievements were the more noteworthy in Los Angeles, whose public schools suffered worse-than-average deterioration as a result of the flight of middle class and white households to secure suburbs.

Adverse Consequences of Entrepreneurship

Although immensely valuable to Los Angeles, Korean entrepreneurship did promote two adverse and usually ignored consequences. First, most Korean-owned garment firms employed undocumented workers. The garment industry in Los Angeles grew rapidly in the 1970s largely as a result of an influx of cheap but undocumented labor from Mexico. By the end of the decade, the garment industry generated more gross sales than the movie industry. Three hundred fifty Korean firms represented about 15 percent of garment factories in Los Angeles in 1979. According to a spokesman for the Korean garment contractors, the Korean firms employed 20,000 women workers in 1980. Like other employers in this industry, Koreans hired undocumented Mexican seamstresses. About 80 percent of workers in the Los Angeles garment industry were undocumented in 1979. Although growth of the garment industry brought welcome income into central Los Angeles, a depressed inner city, the price of this income was augmentation of the illegal worker population. Assuming that Korean garment factories hired the expected share of illegal workers, neither more nor less than the mean for their industry, Korean garment factories provided employment for 16,000 undocumented women, thus encouraging more migration of undocumented workers to Los Angeles. Since Korean-owned garment factories represented about one-tenth of Korean firms in 1980, the proportion of Korean firms that utilized undocumented labor was appreciable, and Korean firms made a small but consequential contribution to the county's population of undocumented workers.

Second, Korean entrepreneurship sometimes entailed violation of laws protecting public morals, health, or labor standards. In 1979 Los Angeles police undertook an investigation of 60 Korean-owned massage parlors mostly located in seedy Hollywood areas. Suspected of fronting for prostitution, the Korean massage parlors represented about 15 percent of massage parlors then licensed in the city of Los Angeles. No convictions resulted, but in April 1984 a Superior Court judge held two Koreans in contempt of court and fined them $1,000 for employing ex-prostitutes in their massage parlor. Police investigations of organized crime in Koreatown also turned up four extortion gangs of which the largest, the Korean Killers, was estimated to have as many as 250 members. According to police, a "favorite" business of Korean gangs was to extort protection payments from operators of massage parlors. A vice squad detective alleged that by 1984 Koreans owned "just about all the massage parlors in Los Angeles." This network of massage parlors required protection. In 1981 the Los Angeles Police Chief charged that a Korean "godfather" operated an organized crime syndicate with 400 hoodlums on the payroll. However, police only arrested three Koreans in a drive to break up this syndicate (whose alleged boss was never named although rumors circulating in Koreatown identified him as the president of a big Koreatown commercial association).

Other violations of law were undramatic but telling. Korean packing houses and restaurants came under investigation for violations of the labor and sanitary code. Inspectors found rat feces and vermin on the premises of Korean packing houses. Korean restaurant workers prepared food on the floor. In the garment industry, state task forces collected evidence of rampant sanitary and labor code violations. More than 95 percent of all garment firms were in violation of state or federal standards. Although Koreans were no more culpable than non-Korean garment factory owners, they were perceived to have participated in a general assault on labor standards characteristic of this industry. Police also charged Koreans with practicing acupuncture without licenses, and investigated allegations that Korean employers in a variety of industries were paying workers less than the statutory minimum wage. Admittedly, many Korean violations of business law arose because of language barriers and unfamiliarity with American law. Indeed, Korean industrial associations usually took as their first task the translation of the business code into Korean for the benefit non-English-speaking members. On the other hand, in order to squeeze into already crowded industries, Korean entrepreneurs sometimes had to shave legal corners. In this sense, Korean sanitary and labor code violations were symptoms of the hard struggle Korean entrepreneurs faced in the competitive sector.

Koreans and Other Immigrants

In the number, rate, and size of businesses, Koreans in Los Angeles represented an outstanding example of immigrant entrepreneurship in the United States. However, Korean entrepreneurship is a social force wherever Koreans settle. Since 47 percent of the nation's 355,000 Korean immigrants resided in seven metropolitan areas (of which two are in Southern California), the Korean impact outside Southern California was concentrated in New York, Chicago, Washington, D.C., and San Francisco. Illsoo Kim has provided a descriptive account of Korean entrepreneurship in New York City,[3] and other accounts have documented the same phenomenon in Chicago, Atlanta, and Philadelphia. Hence, the presumption is strong that Korean immigration had the same entrepreneurial impact in other cities that it had more powerfully in Los Angeles.

Of course, Koreans are not the only entrepreneurially inclined new immigrants. Immigrants have been more frequently self-employed than native whites in every decennial census since 1880.[4] As Conk has also observed: "The proportional representation of the foreign born as traders and dealers is remarkably stable... over time."[5] In 1970, for example, the percentage of self-employed in twenty-two large metropolitan regions was 9.8 among foreign-born men, 9.6 among native-born men of foreign parents, and 6.0 among native-born men of native parents.[6] Some evidence suggests that a heavy concentration of foreign-born workers caused a city's business population to increase beyond national averages. For thirty-six metropolitan areas for which data was available, the 1980 Census indicated a positive and statistically significant correlation between percentage of the labor force self-employed and the percentage foreign born: the higher the percentage foreign born, the higher the percentage self-employed in a city.

Although the foreign born in general have always been more frequently self-employed than the native born in general, some foreign groups have always demonstrated higher rates of self-employment than others. Thus, Higgs found that the rate of retail merchants per 1,000 of population in 1900 was 124 among Russians, 58 among Italians, 29 among Irish, and 20 among Swedes.[7] In their probability sample of Providence, Rhode Island, conducted between 1967 and 1969, Goldscheider and Kobrin found that Jews and Italians were still more frequently self-employed than French Canadians, Portuguese, or Irish.[8] Although rates of self-employment declined in every nativity origin group with successive American-born generations, the intergroup differences persisted. That is, in every generation, Italians and especially Jews demonstrated higher rates of self-employment than the other groups. According to Katzman, "Negroes, Mexicans, and Filipinos contain few entrepreneurs... On the other hand, the Chinese and Japanese... produce an extraordinary number of entrepreneurs as do the Russians (mostly Jewish)."[9] Between 1972 and 1977, Asians formed 20.7 firms per 1,000 population, Hispanics 17.2, and blacks 14.9. The U.S. Bureau of the Census also reported that in 1980 self-employed and unpaid family workers were 6.5 percent of urban Asians, 3.9 percent of urban Spanish-origin, 2.3 percent of urban blacks, and 5.7 percent of all urban persons.[10]

Table 13.1 [*orig. table 1*]   Self-employed workers as a percentage of employed persons by detailed nationality origin: United States, 1980

	Employees of Own Corporation	Self-Employed Workers	Unpaid Family Workers
All Persons	2.1	6.8	0.5
Japanese	na	7.9	0.6
Chinese	na	7.2	1.0
Korean	na	11.9	1.6
Vietnamese	na	2.2	0.5
Mexican	na	3.5	0.3
Cuban	na	5.8	0.4
Irish	2.0	6.6	0.5
Italian	3.5	6.9	0.4
Polish	2.5	5.9	0.4

Source: U.S. Bureau of the Census. *Census of Population*. Vol. 1. *Characteristics of the Population*. Ch. C. *General Social and Economic Characteristics*. Pt. 1. *United States Summary*. PC80-1-C1. (Washington, D.C.: United States Government Printing Office, 1983), pp. 159, 165, 173.

Although uncorrected for urban or rural residence, table 13.1 provides comparative data illustrating the unequal entrepreneurship of nine nationality groups in 1980. The table distinguishes three components of the self-employed population: employees of their own corporation, self-employed workers, and unpaid family workers. Employees of own corporation are chiefly professionals, especially medical doctors. Self-employed workers are predominantly nonprofessional. Unpaid family workers and self-employed workers therefore constitute the small business population, which included 7.3 percent of all employed persons in 1980. Table 13.1 also shows that 13.5 percent of Koreans were in the small business population, the largest proportion of any detailed nationality group shown in the census. Among Asians, Japanese, Chinese, and Koreans were more frequently self-employed than the general population, but Vietnamese were noteworthy exceptions. Within the Spanish-origin population, Cubans were more frequently self-employed than Mexicans. European immigrants clustered around the national mean.

However numerous, immigrants do not fan out over the industrial spectrum, participating equally in every trade.[11] Instead, they concentrate in particular industries where they are usually overrepresented. For example, among Koreans in Los Angeles, three-quarters of firms were retail or service proprietorships. Of these, gasoline service stations, wig stores, grocery stores, and liquor stores were the most common. Although case studies of specific immigrant minorities are sparse, documentation currently available identifies several new immigrant groups who have heavily utilized entrepreneurship in identifiable industries and localities. For example, Greeks dominate the pizza business in Connecticut towns;[12] Dominicans are a power in New York City's garment industry;[13] Soviet Jews operate about half the taxi cabs in Los Angeles;[14] and Arabs have taken over much of the grocery industry on Chicago's South Side.[15] Hong Kong Chinese have doubled the number of Chinese-owned businesses in Toronto.[16] Vietnamese merchants created a little-Saigon in Orange County, California where local merchants sought unsuccessfully to ban the posting of business signs in foreign languages. In Sea Drift, Texas, Vietnamese shrimp-fisherman provided unwelcome competition for the whites some of whom turned to the Ku Klux Klan for protection of their industrial interest. In Detroit and Toledo, 54 percent of Arabic-speaking Christians operate grocery stores.[17] Once mostly professionals, especially medical doctors and engineers, South Indians in Southern California have begun to turn to import-export businesses.[18] Especially in big depressed cities, the entrepreneurship of immigrants has become a consequential economic force. Sassen-Koob observes that New York's potpourri of immigrant entrepreneurs generated employment, saved abandoned buildings, revived deteriorating neighborhoods, and generated tax and cash flows. Although the immigrants' investments were "small scale," Sassen-Koob finds them "not insignificant in the context of a city where economic decline affects large sectors of the economy and the population."[19]

North America is not distinctive in recent reports of extensive entrepreneurship among selected immigrant minorities. In Britain, recent sociological research has called attention to the extensive self-employment of Greeks, Italians, Gujaratis, Sikhs, Pakistanis, and Jews.[20] As in the United States, the entrepreneurship of new immigrants in Britain mostly occurs in central areas of depressed cities such as Manchester, Liverpool, and London. Aldrich et al. declare that minority business expansion is occurring "amid the physical and economic decay of the inner city, cheek-by-jowl with declining activity, employment, and population."[21] But the British experience has turned up one important anomaly. In the United States, West Indians have always enjoyed a reputation for entrepreneurship, and still do in Brooklyn, New York where they are most heavily concentrated. For reasons that are not clear, West Indians in Britain have not established a significant record of entrepreneurship in the last decade.

In the 1970s only the Cubans in Miami had developed a complex, interdependent ethnic economy that rivaled the Korean achievement in Los Angeles. Cuban-owned enterprises in Miami increased from 919 in 1967 to 8,000 in 1976.[22] Like Koreans, Cubans concentrated in identifiable industries rather than fanning out over the industrial spectrum in equal proportion. Textiles, leather, construction, finance, and furniture became Cuban specialities; cigar-making had always been Cuban-dominated. Cubans controlled 40 percent of the construction industry in Miami and 20 percent of the banks, in 1980. Another study found that in 1979, 20 percent of Cubans in Miami were self-employed and 40 percent found employment in Spanish-speaking firms owned by coethnics.[23] Moreover, workers in the coethnic economy received returns on their human capital (education, experience, knowledge) nearly equivalent to those paid in the most advantaged primary labor market and far superior to those paid in the secondary labor market, a junkpile of deadend jobs. Enclave employment did not disadvantage immigrant workers, and probably made better opportunities available than they would have found on the general labor market. These Miami results confirm those uncovered by Jeffrey Reitz who studied the economic performance of Slavs, Italians, and Chinese in Toronto.[24] Among Toronto's immigrants, those who worked in the ethnic economy (e.g., a workplace in which they spoke a language other than English) earned better returns on their human capital than immigrants in the English-speaking economy. "For members of minority groups with low levels of education," Reitz concludes, "work in settings controlled by their own group is quite attractive from the standpoint of income opportunity."[25]

Causes of Immigrant Entrepreneurship

The rediscovery of immigrant entrepreneurship in Britain, Canada, and the United States undermined the position of social scientists who, following C. Wright Mills, widely believed that small business had provided an important avenue of social ascent in the past but, in an era of giant corporations, was no longer of economic or social consequence.[26] The resurgence and profitability of immigrant enterprises partially contradicted Mills' claim that small business was an economic anachronism tottering into oblivion. For example, Gelfand reported that in 1880, 43 percent of Jews in Los Angeles were retail or wholesale proprietors.[27] A century later, 40 percent of Koreans in Los Angeles were proprietors, a level hard to reconcile with the claim that small business had become obsolete in the intervening century.

Indeed, the "enclave sector" emerged as an independent mode of structural incorporation to complement wage earning in the primary and secondary sectors of the labor force. Immigrants who developed a business sector enjoyed two major advantages over immigrants who did not. First, immigrant or ethnic business provided coethnics with an alternative to the general labor market, thus reducing the pressure of their numbers on the job supply. Second, ethnic business provided more secure work and higher incomes, accelerating social mobility of the ethnic or immigrant minority. Since this conclusion rehabilitates the old-fashioned view of small business as a viable route of social ascent, the present has swung into closer compatibility with the past than sociologists had earlier believed possible.

The key element of historical continuity is the use of ethnic resources to support the competitive position of individual firms. This bootstrapping method builds entrepreneurship from elements of ethnic culture. Ethnic resources are the social features of a group, which coethnic business owners utilize in business, or from which their business benefits.[28] Ethnic resources include values, knowledge, skills, information, money and work attitudes, solidarity, an orientation to sojourning, and ethnic institutions. If one says, for example, that immigrants work long hours; assume the risk of criminal victimization; are thrifty; express satisfaction with skimpy money rewards; help one another with business skills, information, and purchase of ethnic commodities; cluster in particular industries; combine easily in restraint of trade; or utilize rotating credit associations, one is calling attention to the economic impact of the immigrants' ethnic resources. After all, if others had these resources, their possession would confer no economic advantage upon immigrants. Because ethnic resources cost no money, they are the natural basis upon which impoverished immigrants develop business firms.

One must distinguish ethnic resources from class resources that may, however, be simultaneously present in the same immigrant group. Class resources are cultural and material. On the material side, class resources are private property in the means of production or distribution, wealth, and investments in human capital. On the cultural side, class resources of entrepreneurship are bourgeois values, attitudes, knowledge, and skills transmitted intergenerationally in the course of primary socialization to a class culture.[29] Although hard to differentiate at the margin, class resources and ethnic resources are as different as class culture and ethnic culture. Either is capable of promoting entrepreneurship. According to currently fashionable speculation, class resources encourage individualistic styles of entrepreneurship whereas ethnic resources encourage collective styles.

In the specific case of Cubans and Mexicans (see table 13.1), the superior class resources of the Cubans probably accounts for the higher rate of entrepreneurship among them. In the case of Cubans and Koreans, both ethnic resources and class resources were simultaneously supporting the entrepreneurship of group members. That is, pre-Mariel Cubans and Koreans alike were highly educated in their countries of origin, well endowed with money upon arrival in the United States, and middle or upper-middle class in social origin. Among the Koreans, surveys found that 70 percent of adult men were college graduates compared with only 15 percent of men in Los Angeles County.[30] Similarly, one-half of Korean men reported that their last occupation in Korea was professional, technical, or managerial. On the other hand, Koreans also worked sixty-hour weeks; saved one-half of their income by dint of painful thrift; accepted the risk of criminal victimization; passed business information among themselves; maintained expected patterns of nepotism and employer paternalism; praised a Calvinist deity; utilized family, alumni, congregational, and network solidarities; thought of themselves as sojourners; expressed satisfaction with poorly remunerated work; and utilized rotating credit associations in financing their small businesses. All of these culturally derived characteristics of the

Korean immigrant community contributed to Korean entrepreneurship, but none required money.

Since the use of rotating credit associations was a particularly noteworthy feature of prewar Asian entrepreneurs, its persistence among the Koreans is a firm element of continuity with the past.[31] Kunae Kim undertook an ethnographic investigation of Korean rotating credit associations in Los Angeles. Eighty percent of Koreans she studied were *kye* (the Korean rotating credit association) participants, and she declared the institution "a significant part" of their strategy for "making it in America."[32] Kim and Hurh interviewed 96 Korean business owners in Chicago. Thirty-four percent of respondents indicated that they had "accumulated some of their own capital through the rotating credit system."[33] In sum, Korean entrepreneurship obviously benefitted from class resources, but Koreans also utilized old-fashioned ethnic resources for supplementation, and a similar conclusion fits the Cuban experience in Miami.

Although the persistence of ethnic resources represents a link with the historic past, old-fashioned verities that the world has not outgrown, the generous endowment of Cubans and Koreans with class resources represents a sharp cleavage with American immigration history. Americans must forego the habit of assuming immigrants were once the "wretched refuse" of benighted countries. With the exception of Mexican and some Latin American immigrants, the general level of socioeconomic status among new immigrants surpasses that of the American common man. As a result, new immigrants possess class resources in excess of the underdog Americans, blacks and Mexicans. This novel situation is called "leapfrog migration" to indicate the lodgement of immigrants in the middle rather than, as previous known, at the bottom of the social ladder.[34] Leapfrog migration arises in substantial measure because U.S. immigration laws have awarded priority to professional and technical workers in "short supply" occupations and to persons prepared to invest in a business enterprise they own and manage. When unable to find suitable employment in the general labor market, educated immigrants have the motive and resources to start their own small business enterprises. Moreover, some proportion of the foreigners investing in business enterprises here do so because entrepreneurship offered them their only access to the United States.

Immigrants of middle or upper-middle class origin react with chagrin to the manual jobs they obtain in the general labor market.

Immigrant doctors, pharmacists, engineers, or attorneys may pump gasoline in service stations, but they are looking for escape from this level of employment. Hence, their labor force disadvantages (poor English, unrecognized professional degrees, under-and unemployment) confer on educated immigrants a motive to open their own businesses. Of course, the entrepreneurship-stimulating effects of disadvantage in the labor force have always been present, and the rate of self-employment among the foreign born has, in consequence, been higher than among the native born since at least 1880. However, as the underutilized human capital of immigrants has risen, a function of their middle and upper-middle class social origins, their motives and capability for entrepreneurship have also risen. Even if the path of small business owners is harder now, contemporary immigrants are better prepared for entrepreneurship than were the unskilled, uneducated immigrants of the prewar epoch. Therefore, new immigrants surmount business hurdles that still obstruct the social mobility of low status blacks, whites, and Hispanics. When the *Wall Street Journal* wondered why Cubans in Miami could open numerous businesses whereas blacks in Miami could not, the newspaper concluded that the question unfairly ignored the money, Latin American import–export connections, and bourgeois social origin of at least a substantial minority of Miami's Cubans. This conclusion underscores the hazard of assuming that intergroup differences in rates of entrepreneurship reflect only ethnic resources. Ethnic resources do affect entrepreneurship, but before their effect can be identified in empirical cases one must discount intergroup differences in class resources.

A neglected and unwelcome point of continuity with the past is the copresence of organized crime and immigrant entrepreneurship in Koreatown. This copresence is reminiscent of Chicago in the 1920s. After all, Al Capone is part of American immigration history and, precisely insofar as one looks for continuity with immigration history, one expects his like among new immigrants. Daniel Bell's "queer ladder of social mobility" still beckons disadvantaged foreigners.[35] Racketeering offers a fast profit for those willing to risk murder or incarceration, unrecognized as forms of entrepreneurial risk. Organized crime has some structural basis in America's free enterprise economy. That is, as entrepreneurial minorities saturate legitimate business opportunities, some ambitious immigrants or, more commonly, the children of immigrants begin to bend, then to stretch, and finally to break the law either to make a living or to make a better living. Unable to comprehend this historical continuity with the past of his adopted country, a Korean-born sociologist expressed his rage and humiliation at the public indictment of racketeers among his countrymen. However, capitalism has allowed the crossing of the boundaries of legality in pursuit of profit, a portion of the bountiful rewards earned being thereupon earmarked for protection. Like Prospero and Caliban, ethnic entrepreneurship and ethnic racketeering often appear together, so that those who applaud the former have ruefully to accept some measure of the latter.

Because the economic benefits of immigrant entrepreneurship are so massive, timely, and well targeted, creating veritable enterprise zones in America's depressed inner cities, people overlook the social costs of excessive entrepreneurship. High rates of immigrant self-employment became necessary because immigrants could not find wage and salary jobs at a level befitting their training and expectations. Obviously, American society benefits more from self-employed immigrants than from unemployed immigrants. However, an economic strategy based on self-employment compels immigrants to find ways to circumvent the normal restraints upon expansion of the business population. Innovation and niche-finding are positive results of this search. Violations of law, decency, and public welfare are negative results. Laws protecting labor standards, sanitation, professional competence, and decency do restrain the expansion of the business population. So do common standards of decency that are not written into law. Someone who cannot squeeze into the business population otherwise can often do so by violating these laws or public standards, thus obtaining a commercial advantage over non-violators. For example, employers who pay less than the minimum wage, a violation of law, obtain a commercial advantage over employers who obey the law. Violating rules is a kind of entrepreneurial risk that, if unpunished could permit otherwise unemployed or under-employed people to operate lucrative businesses. In the long run, however, individual violations of laws turn into endemic violations that, having rendered the laws unenforceable, reintroduce the evils laws were intended to avoid.

As violations become endemic, the social benefits of immigrant entrepreneurship are increasingly counterbalanced by social costs until, in an extreme case, what started as a beneficial influx of entrepreneurial talent in depressed central cities ends up as a destructive and terrifying assault upon labor standards, sanitation, health, child welfare, and human values. Although that tipping point has by no means been reached, reliance upon immigrant entrepreneurship to make jobs for immigrants does move society in that direction. As matters stand, these evils are not hypothetical. They exist now, albeit in moderate amount and heavily overbalanced by the great social and economic contributions of foreign entrepreneurs. However, these evils could grow, and given a policy of central city *laissez faire*, probably will. Like fire, guns, chemicals, and pregnancy, entrepreneurship is both useful and dangerous, but unlike the others, the dangers of entrepreneurship are usually overlooked.

Notes

1 *Los Angeles Times*, April 13, 1980, II, 1.
2 *Los Angeles Times*, February 25, 1979, VIII, 1.
3 Illsoo Kim, *New Urban Immigrants: The Korean Community in New York* (Princeton: Princeton University Press, 1981).
4 Ivan Light, "Immigrant and Ethnic Enterprise in North America," *Ethnic and Racial Studies* 7 (1984): 198.
5 Margo A. Conk, "Immigrant Workers in the City, 1870–1930: Agents of Growth of Threats to Democracy?" *Social Science Quarterly* 62 (1981): 711.
6 U.S. Bureau of the Census, *Census of the Population, 1970. National Origin and Language*. PC2-1A. (Washington, D.C.: U.S. Government Printing Office, 1970), T16.
7 Robert Higgs, "Participation of Blacks and Immigrants in the American Merchant Class, 1890–1910: Some Demographic Relations," *Explorations in Economic History* 13 (1976), T3.
8 Calvin Goldscheider, and Frances Kobrin, "Ethnic Continuity and the Process of Self-Employment," *Ethnicity* 7 (1980): 256–78.
9 Martin T. Katzman, "Urban Racial Minorities and Immigrant Groups: Some Economic Comparisons," *American Journal of Economics and Sociology* 30 (1971): 22.
10 U.S. Bureau of the Census, *1980 Census of Population* Vol. 1. *Characteristics of the Population*. Ch. C. *United States Summary*. PC80-1-C1. Washington, D.C./: U.S. Government Printing Office, p. 72, 99, 119, 263.
11 Sandra Wallman, "The Scope for Ethnicity," pp. 1–14 in Sandra Wallman, ed. *Ethnicity at Work*. (London: Macmillan, 1979).
12 Lovell-Troy, "Ethnic Occupational Structures: Greeks in the Pizza Business," *Ethnicity* 8 (1981): 82–95.
13 Roger Waldinger, "Immigrant Enterprise and Labor Market Structure," Paper presented at the Annual Meeting of the American Sociological Association, San Francisco, Sept. 6th, 1982.
14 Raymond Russell, "Ethnic and Occupational Cultures in the New Taxi Cooperatives of Los Angeles," Paper presented at the Annual Meeting of the American Sociological Association, San Francisco, Sept. 6th, 1982.

15 Kevin B. Blackistone, "Arab Entrepreneurs Take Over Inner City Grocery Stores," *Chicago Reporter* 10 (1982): 1–5.
16 Janet B.L. Chan, and Yuet-Wah Cheung. "Ethnic Resources and Business Enterprise: A Study of Chinese Businesses in Toronto," Paper presented at the Annual Meeting of the American Sociological Association, San Francisco, Sept. 6th, 1982.
17 Walter P. Zenner, "Arabic-Speaking Immigrants in North America as Middleman Minorities," *Ethnic and Racial Studies* 5 (1982): 457–77; and Mary Catherine Sengstock, "Maintenance of Social Interaction Patterns in an Ethnic Group." Ph.D. Diss., Washington University, 1967.
18 Mokkerom Hossain, "South Asians in Southern California: A Sociological Study of Immigrants from India, Pakistan, and Bangladesh," *South Asia Bulletin* 2 (1982): 74–83.
19 Saskia Sassen-Koob, "Recomposition and Peripheralization at the Core," *Contemporary Marxism* 5 (1982): 88–100.
20 Robin Ward, and Richard Jenkins, eds. *Ethnic Communities in Business* (Cambridge: Cambridge University Press, 1984).
21 Howard Aldrich, John C. Cater, Trevor P. Jones, and David McEvoy, "Business Development and Self-Segregation: Asian Enterprise in Three British Cities," pp. 170–90 in Ceri Peach, Vaughan Robinson, and Susan Smith, eds. *Ethnic Segregation in Cities* (Athens, Ga.: University of Georgia, 1981).
22 Kenneth L. Wilson, and Alejandro Portes. "Immigrant Enclaves: An Analysis of the Labor Market Experiences of Cubans in Miami," *American Journal of Sociology* 86 (1980): 303.
23 Alejandro Portes, Juan M. Clark, and Manuel M. Lopez, "Six Years Later: the Process of Incorporation of Cuban Exiles in the United States: 1973–1979," *Cuban Studies* 11–12 (1981–82): 18.
24 Jeffrey Reitz, *The Survival of Ethnic Groups* (Toronto: McGraw Hill, 1980).
25 Ibid., p. 164.
26 C. Wright Mills, *White Collar* (New York: Oxford University Press, 1951).
27 Mitchell Gelfand, "Chutzpah in El Dorado: Social Mobility of Jews in Los Angeles, 1900–1920." Ph.D. Diss., Carnegie-Mellon University, 1981.
28 Ivan Light, "Immigrant and Ethnic Enterprise in North America.'
29 Robert V. Robinson, "Reproducing Class Relations in Industrial Capitalism," *American Sociological Review* 49: 183.
30 Eui-Young Yu, "Occupations and Work Patterns of Korean Immigrants in Los Angeles." Ch. 3 in Eui-Young Yu, Earl H. Phillips, and Eun Sik Yang, eds. *Koreans in Los Angeles* (Los Angeles: Koryo Research Institute and California State University at Los Angeles, 1982), p. 51.
31 See Chapter 2, Ivan Light *Ethnic Enterprise in America* (Berkeley and Los Angeles: University of California, 1972).
32 Kunae Kim, "Rotating Credit Associations among the Korean Immigrants in Los Angeles: Intracultural Diversity Observed in their Economic Adaptation." M.A. Thesis, Department of Anthropology, University of California at Los Angeles, 1982, p. 21.

33 Kwang Chung Kim, and Won Moo Hurh, "The Formation and Maintenance of Korean Small Business in the Chicago Minority Area." Macomb,
III. (1984): Department of Sociology and Anthropology of Western Illinois
University.
34 Ivan Light, *Cities in World Perspective* (New York: Macmillan, 1983), pp. 322–
3, 352.
35 Daniel Bell, *The End of Ideology* (New York: Free Press, 1960), p. 127.

PART IV

COMPARATIVE PERSPECTIVES ON IMMIGRATION

14 Multiculturalism and Immigration: A Comparison of the United States, Germany, and Great Britain

Christian Joppke

"Multiculturalism," the seeking of equal rights and recognition for ethnic, racial, religious, or sexually defined groups, is one of the most pervasive and controversial intellectual and political movements in contemporary Western democracies. In its insistence on equality and emancipation, multiculturalism is clearly a movement of the left. Yet in its defense of particularistic, mostly ascriptively defined group identities, multiculturalism also deviates from the universalist project of the left, and enters a terrain that had previously been held by the political right. Following Charles Taylor,[1] one may characterize multiculturalism as a "politics of difference" that fuses egalitarian rhetoric with a stress on authenticity and rejection of Western universalism, which is seen as falsely homogenizing and a smokescreen for power. Multiculturalism is modern and anti-modern at the same time. It is a thoroughly modern phenomenon in that it reflects the collapse of social hierarchies and the precarious nature of identity in an individualized social structure where traditional, identity-providing milieus of class, religion, or region have melted away. The particularistic identities advocated by multiculturalism are chosen, not received, to be built by means of "consciousness raising" rather than ready-made. At the same time, multiculturalism's identities are primordial, ascribed, and all-encompassing. Ethnic heritage, racial features, or sexual orientation are elevated into exclusive master statuses that totally fix an individual's identity and interests. The world of multiculturalism is populated not by individuals with a multitude of overlapping, and often conflicting, group affiliations and interests, but by groups or "communities" that are inert, homogeneous and mutually exclusive, such as gays, Latinos, or Muslims. This subordination of the individual to one exclusive group runs counter to the modern principles of inclusion and functional differentiation, and makes multiculturalism vulnerable to fundamentalist and anti-modernist extremes. Because multiculturalism, as a kind of chosen primordialism, obviously combines contradictory principles, it may appear in many forms – as the liberal plea for tolerance and mutual understanding in the multiethnic immigrant societies of today, but also as the separatist quest for "black power" or militant attack on "Western imperialism."

For the purpose of the following analysis, I propose to disaggregate the complex phenomenon of multiculturalism along three dimensions: first, multiculturalism as a challenge to the premier cultural community of the modern world, the nation; second, multiculturalism as a quest for recognition and compensatory treatment of historically disadvantaged and discriminated groups in society ("minorities" in Anglo-American parlance); and third, and maybe most importantly, multiculturalism as a generalized form of anticolonial discourse and struggle. With regard to the *first* dimension, the very notion of multiculturalism conveys that not one, but multiple cultures coexist within a limited, state-bounded territory. This goes against the grain of the modern principle of the nation-state, according to which political and cultural boundaries shall be congruent.[2] Multiculturalism reflects a novel situation where culture is no longer contained, controlled, and homogenized by the national state. As Michael Schudson put it, today "cultures flow in, out, around, and through state borders."[3] In response to a host of diverse factors, such as migrations, technological change (enabling instantaneous communications), and the endogenous weakening of national allegiances in postwar western democracies, cultures are either "underinclusive," integrating groups smaller than the national society, or "overinclusive," integrating groups larger than the national society.

While their boundaries do not coincide with the political boundaries of the state, the cultural groups denoted by multiculturalism share some key characteristics of the pivotal cultural community of the modern world, the nation. In contrast to formal, functional organizations like firms, administrations or professions, multiculturalism stipulates culturally integrated associations, i.e., "communities," which penetrate and regulate not only specific aspects, but the entire life conduct of the individual. The patterns of such cultural communities are collectively represented (which is more than individually shared), loaded with emotional significance, and tied to the construction of ingroup–outgroup boundaries. As in the case of nations, exit is generally ruled out, so that the group is endowed with the hallow of fate and interest-transcending loyalty. In contrast to small-scale forms of communal social organization, such as family, neighbourhood or friendship, the communities stipulated by multiculturalism are "imagined": their members do not know one another. In fact, multicultural communities meet all requirements of Benedict Anderson's definition of nations as "imagined communities," except one: multicultural communities do not generally conceive of themselves as "sovereign," a claim obviously reserved to state-aspiring territorial groups, i.e., nations. But notions such as "queer nation" or "black nationalism," however deliberately provocative and mocking, suggest that sovereignty claims are still within the logic of multiculturalism, and are revoked more for lack of practicality than in principle. This points at the major problem of multicultural cohabitation: societal integration. The question if bounded societies are integrated through a common culture, and not through sheer habituation, interest or power, is an open one. But, in contrast to the national model of membership as citizenship, multiculturalism does not provide a group-transcending form of membership or a civic platform for the expression and resolution of interest conflict. Critics have pointed out that multiculturalism's challenge to inclusive national membership entails a tendency toward "balkanization" and "disuniting," which are certainly alarmist but not entirely unfounded labels.

Secondly, only a specific type of cultural group is constitutive of multiculturalism: historically disadvantaged or oppressed groups, which are often referred to as "minorities." The notion of minority refers to more than only a numerical relationship, but to one characterized by unequal power and cultural incompatibility between majority society and minority group. Historically, the existence of minorities is the product of the culturally homogenizing nation-state, and they first appeared in legal and political discourse in the wake of the nationalization of postimperial eastern Europe. Homeland-based minority claims predate explicit multiculturalism, and their affinity to monocultural nationalism makes them somewhat distinct from the later. More relevant for explicit multiculturalism seems to be a second type of migration-based minorities. However, since they haven't been there first and thus cannot claim historical homeland rights, and since they have voluntarily and individually entered the receiving society, migrant claims for public recognition and autonomy rights are on much shakier ground. A special status in this regard is reserved to the archetype of modern non-homeland minorities, the American blacks. Since they owe their existence to forced migration, i.e., overt oppression, their claims are not exhausted by merely symbolical recognition, but extend to material compensations for past wrongs and preferential treatment. Whatever they consist of concretely, multicultural minority claims are always raised by or on behalf of distinct groups qua groups. In this regard, multiculturalism is inherently a quest for group rights. This challenges the liberal rights model dominant in Western democracies, according to which rights are invested in individuals (or "citizens") but not in groups. Liberal defenders of multiculturalism have argued that the exercise of individual rights and liberties depends on "full and unimpeded membership in a respected and flourishing cultural group."[4] But the tension between liberalism and multiculturalism is real, as the latter is based on the ontological primacy of the group over the individual and, if necessary, takes into the bargain the suppression of individual claims.

Along a *third* dimension, multiculturalism inherits the agenda and sensitivity of anticolonial struggle. Multiculturalism takes up W. E. B Du Bois's maxim that "the problem of the twentieth century is the problem of the color line."[5] Multiculturalism shares three characteristics of anticolonial discourse: the centrality of culture for political emancipation; an epistemological relativism that criticizes Western universalism as particularistic power in disguise; and a rejection of the inclusive politics of citizenship in favour of an exclusive politics of identity. Frantz Fanon's anticolonial manifesto *The Wretched of the Earth* may be read as multiculturalism's implicit *Programmschrift*: a colonizing West is juxtaposed to a colonized ethnoracial periphery, which relate to one another like "two different species";[6] because the West exerts its power through destroying the culture of the colonized, liberation comes through the reassertion of indigenous cultures and traditions; and because the West is not the best but mere power in disguise, the direction of liberation cannot be inclusion but separation, ultimately in a romanticized "purging violence." Multiculturalism thus deviates from traditional social movements in the West, which fought for inclusion and citizenship. If traditional social movements sought to abolish the discriminated groups on whose behalf claims are raised (such as "classes"), multiculturalism's opposite thrust is to perpetuate the claims-making groups.

Modern colonialism's imposition of Western culture on periph-
eral cultures, along with the assumed superiority that undergirds
this imposition, is the core grievance for which multiculturalism
seeks belated redress.[7] This explains multiculturalism's preoccupation with the change of self-images through education and a
reformed curriculum. The underlying epistemology is relativistic.
As an intellectual doctrine, multiculturalism reflects the West's
reduced epistemological status after being confronted with its rebel-
lious oriental Other. James Clifford has described the "tectonic"
change in anthropology brought about by the end of empire:
"There is no longer any place of overview (mountaintop) from
which to map human ways of life, no Archimedian point from
which to represent the world."[8] Context-dependence, historicity,
and perspectivism are the new catchwords. If there is no objective
truth or context-independent validity of cultural expressions, one
cultural expression is just as good (or bad) as the other. More
concretely, the universalist claims of the Western enlightenment
tradition are denounced as particularistic power claims, which have
to be countered by the concerted power of the periphery. In
Fanon's words, "Western values . . . produce in the native a sort of
stiffening or muscular lockjaw," so that liberation means to "mock
at these very values, [to] insult them, and [to] vomit them up."[9]
This enterprise of cultural liberation, while consequential on its
own premises, is not without contradictions. As Amy Gutmann
has pointed out, if truth claims and common standards are nothing
but power strategies of dominant groups, "why then bother with
intellectual life at all, which is not the fastest, surest, or even most
satisfying path to political power, if it is political power one is really
after?"[10]

If multiculturalism is a form of generalized Third World liberation, the massive, Third-World-based immigration waves of the
postwar period may be assumed to be one of its driving forces. *The
Empire Strikes Back* is the telling title of a popular treatise on immigrant politics and culture in postwar Britain.[11] Migrations, particularly from the periphery of the modern-world system, have
produced the ethnic and racial diversity that is a central backdrop
of multicultural claims. If related to immigration, multiculturalism
appears as a critique of and alternative to traditional "assimilation,"
which assumed that the cultural difference imported into the
receiving society by immigrants should and would be extinguished
in the long run. Assimilation, whose literal meaning is "making
alike" and originally had biological connotations, is indeed no

longer plausible, for a variety of reasons. Most importantly, in contrast to earlier migrations in the age of empire, contemporary migrations occur within a developed nation-state system, in which there is a stong disinclination on the part of migrants to abandon entrenched national loyalties. Secondly, due to advanced transport and communication technologies migrations are no longer "one-way trips," which Zvetan Todorov considered the basis of the classic immigrant's willingness to become "assimilated."[12] Even if a physical return is postponed or abandoned, symbolical returns are plentiful and permanent in the developed ethnic infrastructure of the modern metropoles, up to a point where even the sense of having departed at all is lost. Thirdly, liberal states are reluctant to impose particular cultural forms on their members, aside from a procedural commitment to basic civic rules. In addition, liberal states today are postimperial states that are not without guilt about their colonial pasts. There is a widely-held sense that forced assimilation or acculturation violates the integrity and dignity of the individual, whose cultural habits should be a matter of his or her choice alone. To a certain degree, liberal states today are necessarily multicultural.

Despite obvious affinities between contemporary immigration and multiculturalism, there are also tensions, if not incompatibilities, between both. The immigrant perspective contradicts the anticolonial perspective advocated by multiculturalism: immigration is voluntary, individual, and in its factual attraction to the host society a powerful reaffirmation of the latter; anticolonialism, by contrast, depicts the incorporation of new members as forced and collective, and it calls for a fundamental transformation of the host society's structure and principles. To put it drastically, immigrants say "we are actors," whereas the anticolonial perspective tells them "you are victims." This is not to deny that both perspectives can move toward one another, especially after the experience of actual discrimination and in view of the benefits that affirmative-action-style minority privileges promise. But it is important to recognize that multiculturalism is in the first a movement of intellectuals, who are offering an interpretation of the immigrant experience that is not necessarily adopted by the immigrants themselves.

This chapter examines the linkage between immigration and multiculturalism in three Western societies that have experienced comparable immigration flows in the postwar period, and where various forms of multiculturalism have emerged as strong intellectual and social currents. But, as I attempt to demonstrate, the concrete meaning of multiculturalism and its linkage to immigration differ significantly across these societies. These differences are conditioned by distinct traditions of nationhood, the specific historical contexts in which immigration has taken place, the existing immigration regimes, and the ethnic immigrant groups themselves.

In the United States, multiculturalism is only indirectly related to the recent immigration waves of non-European origins. Instead, the direct origin of multiculturalism is America's unresolved race problem. Multiculturalism represents only a weak challenge to the prevailing civic concept of nationhood, which allows an accompaniment of a variety of ethnic fillings. Emerging in the historical context of America's civil rights revolution, multiculturalism appears as the quest for group rights, i.e. as the quest for public status by or on behalf of historically oppressed "minority" groups that claim special compensation and privileges. As we will see, this requires the reinterpretation of the immigrant experience along anticolonial lines, an often strained endeavor rife with paradoxes, ambivalences and conflicts, not least with America's premier non-immigrant minority, the Blacks.

In Germany and Britain, multiculturalism is more directly related to immigration, and it also appears as a more direct challenge to established notions of nationhood. In both cases, multiculturalism is an acknowledgment that to be "British" or "German" has thicker, ethnic connotations that – in liberal societies – cannot be easily imposed on culturally remote immigrant groups. But here the convergence ends. In Germany, the multiculturalism debate is really a debate about the protracted problem of nationhood after Nazism, and it is led in virtual absence of the foreigners (*Auslaender*) themselves, who are even denied the very status of immigrants. In Britain, I shall argue, multiculturalism has indigenous roots in the legacy of a multi-racial empire. Multiculturalism is even a deliberate state strategy in the provision of social services and public education, offered as a remedy to Britain's lingering, entirely immigration-based, race problem. Very much a liberal elite strategy, multiculturalism is challenged by an openly racist right that seeks to remodel British nationhood along isolationist, white "little England" lines, and a radical left that prefers "anti-racist" militance over "multicultural" accommodation.

Each of these three cases thus combines the three dimensions of multiculturalism discussed above: challenge to the nation; quest for minority group rights; and the anticolonial perspective. But in each case these dimensions appear in different combinations and orders of relevance. What makes the comparison of the U.S., Germany, and Britain especially attractive is that in each case one particular dimension is predominant, and thus defines the national variant of multiculturalism as a whole: quest for group rights in the U.S. a substitute for the nation in Germany, and the colonial empire making an unexpected return in Britain.

The Quest for Group Rights: The U.S. Case

The American civil rights revolution of the 1960s, which put an end to the dismal postslavery legacy of denying elementary citizenship rights to the American blacks, may be retold in the form of a paradox. What began as the attempt to create a color-blind society turned out to create an increasingly color-conscious society.[13] The Civil Rights Act of 1964, which prohibited any form of discrimination or segregation "on the ground of race, color, religion, sex, or national origin" in employment, education, and public life, deliberately failed to specify which particular group would be affected by it – it spoke of "citizens," "individuals," or "persons" but not of blacks, native Americans, Hispanics, or Asians. However, its implementation required public institutions to identify employees, clients, or other claimants through their ethnic or racial group membership, and thus to carve out race and ethnicity as distinct group categories. This group-emphasis became especially strong once courts and executive agencies, such as the Equal Employment Opportunity Commission, went from a passive registration of actual discriminations to the active mandating of statistical quotas and timetables in the hiring or education of "minorities," which were to be achieved by means of "affirmative action."

More as a matter of expediency and convenience than of explicit legislative fiat, four such "minority" groups emerged as the sole beneficiaries of affirmative-action privileges: Blacks, American Indians, Asians, and Hispanics. Two of these "minorities," Asians and Hispanics, would also provide the large majority of the huge immigration wave that set in shortly after the immigration reforms of the mid-1960s, which represent the second pillar of the civil rights revolution. Replacing the racially motivated national-origins provisions that had been effective since the 1920s, the Immigration Act of 1965 for the first time opened the doors for non-European immigrants, mostly Asians and Hispanics. The affirmative-action framework, however, offered incentives for ethnic leaders to model their constituencies along "minority" lines – thus creating the curious situation that many of the new immigrants automatically qualified for certain benefits that remained foreclosed to most native Americans.

Whereas the civil rights legislation created a strong institutional incentive for the claiming of ethnoracial group rights, an internal transformation of the civil rights movement provided the language in which separate group claims could be raised. Reflecting the disappointment with the slow progress of lower-class Blacks, particularly in the urban ghettos, and fuelled by the anticolonial movements of Africa and Latin America, the separatist, militant creed of "black power" came to replace the civic inclusion gospel of Martin Luther King. This was a significant change, because it set the tone for all the other ethnic identity movements that would become the backbone of multiculturalism. The angry Black Panthers of Oakland, California, not the stoic black reverends of Birmingham, Alabama, provided the model to emulate for the young, impatient student activists that now formed the Asian-American, Chicano, and other ethnic movements on America's college campuses.

As in the case of the Asian-American movement, this required a conscious reinterpretation of the ethnic immigrant experience along anticolonial lines. This was not easy to achieve, because "Asians" do not exist as a homogeneous linguistic or ethnic group, and because Asians – America's proverbial "model minority" – have been extraordinarily successful in occupational and educational regards. The building of an Asian-American "minority" movement thus meant to forge "racial" unity out of "ethnic" diversity and to rewrite a history of success as a history of victimization. Scholar-activist William Wei summarizes this process of movement building: "Gradually, these activists recognized that they belonged to a racial minority subordinated and separated from the dominant society by race-based policies and practices, rejected their previous efforts at assimilating into that society, and reaffirmed their right to an autonomous ethnic identity in a culturally pluralistic society."[14] At the same time, Asian-American student activists had to realize that the immigrant and refugee origins of their ethnic target groups proved severe hurdles to such "consciousness raising," as the latter found no fault with traditional melting pot assimilation.[15]

In the case of Hispanics, the building of an ethnoracial minority movement along the black model was easier to achieve. The common language, the generally low educational and occupational achievement of Hispanics, and – maybe most importantly – the colonialist legacy of the Southwest, which had been Mexican until 1848, provided favorable conditions. The Hispanics have become, to speak with Peter Skerry,[16] America's quintessentially "ambivalent minority," poised between defining themselves as an ethnic immigrant group or ethnoracial minority group. But the culture and political opportunities of the civil rights era pulled Hispanic movement building toward the latter direction.

The Voting Rights Act of 1965, the third pillar of America's civil rights revolution, was a crucial incentive in this regard. While the Act was originally designed to put an end to the disenfranchisement of Blacks in the South through subjecting local elections to federal supervision, a 1975 amendment extended its provisions to four "language minorities," including Hispanics, who were granted the right to cast ballots printed in their native language. Most importantly, in expanding its coverage to more than 375 jurisdictions outside the South, such as Texas, the new act allowed Hispanics to institute via federal mandate ethnic majority, "single member" electoral districts that virtually guarantee ethnic office-holding. This success, however, was conditional on modeling Hispanics as an oppressed minority group, such as equating the provision of voting material in English to the infamous literacy tests in the South. This was no easy task, and a Hispanic lobbyist remembered "being on the phone to Texas with members of the Chicano community, saying, find...a Fannie Lou Hamer, find...a really bad little county with ten little stories, find...someone who's convincing to come up here and testify before Congress... to convince the Congress and the administration...to...change the rules of the game so that Texas will get covered."[17] And these bold Hispanic forays into minority territory, which at that time threatened to provoke a conservative backlash against the entire Voting Rights Act, were resented by the Blacks, who accused the former of "(taking) us back to the dark days of 1963, with lynchings in Mississippi."[18]

An even more important step in unleashing the group-rights logic of the civil rights revolution was a 1982 amendment to the Voting Rights Act. This amendment allowed minority voters nationwide to challenge any method of election (whenever instituted) on the ground of discriminatory "result" rather than "intention." This seemingly innocent change of words applied the "equality of result" maxim of affirmative action to the electoral process, and mandated the drawing of district lines that maximize safe minority seats. The rationale of this amendment is multiculturalism applied to the political process: representation on the basis of group membership. As a result of this amendment, traditional at-large voting and multimember districts are at the point of disappearing, while the number of ethnic office-holders elected from single-member districts has greatly increased. But at the same time, new problems are generated. As critics have pointed out, the stress on group rights in the electoral process inhibits political integration, freezes rather than thaws racial politics, and undermines the sense of common citizenship. Republicans, for instance, have curiously supported the creation of ethnic single-member districts: the concentration of ethnic voters in a few safe districts "whitens" the other districts, thus making Republican victories more likely. At the same time, white representatives may no longer feel compelled to speak for nonwhite minorities.[19]

Affirmative action, which distributes entitlements to ethnic minority groups according to their population share, also creates the interest of ethnic leaders to increase their power base through new immigration. For instance, Hispanic groups such as the League of United Latin American Citizens (LULAC) have traditionally been restrictionist, because new immigrants meant increased competition for scarce jobs and benefits. In the affirmative-action era, where increased numbers translate into increased quota and population totals at census time, Hispanic groups have turned unabashedly pro-immigration. At the same time, the politics of numbers has loosened the links between ethnic constituency and its leadership. In Peter Skerry's sarcastic but pointed words, "Hispanic leaders do not require voters, or even protesters – only bodies."[20] Because the Census, on the basis of which district lines are redrawn, counts "persons" but not eligible voters, even illegal immigrants contribute to the creation of minority districts. The result is "rotten boroughs" with a minimum of eligible voters and elected representatives with a minimum of democratic accountability. For instance, Gloria Molina, the first Hispanic to sit on the powerful Los Angeles County Board of Supervisors, was elected from a "safe" (yet predominantly immigrant) minority district, where only 88,000 votes were cast out of a population of 1.8 million.

Because of loose constituency ties, ethnic leaders often adopt radical positions not shared by the groups for which they claim to speak. The lack of democratic accountability is further increased by the fact that foundations, rather than membership dues, fund most ethnic organizations of the post-civil-rights era. The Mexican-

American Legal Defense and Educational Fund (MALDEF) and the National Council of La Raza, founded in the late 1960s and the most potent Hispanic public policy organizations today, were set up with the help of liberal foundation money, most notably Ford and Rockefeller.[21] Their young leaders, trained in the civil rights movement, have learned to exploit the opportunities of affirmative action, with the result of producing and perpetuating a quasi-racial "minority" status for groups whose members may not actually perceive themselves in these terms. Polls have shown that Hispanic rank-and-file have consistently held more conservative views than their leadership on typical affirmative-action issues such as bussing, employment quota, and bilingual education.[22] Another example of this opinion gap is the debate about employer sanctions in the Immigration Reform and Control Act (IRCA) of 1986. While the Hispanic leadership branded this measure to stop illegal immigration as "racist," the majority of the Hispanic rank-and-file supported employer sanctions.[23] These examples indicate that it is not immigration and ethnic diversification *per se*, but a specific intellectual elite culture in conjunction with the political opportunity structure, which feeds the trend toward group rights and multiculturalism.

The main battleground of the group-rights movement, and of "multiculturalism" proper, is education. After all, as Fanon outlined, "decolonization" begins by reasserting the culture of the colonized. In the hands of the group-rights movement, education has turned from being the "great equalizer" (Horace Mann) between ethnic groups into an ethnic consciousness-raising instrument. Ethnic and racial studies programs, which have been instituted at many American universities and colleges since the late 1960s, are typical examples. They are producing and disseminating the anticolonial view and criticism of assimilation that is typical for multiculturalism. Characteristically, these programs tend to be taught and attended by members of the group that is being studied, and advocacy rather than analysis is their declared purpose. William Wei describes in revealing terms the thrust of the Asian-American Studies Programs, which were instituted in the late 1960s at several West Coast universities after a series of "Third World Strikes": "They instilled pride in students by informing them of their history without the demeaning distortions of Eurocentric scholarship. They emphasized the similarities in the historical experiences of all Asian groups . . ., especially their oppression by European American society and their resistance to it."[24]

The "third-world perspective" (R. Blauner), certainly a provocation in the 1960s, is now well-entrenched. Following the example
of Stanford University, many colleges and universities have
scrapped their mandatory "Western Culture" courses in favor of
courses that stress "diversity" and "cultures" in the plural. Prima
facie, there is nothing unusual about revising the canon in light of
new historical experience. But peculiar is the mindset from which
this revision springs, which is that of a combat against "Eurocentric
hegemony" (M. Asante). Most importantly, the "third-world perspective" is not limited to academia's ivory tower, but has trickled
down to the level of public schools. California and New York, the
two states with the highest ethnic diversity and immigration rates
in the country, are the first states to revise their school curricula
along multicultural lines. In 1989, a task force created by the New
York State Commissioner of Education, Thomas Sobol, released a
new "Curriculum of Inclusion" that recommended a general over-
haul of the history and social studies curriculum at New York
State's public schools. It gave scant attention to reading, mathe-
matics or scientific skills, but opened with a salvo against the evils of
"monocultural" education: "African-Americans, Asian-Americans,
Puerto Ricans/Latinos, and Native Americans have all been the
victims of an intellectual and educational oppression that has characterized the culture and institutions of the United States and the
European American world for centuries."[25] A black school-activist
expressed the rationale of multicultural education in simpler terms:
"We want a program that will produce big black men, not little
white men."[26]

Reviewing the curriculum battles, Arthur Schlesinger wonders
whether the "obsession with difference" will "threaten the idea of
an overarching American nationality."[27] Will it? America's concept
of nationhood is uniquely resilient, because it is politically rather
than ethnically constituted. As Horace Kallen pointed out,[28] the
meaning of "American" is characterized by a "peculiar anonym-
ity": it has no ethnic implications. From this follows that the ethnic
recomposition of American society in the era of Third World immigration is not *per se* a threat to American nationhood. Multiculturalists are fond to point out that the orthodoxy of "melting-pot"
assimilation has always been a myth, and that cultural "pluralism"
has been closer to the American experience. Countering the hys-
terical (anti-German) "Americanization" campaign during World
War I, Horace Kallen codified the "pluralistic" interpretation of
American nationhood as a "democracy of nationalities": "The spirit

of the land is inarticulate, not a voice but a chorus of many voices each singing a rather different tune."[29] Is this so different from a contemporary proponent of multiculturalism, who "seeks to go beyond the model of a nation-state coterminous only with Euro-immigrant America, to one coterminous...with humankind"?[30] Such a model is true to the universalist bent in the American concept of nationhood; but it is also the point at which the very concept of nation collapses, because the necessity of boundaries is denied.

Despite such similarities, multiculturalism deviates from traditional pluralism in one crucial respect. When Horace Kallen devised his pluralistic conception of American nationhood, the existence of a unifying bond was never put in question. Ethnicity and ethnic organization were cushions that stood between the uprooted immigrant and "complete wildness," as W. I. Thomas and Florian Znaniecki put it with reference to the Polish peasant in America.[31] Looking forty years later at ethnic organization and politics in New York City, Nathan Glazer and Daniel Moynihan famously confirmed that "the point about the melting pot...is that it did not happen."[32] However, all these descriptions could take for granted that ethnicity was a matter of private choice; it did not attain public status. This is the novelty of multiculturalism: to claim public status for ethnoracial distinctions. This *does* represent a challenge to American nationhood, because it undermines the color-transcending communality of citizenship. It will not amount to a separatist challenge, because their immigrant origins deny ethnic groups a territorial homeland. But if the idea of a "shared national identity" is denounced as an "evil" that American society can do without,[33] the question arises what will be the common ground that secures the civility of political conflict; where will the group-transcending commitments come from that stand between social organization and "complete wildness," particularly in the Third World metropoles of immigrant America? As Andrew Hacker wrote 18 months after the most serious racial unrest in American history, which happened to occur in the self-styled pioneer city of America's multicultural future, Los Angeles, "a multicultural America may seem benign in a classroom syllabus, but we shouldn't be surprised if the result is conflict in the streets."[34]

To forge a nation out of a heap of immigrants has been conditional upon a willingness to rise above the limitations of one's origins, of "beginning over again on the frontier," as Frederick Turner put it in his famous essay *The Frontier in American History*.

Multiculturalism's preoccupation with remembering one's origins is curiously at odds with the immigrant creed to "never look back" that has given American society its unique dynamism and resilience. This leads us back to our initial question of the relationship between multiculturalism and immigration. Restrictionists like to argue that "the massive Third World immigration is ... the ultimate driving force behind multiculturalism."[35] If my analysis is correct, this is at best a half-truth. The origin of American multiculturalism is the unresolved race question. The new immigrants are mere "junior partners in the fight for multiculturalism."[36] But however junior, the new immigrants are nevertheless partners in the multiculturalism crusade, because the civil rights revolution has given them the incentive to define themselves as ethnoracial "minorities," and thus to trade in the immigrant for the anticolonial perspective. There is no doubt that the quest for group rights is about to fundamentally transform the ethnic pattern in America, with results that are as yet undetermined. But then, indeterminacy has always been the truth of the American experience.

A Substitute for the Nation: The German Case

In a stunning breach of the usually circuitous and polite ways of foreign diplomacy, one of the highest U.S. representatives in Germany has recently launched a sweeping attack on Germany's handling of the foreigner issue, chastising the society for intolerance, self-pity, and "compulsive self-analysis," while rebuking its political leader, Helmut Kohl, for stubbornly insisting that "Germany is not a country of immigration."[37] While certainly refreshing, the can-do pragmatism of the American underestimates the difficulty of a European nation's ability to cope with a fact that has helped America into existence, but which instead is experienced as a disturbing novelty: immigration. But more importantly still, it dismisses too easily the added complication of *German* nationhood that has stood in the way of this country's coming to terms with its embarrassing "foreigner problem."

Since it invited the first Italian "guest workers" in 1955 to feed the insatiable labor needs of its "economic miracle," Germany has insisted that the newcomers were just that: "guests" and "workers" who were expected to return when the job was done and once the contract had expired. As long as these premises were in force, the guest workers were cherished items. The one-millionth labor migrant to arrive at Cologne's train station on September 10, 1964, Armando Rodriguez of Viseo, Portugal, was greeted by a cheerful crowd that included no less a figure than the Federal Minister for Labor Affairs. After rewarding the celebrated, and not a little surprised, new arrival with a shining motorcycle, the Minister intoned a true Ode to the Guest Worker: "These one million persons on the job in Germany help contribute to maintaining production growth while keeping prices stable and maintaining our reputation on world markets. The role of the *Gastarbeiter* will certainly become more significant in the years ahead."[38] To "keep prices stable," to "maintain production growth," and to "maintain our reputation on world markets" – this was how the (West) German nation refashioned itself after its total defeat in 1945. As the economic language indicates, West Germany rebuilt itself in an act of national self-denial. The guest workers were at first welcome in an enterprise whose economic imperatives knew no national markers – and Italy, the home of the first guest workers, was, after all, also the favorite destination of the reborn *Wohlstandsbuerger* to spend their annual *Urlaub*. When the big recession of 1973 inflicted a huge blow to West Germany Inc., and the federal government issued its "recruitment stop" (*Anwerbestop*) that is still in force today, the friendly embracement of guest workers gave way to not-so-friendly reminders to the "guests" to honor their part of the deal – and to go home. By then, most guest workers were not Italians, but Turks, and their alien ways reminded the Germans that they were different – but who were they, the "Germans"?

Multiculturalism in Germany is only secondarily about immigrants; primarily it is about the Germans themselves. In insisting, against the official doctrine, that "Germany is an immigration country," the proponents of multiculturalism are trying to bury the dreadful ghost of the *voelkisch* national tradition and to build a postnational community. The first part of this practical syllogism, which links multiculturalism and immigration, is expressed in the definition of a multicultural society, provided by one of its major proponents, the Green Party: "The 'multicultural society' is not a theory, but a reality. In the Federal Republic immigration has taken place, and immigration will continue to take place." The document then points at the second, and decisive, link between multiculturalism and postnationalism: "Our idea of the 'multicultural society' is not based on [the] concept of the nation-state, but on the indivisibility of human rights. Not citizenship [but where an individual lives] should determine the rights of an individual, (*Lebensmittelpunkt*)."[39] From this the Greens deduce a "general right to stay" (*allgemeines Bleiberecht*) for all who happen to enter the country and stay there for five years, in an explicit "policy of open borders" that patently denies the reality of a world divided into separate nation-states. Also the German debate on multiculturalism is not without its curious blossoms. But they do not spring from the problem of race, as in the United States, but from the peculiarities of German nationhood.

From a historical perspective, Germany's ethnocultural legacy of nationhood and citizenship is responsible for its lack of an explicit immigration policy and the official denial that immigration has taken place. In contrast to the "civic" nations of the West, where nationhood became defined by state territory and adherence to abstract political principles (such as liberty and equality), German nationhood is based on the "ethnic" model of a linguistically and culturally unified group, a "community of destiny" (*Schicksalsgemeinschaft*) transmitting itself from a mystical past into an unknown, sometimes millenarian, sometimes doom-laden future. Because Germany came second and had to assert itself against a Western environment of already established and more advanced nation-states, its concept of nation inhered from the beginning the negative features of *ressentiment* and closure. Whereas the Western nations constituted themselves through intra-state revolutions and their political creeds of secularism, freedom and equality, the German nation came into its own in a succession of inter-state conflicts, especially the wars against France. Not the civic code of equal rights but the ethnic code of "us" versus "them" became constitutive of the German concept of nation. This was no foregone conclusion but conditioned by the difficulties of state building in the "polycephalic" zone of Europe,[40] and, most importantly, by the incapability of, first, an anemic bourgeoisie, and, later, the most powerful working-class movement of Europe, to imbue the nation with the universalistic creed of a successful intra-state revolution.

The ethnic definition of membership in the German nation became codified in the Wilhelmine Citizenship Law of 1913, which decreed that citizenship was to be conferred via descent (*jus sanguinis*) rather than birth on territory (*jus soli*). Blood-based citizenship was a defensive measure against the huge Slavic and Jewish migrations on the open eastern flank of the Reich. In a Reichstag debate of 1912, a government official outlined the rationale of *jus sanguinis*: "The march of nations (*Zug der Nationen*) goes from East to West, and on this march of nations the [Eastern] masses...meet the German Reich with its rule of law, economic prosperity, and free institutions... [A restrictive citizenship policy] is in the national interest, because it erects a barrier to the stream of foreigners flooding our country from the East.'[41] Eight decades later, the West German Minister of the Interior used the exact same rhetoric to defend a restrictive migrant policy that continues to divide the world into "Germans" and "foreigners": "In this time of upheaval and change, it is important that we, as the eastern outpost of the... Western alliance, remain a stable democracy."[42] This is but a small vignette from a debate both formed and deformed by the weight of national history.

Multiculturalism is the attempt to break the "us" versus "them" code in which Germans have traditionally defined themselves. As its multiculturalist critics rightly outline, the *voelkisch* conception of nation as a community of descent, which one cannot become a member of unless one already is one, is anachronistic in the multi-ethnic immigrant societies of today. But the matter is more complicated still. Multiculturalism in Germany is not so much about *redefining* as about *transcending* nationhood altogether. Why? As a result of National Socialism, a positive national identity became impossible in postwar Germany. The left was henceforth inspired by turning this vice into a virtue, setting out on a wholesale crusade against the "mischief of the nation-state."[43] Multiculturalism may be understood as the latest round in this crusade. But more than a fringe phenomenon, postnationalism was a core feature of the Bonn Republic itself. Its foreign policy was not driven by hard "national interest" but by a moralizing quest for peace and European integration. On the domestic side, a prospering economy helped finance a culturally neutralized welfare state that was efficient in maintaining social peace, if spreading a certain complacency. This overall comfortable arrangement was disturbed only by the occasional youth, ecology or peace protest, and a past that would not wither. Habermas's "patriotism of the constitution" came close to being the official doctrine of the Bonn Republic, stipulating a political community kept together by a postnational commitment to abstract constitutional principles.

However, because it failed to engage in a conscious redefinition of German nationhood, the Bonn Republic allowed, underneath its compulsively postnational facade, the *voelkisch* tradition to remain alive and well. In fact, this tradition was further strengthened by the fact that after World War II, like almost always in German history, national and state boundaries did not overlap. The outcome of the war, with the partition of Germany and the existence of a huge and scattered ethnic diaspora in eastern Europe, reinforced the German concept of nation as an ethnocultural community of destiny.[44] The one national fixed-point of the Bonn Republic was its constitutionally enshrined mandate to be the vicarious home of *all* Germans, which amounted to automatic citizenship rights for East or ethnic Germans who managed to escape from Communism. Against this backdrop, the cleverest opponents of immigration argued that only an ethnically homogeneous Germany in the West could maintain its moral and constitutional commitment to the Germans in the East. "What would happen to [German] unity," asks a right-wing advocate of repatriating foreigners in the mid-1980s, with more than a little bit of chuzpah, "if . . . a multiethnic and multicultural Federal Republic would steal itself out of the nation?"[45] To be sure, such openly nationalist reasoning was an anathema to the moderate center, which was nervous not to stir the demons of the past.

When the problem of what to do with the foreigners who would not leave arose with vehemence in the early 1980s (due to the conjunction of the second oil crisis and a first huge wave of asylum-seekers), it met insecure and divided elites that did not dispose of a shared idea of national community from which clear criteria of entry and integration could be derived. Bonn's "foreigner policy" (*Auslaenderpolitik*) is notorious for its lack of consistency and foresight, wavering between impotent attempts to send guest workers home with a check and opposite attempts to "integrate" the second generation through half-hearted education and employment offers, sometimes fusing both approaches in the paradoxical concept of "temporary integration," holding firm only to the one commitment that no new recruitment was to occur. There is, however, an interesting communality between the multicultural left and the national right: both abhor the "assimilation" of foreigners. The conservative state government of Bavaria, for instance, professed its distaste for "Germanizing integration" (H. Maier), and championed the "Bavarian Model" of bilingual education whose pretention was to "maintain the lingual and cultural identity of the foreign children."[46] Only, this seemingly "multicultural" policy was premised on the reverse assumption that education in the mother tongue would facilitate the eventual return of the foreigners to their home countries. Similarly, if a government official insisted that the goal of foreigner policy was not "assimilation" but "integration," understood as "respecting the individual cultural identity [of foreigners]," he was quick to add that too many of such foreign enclaves would feed the "fears of alienation" (*Ueberfrem-dungsaengste*) of the native population, and that *Heimat* was also a "collective human right."[47]

A closer look at the long and contested making of the new Foreigner Law of 1990 reveals the polarization between a crypto-*voelkisch* right and a postnational left, with a wavering liberal center in between, which has marred Germany's immigration debate. But in the end, none of the extremes prevailed, in a cautious vindication of Germany's fabled consensus style of policy-making. The debate began with a powerful opening salvo by a notorious *Aus-laenderfeind*. In 1984, the Interior Ministry, led by ultra-conservative Bavarian hardliner Friedrich Zimmermann, issued a new plan that would limit to six years the maximum age of foreign children entitled to join their parents in Germany. This was an obvious attempt not just to stabilize but to actively reduce the number of foreigners living in Germany, and was in line with official policy at the time. The plan caused a public outcry, and it had to be quickly withdrawn, helped by a most unusual veto of Foreign Minister Genscher. While a reform of foreigner policy had been a declared key issue of his new administration, Chancellor Kohl put it on ice for four more years.

In 1988, the sturdy Bavarian at the helm of the Interior Ministry tried again. Zimmermann's second plan went even further in advocating a rotation system with a maximum stay of eight years. It opened with a solemn and, as it turned out, intolerable reaffirmation of German ethnic nationhood: "The self-understanding of the Federal Republic of Germany as a German state is at stake. A continuing ... migration of foreigners would deeply change the Federal Republic of Germany. It would mean the abandonment of the homogeneity of society, which is defined by membership of the nation ... The Federal Republic of Germany would ... develop into a multinational and multicultural society, which would be permanently plagued by minority problems ... The national interest commands to stop such a development in its very beginning.'[48] By that time, however, a broad extra-party coalition of churches, unions, charity organizations, and employers' associations had emerged that pushed for a liberalization, rather than a hardening, of the Foreigner Law. Zimmermann's reiteration of ethnic nationalism had to appear to them as a serious provocation. Even within the conservative Christian Democratic Party, moderate multiculturalists in line with the Lord Mayor of Stuttgart, Manfred Rommel, and party manager, Heiner Geissler, pressed for more generous offers to integrate foreigners instead of throwing sticks at them. Dieter Oberndoerfer, a CDU-friendly political scientist at Freiburg University, pleaded to abandon the current "nationalist" foreigner policy in favor of a more open "republican" one, pointing his finger at the fateful German division of nationalism and republicanism.[49] Facing such opposition from within and outside his own party, Zimmermann was forced to resign.

The legislation that was finally passed by the Bundestag in 1990, against the votes of the Social Democrats and the Greens, included some important liberalizing measures, while basically perpetuating the non-immigration premises of the old policy. On the positive side, legal entitlements replaced governmental discretion in key areas such as naturalization and the granting of residence permits, and family reunification was eased. What could *not* be achieved, however, indicates the inherent limitations of the maintained framework of foreigner policy: automatic birthright citizenship according to *jus soli*, double citizenship, and the right for foreigners to participate in communal elections. Despite its good intentions, the new Foreigner Law (sic) thus prolonged the previous foreigner–German dualism that remains the enduring legacy of ethnic nationalism. Accordingly, when the chips were down, the new Foreigner Law reopened the old division between the *voelkisch* right and the postnational left. If Minister Schaeuble characterized the law as a "fair compromise between Germans and foreigners (*auslaendische Mitbuerger*)," this was to the point: a compromise between two separate collectivities whose division the law did not do much to overcome.[50] Most interesting to observe are the many mutual allegations and subtle suspicions exchanged between the opponents in this debate, which reveal the dark shadow of history hanging over contemporary foreigner policy. Here one must realize that, when the new Foreigner Law was debated in early 1989/90, Germany was at the point of reunification, while facing the massive inflow of ethnic Germans (*Aussiedler*) from Eastern Europe and an unprecedented wave of asylum-seekers from the Third World and the battle zones of southeastern Europe. In a diabolic twist of history, this dramatic new constellation rehardened the lines between the *voelkisch* right and the postnational left, which – for a brief moment – had seemed to mellow.

The postnational Greens, and parts of the Social Democrats, sided with "immigrants and asylum-seekers," while questioning the automatic citizenship and social welfare privileges granted to the ethnic Germans. Conservative Christian-Democrats, in reverse, defended the constitutional and moral commitments to East Germans and ethnic Germans, and thus were driven into openly nationalist positions. For instance, Johannes Gerster, a Christian-Democratic member of parliament who had helped to make the new Foreigner Law a good deal more liberal than initially deemed possible, stressed that in weighing the claims of political asylum-seekers against the claims of ethnic Germans, "Germans have to be given constitutional and moral-political priority." Evoking the century-old allegation that Social Democrats were nationally unreliable, the CDU-deputy lashed out against the latter: "You are favouring the foreigners and agitating (*hetzen*) against the Germans. This is the reality." On the reverse, a deputy of the postnational Greens found the Social Democrats, as in July 1914, captive to a "nationalist craze" in which "there were only Germans": "This makes you so half-hearted in foreigner policy."[51]

As these small excerpts indicate, multiculturalism in Germany is first and foremost a debate among Germans about the meaning of Germanness. In this regard, our American diplomat's charge of "compulsive self-analysis" is certainly accurate. Compared with the American case, German multiculturalism tends to dwell in rather abstract declarations of, for instance, a "society without cultural center or hegemonic majority."[52] But it has not had any practical impact on college or public school curricula, and it has not led to the establishment of ethnic, race, or women's study programs at German universities. In fact, the experience of Nazism has implanted a strong distaste for cultural relativism in German intellectual discourse, which is unabashedly universalistic.[53] From this angle, the multiculturalism of intellectuals is not driven by the animus against "Eurocentrism," "logocentrism," or "false homogeneity," but by their rejection of the flawed particularism of Germanness. In comparison to Britain or the U.S., the anticolonial impulse is thus largely absent in German multiculturalism.

The Empire Strikes Back: The British Case

In the wake of the Brixton riots of 1981, the worst urban unrest in British history, Salman Rushdie launched a bitter attack on the "new empire" that had arisen within Britain. Branding the government's liberal "race relations" policy as "the latest token gesture towards Britain's blacks," the Indian-born author announced that the "new colony" would rise up against the "one real problem" that aggrieved its involuntary members: "[the racism of] white people."[54] A few years later, Rushdie's *Satanic Verses* were publically burned by an angry Muslim crowd in the city of Bradford; at Westminster, young Muslim demonstrators demanded that "Rushdie Must be Chopped Up."[55] The incriminated author had to go into hiding, protected by Thatcher's police against the anger of his fellow inmates of Britain's "new colony." What became known as the "Rushdie affair" may epitomize more dramatically than elsewhere the seamier side of a multicultural society. But the apparent ethnic assertiveness of parts of Britain's immigrant community is also the result of uniquely British conditions.

While the immigrant and anticolonial perspectives usually exclude one another, they do closely overlap in Britain. This is because former colonial subjects – Caribbean blacks and Asian Indians – formed the bulk of postwar immigration. The legacy of empire created a unique linkage between immigration and multiculturalism. In contrast to the United States, Britain has a race problem because it had immigration – the two are not separate here. This may explain why Britain has opted for an exceptionally restrictionist immigration policy from early on. In contrast to Germany, Britain complemented its restrictionist immigration policy with an American-style liberal "race relations" management, which stopped short of granting affirmative-action privileges to ethnic minorities but saw them as legitimate part of a "multi-racial" society in which "mutual tolerance" should be the norm. The conjunction of a restrictionist immigration policy, which was conditioned by Britain's devolution from multi-racial empire to ethnic nation-state, and liberal race-relations management has both fuelled and frustrated the aspirations of Britain's immigrant minorities. Excluded by Britain's national community as "blacks" or "immigrants," even in the second generation, but endowed with equal citizenship status from the beginning, Britain's immigrant minorities have become more militant and ethnicized than elsewhere, as it became evident from Brixton to Bradford.

The first parameter shaping Britain's treatment of immigration was the devolution from empire to ethnic nation-state. This went along with the exclusion of a "colored" immigrant periphery from an ethnicized British national community. Originally, Britain, with its English national core, had adhered to a "civic" model of nationhood, forged in an inter-state struggle against catholicism and absolute monarchy, with "liberty" as a core value.[56] The acquisition of a vast empire had never been easy to reconcile with the civic-nation model, and according to the national mythology it had occurred in a "fit of absentmindedness."[57] In the postimperial period after World War II, when Britain faced the triple challenge of economic and geopolitical decline and potentially huge postcolonial immigration, Britain refashioned itself from a "civic" to an "ethnic" nation, in which membership became defined by birth and ancestry. Analyzing the anti-immigrant rhetoric of Enoch Powell, Tom Nairn finds that even "in the obscene form of racism, English nationalism has been re-born."[58]

The flat "racism" charge obscures the very real problem of immigration and national membership in postimperial Britain. At the end of World War II, 800 million persons, born outside the U.K. on a territory that covered 25 percent of the land surface of the globe, could claim the equal status of "British subjects," with the concomitant right of settlement in Britain. A shift of membership definition from the feudal-dynastic principle of "allegiance to the crown" to the national principle of territorial citizenship was not only a requirement of political modernization, but also corresponded to the right of a national collectivity to regulate its boundaries.[59] Such a shift of membership definition was necessarily exclusive. Tragically, in the British constellation of a "colored" colonial periphery and a "white" core nation it was impossible to accomplish without, in effect, dividing the "ins" and the "outs" along racial lines.

In a curious counterpoint to a rigid system of immigration control, which had effectively brought new immigration to a halt by the early 1970s, Britain has instituted an exceptionally generous and elaborate regime of harmonizing "race relations." In fact, an official multiculturalism advanced as an enlightened elite strategy to smoothen the relationship between the races (whose separation was by the same token left intact). Home Secretary Roy Jenkins famously expressed this strategy in May 1966: "Integration is perhaps rather a loose word. I do not regard it as meaning the loss, by immigrants, of their own national characteristics and culture. I do not think that we need in this country a 'melting pot,' which will turn everybody out in a common mold, as one of a series of carbon copies of someone's misplaced vision of the stereotypical Englishman . . . I define integration, therefore, not as a flattening process of assimilation but as equal opportunity, accompanied by cultural diversity, in an atmosphere of mutual tolerance."[60]

Earlier than any other immigrant-receiving country in the West, including the United States, Britain rejected the idea of "assimilating" immigrants. Not by accident, but because this rejection could feed upon the legacy of a multi-racial empire. In contrast to France, Britain has never tried to "assimilate" its colonial subjects. According to the system of "indirect rule," the native chiefs were left in charge at the top of native institutions. Sir Ernest Barker has characterized this approach as "trustee imperialism," in which "the African native ... had better be left an African, but aided to become a better African."[61] Certainly, the paternalism of this "civilizing" mission is evident, and the postimperial race-relations regime in Britain could never quite free itself of it – "uneasy paternalism on the one side, a quiet hostility on the other," as David Kirp aptly described the reality of British race relations in the late 1970s.[62] But rather than simply implanting the system of indirect colonial rule into Britain, as Ira Katznelson cynically suggests,[63] the emergent race-relations regime also inherited the consensual tenet of British culture, and it was carried by the genuine impulse to eradicate racial discrimination and to spread "equal opportunities" to disadvantaged ethnic minorities.[64]

As if driven by bad conscience, the major steps in erecting the British race-relations regime were all taken by Labour governments in the wake of restrictive new immigration laws. In addition, the civil rights explosion in the United States provided a negative, ever present, example that was to be avoided in Britain.[65] The first Race Relations Act of 1965 set up a statutory board, with quite modest legal powers, to work against racially motivated discrimination in public facilities like pubs, shops, and the like. While limited in range and effectiveness, the law laid the foundation for what has become known as the "race-relations industry" – professionals paid from public funds to promote better race relations. A second Race Relations Act in 1968 strengthened the powers of the board to conduct investigations on discrimination in employment, housing, and the provision of goods and services. Finally, the third Race Relations Act of 1976 outlawed also "indirect" forms of discrimination, and established the Commission for Racial Equality to conduct formal investigations and advise the government on policy. Parallel to this, a dense network of local Race Relations Councils (RRC) was set up to provide social welfare and monitor racial discrimination at the local level – by 1991, there were approximately 80 of these councils throughout Britain, employing over 600 staff.[66]

Official multiculturalism has expressed itself in a multitude of legal provisions, such as partially exempting Hindus and Muslims from Britain's strict marriage rules, allowing Sikh boys to wear turbans and Asian girls to wear *shalwar* (trousers) at school, or – curiously – excusing Sikhs from wearing crash helmets on motorcycles provided they wear turbans. A short walk along East London's Brick Lane or Southall's South Road conveys authentic images of Islamabad or the Punjab, with Muslim, Hindu and Sikh men, women and children in their traditional dresses; the sight of Mosques; and exotic smells and oriental music from the bazaars and tea houses. Clearly, there is no presumption that these ethnic groups should become "British" in any other sense than their ownership of a British passport.

The main site of official multiculturalism has been the educational system, where it became enshrined in a government report entitled *Education for All*. It tackled the notorious underachievement of black pupils of West Indian descent, and identified "institutional racism" and widespread negative attitudes of teachers toward black pupils as responsible for this. In its opening lines, the so-called Swann Report (named after its principal author, Lord Swann) reiterates the official Government view of Britain as "both multi-racial and culturally diverse." But it goes somewhat further in defining individuals through their membership in different "groups," and in finding the government responsible for "assisting the ethnic minority communities in maintaining their distinct ethnic identities within [a] common framework [of commonly accepted values]." At the same time, "color blindness" is rejected because it "[denies] the validity of an important aspect of a person's identity."[67] While the report provoked no small controversy, it had important ramifications. In response to it, worried immigrant parents sought to establish schools outside the state sector, and local education authorities hired more Asian and black teachers and increased the ethnic component of curricula in order to bolster the positive self-image of immigrant children; following the report's thrust that multicultural education should be "for all," white children were urged to learn the history of blacks and Indians, even to speak Urdu, Creole, or Gujarati; finally, "race-awareness training" was made a required component in the education of teachers.

In his "Myrdal for Britain," E. J. B. Rose suggested that, because they had come as immigrants, "the descendents of Britain's slaves . . . would not be on the conscience of the country in the way that the Negro had for generations been on the conscience of Americans."[68] While this may adequately reflect the complacent disposition of Britain's white majority, ethnic-immigrant politics quickly adopted an anticolonial perspective. This implies negation of the voluntary aspect of this immigration, and recasts it as colonial victimization. "Why did black people come to Britain?" asks a small schoolboy in a cartoon book produced for use in schools by London's radical Institute for Race Relations, *Roots of Racism* (1982). To which this answer is provided: "[Because] white people went over to their countries, robbed them of their land and riches, enslaved their people and taught their children to be more loyal to this country than to their own." The ready acceptance of the anticolonial perspective is the result of the contradictory impulses of exclusion from an ethnicized British national community and a non-assimilationist race-relations approach. It has fuelled an assertive style of ethnic politics, which has gone beyond accommodative "multiculturalism" toward militant "anti-racism."

A peculiarity of ethnic politics in Britain is the forced assembly of the various ethnic groups under the racial fighting-label "black," and the concomitant attempt to outflank moderate "multiculturalism" by militant "anti-racism." A pamphlet on "anti-racist" education by the Institute for Race Relations, whose cynical, race-couched post-Marxism is symptomatic of the British cultural left today, explains the shortcomings of multiculturalism: "We feel...that an ethnic or cultural approach to the educational needs and attainments of racial minorities evades the fundamental reasons for their disabilities – which are the racialist attitudes and the racist practices in the larger society and in the educational system itself."[69] Applying this thinking to the sphere of politics, A. Sivanandan, the fiery leader of IRR, chastises "ethnic pluralism" for "(undermining) the underlying class aspect of black struggle and black politics."[70] In short, the ethnic kaleidoscope of multiculturalism is attacked for obscuring the underlying black–white dualism and the fact that only whites are to be kept at fault for the problems of Britain's blacks. Anti-racism blends class and race into a dichotomic "us" versus "them" fighting creed.

Militant anti-racism has pushed aside the liberal center that has long-dominated British race relations, and provoked an equally militant conservative backlash. A good example for this polarization is a short but flamboyant episode of "municipal socialism" during the early 1980s. In fact, local government has been a major institutional inlet for the anti-racist movement. At about

312   Comparative Perspectives on Immigration

the same time Mrs Thatcher arrived at 10 Downing Street, the British "class of '68" entered the Labour town halls, particularly the Greater London Council and several London borough councils such as Brent and Lambeth. As Ken Livingstone, the charismatic chief of the Greater London Council from 1981 to its abolition in 1986, put it, the new movement was "into all the things she [Mrs Thatcher] didn't like – lesbian and gay rights, black people and feminism."[71] Until the Local Government Act of 1988 and the Poll Tax put an end to it all, local government in Britain had enjoyed, since Elizabethan times, autonomy in fixing budgets and rates for the provision of housing, education, and social services. The new left's entering of town halls and local councils turned them into bastions against, and obvious targets of, Thatcher's crusade to make Britain "safe from socialism."

"Anti-racism" was a major plank of the new left's local agenda. As in the case of the Greater London Council (GLC), the flagship of municipal socialism, a well-staffed "ethnic minorities committee" was established with broad powers to reverse the underrepresentation of blacks in county hall jobs and services. The GLC declared the Greater London area to be an "Anti-Apartheid Zone" and 1984 an "anti-racist year," with festivals, free concerts, and lavish funding for organizations and campaigns engaged in the "combat" against racism, including Rastafarians.[72] As the tabloids eagerly exploited, the local "anti-racist" regime, with professional race advisors, compulsory race-awareness training, and the cleansing of schools and public services of everything that smacked even remotely of "racism," produced a climate of fear and witch-hunts. Topping even "political correctness" *a l'Americaine*, popular headteachers were fired for allegedly "racist" remarks, the nursery rhyme "Baa Baa Black Sheep" was banned as racially offensive, and Brockwell Park in South London was renamed Zephania Mothopeng Park (after the imprisoned anti-Apartheid activist). A 1986 report of Brent council, according to the tabloid *Sun* the "looniest council of the year," found the whole district "permeated with racism overt and covert," with politicians, teachers, and administrators all "outright racists, patronizing, biased, ethnocentric or simply naively ignorant of the racist context in which they work."[73] In the end, the "equal opportunities" to be provided by municipal socialism were reaped by a small core of professional activists, and fights over resources split up the "rainbow" into its components: blacks, Asians, women, gays, the disabled, and so on.[74]

In response to this "racialized" style of ethnic politics, Tories coined the famous notion "Labour calls him Black, we call him British." In fact, "anti-racism" helped produce the demon that it had made it its business to exorcise: a broad "anti-anti-racist" coalition of populist tabloids, conservative intellectuals around the *Salisbury Review*, and back-bench Tories, who mobilized a flag-waving notion of "Britishness" which hardly included multicultural identities. In this polarized confrontation between "anti-racists" and white majority defenders the liberal center became almost invisible, which thus payed the price for its neglect to link racial pluralism with an insistence to become "British" in more than mere passport ownership. In fact, by rejecting the "assimilation" endeavor from early on, the liberal center kept both core and periphery equally "ethnic," and thus apart from one another.

The unintended consequences of official multiculturalism became even more dramatically revealed during the Rushdie affair. Roy Jenkins himself, the architect of Britain's liberal race-relations regime, felt obliged to reconsider the "assumptions of the sixties," admonishing the protesting Muslims that "acceptance of British law and of British liberties is expected by all who wish to live in this country."[75] Muslims, in turn, complained that "when it comes to the test, a great deal that is spoken about Britain being a multicultural society is only words."[76] As if to make up for years of neglect, the Home Office Minister of State, John Patten, addressed British Muslim leaders in an unprecedented letter about "what it means to be British."[77] In moderate language that does by no means revokes the previous pluralism in race relations, the minister draws the picture of a "Britain where Christians, Muslims, Jews, Hindus, Sikhs and others can all work and live together, each retaining proudly their own faith and identity, but each sharing in common the bond of being, by birth or choice, British." Unfortunately, it is exactly the "proud" retention of "own faith and identity" that seems to stand in the way of being "British." The rejection of their demand to reactivate and amend an outdated "blasphemy law" for their purposes has deeply embittered the British Muslim community, which has taken a sharp separatist turn toward setting up its own schools and even founding its own Muslim "parliament." As Tariq Modood put it sarcastically, Muslims are "the group that British society is currently being forced to adjust to or defeat."[78] The call has been heard. At the height of the Rushdie affair, a conservative columnist of *The Times* threatened that "the white tribes of Britain can be every bit as stubborn and intransigent, and no less forceful in defence of their beliefs, as the brown tribes."[79]

Conclusion

If there is one general conclusion to be drawn from these case histories, it is this: having accepted significant amounts of immigrants at one point or more in the postwar period, liberal states have to tolerate the multicultural transformation of their societies. This is because liberal states, while notionally tied to particular nations, are still hesitant to impose particular cultural ways on their members. Liberal states are neutral *vis-à-vis* substantive life forms and world-views, which proved to be the major inroad for multiculturalism. This communality of liberal states is revealed if one compares them to the illiberal, increasingly immigrant-receiving states of the Near and Middle East or East Asia: states that practice caning of illegal entrants and forced repatriation of labor migrants. This does not mean that, in confrontation with radical challenges to its very premises, liberalism can itself turn into a "fighting creed," as Charles Taylor put it. It did this during the Rushdie Affair, which remains the most dramatic demonstration of the limits to multiculturalism in a liberal society. The "British liberties" held against protesting Muslims were "liberties" first, and "British" second – the national marker being exchangeable, the commitment to universal (Western) principles, like freedom of speech and expression, emphatically not. As a result of the multicultural challenge, Western nations are increasingly stripped of their particular cultural contents and reduced to civic communities committed to the same procedural rules. This is why a second-generation Turkish-German intellectual could say that immigration offered a (however ignored) "opportunity" for the German nation to ease its historical burdens.[80] In sum, liberal states have multiculturalism because they have given up the idea of assimilating their members beyond basic procedural commitments.

Such empirical multiculturalism, while heavily reinforced by immigration, is in principle independent of the latter, and applies equally to non-migrant minorities, such as sexual or religious ones. However, multiculturalism proper is not just an empirical description of culturally diverse societies, but a normative claim that cultural difference is to be publically recognized and instituted, and thus to be made the business of state rather than private initiative. To this an exasperated Juergen Habermas responded that "the ecological perspective on species conservation cannot be transferred to cultures," insisting on the group-indifferent neutrality of modern law.[81] Such normative multiculturalism, according to which the state is to be more than neutral, but actively protective of cultural difference, is especially problematic if applied to migrant minorities. "If in Rome, do as the Romans do" is one of the oldest and most constant expectations that settled groups have brought against nomadic ones. The liberal state has in fact abandoned the factual "this is how we do things here" in favor of abstract civic rules to be followed by everyone equally. But multicultural claims for group rights, which tend to be backed by an anticolonial critique of host society institutions, go beyond expectations for equal treatment toward preferential treatment for migrant "minority" groups. This is no easily sellable package, and its rejection seems to partially fire the current immigration-cum-affirmative action backlash in the United States.

Multiculturalism entails two opposite visions, articulated by its respective proponents and opponents: syncretism and fragmentation. The syncretist vision is eloquently outlined by Salman Rushdie, who sees mass migration as a possibility to "(celebrate) hybridity, impurity, intermingling, [and] the transformation that comes from new and unexpected combinations of human beings, cultures, ideas, politics, movies, songs," the migrant condition as a "metaphor for all humanity."[82] In this benign vision, multiculturalism realizes the old enlightenment dream of the unbounded "perfectibility of the human race."[83] The postcolonial literary imagination of Rushdie or Vikram Seth, popular "world music," or the vibrant art world of Los Angeles, gives a hint at the syncretist riches of multiculturalism.

But in the realm of politics, multiculturalism is more likely to entail the less benign vision of fragmentation. Post-riot Los Angeles, with its bitter inter-ethnic rivalries between Blacks, Koreans, and Latinos for scarce "rebuilding" resources, and with its dismal trend toward color-conscious "Balkan justice" in the legal system, gives a hint at the seamier side of multiculturalism. In fact, the current flurry of inter-racial activism tries to put back together what multiculturalism has helped to tear apart. In his bleak survey of ethnocentric "identity politics" in various arenas of American polity and society, Jim Sleeper seeks to distinguish between "benign multiculturalism" and "dangerous ethnocentrism."[84] Multiculturalism itself cannot generate the "civic" commitments that would allow it to transcend narrow ethnic group boundaries. Here it is worth pointing out that citizenship and "civic culture" have historically been tied to the institution of nationhood as the fixed-point of an individual's highest loyalties. When he discussed the evolution of citizenship rights in modern Britain, T. H. Marshall mentioned in passing that it was tied to the development of "national consciousness."[85] Citizenship, so Marshall argued, requires a "sense of community membership." Historically, this "community" has been the nation. If multiculturalism challenges the nation, it fails to offer a substitute for it. In this regard, recent analyses of "postnational" citizenship may be precipitate. Yasemin Soysal argues that European guest workers have pioneered a new form of membership based on a transnational "logic of personhood" superseding the "logic of national citizenship." But she has to admit that the implementation of "universalistic rights" remains "tied to specific states and their institutions."[86] Short of a world state, the world's states will remain nation-states. Paradoxically, multiculturalism remains dependent upon the nation-state, while undermining it at the same time.

Notes

1 Charles Taylor, *Multiculturalism and the Politics of Recognition* (Princeton, N.J.: Princeton University Press, 1992; 2nd edn, 1994).

2 See Ernest Gellner, *Nations and Nationalism* (Ithaca, N.Y.: Cornell University Press, 1983).

3 Michael Schudson, "Culture and the Integration of National Societies," *International Social Science Journal* 139, 1994, p. 77.

4 Joseph Raz, "Multiculturalism: A Liberal Perspective," *Dissent*, Winter 1994, p. 69.

5 Quoted in Cornel West, *Race Matters* (New York: Vintage, 1994), p. xiv.

6 Frantz Fanon, *The Wretched of the Earth* (New York: Grove Press, 1963), p. 39f.

7 Charles Taylor, *Multiculturalism*, p. 63 (see note 1), has made this point.

8 James Clifford, "Introduction: Partial Truths," in: J. Clifford/George Marcus, eds, *Writing Culture* (Berkeley: University of California Press, 1986).

9 Fanon, *Wretched of the Earth*, p. 43.

10 Amy Gutmann, "Introduction," in: Charles Taylor, *Multiculturalism*, p. 19 (see note 1).

11 Centre for Contemporary Cultural Studies, *The Empire Strikes Back* (London: Hutchinson, 1982).

12 See Todorov's suggestive "portraits of travelers" in his *On Human Diversity* (Cambridge, Mass.: Harvard University Press, 1993), pp. 341–52.

13 This paradox is brilliantly scrutinized by Nathan Glazer, *Affirmative Discrimination* (Cambridge: Harvard University Press, 1975), and *Ethnic Dilemmas, 1964–1982* (Cambridge, Mass.: Harvard University Press, 1983).

14 William Wei, *The Asian American Movement* (Philadelphia: Temple University Press, 1992), p. 9.

15 Ibid., p. 136.

16 Peter Skerry, *Mexican Americans: The Ambivalent Minority* (New York: Free Press, 1993).

17 Quoted in Abigail Thernstrom, *Whose Votes Count? Affirmative Action and Minority Voting Rights* (Cambridge Mass: Harvard University Press, 1987), p. 54.

18 Ibid., p. 50.

19 See Linda Chavez, "Party Lines," *New Republic*, 24 June 1991, pp. 14–16.

20 Peter Skerry, "Keeping Immigrants in the Political Sweatshop," *Wall Street Journal*, 6 November 1989, p. 16.

21 See Linda Chavez, *Out of the Barrio* (New York: Basic Books, 1991).

22 Peter Skerry, *Mexican Americans*, ch. 9.

23 "Black and Hispanic Opinion on Immigration Reform," *Immigration Report* (Federation of Americans for Immigration Reform, Washington D.C.) 4(11), August 1983.

24 Wei, *Asian Americans*, p. 136.

25 Quoted in Diane Ravitch, "Multiculturalism: E Pluribus Plures," in: P. Berman, *Debating P.C.*, p. 291.

26 Quoted in Jim Sleeper, *The Closest of Strangers* (New York: Norton, 1990), p. 219.

27 Arthur Schlesinger, *The Disuniting of America* (New York: Norton, 1992), p. 74.

28 Horace Kallen, *Culture and Democracy in the United States* (New York: Boni and Liveright, 1924), p. 51.

29 Ibid., p. 124.

30 Quoted in Robert Reinhold, "Class Struggle," *New York Times Magazine*, 29 September 1991, p. 47.

31 William I. Thomas and Florian Znaniecki, *The Polish Peasant in Europe and America* (edited and abridged by Eli Zaretsky). Urbana: University of Illinois Press, 1984, p. 289.

32 Nathan Glazer and Daniel P. Moynihan, *Beyond the Melting Pot* (Cambridge: MIT Press, 1970; 2nd edn), p. xcvii.

33 Richard Sennett, "The Identity Myth," *New York Times*, 30 January 1994, p. E17.

34 Andrew Hacker, " 'Diversity' and its Dangers," *New York Review of Books*, 7 October 1993, p. 22.

35 Lawrence Auster, "The Forbidden Topic," *National Review*, 27 April 1992, p. 42.

36 Nathan Glazer, "In Defense of Multiculturalism," *The New Republic*, 2 September 1991, p. 19.

37 'U.S. Envoy Rebukes Germans and Kohl on Foreigner Issue," *International Herald Tribune*, 16/17 April 1994, p. 2.

38 Quoted in Ulrich Herbert, *A History of Foreign Labor in Germany, 1880–1980* (Ann Arbor: University of Michigan Press, 1990), p. 212.

Comparative Perspectives on Immigration

39 The Greens, *Die multikulturelle Gesellschaft* (Bonn: Die Gruenen im Bundestag, 1990), pp. 88 and 90.

40 Stein Rokkan, "Dimensions of State Formation and Nation-Building," in: Charles Tilly, ed. *The Foundation of National States in Western Europe* (Princeton University Press, 1975).

41 In Lutz Hoffmann, *Die unvollendete Republik* (Cologne: Papy Rossa, 1990), p. 97.

42 "Sind wir ein Einwanderungsland?" *Das Parlament* (Bonn), no. 9–10, 1990, p. 11.

43 Peter Glotz, *Der Irrweg des Nationalstaats* (Stuttgart: DVA, 1990).

44 Rogers Brubaker, *Citizenship and Nationhood in France and Germany* (Cambridge, MASS.: Harvard University Press, 1992) makes this point (pp. 168 ff).

45 Juergen Schilling, "Multikulturelle Gesellschaft oder Repatriierung?" in: Heiner Geissler, ed. *Auslaender in Deutschland* vol. 2 (Munich: Olzog, 1984), p. 127.

46 Hans Maier, "Bildungspolitische Integration 'Modell Bayern'," *Das Parlament*, 29 August/5 September 1981, p. 13.

47 Eckart Schiffer, "Auslaenderintegration und/oder multikulturelle Gesellschaft," *Politische Studien* 43(321), 1992.

48 Quoted in Christian Schneider, "Aus Fremden werden Mitbuerger und Landsleute," *Sueddeutsche Zeitung*, 10/11 September 1988, p. 9.

49 Dieter Oberndoerfer, "Nationalismus und Republikanismus im Grundgesetz der Bundesrepublik Deutschland," in: Klaus J. Bade, ed., *Auslaender, Aussiedler, Asyl in der Bundesrepublik Deutschland* (Hanover: Landeszentrale fuer politische Bildung, 1992).

50 This and the following statements are reprinted in "Neues Auslaenderrecht vom Bundestag verabschiedet," *Das Parlament*, 18 May 1990, p. 8.

51 'Sind wir ein Einwanderungsland?" *Das Parlament*, 23 February/2 March 1990, pp. 12 and 13.

52 Claus Leggewie, *Multi Kulti* (Berlin: Rotbuch, 1993), p. xiii.

53 The best example is the work and politics of Juergen Habermas, Germany's first and foremost intellectual.

54 Salman Rushdie, "The New Empire Within Britain," *New Society*, 9 December 1982, p. 421.

55 "March ends in battle at Westminster," *The Guardian*, 29 May 1989, p. 2.

56 "Liberty was the hallmark of Englishness," in: Linda Colley, *Britons* (New Haven: Yale University Press), p. 111).

57 See Sir Ernest Barker's telling characterization of the empire as "something outside ourselves which is yet a part of ourselves," in his *The Ideas and Ideas of the British Empire* (Cambridge, Cambridge University Press, 1951), p. 7.

58 Tom Nairn, *The Break-Up of Britain* (London: Verso, 1981), p. 269.

59 See the normative discussion by Michael Walzer, *Spheres of Justice* (New York: Basic Books), ch. 3.

60 Quoted in Sheila Patterson, *Immigration and Race Relations in Britain 1960–1967* (London: Oxford University Press, 1969), p. 112f.

61 Ernest Barker, *The Ideas and Ideals of the British Empire*, p. 155.

62 David L. Kirp, *Doing Good by Doing Little: Race and Schooling in Britain* (Berkeley: University of California Press, 1979), p. 29.

63 Ira Katznelson, *Black Men, White Cities* (London: Oxford University Press, 1973).

64 This partial break with colonialism is stressed by Gary Freeman, *Immigrant Labor and Racial Conflict*, p. 148.

65 Characteristically, the first (and largest) survey undertaken on the situation of New Commonwealth immigrants in Britain, E. J. B. Rose's *Colour and Citizenship* (London: Oxford University Press, 1969), was framed as "a Myrdal for Britain while there is still time" (p. xix).

66 Central Office of Information, *Ethnic Minorities*, p. 32.

67 Lord Swann, *Education for All* (London: HMSO, 1985), pp. 5 and 26f.

68 Rose, *Colour and Citizenship*, p. 5.

69 IRR, "Anti-Racist Not Multicultural Education," *Race and Class* 21(1), 1980, pp. 81–3.

70 A. Sivanandan, "Challenging Racism," *Searchlight*, no. 95, May 1983, p. 17.

71 Quoted by Russell Lewis, *Anti-Racism: A Mania Exposed* (London: Quartet 1988), p. 132.

72 See Greater London Council, *Ethnic Minorities and the Abolition of the GLC* (London: GLC, 1984), p. 1.

73 Quoted in Stewart Lansley et al., *Councils in Conflict* (London: Macmillan, 1989), p. 135.

74 See Herman Ouseley, "Resisting Institutional Change," in: Wendy Ball and John Solomos, eds, *Race and Local Politics* (London: Macmillan, 1990).

75 Roy Jenkins, "On Race Relations and the Rushdie Affair," *The Independent*, 4 March 1989.

76 So said a Muslim member of Bradford City Council Labour group, quoted in *Financial Times*, 24 June 1989, p. 5.

77 The letter is reprinted as "The Muslim Community in Britain" in *The Times*, 5 July 1989, p. 13.

78 Tariq Modood, "British Asian Muslims and the Rushdie Affair," *Political Quarterly* 61(2), 1990, p. 144.

79 Clifford Longley, "A very British lesson Muslims must learn," *The Times*, 8 July 1989.

80 Interview with Zafer Senocak, 13 June 1994, Berlin.

81 Juergen Habermas, "Struggles for Recognition in the Democratic Constitutional State," in: Charles Taylor, *Multiculturalism*, p. 130 (see note 1).

82 Quoted in Kaushika Amin and Robin Richardson, *Politics for All* (London: Runnymede Trust, 1992), p. 47.

83 The most eloquent version of this dream can be found in Condorcet's "Tenth Stage" of his *Sketch for a Historical Picture of the Progress of the Human Mind*.

84 Jim Sleeper, *In Defense of Civic Culture* (Washington, D.C.: Progressive Foundation, 1993).

85 T. H. Marshall, *Citizenship and Social Class* (London: Pluto Press, 1992), p. 25.

86 Yasemin Soysal, *Limits to Citizenship* (Chicago: University of Chicago Press, 1994), p. 164 and p. 157, respectively.

15 Immigration and Group Relations in France and America

Donald L. Horowitz

International migration is often thought of as something new in world history. In receiving countries, the immigrants, their place in the new society, and their ties to the old are rediscovered by each generation as issues to be faced afresh. Since World War II, there has been a new surge of movement across international boundaries. The need for labor in industrial countries, the gap in standards of living, turbulence and warfare in many newly independent countries, and the greater ease and reduced cost of transportation have all contributed to increased migrant flows, particularly increased flows over longer distances. Yet, despite ebbs and flows, the world-wide movement of peoples is of long standing.

So, too, are the characteristic issues raised by international migration in the receiving countries. How do the immigrants fit into and affect the receiving polity and society? What changes can or must the receiving country make to accommodate them? What changes do immigrants and their descendants experience, in culture and ethnic identity? What are the relations of immigrant groups to the mix of peoples already present in the receiving country? What determines the policies that govern the reception and treatment of immigrants? What determines the success and satisfaction of immigrants over time? Everywhere questions such as these have been asked.

Uniform questions, however, do not elicit uniform answers, even among countries with relatively similar institutions, ideologies, and histories of immigration. Two of the world's oldest democracies, the United States and France, have traditionally welcomed immigrants. With strongly entrenched official doctrines of equality, traceable to common sources in the European Enlightenment, both countries have long received immigrants seeking economic opportunity, and both pride themselves on their hospitality to political refugees and dissidents. Both experienced large immigrant flows in the late nineteenth and early twentieth centuries, followed by a hiatus and then resumed flows from different source countries in recent decades. Both have become home to large numbers of immigrants from countries outside of Europe and North America. Both need to accommodate greater racial and religious heterogeneity than they were previously accustomed to accommodating.

France and the United States are attempting to come to grips with the effects of immigration on the economy, on political integration, and on culture. France has experienced an anti-immigrant backlash and a debate on the place of immigrants and ethnic minorities in French society. In France, as elsewhere in Europe, immigrant groups are now perceived as a major "problem." In the United States, passage of the Immigration Reform and Control Act of 1986 and of the Immigration Act of 1990 has by no means ended debate on such matters. On the contrary, the United States may be in the process of redefining the nature of its society and polity – a process prompted by the conjunction of large-scale immigration with the increased economic and political participation of preexisting racial minorities. In both countries, immigration has wrought profound change. In neither has the process of change run its course.

The many similarities between France and the United States make a comparison of the two countries particularly feasible and intriguing. Despite the similarities, what is striking is how different many of the results of immigration have been thus far. In both countries, there is an interplay of popular conceptions about immigrants (and about the pluralism they engender) with national history and ideology, as well as with official policy and thought about the nature of the society being created. Yet, whereas the United States is overtly a country of immigrants, France is only covertly and partially such a country. The French do not regard themselves, in the way that Americans do, as the descendants of immigrants. Subtle differences in doctrines of equality yield different relations of citizens to the state, and a different configuration of political institutions also produces divergent conceptions of the role of immigrant and minority groups in the polity. Many of the same roots grow into quite different branches.

Immigration: Parallel Histories

About 7 percent of the United States population and about 8 percent of the French population were born in foreign countries. Although the French percentage is the highest in Europe, other countries of immigration, such as Australia, have much higher percentages. Perhaps as much as one-third of the population of France can trace its origins to the immigration of a grandparent (Girard 1971). *"France, terre d'accueil"* – "a welcoming country" – is a boast with considerable historical validity. Moreover, as previous generations of immigrants became "just Americans" (Lieberson and Waters 1988), their counterparts became just French, to the point where Gérard Noiriel (1988, 19) speaks of a "collective amnesia" about immigrant origins.

France, too, has a population traditionally enriched by immigration. Mass immigration to France began in the mid nineteenth century. Among the main source countries were Belgium, Italy, and Poland. By 1930, France had the world's highest rate of immigration, 515 per one hundred thousand inhabitants, higher than the United States, with 492 (Noiriel 1987, 3). Following World War II, immigration resumed, putting France near the top of the world's countries in terms of foreign-born population. To the earlier central European immigrants who staffed the mines and factories in which French peasants were reluctant to work was added a new wave of Iberian, Asian, and North African immigrants. In 1901, nearly two-thirds of the foreign population in France was Belgian or Italian. During the interwar period, a good many Slavs came as well: Poles, Czechs, and Ukrainians. By 1975, a year after the French border was closed to most immigration, more than four-fifths of all foreigners had come from North Africa or the Iberian peninsula, with more than a fifth each from Portugal and Algeria. Like the United States, France has its old immigrants and its new, and by some estimates (*Figaro*, 16 October 1989) nearly a million illegal immigrants. In both countries, restrictions on immigration have increased the numbers of those seeking entry in special categories: refugees in the United States, asylees in France (OECD 1990, 37).

In France, as in the United States, immigrants are not distributed randomly across the country. As the favored American destinations of central and eastern Europeans were the industrial cities of the Midwest, so the favored destination of Mexicans has been California, that of Cubans has been Florida, and that of a great many other groups has been New York City and its environs. Belgians congregated in nineteenth-century French factory towns, and Poles sought work in the mines of Lorraine and Languedoc. North Africans have been heavily concentrated in and around several major cities: Paris, Lyon, and Marseilles.

Americans like to think that the United States is distinctive in its creation through immigration. In this, of course, they are quite mistaken. Not only have Canada, Australia, and Argentina been equally affected by immigration, but so have several European countries, none more than France. The difference between France and the United States has not been so much in immigration but in ideas about immigration – and hence about ethnicity – and in the institutions that govern the reception of immigrants and their descendants.

National Ideas: Divergent Histories

Both France and the United States share a conception of open admission to the political community. The French census and other officially gathered statistics divide the population into "French" and "foreigners." Earlier generations of immigrants, especially European immigrants but not merely Europeans, have moved over into the "French" column, in much the same way as previous immigrants to the United States were "Americanized" – and by many of the same methods. In both countries, the public schools were taken to be important vehicles of acculturation. Mastery of the French and English languages also played roughly similar roles in the transformation of immigrants into citizens. Although France has not had the same liberal *jus soli* rules of citizenship that the United States has had, it nevertheless has made naturalization liberally available to immigrants and their children, and there are forces working for further liberalization of citizenship rules (see the report of the so-called *Commission des Sages*: Long 1988).

At the same time, the division of the population into French and foreign implies something that goes to the heart of differences between France and the United States. The dichotomization of identity means that immigrants who are no longer "foreigners" are presumed to exchange their former identity for a French identity. Hyphenation, the hardy perennial of American ethnic studies, is logically foreclosed in France (with exceptions to be noted later).

It is possible to be an Italian in France, but it is not possible to be an Italian-Frenchman in the same easy way as it is possible to be an Italian-American.

Right at this point, one can glimpse some central differences in French and American thought. These relate to the concept of a core identity, the relation of people to the land and the community, and the relative spheres of the state and civil society.

At the time of the French Revolution, the French language and French identity certainly did not occupy the same geographic space that they do today. Both have spread out from the center to most parts of the periphery. Still, the core identity has not been in doubt. There was a French nation, defined largely by blood and later by conceptions of "our ancestors, the Gauls" – a conception taken a bit more literally than the rather metaphorically invoked "pilgrim fathers" in the United States. After the Revolution, to be sure, powerful doctrines of equality bonded citizens to that nation, irrespective of blood. The concept of the nation was not, however, wholly drained of its organic character (Safran 1989a) – as Gérard Noiriel points out. 1789 was said to mark the victory of the Gauls over the aristocratic Franks – and immigrants were often greeted with a considerable measure of xenophobia. Anti-Belgian feeling ran very strong in northern France in the mid-nineteenth century (Noiriel 1988, 258). In the 1870s, Italians were viewed as "parasites on the economic system" and thought to be utterly unassimilable (Morsy 1984, 33). The same objections are raised today for the Maghrébins.

In the United States during the revolutionary period, the various colonies were composed of differing ethnic and religious mixes. Often, there was mutual enmity within colonies, as between, for example, Scots-Irish Presbyterians and English Quakers in Pennsylvania. Political positions taken toward the American Revolution were frequently explicable in terms of such ethnic and religious rivalries (Alger 1974). No doubt, earlier migrants from Great Britain often were acknowledged as a founding population, but the fact that the Revolutionary War was fought against Britain diluted any stronger claims that might have been made over the long term. Ultimately, the sense of the United States as a country formed and re-formed by immigration precluded the creation of a permanent core identity to which outsiders could only aspire.

There were, to be sure, powerful waves of nativist sentiment, triggered by each new wave of immigration (see Higham 1968). At various times, those who arrived earlier pursued conflict against foreigners, against Catholics, against Irish, and against eastern and southern Europeans. These conflicts were punctuated by lethal episodes of ethnic violence (Horowitz 1983). As Italians were killed in a southern French city in 1893, they were also lynched in a southern American city in 1891 (Higham 1968, 91). Yet, in the end, yesterday's immigrants became today's natives, precisely because there was no fixed notion of who – among Whites – could claim indigenous status. A study in a small Vermont city in the 1930s found that more recent immigrants accorded a mild form of deference toward the established "Yankee" families of the city, who were acknowledged by their Irish and French Canadian neighbors as a "Charter Group," people associated with the founding (Anderson 1937). Beyond that, at least for Whites, the society could make no permanently fixed distinctions between indigenes and immigrants. It had no strongly organic conception of Americanness.

The United States was also conceived as a great adventure in the conquest and taming of a vast land. It was a country in the making, and immigration was essential to settling it. Gérard Noiriel (1988) points out that immigration was encouraged not in order to settle France, but to provide labor. Still, in France, there was – and is – some notion, however fictitious, that immigrants may actually return to their countries of origin, and there has been no notion that immigrants have been in any sense creating the country. The nation and the republican polity were created by 1789. Unlike the American Revolution, which was a beginning, the French Revolution was a culmination. Immigrants could cleave to a France already established, but they could neither make nor remake it.

Equally republican, France and the United States nevertheless entertain diametrically opposed conceptions of state and society. French revolutionary norms provide for a direct relationship between the citizen and the state. Jacobin ideals are hostile to organizations that mediate this relationship. Hence the suspicion of ethnic interest groups. Until 1981, there was actually in force a statute that prohibited formation of organizations of foreigners. There is no denying that various interest organizations exist and that they sometimes lobby government, but the phenomenon gives rise to theoretical discomfort. Interests, which are inevitably partial, are a contradiction of Rousseauean notions of the general will (Ehrmann and Schain 1991, 165). In such an ideological climate, ethnic pluralism does not flourish easily. It is not surprising that even the term *ethnicity*, with its connotations of competing, substate loyalty, is regarded with considerable suspicion.

The United States, on the other hand, is beholden more to Montesquieu than to Rousseau. Madison, too, was suspicious of interests, but he saw them as inevitable, indeed natural, and his response was to balance them rather than to delegitimize them (Hamilton, Jay, and Madison 1888, nos. 10, 51). There has always been a legitimate place in American political thought for mediary institutions between the citizen and the state. Speaking of the multitude of American voluntary associations, Alexis de Tocqueville (1945, 198) aptly linked them to "mistrust" of "social authority." American theorists often regard a rich array of interests as supportive of democracy (Key 1956, 10–11; Diamond et al. 1988), partly because they help to limit state power. Traditional American liberalism has been thoroughly hostile to state power (and "big government"), which it placed in opposition to the popular will (Hartz 1955, 211–18). For this among other reasons, voluntary associations are not suspect. The assortment of American ethnic organizations active in lobbying on policy matters seems thoroughly bewildering in France (see Weiner, 1989).

As William Safran (1989a, 6) has well said, the United States favors civil society against the state, whereas France favors the state over civil society. Is it any wonder that France habitually forgets its previous waves of immigration and provides little or no space for ethnic groups, whereas the United States has made the recollection of immigration and the exaltation of ethnicity something of a cottage industry?

The Foulard Affair: Immigrants and Two Secular Religions

Ethnic pluralism is not in favor in France, largely because of long-standing ideas about the relationships of citizens to the state. There are other forces that point in the same direction, most notably the singular secularism of the French state, with its origins in the thought of Voltaire and the *philosophes* (see, e.g., Cobban 1961, 83–4).

A revealing example of the powerful challenge immigrants are thought to present to some fundamental conceptions of French nationhood is provided by the great *foulard* controversy of 1989.

A furor was created when three North African students in a state school north of Paris refused to remove the head coverings (*chadors*) worn by Muslim women, in order to attend class. School authorities prevented their attendance. In a compromise, the students then agreed to remove the head coverings in class but not at recreation, but they subsequently reneged. Muslim students elsewhere in France took a similar position, and the matter quickly became a *cause célèbre* (see, e.g., the several articles in the right-wing newspaper *Figaro*, 20 October 1989). Eventually, French educational authorities relented, but it was widely agreed that the episode epitomized serious tensions.

In the United States, the *foulard* dispute would quickly have been perceived to implicate only the right to religious freedom. That is not to say that the courts would under all circumstances have upheld the right to wear the *chador* (cf. *Employment Division v. Smith* [1990]), only that the matter would have been cast instantly in the discourse of rights. The *chador* might make a variety of groups uneasy, for a variety of reasons, none of which – certainly not the secularization of the schools – could compete with a formulation in terms of rights. A public school that excluded a student on grounds of religiously motivated costume would have been widely denounced as bigoted. If France worships at the shrine of the undifferentiated citizen, the United States worships at the shrine of constitutional rights.

This is particularly so in ethnic and racial relations, where rights discourse furnishes strong support for the entrenchment of heterogeneity. The Constitution and several civil rights statutes have produced an elaborate jurisprudence of ethnic and racial equality, about which I shall say more later. An important illustration of the reach of such doctrine is the decision of the United States Supreme Court that aliens are a "protected class," so that legal classifications based on alienage receive "close judicial scrutiny" for their conformity to the principles of equal treatment embodied in the Constitution and in a plethora of judicial decisions (*Graham v. Richardson* [1971]).

To be sure, the law is not silent on such matters in France. There are ongoing efforts to make legal procedures affecting immigrants more fair (see, e.g., *Libération*, 14 October 1989, on stays of deportation), and there are statutes prohibiting ethnic and racial discrimination in employment, provision of goods and services, including housing, and treatment by public authorities (Costa-Lascoux 1990). But discrimination is difficult to prove, the law has been effective only "where the discrimination is manifest and specific," and the number of cases remains small: well under one hundred that reach final adjudication each year (Costa-Lascoux 1990, 17, 18).

Moreover, the scope of the interests protected by French law is relatively narrow. Foreigners are excluded from French civil service employment and membership in the professions – both areas opened up to aliens by the Supreme Court of the United States (*Sugarman v. Dougall* [1973]; *In re Griffiths* [1973]) – and immigrants are frequently subject to arbitrary police action. The range of matters conceived in legal terms is completely different, as indeed the remedies are as well. Whereas the British Race Relations Act of 1976 makes limited provision for positive discrimination (affirmative action), French law has no such provision.

More to the point, however, is the judicialization of the whole subject in the United States in a way that is completely unheard of in France or anywhere else. If Congress passes an act forbidding discrimination in employment, as indeed it has in Title 7 of the Civil Rights Act of 1964, the cases number annually in the many thousands. Title 7 law is voluminous and elaborate; it engages the attention of thousands of lawyers and administrators in the private and public sectors. If there are thought to be too few television programs catering to minority tastes, then the Federal Communications Commission may set aside a certain share of television licenses for applicants who are "Black, Hispanic Surnamed, American Eskimo, Aleut, American Indian and Asiatic American," and the courts will decide whether the set-aside is lawful (*Metro Broadcasting v. FCC* [1990]). It was, again, Tocqueville (1945, 290) who first noted the powerful impact of law and legal thinking on Americans. In the United States, he said, everyone speaks "the language of the magistrate." Tocqueville's insight applies to immigration, race, and ethnicity, as much as it does to any other field.

In the United States, then, ethnic and racial politics wears the clothing of the law. This means, first of all, that ethnicity and ethnic politics are legitimate – indeed, legally protected – in ways that are inconceivable in France. There is, for example, a role for ethnic groups in American foreign policy toward Northern Ireland, Israel, Cyprus, South Africa, and Cuba, among others, that would be anathema in France (see Glazer 1987). It also means that the law and often the Constitution are on the side of ethnic pluralism, and those who question the rights of immigrants and minorities start out at a considerable disadvantage.

None of this implies that the United States is a happier multi-ethnic society than France is. It does suggest that quite different paradigms are at work.

The most direct manifestation of the two paradigms is the different meaning of equality in the two countries, despite the common sources of the very concept of equality. In France, the attainment of equality implied erasing blood privileges and therefore more generally erasing traces of origins. In the United States, with no aristocracy, stripping citizens of birth origins before their encounter with the state was a less pressing task. It is thus possible to say that Americans are equal despite remaining differences (and, more recently, that the differences, irrespective of their content, are enriching). If the *bête noire* of ethnic activists in the United States is "Anglo conformity," much of the society – even much of what remains of discernible Anglo-Saxon society – opposes that conformity. But if an equivalent *bête noire* should emerge in France – call it "Franco conformity" – the mainstream population is unlikely to understand why this should be regarded as any kind of beast at all. The very epithet sounds highly improbable. When the French government speaks of "integration," it is safe to assume that something like conformity to French cultural norms forms a major part of such a program. Americans, on the other hand, no longer speak of either "Americanization" or integration.

The Configuration of Institutions

In any inventory of French-American differences bearing on immigration and group relations, the political institutions of the two countries must rank high. To some extent, of course, the institutions are the product of the national ideologies. The importance of the central government in France reflects the *étatisme* of France (Wilson 1989); federalism in the United States reflects the desire for complex institutions to prevent the concentration of power in any one of them. Yet institutions structure the way groups relate to the polity.

For the United States, federalism historically meant that ethnic groups that opposed each other in one state did not necessarily meet the same antagonists in the next. Federalism compartmentalized tensions and made identities relevant at the state level that could never have been relevant at the national level. It reinforced the fragmented character of ethnic cleavages and precluded the ultimate ascendancy of any one of them, save the White-Black cleavage. It also permitted groups to attain a measure of satisfaction by attaining local power when national power was far from their grasp.

Lacking federalism, France's immigration problems are national – in many ways, uniform – problems. The decentralization of power beginning in 1982 has, however, allowed some scope for local management of minority problems (Ireland 1989, 323), not always felicitous management. The same was true historically in the United States, for state control made possible the maintenance of racial segregation in the southern states until the issue of racial equality was nationalized, first by the Supreme Court and then by Congress.

Political party systems are crucial to patterns of immigrant and ethnic politics. French parties are centrally directed; voter identification with parties is not overwhelming; voters can be volatile; and the party system is fragmented across a wide spectrum, so that no party approaches a majority. The party system is therefore "susceptible to single-issue movements, such as the *Front National*" (Hollifield 1989, 7). As established parties sense the saliency of the immigrant issue, they respond by making it their issue, as the Socialist government did soon after the *foulard* controversy. Indeed, the Communists, who controlled some local authorities with heavy concentrations of immigrants, began to implement anti-immigrant policies in the late 1970s and early 1980s (Schain 1988, 605). That the left proved soft on xenophobia despite its class commitments is testimony to the power of the immigrant issue in electoral politics. The decline of the Communist vote was indeed paralleled by the growth of the *Front National*, often in the same urban areas.

In certain areas heavily populated by immigrants, the FN has gained seats overwhelmingly, by winning a majority of the vote. Nowhere else in Western Europe does anti-immigrant sentiment, strong though it may be, have such a promising electoral foothold. With two relatively strong parties, Germany has some extremist parties as well, but none with such an exclusive focus on immigrant groups or with as much electoral appeal. The FN has no strong electoral counterpart in two-party-dominant Britain. The anti-immigrant cause has been taken up in Italy by regional parties, such as the Lombardy League, their national strength limited by their parochial appeal. In France, the combination of a spectrum of opinion, concomitantly weak parties, and a strong center undiluted by Italy's pervasive regionalism provides no barrier to the power of the immigrant issue.

The American system is, of course, completely different. Parties are decentralized, and candidates operate as sovereign political entrepreneurs, which means that they are open to ethnic and racial interest groups on an individual basis. Two parties are dominant, and plurality elections pull both of them to the center. Occasionally, extreme candidates can win elections, but it is difficult to imagine an ethnically or racially extremist party with power at the polls. In the United States, where ethnic and racial politics pervades the system, the issues still do not quite have the clarity that they have in France. Some issues are localized, and others find their way to the courts. In France, immigration issues ebb and flow, but the politics of integration or exclusion has a bluntness and a resonance denied to it by the complexity of American institutions as well as by American ideology.

What Kind of Society?

Both France and America may be on the verge of redefining the relationships of groups to each other and possibly to the state. But the differing directions of the redefinition are suggested by two French events. In September 1989, French demonstrators protested plans to build a mosque in Lyon. The mayor declined to retract the building permit, but he did say that no call to prayer would be allowed from the minaret. A year later, a mosque was built in Lorraine, with an eighty-foot minaret, from which, the mosque's builders volunteered at the outset, no amplified call to prayer would issue, for fear of drowning out church bells nearby (*New York Times*, 29 November 1990). There have been Maghrébin protest marches, but at bottom the cautious etiquette of group relations in France reflects deference of the immigrants to the indigenous population and a model that still differentiates, in some measure, hosts and guests.

To be sure, there are many proposals by distinguished students of French immigration for a new French pluralism. But what is emphasized in such proposals is, first of all, to redress the failure to remember the long French history of immigration and to acknowledge France as the home of xenophobia as well as of the Rights of Man, not merely for historical accuracy but to ameliorate the plight of today's immigrants, who suffer from a debilitating sense of difference (Noiriel in *Le Monde*, 20 October 1989). Beyond that, the demand for a *"multiculturalisme à la française"* is generally an argument for the integration of "foreign origin populations by universal institutions" (Schnapper 1989, 107) – which is to say that it is an argument for liberal equality and against balkanization along ethnic lines. Here, too, the American experience enters, for differential treatment, including what are seen in France as ethnic "quotas," is believed to produce only a "false equality." The United States provides again a contrast for France to avoid.

Now, however, as France moves haltingly to a recognition of pluralism, with a strong admixture of integration and acculturation, the United States may be moving to something different: a more truly plural or mosaic society, with many compartments.

Such an impetus derives, above all, from a combination of subjective and objective developments in race relations. There is a gap between White and Black attitudes. In recent years, Whites increasingly believe a great deal of progress has been made in race relations. Blacks decreasingly believe that (Schuman et al. 1988, xiv, 141–2). At the same time, there has been some tendency toward separate Black institutions – some separately run schools based on voucher plans and a certain elite enthusiasm for so-called Afrocentric curricula. All of this is concurrent, of course, with increasing representation of Blacks in formerly White institutions, from universities to corporations, professions, and governmental bodies. As the society has moved from racial subordination, the claim has increasingly been made by Black elites that the United States is a truly "multicultural society." In place of the previous horizontal cleavage, one or more vertical cleavages may be emerging.

Here, again, the connection between the Afro-American experience and the recent immigrant experience becomes crucial. It is open to Hispanics and Asians to take up this invitation for a reconstruction of American society along genuinely plural or multicultural lines. Presumably, the implication of such a formulation is that groups would have considerable autonomy in regulating their own affairs, and there would be shares of rewards and opportunities apportioned in advance by a political process involving negotiations among group representatives and doubtless by a legal process involving new rights. Needless to say, there are societies organized along such lines, but the United States has not been one of them.

Whether it will become such a society depends on many things, including political and legal institutions. One thing it also depends on is the emerging perceptions and social constructions of the Hispanic and Asian groups. Thus far there is little in the ideology or behavior of these groups that would suggest that such a formulation is congenial to them (see, e.g., Horowitz 1985, 77–92). But if anything like such a conception should prevail, France will observe this experience with keen interest, the French-American contrast will be extended, and French fears of "ethnicity" will undoubtedly be confirmed.

Cases Cited

Allen v. Board of Elections, 393 U.S. 544, 549 (1969).
Employment Division v. Smith, 108 L. Ed. 2d 876 (1990).
Farrington v. Tokushige, 284 U.S. 298 (1926).
Graham v. Richardson, 403 U.S. 365 (1971).
In re Griffiths, 413 U.S. 717 (1973).
Metro Broadcasting v. FCC, 110 S. Ct. 2997 (1990).
Meyer v. Nebraska, 262 U.S. 390 (1923).
Pierce v. Society of Sisters, 268 U.S. 510 (1925).
Plyler v. Doe, 457 U.S. 202 (1982).
Sugarman v. Dougall, 413 U.S. 634 (1973).

Statutes Cited

Civil Rights Act of 1964, Title 7, as amended, 42 U.S.C. $$ 2000e et seq.
Immigration Act of 1990, Pub. L. 101–649, 104 Stat. 4978 (29 November 1990).
Immigration Reform and Control Act of 1986, Pub. L. 99–603, 100 Stat. 3359.
Voting Rights Act of 1965, as amended, 42 U.S.C. $$ 1971 et seq.

References

Alba, Richard. 1990. *Ethnic Identity: The Transformation of White America*. New Haven, CT: Yale University Press.
Alger, Janet Merrill. 1974. "The Impact of Ethnicity and Religion on Social Development in Revolutionary America." In *Ethnicity and Nation-Building*, edited by Wendell Bell and Walter E. Freeman, 327–39. Beverly Hills, CA: Sage.
Anderson, Elin. 1937. *We Americans: A Study of Cleavage in an American City*. Cambridge, MA: Harvard University Press.
Antunes, George, and Charles M. Gaitz. 1975. "Ethnicity and Participation: A Study of Mexican Americans, Blacks, and Whites." *American Journal of Sociology* 80, no. 5 (March): 1192–211.
Bean, Frank D., and Marta Tienda. 1987. *The Hispanic Population of the United States*. New York: Russell Sage.
Begag, Azouz. 1988. "Les filles Maghrébines et les Symboliques de la Mobilité." *Hommes et Migrations Documents*, no. 1113: 9–13.

———.1990. "The 'Beurs,' Children of North-African Immigrants in France: The Issue of Integration." *Journal of Ethnic Studies* 18, no. 1 (Spring): 1–14.

Bonilla, Frank, and Ricardo Campos. 1981. "A Wealth of Poor: Puerto Ricans in the New Economic Order." *Daedalus* 110, no. 2 (Spring): 133–76.

Borjas, George J. 1990. *Friends or Strangers: The Impact of Immigrants on the U.S. Economy*. New York: Basic Books.

Boulot, Serge, and Danielle Boyzon-Fradet. 1985. "L'échec scolaire des enfants de travailleurs immigrés (un problème mal posé)." In *L'immigration Maghrébine en France*, 212–24. Paris: Denoël.

———.1988. "L'Ecole Francaise: Egalité des chances et logiques d'une institution." Unpublished paper presented at the Conference on the Politics of Immigration in Europe and the United States, Centre d'Etudes et de Recherches Internationales, 21–22 April.

Brubaker, [William] Rogers. 1988. "Immigration and the Nation-State in France and Germany." Unpublished paper.

Bryce-Laporte, Roy Simon, ed. 1980. *Sourcebook on the New Immigration*. New Brunswick, NJ: Transaction Books.

Caillot, R. 1969. *L'insertion des étrangers dans l'aire métropolitaine Lyon-Saint-Etienne*, 64–145. Paris: Hommes et Migrations Etudes no. 113.

Cain, Bruce, and D. Roderick Kiewiet. 1986a. "California's Coming Minority Majority." *Public Opinion*, March 1986, 50–2.

———. 1986b. "Minorities in California." California Institute of Technology, Division of Humanities and Social Sciences. Mimeographed.

Castles, Stephen. 1984. *Here for Good: Western Europe's New Ethnic Minorities*. London: Pluto Press.

Cobban, Alfred. 1961. *A History of Modern France*. Vol. 1. Baltimore: Penguin Books.

Connor, John W. 1977. *Tradition and Change in Three Generations of Japanese Americans*. Chicago: Nelson-Hall.

Cordeiro, Albano. 1987. *L'immigration*. 3d ed. Paris: Editions la Découverte.

Costa-Lascoux, Jacqueline. 1990. "Anti-Discrimination Legislation: Belgium, France, Netherlands." Council of Europe, Strasbourg, Committee of Experts on Community Relations (mimeo., EMG-CR 2.90).

Daniels, Roger. 1973. *The Politics of Prejudice: The Anti-Japanese Movement in California and the Struggle for Japanese Exclusion*. New York: Atheneum. Originally published 1962.

de la Garza, Rodolfo, and Janet Weaver. 1985. "Chicano and Anglo Public Policy Preferences in San Antonio: Does Ethnicity Make a Difference?" *Social Science Quarterly* 66: 576–86.

Diamond, Larry, et al. 1988. *Democracy in Developing Countries*. Vol. 2, *Africa*. Boulder, CO; Lynne Rienner.

Ehrmann, Henry W., and Martin A. Schain. 1991. *Politics in France*, 5th ed. New York: Harper Collins.

Fijalkowski, Jurgen. 1989. "Les obstacles à la citoyenneté: Immigration et naturalisation en République fédérale d'Allemagne." *Revue européenne des migrations internationales* 5, no. 1 (2ème trimestre): 33–46.

Fuchs, Lawrence H. 1990. *The American Kaleidoscope: Race, Ethnicity, and the Civic Culture*. Hanover, NH: University Press of New England.

Gans, Herbert. 1979. "Symbolic Ethnicity: The Future of Ethnic Groups and Cultures in America." *Ethnic and Racial Studies* 2, no. 1 (January): 1–19.

Gephart, Martha A., and Robert W. Pearson. 1988. "Contemporary Research on the Urban Underclass." Social Science Research Council, *Items* (June): 1–10.

Gibney, James S. 1988. "The Berkeley Squeeze." *The New Republic*, 11 April 1988, 15–17.

Girard, Alain. 1971. "Attitudes des Francais à l'égard de l'immigration étrangère." *Population* 26, no. 5: 827–76.

Glazer, Nathan. 1987. "New Rules of the Game." *The National Interest*, no. 8 (Summer): 62–70.

Grillo, R. D. 1985. *Ideologies and Institutions in Urban France: The Representation of Immigrants*. Cambridge: Cambridge University Press.

Hamilton, Alexander, John Jay, and James Madison. 1888. *The Federalist*. New York: G. P. Putnam. Originally published 1788.

Hamonet, France, and Michèle Proux. 1984. "L'enfant maghrébin en milieu scolaire." In *Les Nord-Africans en France*, edited by Magali Morsy, 105–8. Paris: Centre des Hautes Etudes sur l'Afrique et l'Asie Modernes.

Hartz, Louis. 1955. *The Liberal Tradition in America*. New York: Harcourt, Brace & World.

Higham, John. 1968. *Strangers in the Land: Patterns of American Nativism, 1860–1925*. New York: Atheneum. Originally published in 1955.

———. 1977. "Disjunction and Diversity in American Ethnic History." Unpublished paper presented at the Woodrow Wilson International Center for Scholars, April.

Hollifield, James F. 1989. "Migrants into Citizens: The Politics of Immigration in France and the United States." Unpublished paper presented at the Annual Meeting of the American Political Science Association.

Horowitz, Donald L. 1975. "Ethnic Identity." *Ethnicity: Theory and Experience*, edited by Nathan Glazer and Daniel P. Moynihan, 111–40. Cambridge, MA: Harvard University Press.

———. 1983. "Racial Violence in the United States." In *Ethnic Pluralism and Public Policy: Achieving Equality in the United States and Britain*, edited by Nathan Glazer and Ken Young, 187–211. London: Heinemann.

———. 1985. "Conflict and Accommodation: Mexican-Americans in the Cosmopolis." In *Mexican-Americans in Comparative Perspective*, edited by Walker Connor. Washington, DC: Urban Institute.

———. 1989. "Europe and America: A Comparative Analysis of 'Ethnicity.'" *Revue européenne des migrations internationales* 5, no. 1 (2ème trimestre): 47–61.

Houston, Jeanne Wakatsuki, and James D. Houston. 1973. *Farewell to Manzanar*. New York: Bantam Books.

Ireland, Patrick R. 1989. "The State and the Political Participation of the 'New' Immigrants in France and the United States." *Revue francaise d'etudes américaines* 14, no. 41 (Juillet): 315–28.

Jacob, James E. 1978. "Two Types of Ethnic Militancy in France." Unpublished paper presented at the Annual Meeting of the International Studies Association.

Jiobu, Robert M. 1988. *Ethnicity and Assimilation: Blacks, Chinese, Filipinos, Japanese, Koreans, Mexicans, Vietnamese, and Whites*. Albany: State University of New York Press.

Keller, Phyllis. 1979. *States of Belonging: German-American Intellectuals and the First World War*. Cambridge, MA: Harvard University Press.

Key, V. O., Jr. 1956. *Politics, Parties, and Pressure Groups*. 3d ed. New York: Thomas Y. Crowell.

Kikumura, Akemi. 1981. *Through Harsh Winters: The Life of a Japanese Immigrant Woman*. Novato, CA: Chandler & Sharp.

Lapeyronnie, Didier. 1987. "Assimilation, mobilisation, et action collective chez les jeunes de la seconde génération de l'immigration maghrébine." *Revue francaise de sociologie* 28: 287–318.

Leonhard-Spark, Philip J., and Parmatma Saran. 1980. "The Indian Immigrant in America: A Demographic Profile." In *The New Ethnics: Asian Indians in the United States*, edited by Parmatma Saran and Edwin Eames, 136–62. New York: Praeger.

Lieberson, Stanley, and Mary Waters. 1988. *From Many Strands: Ethnic and Racial Groups in Contemporary America*. New York: Russell Sage.

Long, Marceau. 1988. *Etre français aujourd'hui et demain*. Paris: Documentation française.

Lopez, David E. 1978. "Chicano Language Loyalty in an Urban Setting." *Sociology and Social Research* 62: 267–78.

Malewska-Peyre, Hanna, and M. Zaleska. 1980. "Identités et conflits de valeurs chez les jeunes immigrés Maghrébins." *Psychologie française* 25, no. 2.

Massey, Douglas S., and Brendan P. Mullen. 1984. "Processes of Hispanic and Black Spatial Assimilation." *American Journal of Sociology* 89: 836–73.

Meier, Kenneth J., and Joseph Stewart, Jr. 1989. "In Search of Rainbow Coalitions: Racial/Ethnic Representation on Public School Boards." Unpublished paper presented at the Annual Meeting of the American Political Science Association.

Morsy, Magali. 1984. "La migration: dimension et révélateur de la vie nationale." In *Les Nord-Africains en France*, edited by Magali Morsy. Paris: Centre des Hautes Etudes sur l'Afrique et l'Asie Modernes.

Murguia, Edward, and W. Parker Frisbie. 1977. "Trends in Mexican American Intermarriage." *Social Science Quarterly* 58:374–89.

Muxel, Anne. 1988. "Les attitudes socio-politiques des jeunes issus de l'immigration maghrébine en région parisienne." *Revue française de la science politique* 38, no. 6 (Décembre): 925–39.

Noiriel, Gérard. 1987. "Proposals for a Comparative Research Program on Immigration in France and the United States." Unpublished paper, Paris.

Noiriel, Gérard. 1988. *Le Creuset Français*. Paris: Seuil.

Nouschi, André. 1984. "Esquisse d'une histoire de l'immigration maghrébine." In *Les Nord-Africains en France*, edited by Magali Morsy. Paris: Centre des Hautes Etudes sur l'Afrique et l'Asie Modernes.

OECD (Organization for Economic Cooperation and Development). 1987. *Immigrants' Children at School.* Paris: OECD Directorate for Social Affairs, Manpower and Education.

———. 1990. *Continuous Reporting System on Migration, SOPEMI, 1989.* Paris: OECD Directorate for Social Affairs, Manpower and Education.

Portes, Alejandro, and Rubén G. Rumbaut, 1989. *Immigrant America: A Portrait.* Berkeley: University of California Press.

Rose Institute. 1988. "Selected Cross-Tabulations: A Survey of California Latinos, 1988." Claremont: Rose Institute of Claremont McKenna College.

Rudwick, Elliot. 1964. *Race Riot in East St. Louis, 1917.* Carbondale: Southern Illinois University Press.

Safran, William. 1989a. "Nationality and Citizenship in France and the United States: Concepts of Membership in the Political Community." Unpublished paper presented at the Annual Meeting of the American Political Science Association.

———. 1989b. "The French State and Ethnic Minority Cultures: Policy Dimensions and Problems." In *Ethnoterritorial Politics, Policy, and the Western World,* edited by Joseph R. Rudolph, Jr., and Robert J. Thompson. Boulder, CO: Lynne Rienner.

Schain, Martin A. 1988. "Immigration and Changes in the French Party System." *European Journal of Political Research* 16:597–621.

Schnapper, Dominique. 1989. "Un pays d'immigration qui s'ignore." *Le genre humain* (printemps): 99–109.

Schuman, Howard, et al. 1988. *Racial Attitudes in America.* 2d ed. Cambridge, MA: Harvard University Press.

Shastri, Amita. 1986. "Social Welfare and Social Service Recipients in California by Ethnic Origin." California Institute of Technology, Division of Humanities and Social Sciences. Mimeographed.

Strand, Paul J. 1989. "The Indochinese Refugee Experience: The Case of San Diego." In *Refugees as Immigrants: Cambodians, Laotians, and Vietnamese in America,* edited by David W. Haines, 105–20. Totowa, NJ: Rowman & Littlefield.

Thernstrom, Abigail M. 1987. *Whose Votes Count? Affirmative Action and Minority Voting Rights.* Cambridge, MA: Harvard University Press.

Tocqueville, Alexis de. 1945. *Democracy in America.* Vol. 1. Translated by Francis Bowen. New York: Knopf. Originally published 1835.

Tuttle, William M., Jr. 1972. *Race Riot: Chicago in the Red Summer of 1919.* New York: Atheneum.

U.S. Commission on Civil Rights. 1988. *The Economic Status of Americans of Asian Descent.* Washington, DC: U.S. Government Printing Office.

Warren, Robert. 1980. "Volume and Composition of U.S. Immigration and Emigration." In *Sourcebook on the New Immigration,* edited by Roy Simon Bryce-Laporte, 1–14. New Brunswick, NJ: Transaction Books.

Waters, Mary C. 1990. *Ethnic Options: Choosing Identities in America.* Berkeley: University of California Press.

Weiner, Myron. 1989. "Asian-Americans and American Foreign Policy." *Revue Européenne des Migrations Internationales* 5, no. 1 (2d trimestre):71–112.

——. 1990. "Immigration: Perspectives from Receiving Countries." *Third World Quarterly* 12, no. 1: 140–65.

Whitmore, John K., Marcella Trautmann, and Nathan Caplan, 1989. "The Socio-Cultural Basis for the Economic and Educational Success of Southeast Asian Refugees (1978–1982 Arrivals)." In *Refugees as Immigrants: Cambodians, Laotians, and Vietnamese in America*, edited by David W. Haines, 121–37. Totowa, NJ: Rowman & Littlefield.

Wieviorka, Michel. 1991. *L'espace du Racisme*. Paris: Seuil.

Wilpert, Czarina. 1988. "Associations of Turks in the Federal Republic of Germany: Between Guestworker Policy, European Integration and Ataturk's Aspiration to a Secular and Monocultural Nation State." Paper presented at the Conference on the Politics of Immigration in Europe and the United States, Centre d'Etudes et de Recherches Internationales, Paris, 21–22 April.

Wilson, Frank L. 1989. "France: Group Politics in a Strong State." Unpublished paper presented at the Annual Meeting of the American Political Science Association.

PART V

POLITICAL DEBATE ON IMMIGRATION

16 Membership

Michael Walzer

Members and Strangers

Men and women without membership anywhere are stateless persons. That condition doesn't preclude every sort of distributive relation: markets, for example, are commonly open to all comers. But non-members are vulnerable and unprotected in the marketplace. Although they participate freely in the exchange of goods, they have no part in those goods that are shared. They are cut off from the communal provision of security and welfare. Even those aspects of security and welfare that are, like public health, collectively distributed are not guaranteed to non-members: for they have no guaranteed place in the collectivity and are always liable to expulsion. Statelessness is a condition of infinite danger.

But membership and non-membership are not the only – or, for our purposes, the most important – set of possibilities. It is also possible to be a member of a poor or a rich country, to live in a densely crowded or a largely empty country, to be the subject of an authoritarian regime or the citizen of a democracy. Since human beings are highly mobile, large numbers of men and women regularly attempt to change their residence and their membership, moving from unfavored to favored environments. Affluent and free countries are, like élite universities, besieged by applicants. They have to decide on their own size and character. More precisely, as citizens of such a country, we have to decide: Whom should we admit? Ought we to have open admissions? Can we choose among applicants? What are the appropriate criteria for distributing membership?

The plural pronouns that I have used in asking these questions suggest the conventional answer to them: we who are already

members do the choosing, in accordance with our own understanding of what membership means in our community and of
what sort of a community we want to have. Membership as a social
good is constituted by our understanding; its value is fixed by our
work and conversation; and then we are in charge (who else could
be in charge?) of its distribution. But we don't distribute it among
ourselves; it is already ours. We give it out to strangers. Hence the
choice is also governed by our relationships with strangers – not
only by our understanding of those relationships but also by the
actual contacts, connections, alliances we have established and
the effects we have had beyond our borders. But I shall focus first
on strangers in the literal sense, men and women whom we meet,
so to speak, for the first time. We don't know who they are or what
they think, yet we recognize them as men and women. Like us but
not of us: when we decide on membership, we have to consider
them as well as ourselves.

I won't try to recount here the history of Western ideas about
strangers. In a number of ancient languages, Latin among them,
strangers and enemies were named by a single word. We have
come only slowly, through a long process of trial and error, to
distinguish the two and to acknowledge that, in certain circumstances, strangers (but not enemies) might be entitled to our hospitality, assistance, and good will. This acknowledgment can be
formalized as the principle of mutual aid, which suggests the duties
that we owe, as John Rawls has written, "not only to definite
individuals, say to those cooperating together in some social
arrangement, but to persons generally."[1] Mutual aid extends across
political (and also cultural, religious, and linguistic) frontiers. The
philosophical grounds of the principle are hard to specify (its
history provides its practical ground). I doubt that Rawls is right
to argue that we can establish it simply by imagining "what a
society would be like if this duty were rejected"[2] – for rejection is
not an issue within any particular society; the issue arises only
among people who don't share, or don't know themselves to
share, a common life. People who do share a common life have
much stronger duties.

It is the absence of any cooperative arrangements that sets the
context for mutual aid: two strangers meet at sea or in the desert or,
as in the Good Samaritan story, by the side of the road. What
precisely they owe one another is by no means clear, but we
commonly say of such cases that positive assistance is required if
(1) it is needed or urgently needed by one of the parties; and (2) if

the risks and costs of giving it are relatively low for the other party. Given these conditions, I ought to stop and help the injured stranger, wherever I meet him, whatever his membership or my own. This is our morality; conceivably his, too. It is, moreover, an obligation that can be read out in roughly the same form at the collective level. Groups of people ought to help necessitous strangers whom they somehow discover in their midst or on their path. But the limit on risks and costs in these cases is sharply drawn. I need not take the injured stranger into my home, except briefly, and I certainly need not care for him or even associate with him for the rest of my life. My life cannot be shaped and determined by such chance encounters. Governor John Winthrop, arguing against free immigration to the new Puritan commonwealth of Massachusetts, insisted that this right of refusal applies also to collective mutual aid: "As for hospitality, that rule does not bind further than for some present occasion, not for continual residence."[3] Whether Winthrop's view can be defended is a question that I shall come to only gradually. Here I only want to point to mutual aid as a (possible) external principle for the distribution of membership, a principle that doesn't depend upon the prevailing view of membership within a particular society. The force of the principle is uncertain, in part because of its own vagueness, in part because it sometimes comes up against the internal force of social meanings. And these meanings can be specified, and are specified, through the decision-making processes of the political community.

We might opt for a world without particular meanings and without political communities: where no one was a member or where everyone "belonged" to a single global state. These are the two forms of simple equality with regard to membership. If all human beings were strangers to one another, if all our meetings were like meetings at sea or in the desert or by the side of the road, then there would be no membership to distribute. Admissions policy would never be an issue. Where and how we lived, and with whom we lived, would depend upon our individual desires and then upon our partnerships and affairs. Justice would be nothing more than non-coercion, good faith, and Good Samaritanism – a matter entirely of external principles. If, by contrast, all human beings were members of a global state, membership would already have been distributed, equally; and there would be nothing more to do. The first of these arrangements suggests a kind of global libertarianism; the second, a kind of global socialism. These are the two conditions under which the distribution of membership would never arise. Either there would be no such status to distribute, or it would simply come (to everyone) with birth. But neither of these arrangements is likely to be realized in the foreseeable future; and there are impressive arguments, which I will come to later, against both of them. In any case, so long as members and strangers are, as they are at present, two distinct groups, admissions decisions have to be made, men and women taken in or refused. Given the indeterminate requirements of mutual aid, these decisions are not constrained by any widely accepted standard. That's why the admissions policies of countries are rarely criticized, except in terms suggesting that the only relevant criteria are those of charity, not justice. It is certainly possible that a deeper criticism would lead one to deny the member/stranger distinction. But I shall try, nevertheless, to defend that distinction and then to describe the internal and the external principles that govern the distribution of membership.

The argument will require a careful review of both immigration and naturalization policy. But it is worth noting first, briefly, that there are certain similarities between strangers in political space (immigrants) and descendants in time (children). People enter a country by being born to parents already there as well as, and more often than, by crossing the frontier. Both these processes can be controlled. In the first case, however, unless we practice a selective infanticide, we will be dealing with unborn and hence unknown individuals. Subsidies for large families and programs of birth control determine only the size of the population, not the characteristics of its inhabitants. We might, of course, award the right to give birth differentially to different groups of parents, establishing ethnic quotas (like country-of-origin quotas in immigration policy) or class or intelligence quotas, or allowing right-to-give-birth certificates to be traded on the market. These are ways of regulating who has children and of shaping the character of the future population. They are, however, indirect and inefficient ways, even with regard to ethnicity, unless the state also regulates intermarriage and assimilation. Even well short of that, the policy would require very high, and surely unacceptable, levels of coercion: the dominance of political power over kinship and love. So the major public policy issue is the size of the population only – its growth, stability, or decline. To how many people do we distribute membership? The larger and philosophically more interesting questions – To what sorts of people?, and To what particular people? – are most clearly confronted when we turn to the problems involved in admitting or excluding strangers.

Analogies: Neighborhoods, Clubs, and Families

Admissions policies are shaped partly by arguments about economic and political conditions in the host country, partly by arguments about the character and "destiny" of the host country, and partly by arguments about the character of countries (political communities) in general. The last of these is the most important, in theory at least; for our understanding of countries in general will determine whether particular countries have the right they conventionally claim: to distribute membership for (their own) particular reasons. But few of us have any direct experience of what a country is or of what it means to be a member. We often have strong feelings about our country, but we have only dim perceptions of it. As a political community (rather than a place), it is, after all, invisible; we actually see only its symbols, offices, and representatives. I suspect that we understand it best when we compare it to other, smaller associations whose compass we can more easily grasp. For we are all members of formal and informal groups of many different sorts; we know their workings intimately. And all these groups have, and necessarily have, admissions policies. Even if we have never served as state officials, even if we have never emigrated from one country to another, we have all had the experience of accepting or rejecting strangers, and we have all had the experience of being accepted or rejected. I want to draw upon this experience. My argument will be worked through a series of rough comparisons, in the course of which the special meaning of political membership will, I think, become increasingly apparent.

Consider, then, three possible analogues for the political community: we can think of countries as neighborhoods, clubs, or families. The list is obviously not exhaustive, but it will serve to illuminate certain key features of admission and exclusion. Schools, bureaucracies, and companies, though they have some of the characteristics of clubs, distribute social and economic status as well as membership; I will take them up separately. Many domestic associations are parasitic for their memberships, relying on the procedures of other associations: unions depend upon the hiring policies of companies; parent-teacher organizations depend upon the openness of neighborhoods or upon the selectiveness of private schools. Political parties are generally like clubs; religious congregations are often designed to resemble families. What should countries be like?

The neighborhood is an enormously complex human association, but we have a certain understanding of what it is like – an understanding at least partially reflected (though also increasingly challenged) in contemporary American law. It is an association without an organized or legally enforceable admissions policy. Strangers can be welcomed or not welcomed; they cannot be admitted or excluded. Of course, being welcomed or not welcomed is sometimes effectively the same thing as being admitted or excluded, but the distinction is theoretically important. In principle, individuals and families move into a neighborhood for reasons of their own; they choose but are not chosen. Or, rather, in the absence of legal controls, the market controls their movements. Whether they move is determined not only by their own choice but also by their ability to find a job and a place to live (or, in a society different from our own, to find a factory commune or a cooperative apartment house ready to take them in). Ideally, the market works independently of the existing composition of the neighborhood. The state upholds this independence by refusing to enforce restrictive covenants and by acting to prevent or minimize discrimination in employment. There are no institutional arrangements capable of maintaining "ethnic purity" – though zoning laws sometimes maintain class segregation.[4] The use of zoning laws to bar from neighborhoods (boroughs, villages, towns) certain sorts of people – namely, those who don't live in conventional families – is a new feature of our political history, and I shall not try to comment on it here.[5] With reference to any formal criteria, the neighborhood is a random association, "not a selection, but rather a specimen of life as a whole . . . By the very indifference of space," as Bernard Bosanquet has written, "we are liable to the direct impact of all possible factors."[6]

It was a common argument in classical political economy that national territory should be as "indifferent" as local space. The same writers who defended free trade in the nineteenth century also defended unrestricted immigration. They argued for perfect freedom of contract, without any political restraint. International society, they thought, should take shape as a world of neighborhoods, with individuals moving freely about, seeking private advancement. In their view, as Henry Sidgwick reported it in the 1890s, the only business of state officials is "to maintain order over [a] particular territory . . . but not in any way to determine who is to inhabit this territory, or to restrict the enjoyment of its natural advantages to any particular portion of the human race."[7] Natural advantages (like markets) are open to all comers, within the limits of private property rights; and if they are used up or devalued by overcrowding, people presumably will move on, into the jurisdiction of new sets of officials.

Sidgwick thought that this is possibly the "ideal of the future," but he offered three arguments against a world of neighborhoods in the present. First of all, such a world would not allow for patriotic sentiment, and so the "casual aggregates" that would probably result from the free movement of individuals would "lack internal cohesion." Neighbors would be strangers to one another. Second, free movement might interfere with efforts "to raise the standard of living among the poorer classes" of a particular country, since such efforts could not be undertaken with equal energy and success everywhere in the world. And, third, the promotion of moral and intellectual culture and the efficient working of political institutions might be "defeated" by the continual creation of heterogeneous populations.[8] Sidgwick presented these three arguments as a series of utilitarian considerations that weigh against the benefits of labor mobility and contractual freedom. But they seem to me to have a rather different character. The last two arguments draw their force from the first, but only if the first is conceived in non-utilitarian terms. It is only if patriotic sentiment has some moral basis, only if communal cohesion makes for obligations and shared meanings, only if there are members as well as strangers, that state officials would have any reason to worry especially about the welfare of their own people (and of *all* their own people) and the success of their own culture and politics. For it is at least dubious that the average standard of living of the poorer classes throughout the world would decline under conditions of perfect labor mobility. Nor is there firm evidence that culture cannot thrive in cosmopolitan environments, nor that it is impossible to govern casual aggregations of people. As for the last of these, political theorists long ago discovered that certain sorts of regimes – namely, authoritarian regimes – thrive in the absence of communal cohesion. That perfect mobility makes for authoritarianism might suggest a utilitarian argument against mobility; but such an argument would work only if individual men and women, free to come and go, expressed a desire for some other form of government. And that they might not do.

Perfect labor mobility, however, is probably a mirage, for it is almost certain to be resisted at the local level. Human beings, as I have said, move about a great deal, but not because they love to move. They are, most of them, inclined to stay where they are unless their life is very difficult there. They experience a tension between love of place and the discomforts of a particular place. While some of them leave their homes and become foreigners in new lands, others stay where they are and resent the foreigners in their own land. Hence, if states ever become large neighborhoods, it is likely that neighborhoods will become little states. Their members will organize to defend the local politics and culture against strangers. Historically, neighborhoods have turned into closed or parochial communities (leaving aside cases of legal coercion) whenever the state was open: in the cosmopolitan cities of multinational empires, for example, where state officials don't foster any particular identity but permit different groups to build their own institutional structures (as in ancient Alexandria), or in the receiving centers of mass immigration movements (early twentieth century New York) where the country is an open but also an alien world – or, alternatively, a world full of aliens. The case is similar where the state doesn't exist at all or in areas where it doesn't function. Where welfare monies are raised and spent locally, for example, as in a seventeenth-century English parish, the local people will seek to exclude newcomers who are likely welfare recipients. It is only the nationalization of welfare (or the nationalization of culture and politics) that opens the neighborhood communities to whoever chooses to come in.

Neighborhoods can be open only if countries are at least potentially closed. Only if the state makes a selection among would-be members and guarantees the loyalty, security, and welfare of the individuals it selects, can local communities take shape as "indifferent" associations, determined solely by personal preference and market capacity. Since individual choice is most dependent upon local mobility, this would seem to be the preferred arrangement in a society like our own. The politics and the culture of a modern democracy probably require the kind of largeness, and also the kind of boundedness, that states provide. I don't mean to deny the value of sectional cultures and ethnic communities; I mean only to suggest the rigidities that would be forced upon both in the absence of inclusive and protective states. To tear down the walls of the state is not, as Sidgwick worriedly suggested, to create a world without walls, but rather to create a thousand petty fortresses.

The fortresses, too, could be torn down: all that is necessary is a global state sufficiently powerful to overwhelm the local communities. Then the result would be the world of the political economists, as Sidgwick described it – a world of radically deracinated men and women. Neighborhoods might maintain some cohesive culture for a generation or two on a voluntary basis, but people would move in, people would move out; soon the cohesion would be gone. The distinctiveness of cultures and groups depends upon closure and, without it, cannot be conceived as a stable feature of human life. If this distinctiveness is a value, as most people (though some of them are global pluralists, and others only local loyalists) seem to believe, then closure must be permitted somewhere. At some level of political organization, something like the sovereign state must take shape and claim the authority to make its own admissions policy, to control and sometimes restrain the flow of immigrants.

But this right to control immigration does not include or entail the right to control emigration. The political community can shape its own population in the one way, not in the other: this is a distinction that gets reiterated in different forms throughout the account of membership. The restraint of entry serves to defend the liberty and welfare, the politics and culture of a group of people committed to one another and to their common life. But the restraint of exit replaces commitment with coercion. So far as the coerced members are concerned, there is no longer a community worth defending. A state can, perhaps, banish individual citizens or expel aliens living within its borders (if there is some place ready to receive them). Except in times of national emergency, when everyone is bound to work for the survival of the community, states cannot prevent such people from getting up and leaving. The fact that individuals can rightly leave their own country, however, doesn't generate a right to enter another (any other). Immigration and emigration are morally asymmetrical.[9] Here the appropriate analogy is with the club, for it is a feature of clubs in domestic society – as I have just suggested it is of states in international society – that they can regulate admissions but cannot bar withdrawals.

Like clubs, countries have admissions committees. In the United States, Congress functions as such a committee, though it rarely makes individual selections. Instead, it establishes general qualifications, categories for admission and exclusion, and numerical quotas (limits). Then admissible individuals are taken in, with varying degrees of administrative discretion, mostly on a first-come, first-served basis. This procedure seems eminently defensible, though that does not mean that any particular set of qualifications and categories ought to be defended. To say that states have a right to act in certain areas is not to say that anything they do in those areas is right. One can argue about particular admissions standards by appealing, for example, to the condition and character of the host country and to the shared understandings of those who are already members. Such arguments have to be judged morally and politically as well as factually. The claim of American advocates of restricted immigration (in 1920, say) that they were defending a homogeneous white and Protestant country, can plausibly be called unjust as well as inaccurate: as if non-white and non-Protestant citizens were invisible men and women, who didn't have to be counted in the national census![10] Earlier Americans, seeking the benefits of economic and geographic expansion, had created a pluralist society; and the moral realities of that society ought to have guided the legislators of the 1920s. If we follow the logic of the club analogy, however, we have to say that the earlier decision might have been different, and the United States might have taken shape as a homogeneous community, an Anglo-Saxon nation-state (assuming what happened in any case: the virtual extermination of the Indians who, understanding correctly the dangers of invasion, struggled as best they could to keep foreigners out of their native lands). Decisions of this sort are subject to constraint, but what the constraints are I am not yet ready to say. It is important first to insist that the distribution of membership in American society, and in any ongoing society, is a matter of political decision. The labor market may be given free rein, as it was for many decades in the United States, but that does not happen by an act of nature or of God; it depends upon choices that are ultimately political. What kind of community do the citizens want to create? With what other men and women do they want to share and exchange social goods?

These are exactly the questions that club members answer when they make membership decisions, though usually with reference to a less extensive community and to a more limited range of social goods. In clubs, only the founders choose themselves (or one another); all other members have been chosen by those who were members before them. Individuals may be able to give good reasons why they should be selected, but no one on the outside has a right to be inside. The members decide freely on their future associates, and the decisions they make are authoritative and final. Only when clubs split into factions and fight over property can the state intervene and make its own decision about who the members are. When states split, however, no legal appeal is possible; there is no superior body. Hence, we might imagine states as perfect clubs, with sovereign power over their own selection processes. (Winthrop made the point clearly: "If we here be a corporation established by free consent, if the place of our habitation be our own, then no man hath right to come into us...without our consent."[11] I will come back to the question of "place" later.)

But if this description is accurate in regard to the law, it is not an accurate account of the moral life of contemporary political communities. Clearly, citizens often believe themselves morally bound to open the doors of their country – not to anyone who wants to come in, perhaps, but to a particular group of outsiders, recognized as national or ethnic "relatives." In this sense, states are like families rather than clubs, for it is a feature of families that their members are morally connected to people they have not chosen, who live outside the household. In time of trouble, the household is also a refuge. Sometimes, under the auspices of the state, we take in fellow citizens to whom we are not related, as English country families took in London children during the blitz; but our more spontaneous beneficence is directed at our own kith and kin. The state recognizes what we can call the "kinship principle" when it gives priority in immigration to the relatives of citizens. That is current policy in the United States, and it seems especially appropriate in a political community largely formed by the admission of immigrants. It is a way of acknowledging that labor mobility has a social price: since laborers are men and women with families, one cannot admit them for the sake of their labor without accepting some commitment to their aged parents, say, or to their sickly brothers and sisters.

In communities differently formed, where the state represents a nation largely in place, another sort of commitment commonly develops, along lines determined by the principle of nationality. In time of trouble, the state is a refuge for members of the nation, whether or not they are residents and citizens. Perhaps the border of the political community was drawn years ago so as to leave their villages and towns on the wrong side; perhaps they are the children or grandchildren of emigrants. They have no legal membership rights, but if they are persecuted in the land where they live, they look to their homeland not only with hope but also with expectation. I am inclined to say that such expectations are legitimate. Greeks driven from Turkey, Turks from Greece, after the wars and revolutions of the early twentieth century, had to be taken in by the states that bore their collective names. What else are such states for? They don't only preside over a piece of territory and a random collection of inhabitants; they are also the political expression of a common life and (most often) of a national "family" that is never entirely enclosed within their legal boundaries. After the Second World War, millions of Germans, expelled by Poland and Czechoslovakia, were received and cared for by the two Germanies. Even if these states had been free of all responsibility in the expulsions, they would still have had a special obligation to the refugees. Most states recognize obligations of this sort in practice; some do so in law.

Territory

We might, then, think of countries as national clubs or families. But countries are also territorial states. Although clubs and families own property, they neither require nor (except in feudal systems) possess jurisdiction over territory. Leaving children aside, they do not control the physical location of their members. The state does control physical location – if only for the sake of clubs and families and the individual men and women who make them up; and with this control there come certain obligations. We can best examine these if we consider once again the asymmetry of immigration and emigration.

The nationality principle has one significant limit, commonly accepted in theory, if not always in practice. Though the recognition of national affinity is a reason for permitting immigration, nonrecognition is not a reason for expulsion. This is a major issue in the modern world, for many newly independent states find themselves in control of territory into which alien groups have been admitted under the auspices of the old imperial regime. Sometimes these people are forced to leave, the victims of a popular hostility that the new government cannot restrain. More often the government itself fosters such hostility, and takes positive action to drive out the "alien elements," invoking when it does so some version of the club or the family analogy. Here, however, neither analogy applies: for though no "alien" has a right to be a member of a club or a family, it is possible, I think, to describe a kind of territorial or locational right.

Hobbes made the argument in classical form when he listed those rights that are given up and those that are retained when the social contract is signed. The retained rights include self-defense and then "the use of fire, water, free air, *and place to live in,* and ... all things necessary for life" (italics mine).[12] The right is not, indeed, to a particular place, but it is enforceable against the state, which exists to protect it; the state's claim to territorial jurisdiction derives ultimately from this individual right to place. Hence the right has a collective as well as an individual form, and these two can come into conflict. But it can't be said that the first always or necessarily supercedes the second, for the first came into existence for the sake of the second. The state owes something to its inhabitants simply, without reference to their collective or national identity. And the first place to which the inhabitants are entitled is surely the place where they and their families have lived and made a life. The attachments and expectations they have formed argue against a forced transfer to another country. If they can't have this particular piece of land (or house or apartment), then some other must be found for them within the same general "place." Initially, at least, the sphere of membership is given: the men and women who determine what membership means, and who shape the admissions policies of the political community, are simply the men and women who are already there. New states and governments must make their peace with the old inhabitants of the land they rule. And countries are likely to take shape as closed territories dominated, perhaps, by particular nations (clubs or families), but always including aliens of one sort or another – whose expulsion would be unjust.

This common arrangement raises one important possibility: that many of the inhabitants of a particular country won't be allowed full membership (citizenship) because of their nationality. I will consider that possibility, and argue for its rejection, when I turn to the specific problems of naturalization. But one might avoid such problems entirely, at least at the level of the state, by opting for a radically different arrangement. Consider once again the neighborhood analogy: perhaps we should deny to national states, as we deny to churches and political parties, the collective right of territorial jurisdiction. Perhaps we should insist upon open countries and permit closure only in non-territorial groups. Open neighborhoods together with closed clubs and families: that is the structure of domestic society. Why can't it, why shouldn't it be extended to the global society?

An extension of this sort was actually proposed by the Austrian socialist writer Otto Bauer, with reference to the old multinational empires of Central and Eastern Europe. Bauer would have organized nations into autonomous corporations permitted to tax their members for educational and cultural purposes, but denied any territorial dominion. Individuals would be free to move about in political space, within the empire, carrying their national memberships with them, much as individuals move about today in liberal and secular states, carrying their religious memberships and partisan affiliations. Like churches and parties, the corporations could admit or reject new members in accordance with whatever standards their old members thought appropriate.[13]

The major difficulty here is that all the national communities that Bauer wanted to preserve came into existence, and were sustained over the centuries, on the basis of geographical coexistence. It isn't any misunderstanding of their histories that leads nations newly freed from imperial rule to seek a firm territorial status. Nations look for countries because in some deep sense they already have countries: the link between people and land is a crucial feature of national identity. Their leaders understand, moreover, that because so many critical issues (including issues of distributive justice, such as welfare, education, and so on) can best be resolved within geographical units, the focus of political life can never be established elsewhere. "Autonomous" corporations will always be adjuncts, and probably parasitic adjuncts, of territorial states; and to give up the state is to give up any effective self-determination. That's why borders, and the movements of individuals and groups across borders, are bitterly disputed as soon as imperial rule recedes and nations begin the process of "liberation." And, once again, to reverse this process or to repress its effects would require massive coercion on a global scale. There is no easy way to avoid the country (and the proliferation of countries) as we currently know it. Hence the theory of justice must allow for the territorial state, specifying the rights of its inhabitants and recognizing the collective right of admission and refusal.

The argument cannot stop here, however, for the control of territory opens the state to the claim of necessity. Territory is a social good in a double sense. It is living space, earth and water, mineral resources and potential wealth, a resource for the destitute and the hungry. And it is protected living space, with borders and police, a resource for the persecuted and the stateless. These two resources are different, and we might conclude differently with regard to the kinds of claim that can be made on each. But the issue at stake should first be put in general terms. Can a political community exclude destitute and hungry, persecuted and stateless – in a word, necessitous – men and women simply because they are foreigners? Are citizens bound to take in strangers? Let us assume that the citizens have no formal obligations; they are bound by nothing more stringent than the principle of mutual aid. The principle must be applied, however, not to individuals directly but to the citizens as a group, for immigration is a matter of political decision. Individuals participate in the decision making, if the state is democratic; but they decide not for themselves but for the community generally. And this fact has moral implications. It replaces immediacy with distance and the personal expense of time and energy with impersonal bureaucratic costs. Despite John Winthrop's claim, mutual aid is more coercive for political communities than it is for individuals because a wide range of benevolent actions is open to the community which will only marginally affect its present members considered as a body or even, with possible exceptions, one by one or family by family or club by club. (But benevolence will, perhaps, affect the children or grandchildren or great-grandchildren of the present members – in ways not easy to measure or even to make out. I'm not sure to what extent considerations of this sort can be used to narrow the range of required actions.) These actions probably include the admission of strangers, for admission to a country does not entail the kinds of intimacy that could hardly be avoided in the case of clubs and families. Might not admission, then, be morally imperative, at least for *these* strangers, who have no other place to go?

Some such argument, turning mutual aid into a more stringent charge on communities than it can ever be on individuals, probably underlies the common claim that exclusion rights depend upon the territorial extent and the population density of particular countries. Thus, Sidgwick wrote that he "cannot concede to a state possessing large tracts of unoccupied land an absolute right of excluding alien elements."[14] Perhaps, in his view, the citizens can make some selection among necessitous strangers, but they cannot refuse entirely to take strangers in so long as their state has (a great deal of) available space. A much stronger argument might be made from the other side, so to speak, if we consider the necessitous strangers not as objects of beneficent action but as desperate men and women, capable of acting on their own behalf. In *Leviathan*, Hobbes argued that such people, if they cannot earn a living in their own countries, have a right to move into "countries not sufficiently inhabited: where nevertheless they are not to exterminate those they find there, but constrain them to inhabit closer together and not range a great deal of ground to snatch what they find."[15] Here the "Samaritans" are not themselves active but acted upon and (as we shall see in a moment) charged only with nonresistance.

"White Australia" and the claim of necessity

The Hobbesian argument is clearly a defense of European coloniza- tion – and also of the subsequent "constraint" of native hunters and gatherers. But it has a wider application. Sidgwick, writing in 1891, probably had in mind the states the colonists had created: the United States, where agitation for the exclusion of immigrants had been at least a sporadic feature of political life all through the nineteenth century; and Australia, then just beginning the great debate over immigration that culminated in the "White Australia" policy. Years later, an Austrialian minister of immigration defended that policy in terms that should by now be familiar: "We seek to create a homogeneous nation. Can anyone reasonably object to that? Is not this the elementary right of every government, to decide the composition of the nation? It is just the same prerogative as the head of a family exercises as to who is to live in his own house."[16] But the Australian "family" held a vast territory of which it occupied (and I shall assume, without further factual reference, still occupies) only a small part. The right of white Australians to the great empty spaces of the subcontinent rested on nothing more than the claim they had staked, and enforced against the aboriginal population, before anyone else. That does not seem a right that one would readily defend in the face of necessitous men and women, clamoring for entry. If, driven by famine in the densely populated lands of Southeast Asia, thousands of people were to fight their way into an Australia otherwise closed to them, I doubt that we would want to charge the invaders with aggression. Hobbes's charge might make more sense: "Seeing every man, not only by Right, but also by necessity of Nature, is supposed to endeavor all he can, to obtain that which is necessary for his conservation; he that shall oppose himself against it, for things superfluous, is guilty of the war that thereupon is to follow."[17]

But Hobbes's conception of "things superfluous" is extraordina- rily wide. He meant, superfluous to life itself, to the bare require- ments of physical survival. The argument is more plausible, I think, if we adopt a more narrow conception, shaped to the needs of particular historical communities. We must consider "ways of life" just as, in the case of individuals, we must consider "life plans." Now let us suppose that the great majority of Australians could maintain their present way of life, subject only to marginal shifts, given a successful invasion of the sort I have imagined. Some individuals would be more drastically affected, for they have come to "need" hundreds or even thousands of empty miles for the life they have chosen. But such needs cannot be given moral priority over the claims of necessitous strangers. Space on that scale is a luxury, as time on that scale is a luxury in more conventional Good Samaritan arguments; and it is subject to a kind of moral encroachment. Assuming, then, that there actually is superfluous land, the claim of necessity would force a political community like that of White Australia to confront a radical choice. Its members could yield land for the sake of homogeneity, or they could give up homogeneity (agree to the creation of a multiracial society) for the sake of the land. And those would be their only choices. White Australia could survive only as Little Australia.

I have put the argument in these forceful terms in order to suggest that the collective version of mutual aid might require a limited and complex redistribution of membership and/or territory. Farther than this we cannot go. We cannot describe the littleness of Little Australia without attending to the concrete meaning of "things superfluous." To argue, for example, that living space should be distributed in equal amounts to every inhabitant of the globe would be to allow the individual version of the right to a place in the world to override the collective version. Indeed, it would deny that national clubs and families can ever acquire a firm title to a particular piece of territory. A high birthrate in a neighboring land would immediately annul the title and require territorial redistribution.

The same difficulty arises with regard to wealth and resources. These, too, can be superfluous, far beyond what the inhabitants of a particular state require for a decent life (even as they themselves define the meaning of a decent life). Are those inhabitants morally bound to admit immigrants from poorer countries for as long as superfluous resources exist? Or are they bound even longer than that, beyond the limits of mutual aid, until a policy of open admissions ceases to attract and benefit the poorest people in the world? Sidgwick seems to have opted for the first of these possibilities; he proposed a primitive and parochial version of Rawls's difference principle: immigration can be restricted as soon as failure to do so would "interfere materially ... with the efforts of the government to maintain an adequately high standard of life among the members of the community generally – especially the poorer classes."[18] But the community might well decide to cut off immigration even before that, if it were willing to export (some of) its superfluous wealth. Its members would face a choice similar to that of the Australians: they could share their wealth with necessitous strangers outside their country or with necessitous strangers inside their country. But just how much of their wealth do they have to share? Once again, there must be some limit, short (and probably considerably short) of simple equality, else communal wealth would be subject to indefinite drainage. The very phrase "communal wealth" would lose its meaning if all resources and all products were globally common. Or, rather, there would be only one community, a world state, whose redistributive processes would tend over time to annul the historical particularity of the national clubs and families.

If we stop short of simple equality, there will continue to be many communities, with different histories, ways of life, climates, political structures, and economies. Some places in the world will still be more desirable than others, either to individual men and women with particular tastes and aspirations, or more generally. Some places will still be uncomfortable for at least some of their inhabitants. Hence immigration will remain an issue even after the claims of distributive justice have been met on a global scale – assuming, still, that global society is and ought to be pluralist in form and that the claims are fixed by some version of collective mutual aid. The different communities will still have to make admissions decisions and will still have a right to make them. If we cannot guarantee the full extent of the territorial or material base on which a group of people build a common life, we can still say that the common life, at least, is their own and that their comrades and associates are theirs to recognize or choose.

Refugees

There is, however, one group of needy outsiders whose claims cannot be met by yielding territory or exporting wealth; they can be met only by taking people in. This is the group of refugees whose need is for membership itself, a non-exportable good. The liberty that makes certain countries possible homes for men and women whose politics or religion isn't tolerated where they live is also non-exportable: at least we have found no way of exporting it. These goods can be shared only within the protected space of a particular state. At the same time, admitting refugees doesn't necessarily decrease the amount of liberty the members enjoy within that space. The victims of political or religious persecution, then, make the most forceful claim for admission. If you don't take me in, they say, I shall be killed, persecuted, brutally oppressed by the rulers of my own country. What can we reply?

Toward some refugees, we may well have obligations of the same sort that we have toward fellow nationals. This is obviously the case with regard to any group of people whom we have helped turn into refugees. The injury we have done them makes for an affinity between us: thus Vietnamese refugees had, in a moral sense, been effectively Americanized even before they arrived on these shores. But we can also be bound to help men and women persecuted or oppressed by someone else – if they are persecuted or oppressed because they are like us. Ideological as well as ethnic affinity can generate bonds across political lines, especially, for example, when we claim to embody certain principles in our communal life and encourage men and women elsewhere to defend those principles. In a liberal state, affinities of this latter sort may be highly attenuated and still morally coercive. Nineteenth-century political refugees in England were generally not English liberals. They were heretics and oppositionists of all sorts, at war with the autocracies of Central and Eastern Europe. It was chiefly because of their enemies that the English recognized in them a kind of kin. Or, consider the thousands of men and women who fled Hungary after the failed revolution of 1956. It is hard to deny them a similar recognition, given the structure of the Cold War, the character of Western propaganda, the sympathy already expressed with East European "freedom fighters." These refugees probably had to be taken in by countries like Britain and the United States. The repression of political comrades, like the persecution of co-religionists, seems to generate an obligation to help, at least to provide a refuge for the most exposed and endangered people. Perhaps every victim of authoritarianism and bigotry is the moral comrade of a liberal citizen: that is an argument I would like to make. But that would press affinity too hard, and it is in any case unnecessary. So long as the number of victims is small, mutual aid will generate similar practical results; and when the number increases, and we are forced to choose among the victims, we will look, rightfully, for some more direct connection with our own way of life. If, on the other hand, there is no connection at all with particular victims, antipathy rather than affinity, there can't be a requirement to choose them over other people equally in need. Compare Bruce Ackerman's claim that "the *only* reason for restricting immigration is to protect the ongoing process of liberal conversation itself" (the italics are Ackerman's).[19] People publicly committed to the destruction of "liberal conversation" can rightfully be excluded – or perhaps Ackerman would say that they can be excluded only if their numbers or the strength of their commitment poses a real threat. In any case, the principle stated in this way applies only to liberal states. But surely other sorts of political communities also have a right to protect their members' shared sense of what they are about. Britain and the United States could hardly have been required, for example, to offer refuge to Stalinists fleeing Hungary in 1956, had the revolution triumphed. Once again, communities must have boundaries; and however these are determined with regard to territory and resources, they depend with regard to population on a sense of relatedness and mutuality. Refugees must appeal to that sense. One wishes them success; but in particular cases, with reference to a particular state, they may well have no right to be successful.

Since ideological (far more than ethnic) affinity is a matter of mutual recognition, there is a lot of room here for political choice – and thus, for exclusion as well as admission. Hence it might be said that my argument doesn't reach to the desperation of the refugee. Nor does it suggest any way of dealing with the vast numbers of refugees generated by twentieth-century politics. On the one hand, everyone must have a place to live, and a place where a reasonably secure life is possible. On the other hand, this is not a right that can be enforced against particular host states. (The right can't be enforced in practice until there is an international authority capable of enforcing it; and were there such an authority, it would certainly do better to intervene against the states whose brutal policies had driven their own citizens into exile, and so enable them all to go home.) The cruelty of this dilemma is mitigated to some degree by the principle of asylum. Any refugee who has actually made his escape, who is not seeking but has found at least a temporary refuge, can claim asylum – a right recognized today, for example, in British law; and then he cannot be deported so long as the only available country to which he might be sent "is one to which he is unwilling to go owing to well-founded fear of being persecuted for reasons of race, religion, nationality...or political opinion."[20] Though he is a stranger, and newly come, the rule against expulsion applies to him as if he had already made a life where he is: for there is no other place where he can make a life.

But this principle was designed for the sake of individuals, considered one by one, where their numbers are so small that they cannot have any significant impact upon the character of the political community. What happens when the numbers are not small? Consider the case of the millions of Russians captured or enslaved by the Nazis in the Second World War and overrun by Allied armies in the final offensives of the war. All these people were returned, many of them forcibly returned, to the Soviet Union, where they were immediately shot or sent on to die in labor camps.[21] Those of them who foresaw their fate pleaded for asylum in the West, but for expediential reasons (having to do with war and diplomacy, not with nationality and the problems of assimilation), asylum was denied them. Surely, they should not have been forcibly returned – not once it was known that they would be murdered; and that means that the Western allies should have been ready to take them in, negotiating among themselves, I suppose, about appropriate numbers. There was no other choice: at the extreme, the claim of asylum is virtually undeniable. I assume that there are in fact limits on our collective liability, but I don't know how to specify them.

This last example suggests that the moral conduct of liberal and humane states can be determined by the immoral conduct of authoritarian and brutal states. But if that is true, why stop with asylum? Why be concerned only with men and women actually on our territory who ask to remain, and not with men and women oppressed in their own countries who ask to come in? Why mark off the lucky or the aggressive, who have somehow managed to make their way across our borders, from all the others? Once again, I don't have an adequate answer to these questions. We seem bound to grant asylum for two reasons: because its denial would require us to use force against helpless and desperate people, and because the numbers likely to be involved, except in unusual cases, are small and the people easily absorbed (so we would be using force for "things superfluous"). But if we offered a refuge to everyone in the world who could plausibly say that he needed it, we might be overwhelmed. The call "Give me ... your huddled masses yearning to breathe free" is generous and noble; actually to take in large numbers of refugees is often morally necessary; but the right to restrain the flow remains a feature of communal self-determination. The principle of mutual aid can only modify and not transform admissions policies rooted in a particular community's understanding of itself.

Membership and Justice

The distribution of membership is not pervasively subject to the constraints of justice. Across a considerable range of the decisions that are made, states are simply free to take in strangers (or not) – much as they are free, leaving aside the claims of the needy, to share their wealth with foreign friends, to honor the achievements of foreign artists, scholars, and scientists, to choose their trading partners, and to enter into collective security arrangements with foreign states. But the right to choose an admissions policy is more basic than any of these, for it is not merely a matter of acting in the world, exercising sovereignty, and pursuing national interests. At stake here is the shape of the community that acts in the world, exercises sovereignty, and so on. Admission and exclusion are at the core of communal independence. They suggest the deepest meaning of self-determination. Without them, there could not be *communities of character*, historically stable, ongoing associations of men and women with some special commitment to one another and some special sense of their common life.[31]

But self-determination in the sphere of membership is not absolute. It is a right exercised, most often, by national clubs or families, but it is held in principle by territorial states. Hence it is subject both to internal decisions by the members themselves (*all* the members, including those who hold membership simply by right of place) and to the external principle of mutual aid. Immigration, then, is both a matter of political choice and moral constraint. Naturalization, by contrast, is entirely constrained: every new immigrant, every refugee taken in, every resident and worker must be offered the opportunities of citizenship. If the community is so radically divided that a single citizenship is impossible, then its territory must be divided, too, before the rights of admission and exclusion can be exercised. For these rights are to be exercised only by the community as a whole (even if, in practice, some national majority dominates the decision making) and only with regard to foreigners, not by some members with regard to others. No community can be half-metic, half-citizen and claim that its admissions policies are acts of self-determination or that its politics is democratic.

The determination of aliens and guests by an exclusive band of citizens (or of slaves by masters, or women by men, or blacks by whites, or conquered peoples by their conquerors) is not communal freedom but oppression. The citizens are free, of course, to set up a club, make membership as exclusive as they like, write a constitution, and govern one another. But they can't claim territorial jurisdiction and rule over the people with whom they share the territory. To do this is to act outside their sphere, beyond their rights. It is a form of tyranny. Indeed, the rule of citizens over non-citizens, of members over strangers, is probably the most common form of tyranny in human history. I won't say much more than this about the special problems of non-citizens and strangers: henceforth, whether I am talking about the distribution of security and welfare or about hard work or power itself, I shall assume that all the eligible men and women hold a single political status. This assumption doesn't exclude other sorts of inequality further down the road, but it does exclude the piling up of inequalities that is characteristic of divided societies. The denial of membership is always the first of a long train of abuses. There is no way to break the train, so we must deny the rightfulness of the denial. The theory of distributive justice begins, then, with an account of membership rights. It must vindicate at one and the same time the (limited) right of closure, without which there could be no communities at all, and the political inclusiveness of the existing communities. For it is only as members somewhere that men and women can hope to share in all the other social goods – security, wealth, honor, office, and power – that communal life makes possible.

Notes

1 John Rawls, *A Theory of Justice* (Cambridge, Mass., 1971), p. 115. For a useful discussion of mutual aid as a possible right, see Theodore M. Benditt, *Rights* (Totowa, N. J., 1982), chap. 5.
2 Rawls, *Theory of Justice* [1], p. 339.
3 John Winthrop, in *Puritan Political Ideas: 1558–1794*, ed. Edmund S. Morgan (Indianapolis, 1965), p. 146.
4 On zoning, see Robert H. Nelson, *Zoning and Property Rights: An Analysis of the American System of Land Use Regulation* (Cambridge, Mass., 1977), pp. 120–1.
5 See the U.S. Supreme Court's decision in *Village of Belle Terre v. Boraas* (October term, 1973).
6 Bernard Bosanquet, *The Philosophical Theory of the State* (London, 1958), p. 286.
7 Henry Sidgwick, *Elements of Politics* (London, 1881), pp. 295–96.
8 Ibid., p. 296.
9 Cf. Maurice Cranston, on the common understanding of the right to move, in *What Are Human Rights?* (New York, 1973), p. 32.
10 See John Higham's account of these debates, *Strangers in the Land* (New York, 1968).

364   Political Debate on Immigration

11 Winthrop, *Puritan Political Ideas* [3], p. 145.
12 Thomas Hobbes, *The Elements of Law*, ed. Ferdinand Tönnies (2nd ed., New York, 1969), p. 88, (part I, chap. 17, para. 2).
13 Bauer made his argument in *Die Nationalitätenfrage und die Sozialdemokratie* (1907); parts of it are excerpted in *Austro-Marxism*, ed. Tom Bottomore and Patrick Goode (Oxford, England, 1978), pp. 102–25.
14 Sidgwick, *Elements of Politics* [7], p. 295. Cf. John Stuart Mill's letter to Henry George on Chinese immigration to America, quoted in Alexander Saxton, *The Indispensable Enemy: Labor and the Anti-Chinese Movement in California* (Berkeley, 1971), p. 103.
15 Thomas Hobbes, *Leviathan*, part II, chap. 30.
16 Quoted in H. I. London, *Non-White Immigration and the "White Australia" Policy* (New York, 1970), p. 98.
17 Hobbes, *Leviathan*, part I, chap. 15.
18 Sidgwick, *Elements of Politics* [7], pp. 296–7.
19 Bruce Ackerman, *Social Justice in the Liberal State* (New Haven, 1980), p. 95.
20 E. C. S. Wade, and G. Godfrey Phillips, *Constitutional and Administrative Law*, 9th ed. revised by A. W. Bradley (London, 1977), p. 424.
21 For the whole ugly story, see Nikolai Tolstoy, *The Secret Betrayal: 1944–1947* (New York, 1977).
22 I have taken the term "communities of character" from Otto Bauer (see *Austro-Marxism* [13], p. 107).

17 Aliens and Citizens: The Case for Open Borders

Joseph H. Carens

Borders have guards and the guards have guns. This is an obvious fact of political life but one that is easily hidden from view – at least from the view of those of us who are citizens of affluent Western democracies. To Haitians in small, leaky boats confronted by armed Coast Guard cutters, to Salvadorans dying from heat and lack of air after being smuggled into the Arizona desert, to Guatemalans crawling through rat-infested sewer pipes from Mexico to California – to these people the borders, guards and guns are all too apparent. What justifies the use of force against such people? Perhaps borders and guards can be justified as a way of keeping out criminals, subversives, or armed invaders. But most of those trying to get in are not like that. They are ordinary, peaceful people, seeking only the opportunity to build decent, secure lives for themselves and their families. On what moral grounds can these sorts of people be kept out? What gives anyone the right to point guns at *them*?

To most people the answer to this question will seem obvious. The power to admit or exclude aliens is inherent in sovereignty and essential for any political community. Every state has the legal and moral right to exercise that power in pursuit of its own national interest, even if that means denying entry to peaceful, needy foreigners. States may choose to be generous in admitting immigrants, but they are under no obligation to do so.[1]

I want to challenge that view. In this essay I will argue that borders should generally be open and that people should normally be free to leave their country of origin and settle in another, subject only to the sorts of constraints that bind current citizens in their new country. The argument is strongest, I believe, when applied to the migration of people from third world countries to those of the first world. Citizenship in Western liberal democracies is the modern equivalent of feudal privilege – an inherited status that greatly enhances one's life chances. Like feudal birthright privileges, restrictive citizenship is hard to justify when one thinks about it closely.

In developing this argument I will draw upon three contemporary approaches to political theory: first that of Robert Nozick; second that of John Rawls; third that of the utilitarians. Of the three, I find Rawls the most illuminating, and I will spend the most time on the arguments that flow from his theory. But I do not want to tie my case too closely to his particular formulations (which I will modify in any event). My strategy is to take advantage of three well-articulated theoretical approaches that many people find persuasive to construct a variety of arguments for (relatively) open borders. I will argue that all three approaches lead to the same basic conclusion: there is little justification for restricting immigration. Each of these theories begins with some kind of assumption about the equal moral worth of individuals. In one way or another, each treats the individual as prior to the community. These foundations provide little basis for drawing fundamental distinctions between citizens and aliens who seek to become citizens. The fact that all three theories converge upon the same basic result with regard to immigration despite their significant differences in other areas strengthens the case for open borders. In the final part of the essay I will consider communitarian objections to my argument, especially those of Michael Walzer, the best contemporary defender of the view I am challenging.

Aliens and Property Rights

One popular position on immigration goes something like this: "It's our country. We can let in or keep out whomever we want." This could be interpreted as a claim that the right to exclude aliens is based on property rights, perhaps collective or national property rights. Would this sort of claim receive support from theories in which property rights play a central role? I think not, because those theories emphasize *individual* property rights and the concept of collective or national property rights would undermine the individual rights that these theories wish to protect.

Consider Robert Nozick as a contemporary representative of the property rights tradition. Following Locke, Nozick assumes that individuals in the state of nature have rights, including the right to acquire and use property. All individuals have the same natural rights – that is the assumption about moral equality that underlies this tradition – although the exercise of those rights leads to material inequalities. The "inconveniences" of the state of nature justify the creation of a minimal state whose sole task is to protect people within a given territory against violations of their rights.[2]

Would this minimal state be justified in restricting immigration? Nozick never answers this question directly, but his argument at a number of points suggests not. According to Nozick the state has no right to do anything other than enforce the rights which individuals already enjoy in the state of nature. Citizenship gives rise to no distinctive claim. The state is obliged to protect the rights of citizens and noncitizens equally because it enjoys a *de facto* monopoly over the enforcement of rights within its territory. Individuals have the right to enter into voluntary exchanges with other individuals. They possess this right as individuals, not as citizens. The state may not interfere with such exchanges so long as they do not violate someone else's rights.[3]

Note what this implies for immigration. Suppose a farmer from the United States wanted to hire workers from Mexico. The government would have no right to prohibit him from doing this. To prevent the Mexicans from coming would violate the rights of both the American farmer and the Mexican workers to engage in voluntary transactions. Of course, American workers might be disadvantaged by this competition with foreign workers. But Nozick explicitly denies that anyone has a right to be protected against competitive disadvantage. (To count that sort of thing as a harm would undermine the foundations of *individual* property rights.) Even if the Mexicans did not have job offers from an American, a Nozickean government would have no grounds for preventing them from entering the country. So long as they were peaceful and did not steal, trespass on private property, or otherwise violate the rights of other individuals, their entry and their actions would be none of the state's business.

Does this mean that Nozick's theory provides no basis for the exclusion of aliens? Not exactly. It means rather that it provides no basis for the *state* to exclude aliens and no basis for individuals to exclude aliens that could not be used to exclude citizens as well. Poor aliens could not afford to live in affluent suburbs (except in the servants' quarters), but that would be true of poor citizens too. Individual property owners could refuse to hire aliens, to rent them houses, to sell them food, and so on, but in a Nozickean world they could do the same things to their fellow citizens. In other words, individuals may do what they like with their own personal property. They may normally exclude whomever they want from land they own. But they have this right to exclude as individuals, not as members of a collective. They cannot prevent other individuals from acting differently (hiring aliens, renting them houses, etc.).[4]

Is there any room for collective action to restrict entry in Nozick's theory? In the final section of his book, Nozick draws a distinction between nations (or states) and small face-to-face communities. People may voluntarily construct small communities on principles quite different from the ones that govern the state so long as individuals are free to leave these communities. For example, people may choose to pool their property and to make collective decisions on the basis of majority rule. Nozick argues that this sort of community has a right to restrict membership to those whom it wishes to admit and to control entry to its land. But such a community may also redistribute its jointly held property as it chooses. This is not an option that Nozick (or any other property rights theorist) intends to grant to the state.[5]

This shows why the claim "It's our country. We can admit or exclude whomever we want" is ultimately incompatible with a property rights theory like Nozick's. Property cannot serve as a protection for individuals *against* the collective if property is collectively owned. If the notion of collective ownership is used to justify keeping aliens out, it opens the possibility of using the same notion to justify redistributing income or whatever else the majority decides. Nozick explicitly says that the land of a nation is not the collective property of its citizens. It follows that the control that the state can legitimately exercise over that land is limited to the enforcement of the rights of individual owners. Prohibiting people from entering a territory because they did not happen to be born there or otherwise gain the credentials of citizenship is no part of any state's legitimate mandate. The state has no right to restrict immigration.

Migration and the Original Position

In contrast to Nozick, John Rawls provides a justification for an activist state with positive responsibilities for social welfare. Even so, the approach to immigration suggested by *A Theory of Justice* leaves little room for restrictions in principle. I say "suggested" because Rawls himself explicitly assumes a closed system in which questions about immigration could not arise. I will argue, however, that Rawls's approach is applicable to a broader context than the one he considers.

Rawls asks what principles people would choose to govern society if they had to choose from behind a "veil of ignorance," knowing nothing about their own personal situations (class, race, sex, natural talents, religious beliefs, individual goals and values, and so on). He argues that people in this original position would choose two principles. The first principle would guarantee equal liberty to all. The second would permit social and economic inequalities so long as they were to the advantage of the least well off (the difference principle) and attached to positions open to all under fair conditions of equal opportunity. People in the original position would give priority to the first principle, forbidding a reduction of basic liberties for the sake of economic gains.[6]

Rawls also draws a distinction between ideal and nonideal theory. In ideal theory one assumes that, even after the "veil of ignorance" is lifted, people will accept and generally abide by the principles chosen in the original position and that there are no historical obstacles to the realization of just institutions. In nonideal theory, one takes account of both historical obstacles and the unjust actions of others. Nonideal theory is thus more immediately relevant to practical problems, but ideal theory is more fundamental, establishing the ultimate goal of social reform and a basis for judging the relative importance of departures from the ideal (e.g. the priority of liberty).[7]

Like a number of other commentators, I want to claim that many of the reasons that make the original position useful in thinking about questions of justice within a given society also make it useful for thinking about justice across different societies.[8] Cases like migration and trade, where people interact across governmental boundaries, raise questions about whether the background conditions of the interactions are fair. Moreover, anyone who wants to be moral will feel obliged to justify the use of force against other human beings, whether they are members of the same society or not. In thinking about these matters we don't want to be biased by self-interested or partisan considerations, and we don't want existing injustices (if any) to warp our reflections. Moreover, we can take it as a basic presupposition that we should treat all human beings, not just members of our own society, as free and equal moral persons.[9]

The original position offers a strategy of moral reasoning that helps to address these concerns. The purpose of the "veil of ignorance" is "to nullify the effects of specific contingencies which put men at odds" because natural and social contingencies are "arbitrary from a moral point of view" and therefore are factors which ought not to influence the choice of principles of justice.[10] Whether one is a citizen of a rich nation or a poor one, whether one is already a citizen of a particular state or an alien who wishes to become a citizen – this is the sort of specific contingency that could set people at odds. A fair procedure for choosing principles of justice must therefore exclude knowledge of these circumstances, just as it excludes knowledge of one's race or sex or social class. We should therefore take a global, not a national, view of the original position.

One objection to this global approach is that it ignores the extent to which Rawls's use of the original position and the "veil of ignorance" depends upon a particular understanding of moral personality that is characteristic of modern democratic societies but may not be shared by other societies.[11] Let us grant the objection and ask whether it really matters.

The understanding of moral personality in question is essentially the view that all people are free and equal moral persons. Even if this view of moral personality is not shared by people in other societies, it is not a view that applies only to people who share it. Many members of our own society do not share it, as illustrated by the recent demonstrations by white racists in Forsythe County, Georgia. We criticize the racists and reject their views but do not deprive them of their status as free and equal citizens because of their beliefs. Nor is our belief in moral equality limited to members of our own society. Indeed our commitment to civic equality is derived from our convictions about moral equality, not vice versa. So, whatever we think about the justice of borders and the limitations of the claims of aliens, our views must be compatible with a respect for all other human beings as moral persons.

A related objection emphasizes the "constructivist" nature of Rawls's theory, particularly in its later formulations.[12] The theory only makes sense, it is said, in a situation where people already share liberal-democratic values. But if we presuppose a context of shared values, what need have we for a "veil of ignorance'? Why not move directly from the shared values to an agreement on principles of justice and corresponding institutions? The "veil of ignorance" offers a way of thinking about principles of justice in a context where people have deep, unresolvable disagreements about matters of fundamental importance and yet still want to find a way to live together in peaceful cooperation on terms that are fair to all. That seems to be just as appropriate a context for considering the problem of worldwide justice as it is considering the problem of domestic justice.

To read Rawls's theory only as a constructive interpretation of existing social values is to undermine its potential as a constructive critique of those values. For example, racism has deep roots in American public culture, and in the not-too-distant past people like those in Forsythe County constituted a majority in the United States. If we think the racists are wrong and Rawls is right about our obligation to treat all members of our society as free and equal moral persons, it is surely not just because the public culture has changed and the racists are now in the minority. I gladly concede that I am using the original position in a way that Rawls himself does not intend, but I think that this extension is warranted by the nature of the questions I am addressing and the virtues of Rawls's approach as a general method of moral reasoning.

Let us therefore assume a global view of the original position. Those in the original position would be prevented by the "veil of ignorance" from knowing their place of birth or whether they were members of one particular society rather than another. They would presumably choose the same two principles of justice. (I will simply assume that Rawls's argument for the two principles is correct, though the point is disputed.) These principles would apply globally, and the next task would be to design institutions to implement the principles – still from the perspective of the original position. Would these institutions include sovereign states as they currently exist? In ideal theory, where we can assume away historical obstacles and the dangers of injustice, some of the reasons for defending the integrity of existing states disappear. But ideal theory does not require the elimination of all linguistic, cultural, and historical differences. Let us assume that a general case for decentralization of power to respect these sorts of factors would justify the existence of autonomous political communities comparable to modern states.[13] That does not mean that all the existing features of state sovereignty would be justified. State sovereignty would be (morally) constrained by the principles of justice. For example, no state could restrict religious freedom and inequalities among states would be restricted by an international difference principle.

What about freedom of movement among states? Would it be regarded as a basic liberty in a global system of equal liberties, or would states have the right to limit entry and exit? Even in an ideal world people might have powerful reasons to want to migrate from one state to another. Economic opportunities for particular individuals might vary greatly from one state to another even if economic inequalities among states were reduced by an international difference principle. One might fall in love with a citizen from another land, one might belong to a religion which has few followers in one's native land and many in another, one might seek cultural opportunities that are only available in another society. More generally, one has only to ask whether the right to migrate freely *within* a given society is an important liberty. The same sorts of considerations make migration across state boundaries important.[14]

Behind the "veil of ignorance," in considering possible restrictions on freedom, one adopts the perspective of the one who would be most disadvantaged by the restrictions, in this case the perspective of the alien who wants to immigrate. In the original position, then, one would insist that the right to migrate be included in the system of basic liberties for the same reasons that one would insist that the right to religious freedom be included: it might prove essential to one's plan of life. Once the "veil of ignorance" is lifted, of course, one might not make use of the right, but that is true of other rights and liberties as well. So, the basic agreement among those in the original position would be to permit no restrictions on migration (whether emigration or immigration).

There is one important qualification to this. According to Rawls, liberty may be restricted for the sake of liberty even in ideal theory and all liberties depend on the existence of public order and security.[15] (Let us call this the public order restriction.) Suppose that unrestricted immigration would lead to chaos and the breakdown of order. Then all would be worse off in terms of their basic liberties. Even adopting the perspective of the worst-off and recognizing the priority of liberty, those in the original position would endorse restrictions on immigration in such circumstances. This would be a case of restricting liberty for the sake of liberty and every individual would agree to such restrictions even though, once the "veil of ignorance" was lifted, one might find that it was one's own freedom to immigrate which had been curtailed.

Rawls warns against any attempt to use this sort of public order argument in an expansive fashion or as an excuse for restrictions on liberty undertaken for other reasons. The hypothetical possibility of a threat to public order is not enough. Restrictions would be justified only if there were a "reasonable expectation" that unlimited immigration would damage the public order and this expectation would have to be based on "evidence and ways of reasoning acceptable to all."[16] Moreover, restrictions would be justified only to the extent necessary to preserve public order. A need for some restrictions would not justify any level of restrictions whatsoever. Finally, the threat to public order posed by unlimited immigration could not be the product of antagonistic reactions (e.g., riots) from current citizens. This discussion takes place in the context of ideal theory and in this context it is assumed that people try to act justly. Rioting to prevent others from exercising legitimate freedoms would not be just. So, the threat to public order would have to be one that emerged as the unintended cumulative effect of individually just actions.

In ideal theory we face a world of just states with an international difference principle. Under such conditions, the likelihood of mass migrations threatening to the public order of any particular state seems small. So, there is little room for restrictions on immigration in ideal theory. But what about nonideal theory, where one takes into account both historical contingencies and the unjust actions of others?

In the nonideal, real world there are vast economic inequalities among nations (presumably much larger than would exist under an international difference principle). Moreover, people disagree about the nature of justice and often fail to live up to whatever principles they profess. Most states consider it necessary to protect themselves against the possibility of armed invasion or covert subversion. And many states deprive their own citizens of basic rights and liberties. How does all this affect what justice requires with regard to migration?

First, the conditions of the real world greatly strengthen the case for state sovereignty, especially in those states that have relatively just domestic institutions. National security is a crucial form of public order. So, states are clearly entitled to prevent the entry of people (whether armed invaders or subversives) whose goal is the overthrow of just institutions. On the other hand, the strictures against an expansive use of the public order argument also apply to claims about national security.

A related concern is the claim that immigrants from societies where liberal democratic values are weak or absent would pose a threat to the maintenance of a just public order. Again the distinction between reasonable expectations and hypothetical speculations is crucial. These sorts of arguments were used during the nineteenth century against Catholics and Jews from Europe and against all Asians and Africans. If we judge those arguments to have been proven wrong (not to say ignorant and bigoted) by history, we should be wary of resurrecting them in another guise.

A more realistic concern is the sheer size of the potential demand. If a rich country like the United States were simply to open its doors, the number of people from poor countries seeking to immigrate might truly be overwhelming, even if their goals and beliefs posed no threat to national security or liberal democratic values.[17] Under these conditions, it seems likely that some restrictions on immigration would be justified under the public order principle. But it is important to recall all the qualifications that apply to this. In particular, the need for some restriction would not justify any level of restriction whatsover or restrictions for other reasons, but only that level of restriction essential to maintain public order. This would surely imply a much less restrictive policy than the one currently in force which is shaped by so many other considerations besides the need to maintain public order.

Rawls asserts that the priority accorded to liberty normally holds under nonideal conditions as well. This suggests that, if there are restrictions on immigration for public order reasons, priority should be given to those seeking to immigrate because they have been denied basic liberties over those seeking to immigrate simply for economic opportunities. There is a further complication, however. The priority of liberty holds absolutely only in the long run. Under nonideal conditions it can sometimes be justifiable to restrict liberty for the sake of economic gains, if that will improve the position of the worst-off and speed the creation of conditions in which all will enjoy equal and full liberties. Would it be justifiable to restrict immigration for the sake of the worst-off?

We have to be wary of hypocritical uses of this sort of argument. If rich states are really concerned with the worst-off in poor states, they can presumably help more by transferring resources and reforming international economic institutions than by restricting immigration. Indeed, there is reason to suppose more open immigration would help some of the worst-off, not hurt them. At the least, those who immigrate presumably gain themselves and often send money back home as well.

Perhaps the ones who come are not the worst-off, however. It is plausible to suppose that the worst-off don't have the resources to leave. That is still no reason to keep others from coming unless their departure hurts those left behind. But let's suppose it does, as the brain-drain hypothesis suggests. If we assume some restrictions on immigration would be justified for public order reasons, this would suggest that we should give priority to the least skilled among potential immigrants because their departure would presumably have little or no harmful effect on those left behind. It might also suggest that compensation was due to poor countries when skilled people emigrate. But to say that we should actually try to keep people from emigrating (by denying them a place to go) because they represent a valuable resource to their country of origin would be a dramatic departure from the liberal tradition in general and from the specific priority that Rawls attaches to liberty even under nonideal conditions.[18]

Consider the implications of this analysis for some of the conventional arguments for restrictions on immigration. First, one could not justify restrictions on the grounds that those born in a given territory or born of parents who were citizens were more entitled to the benefits of citizenship than those born elsewhere or born of alien parents. Birthplace and parentage are natural contingencies that are "arbitrary from a moral point of view." One of the primary goals of the original position is to minimize the effects of such contingencies upon the distribution of social benefits. To assign citizenship on the basis of birth might be an acceptable procedure, but only if it did not preclude individuals from making different choices later when they reached maturity.

Second, one could not justify restrictions on the grounds that immigration would reduce the economic well-being of current citizens. That line of argument is drastically limited by two considerations: the perspective of the worst-off and the priority of liberty. In order to establish the current citizens' perspective as the relevant worst-off position, it would be necessary to show that immigration would reduce the economic well-being of current citizens below the level the potential immigrants would enjoy if they were not permitted to immigrate. But even if this could be established, it would not justify restrictions on immigration because of the priority of liberty. So, the economic concerns of current citizens are essentially rendered irrelevant.

Third, the effect of immigration on the particular culture and history of the society would not be a relevant moral consideration, so long as there was no threat to basic liberal democratic values. This conclusion is less apparent from what I have said so far, but it follows from what Rawls says in his discussion of perfectionism.[19] The principle of perfectionism would require social institutions to be arranged so as to maximize the achievement of human excellence in art, science, or culture regardless of the effect of such arrangements on equality and freedom. (For example, slavery in ancient Athens has sometimes been defended on the grounds that it was essential to Athenian cultural achievements.) One variant of this position might be the claim that restrictions on immigration would be necessary to preserve the unity and coherence of a culture (assuming that the culture was worth preserving). Rawls argues that in the original position no one would accept any perfectionist standard because no one would be willing to risk the possibility of being required to forego some important right or freedom for the sake of an ideal that might prove irrelevant to one's own concerns. So, restrictions on immigration for the sake of preserving a distinctive culture would be ruled out.

In sum, nonideal theory provides more grounds for restricting immigration than ideal theory, but these grounds are severely limited. And ideal theory holds up the principle of free migration as an essential part of the just social order toward which we should strive.

Aliens in the Calculus

A utilitarian approach to the problem of immigration can take into account some of the concerns that the original position excludes but even utilitarianism does not provide much support for the sorts of restrictions on immigration that are common today. The fundamental principle of utilitarianism is "maximize utility," and the utilitarian commitment to moral equality is reflected in the assumption that everyone is to count for one and no one for more than one when utility is calculated. Of course, these broad formulations cover over deep disagreements among utilitarians. For example, how is "utility" to be defined? Is it subjective or objective? Is it a question of happiness or welfare as in classical utilitarianism or preferences or interests as in some more recent versions?[20]

However these questions are answered, any utilitarian approach would give more weight to some reasons for restricting immigration than Rawls's approach would. For example, if more immigration would hurt some citizens economically, that would count against a more open immigration policy in any utilitarian theory I am familiar with. But that would not settle the question of whether restrictions were justified, for other citizens might gain economically from more immigration and that would count in favor of a more open policy. More importantly, the economic effects of more immigration on noncitizens would also have to be considered. If we focus only on economic consequences, the best immigration policy from a utilitarian perspective would be the one that maximized overall economic gains. In this calculation, current citizens would enjoy no privileged position. The gains and losses of aliens would count just as much. Now the dominant view among both classical and neoclassical economists is that the free mobility of capital and labor is essential to the maximization of overall economic gains. But the free mobility of labor requires open borders. So, despite the fact that the economic costs to current citizens are morally relevant in the utilitarian framework, they would probably not be sufficient to justify restrictions.

Economic consequences are not the only ones that utilitarians consider. For example, if immigration would affect the existing culture or way of life in a society in ways that current citizens found undesirable, that would count against open immigration in many versions of utilitarianism. But not in all. Utilitarians disagree about whether all pleasures (or desires or interests) are to count or only some. For example, should a sadist's pleasure be given moral weight and balanced against his victim's pain or should that sort of pleasure be disregarded? What about racial prejudice? That is clearly relevant to the question of immigration. Should a white racist's unhappiness at the prospect of associating with people of color be counted in the calculus of utility as an argument in favor of racial exclusion as reflected, say, in the White Australia policy? What about the desire to preserve a distinctive local culture as a reason for restricting immigration? That is sometimes linked to racial prejudice but by no means always.

Different utilitarians will answer these sorts of questions in different ways. Some argue that only long-term, rational, or otherwise refined pleasures (or desires or interests) should count. Others insist that we should not look behind the raw data in making our calculations. Everyone's preferences should count, not merely the preferences someone else finds acceptable. I favor the former approach, a reconstructive or filtering approach to utility, but I won't try to defend that here. Even if one takes the raw data approach, which seems to leave more room for reasons to restrict immigration, the final outcome is still likely to favor much more open immigration than is common today. Whatever the method of calculation, the concerns of aliens must be counted too. Under current conditions, when so many millions of poor and oppressed people feel they have so much to gain from migration to the advanced industrial states, it seems hard to believe that a utilitarian calculus which took the interests of aliens seriously would justify significantly greater limits on immigration than the ones entailed by the public order restriction implied by the Rawlsian approach.

The Communitarian Challenge

The three theories I have discussed conflict with one another on many important issues but not (deeply) on the question of immigration. Each leads on its own terms to a position far more favorable to open immigration than the conventional moral view. It is true that, in terms of numbers, even a public order restriction might exclude millions of potential immigrants given the size of the potential demand. Nevertheless, if the arguments I have developed here were accepted, they would require a radical transformation both of current immigration policies and of conventional moral thinking about the question of immigration.

Some may feel that I have wrenched these theories out of context. Each is rooted in the liberal tradition. Liberalism, it might be said, emerged with the modern state and presupposes it. Liberal theories were not designed to deal with questions about aliens. They assumed the context of the sovereign state. As a historical observation this has some truth, but it is not clear why it should have normative force. The same wrenching out of context complaint could as reasonably have been leveled at those who first constructed liberal arguments for the extension of full citizenship to women and members of the working class. Liberal theories also assumed the right to exclude them. Liberal theories focus attention on the need to justify the use of force by the state. Questions about the exclusion of aliens arise naturally from that context. Liberal principles (like most principles) have implications that the original advocates of the principles did not entirely foresee. That is part of what makes social criticism possible.

Others may think that my analysis merely illustrates the inadequacy of liberal theory, especially its inability to give sufficient weight to the value of community.[21] That indictment of liberal theory may or may not be correct, but my findings about immigration rest primarily on assumptions that I think no defensible moral theory can reject: that our social institutions and public policies must respect all human beings as moral persons and that this respect entails recognition, in some form, of the freedom and equality of every human being. Perhaps some other approach can accept these assumptions while still making room for greater restrictions on immigration. To test that possibility, I will consider the views of the theorist who has done the most to translate the communitarian critique into a positive alternative vision: Michael Walzer.

Unlike Rawls and the others, Walzer treats the question of membership as central to his theory of justice, and he comes to the opposite conclusion about immigration from the one that I have defended:

> Across a considerable range of the decisions that are made, states are simply free to take strangers in (or not).[22]

Walzer differs from the other theorists I have considered not only in his conclusions but also in his basic approach. He eschews the search for universal principles and is concerned instead with "the particularism of history, culture, and membership."[23] He thinks that questions of distributive justice should be addressed not from behind a "veil of ignorance" but from the perspective of membership in a political community in which people share a common culture and a common understanding about justice.

I cannot do full justice here to Walzer's rich and subtle discussion of the problem of membership, but I can draw attention to the main points of his argument and to some of the areas of our disagreement. Walzer's central claim is that exclusion is justified by the right of communities to self-determination. The right to exclude is constrained in three important ways, however. First, we have an obligation to provide aid to others who are in dire need, even if we have no established bonds with them, provided that we can do so without excessive cost to ourselves. So, we may be obliged to admit some needy strangers or at least to provide them with some of our resources and perhaps even territory. Second, once people are admitted as residents and participants in the economy, they must be entitled to acquire citizenship, if they wish. Here the constraint flows from principles of justice not mutual aid. The notion of permanent "guest workers" conflicts with the underlying rationale of communal self-determination which justified the right to exclude in the first place. Third, new states or governments may not expel existing inhabitants even if they are regarded as alien by most of the rest of the population.[24]

In developing his argument, Walzer compares the idea of open states with our experience of neighborhoods as a form of open association.[25] But in thinking about what open states would be like, we have a better comparison at hand. We can draw upon our experience of cities, provinces, or states in the American sense. These are familiar political communities whose borders are open. Unlike neighborhoods and like countries, they are formally organized communities with boundaries, distinctions between citizens and noncitizens, and elected officials who are expected to pursue policies that benefit the members of the community that elected them. They often have distinctive cultures and ways of life. Think of the differences between New York City and Waycross, Georgia, or between California and Kansas. These sorts of differences are often much greater than the differences across nation-states. Seattle has more in common with Vancouver than it does with many American communities. But cities and provinces and American states cannot restrict immigration (from other parts of the country). So, these cases call into question Walzer's claim that distinctiveness depends on the possibility of formal closure. What makes for distinctiveness and what erodes it is much more complex than political control of admissions.

This does not mean that control over admissions is unimportant. Often local communities would like to restrict immigration. The people of California wanted to keep out poor Oklahomans during the Depression. Now the people of Oregon would like to keep out the Californians. Internal migrations can be substantial. They can transform the character of communities. (Think of the migrations from the rural South to the urban North.) They can place strains on the local economy and make it difficult to maintain locally funded social programs. Despite all this, we do not think these political communities should be able to control their borders. The right to free migration takes priority.

Why should this be so? Is it just a choice that we make as a larger community (i.e., the nation state) to restrict the self-determination of local communities in this way? Could we legitimately permit them to exclude? Not easily. No liberal state restricts internal mobility. Those states that do restrict internal mobility are criticized for denying basic human freedoms. If freedom of movement within the state is so important that it overrides the claims of local political communities, on what grounds can we restrict freedom of movement across states? This requires a stronger case for the *moral* distinctiveness of the nation-state as a form of community than Walzer's discussion of neighborhoods provides.

Walzer also draws an analogy between states and clubs.[26] Clubs may generally admit or exclude whomever they want, although any particular decision may be criticized through an appeal to the character of the club and the shared understandings of its members. So, too, with states. This analogy ignores the familiar distinction between public and private, a distinction that Walzer makes use of elsewhere.[27] There is a deep tension between the right of freedom of association and the right to equal treatment. One way to address this tension is to say that in the private sphere freedom of association prevails and in the public sphere equal treatment does. You can pick your friends on the basis of whatever criteria you wish, but in selecting people for offices you must treat all candidates fairly. Drawing a line between public and private is often problematic, but it is clear that clubs are normally at one end of the scale and states at the other. So, the fact that private clubs may admit or exclude whomever they choose says nothing about the appropriate admission standards for states. When the state acts it must treat individuals equally.

Against this, one may object that the requirement of equal treatment applies fully only to those who are already *members* of the community. That is accurate as a description of practice but the question is why it should be so. At one time, the requirement of equal treatment did not extend fully to various groups (workers, blacks, women). On the whole, the history of liberalism reflects a tendency to expand both the definition of the public sphere and the requirements of equal treatment. In the United States today, for example, in contrast to earlier times, both public agencies and private corporations may not legally exclude women simply because they are women (although private clubs still may). A white shopkeeper may no longer exclude blacks from his store (although he may exclude them from his home). I think these recent developments, like the earlier extension of the franchise, reflect something fundamental about the inner logic of liberalism.[28] The extension of the right to immigrate reflects the same logic: equal treatment of individuals in the public sphere.

As I noted at the beginning of this section, Walzer asserts that the political community is constrained by principles of justice from admitting permanent guest workers without giving them the opportunity to become citizens. There is some ambiguity about whether this claim is intended to apply to all political communities or only to ones like ours. If states have a right to self-determination, broadly conceived, they must have a right to choose political forms and political practices different from those of libeal democracies. That presumably includes the right to establish categories of second-class citizens (or, at least, temporary guest workers) and also the right to determine other aspects of admissions policy in accordance with their own principles.[29] But if the question is what *our* society (or one with the same basic values) ought to do, then the matter is different both for guest workers and for other aliens. It is right to assert that *our* society ought to admit guest workers to full citizenship. Anything else is incompatible with our liberal democratic principles. But so is a restrictive policy on immigration.

Any approach like Walzer's that seeks its ground in the tradition and culture of *our* community must confront, as a methodological paradox, the fact that liberalism is a central part of our culture. The enormous intellectual popularity of Rawls and Nozick and the enduring influence of utilitarianism attest to their ability to communicate contemporary understandings and shared meanings in a language that has legitimacy and power in our culture. These theories would not make such sense to a Buddhist monk in medieval Japan. But their individualistic assumptions and their language of universal, ahistorical reason makes sense to us because of *our* tradition, *our* culture, *our* community. For people in a different moral tradition, one that assumed fundamental moral differences between those inside the society and those outside, restrictions on immigration might be easy to justify. Those who are *other* simply might not count, or at least not count as much. But we cannot dismiss the aliens on the ground that they are other, because *we* are the products of a liberal culture.

The point goes still deeper. To take *our* community as a starting point is to take a community that expresses its moral views in terms of universal principles. Walzer's own arguments reflect this. When he asserts that states may not expel existing inhabitants whom the majority or the new government regards as alien, he is making a claim about what is right and wrong for *any* state not just our own or one that shares our basic values. He develops the argument by drawing on Hobbes. That is an argument from a particular tradition, one that may not be shared by new states that want to expel some of their inhabitants. Nonetheless, Walzer makes a universal claim (and one I consider correct). He makes the same sort of argument when he insists that states may not legitimately restrict emigration.[30] This applies to all political communities not just those that share our understanding of the relation of individual and collective.

Recognition of the particularity of our own culture should not prevent us from making these sorts of claims. We should not try to force others to accept our views, and we should be ready to listen to others and learn from them. But respect for the diversity of communities does not require us to abandon all claims about what other states ought to do. If my arguments are correct, the general case for open borders is deeply rooted in the fundamental values of our tradition. No moral argument will seem acceptable to *us*, if it directly challenges the assumption of the equal moral worth of all individuals. If restrictions on immigration are to be justified, they have to be based on arguments that respect that principle. Walzer's theory has many virtues that I have not explored here, but it does not supply an adequate argument for the state's right to exclude.

Conclusion

Free migration may not be immediately achievable, but it is a goal toward which we should strive. And we have an obligation to open our borders much more fully than we do now. The current restrictions on immigration in Western democracies – even in the most open ones like Canada and the United States – are not justifiable. Like feudal barriers to mobility, they protect unjust privilege.

Does it follow that there is *no* room for distinctions between aliens and citizens, no theory of citizenship, no boundaries for the community? Not at all. To say that membership is open to all who wish to join is not to say that there is no distinction between members and nonmembers. Those who choose to cooperate together in the state have special rights and obligations not shared by noncitizens. Respecting the particular choices and commitments that individuals make flows naturally from a commitment to the idea of equal moral worth. (Indeed, consent as a justification for political obligation is least problematic in the case of immigrants.) What is *not* readily compatible with the idea of equal moral worth is the exclusion of those who want to join. If people want to sign the social contract, they should be permitted to do so.

Open borders would threaten the distinctive character of different political communities only because we assume that so many people would move if they could. If the migrants were few, it would not matter. A few immigrants could always be absorbed without changing the character of the community. And, as Walzer observes, most human beings do not love to move.[31] They normally feel attached to their native land and to the particular language, culture, and community in which they grew up and in which they feel at home. They seek to move only when life is very difficult where they are. Their concerns are rarely frivolous. So, it is right to weigh the claims of those who want to move against the claims of those who want to preserve the community as it is. And if we don't unfairly tip the scales, the case for exclusion will rarely triumph.

People live in communities with bonds and bounds, but these may be of different kinds. In a liberal society, the bonds and bounds should be compatible with liberal principles. Open immigration would change the character of the community but it would not leave the community without any character. It might destroy old ways of life, highly valued by some, but it would make possible new ways of life, highly valued by others. The whites in Forsythe County who want to keep out blacks are trying to preserve a way of life that is valuable to them. To deny such communities the right to exclude does limit their ability to shape their future character and destiny, but it does not utterly destroy their capacity for self-determination. Many aspects of communal life remain potentially subject to collective control. Moreover, constraining the kinds of choices that people and communities may make is what principles of justice are for. They set limits on what people seeking to abide by these principles may do. To commit ourselves to open borders would not be to abandon the idea of communal character but to reaffirm it. It would be an affirmation of the liberal character of the community and of its commitment to principles of justice.

Acknowledgments

This paper was first written for an APSA seminar on citizenship directed by Nan Keohane. Subsequent versions were presented to seminars at the University of Chicago, the Institute for Advanced Study, and Columbia University. I would like to thank the members of these groups for their comments. In addition I would like to thank the following individuals for helpful comments on one of the many drafts: Sot Barber, Charles Beitz, Michael Doyle, Amy Gutmann, Christine Korsgaard, Charles Miller, Donald Moon, Jennifer Nedelsky, Thomas Pogge, Peter Schuck, Rogers Smith, Dennis Thompson, and Michael Walzer.

Notes

1 The conventional assumption is captured by the Select Commission on Immigration and Refugee Policy: "Our policy – while providing opportunity to a portion of the world's population – must be guided by the basic national interests of the people of the United States." From *U.S. Immigration Policy and the National Interest: The Final Report and Recommendations of the Select Commission on Immigration and Refugee Policy to the Congress and the President of the United States* (1 March 1981). The best theoretical defense of the conventional assumption (with some modifications) is Michael Walzer, *Spheres of Justice* (New York: Basic Books, 1983), pp. 31–63. A few theorists have challenged the conventional assumption. See Bruce Ackerman, *Social Justice in the Liberal State* (New Haven: Yale University Press, 1980), pp. 89–95; Judith Lichtenberg, "National Boundaries and Moral Boundaries: A Cosmopolitan View" in *Boundaries: National Autonomy and Its Limits*, ed. Peter G. Brown and Henry Shue (Totowa, NJ: Rowman and Littlefield, 1981), pp. 79–100, and Roger Nett, "The Civil Right We Are Not Ready For: The Right of Free Movement of People on the Face of the Earth," *Ethics* 81:212–27. Frederick Whelan has also explored these issues in two interesting unpublished papers.
2 Robert Nozick, *Anarchy, State, and Utopia* (New York: Basic Books, 1974), pp. 10–25, 88–119.
3 Ibid., pp. 108–113. Citizens, in Nozick's view, are simply consumers purchasing impartial, efficient protection of preexisting natural rights. Nozick uses the terms "citizen," "client" and "customer" interchangeably.
4 Nozick interprets the Lockean proviso as implying that property rights in land may not so restrict an individual's freedom of movement as to deny him effective liberty. This further limits the possibility of excluding aliens. See p. 55.
5 Ibid., pp. 320–3.
6 John Rawls, *A Theory of Justice* (Cambridge, MA.: Harvard University Press, 1971), pp. 60–5, 136–42, 243–8.
7 Ibid., pp. 8–9, 244–8.
8 The argument for a global view of the original position has been developed most fully in Charles Beitz, *Political Theory and International Relations* (Princeton, NJ: Princeton University Press, 1979), pp. 125–76, especially 129–36 and 143–53. For earlier criticisms of Rawls along the same lines, see Brian Barry, *The Liberal Theory of Justice* (Oxford: Clarendon Press, 1973), pp. 128–33 and Thomas M. Scanlon, "Rawls's Theory of Justice," *University of Pennsylvania Law Review* 121, no. 5 (May 1973): 1066–7. For more recent discussions, see David A. J. Richards, "International Distributive Justice," in *Ethics, Economics, and the Law*, eds. J. Roland Pennock and John Chapman

(New York: New York University Press, 1982), pp. 275–99 and Charles Beitz, "Cosmopolitan Ideals and National Sentiments," *The Journal of Philosophy* 80, no. 10 (October 1983): 591–600. None of these discussions fully explores the implications of a global view of the original position for the issue of immigration, although the recent essay by Beitz touches on the topic.

9 Respecting others as free and equal moral persons does not imply that one cannot distinguish friends from strangers or citizens from aliens. See the conclusion for an elaboration.

10 Rawls, *Justice*, pp. 136, 72.

11 John Rawls, "Kantian Constructivism in Moral Theory," *The Journal of Philosophy* 77, no. 9 (September 1980): 515–72.

12 Ibid. See also John Rawls, "Justice as Fairness: Political not Metaphysical," *Philosophy and Public Affairs* 14 (Summer 1985): 223–51.

13 Compare Beitz, *Political Theory*, p. 183.

14 For more on the comparison of mobility within a country and mobility across countries, see Joseph H. Carens, "Migration and the Welfare State" in *Democracy and the Welfare State*, ed. Amy Gutmann (Princeton: Princeton University Press, 1987).

15 Rawls, *Justice*, pp. 212–13.

16 Ibid., p. 213.

17 For statistics on current and projected levels of immigration to the U.S., see Michael S. Teitelbaum, "Right Versus Right: Immigration and Refugee Policy in the United States," *Foreign Affairs* 59 (1980): 21–59.

18 For the deep roots of the right to emigrate in the liberal tradition, see Frederick Whelan, "Citizenship and the Right to Leave," *American Political Science Review* 75, no. 3 (September 1981): 636–53.

19 Rawls, *Justice*, pp. 325–32.

20 For recent discussions of utilitarianism, see Richard Brandt, *A Theory of the Good and the Right* (Oxford: Oxford University Press, 1979); Peter Singer, *Practical Ethics* (Cambridge: Cambridge University Press, 1979); R. M. Hare, *Moral Thinking* (Oxford: Oxford University Press, 1981); and Amartya Sen and Bernard Williams, eds., *Utilitarianism and Beyond* (Cambridge: Cambridge University Press, 1982).

21 For recent communitarian critiques of liberalism, see Alasdair MacIntyre, *After Virtue* (Notre Dame: Notre Dame University Press, 1981) and Michael Sandel, *Liberalism and the Limits of Justice* (New York: Cambridge University Press, 1982). For a critique of the critics, see Amy Gutmann, "Communitarian Critics of Liberalism," *Philosophy and Public Affairs* 14 (Summer 1985): 308–22.

22 Walzer, *Spheres*, p. 61.

23 Ibid., p. 5.

24 Ibid., pp. 33, 45–8, 55–61, 42–4.

25 Ibid., pp. 36–9.

26 Ibid., pp. 39–41.

27 Ibid., pp. 129–64.

28 I am not arguing that the changes in treatment of women, blacks, and workers were *brought about* by the inner logic of liberalism. These changes

resulted from changes in social conditions and from political struggles, including ideological struggles in which arguments about the implications of liberal principles played some role, though not necessarily a decisive one. But from a philosophical perspective, it is important to understand where principles lead, even if one does not assume that people's actions in the world will always be governed by the principles they espouse.

29 Compare Walzer's claim that the caste system would be just if accepted by the villages affected ibid., pp. 313–15).

30 Ibid., pp. 39–40.

31 Ibid., p. 38.

18 Immigrants and Family Values

Francis Fukuyama

At the Republican convention in Houston in 1992, Patrick J. Buchanan announced the coming of a block-by-block war to "take back our culture." Buchanan is right that a cultural war is upon us, and that this fight will be a central American preoccupation now that the cold war is over. What he understands less well, however, is that the vast majority of the non-European immigrants who have come into this country in the past couple of decades are not the enemy. Indeed, many of them are potentially on his side.

Conservatives have for long been sharply divided on the question of immigration. Many employers and proponents of free-market economics, like Julian Simon or the editorial page of the *Wall Street Journal*, are strongly pro-immigration; they argue for open borders because immigrants are a source of cheap labor and ultimately create more wealth than they consume. Buchanan and other traditional right-wing Republicans, by contrast, represent an older nativist position. They dispute the economic benefits of immigration, but more importantly look upon immigrants as bearers of foreign and less desirable cultural values. It is this group of conservatives who forced the inclusion of a plank in the Republican platform last August calling for the creation of "structures" to maintain the integrity of America's southern border.

Indeed, hostility to immigration has made for peculiar bedfellows. The Clinton administration's difficulties in finding an attorney general who had not at some point hired an illegal-immigrant babysitter is testimony to the objective dependence of liberal yuppies on immigration to maintain their life-styles, and they by and large would support the *Wall Street Journal*'s open-borders position.

On the other hand, several parts of the liberal coalition – blacks and environmentalists – have been increasingly vocal in recent years in opposition to further immigration, particularly from Latin America. The Black Leadership Forum, headed by Coretta Scott King and Congressman Walter Fauntroy, has lobbied to maintain sanctions against employers hiring illegal immigrant labor on the ground that this takes away jobs from blacks and "legal" browns. Jack Miles, a former *Los Angeles Times* book-review editor with impeccable liberal credentials, has in a recent article in the *Atlantic* lined up with the Federation for American Immigration Reform (FAIR) in calling for a rethinking of open borders, while liberal activist groups like the Southern California Interfaith Task Force on Central America have supported Senator Orrin Hatch's legislation strengthening employer sanctions. Environmental groups like the Sierra Club, for their part, oppose immigration because it necessitates economic growth, use of natural resources, and therefore environmental degradation.

But if much of the liberal opposition to immigration has focused on economic issues, the conservative opposition has concentrated on the deeper cultural question; and here the arguments made by the Right are very confused. The symptoms of cultural decay are all around us, but the last people in the world we should be blaming are recent immigrants.

II

The most articulate and reasoned recent conservative attack on immigration came in an 1992 article in *National Review* by Peter Brimelow. Brimelow, a senior editor at *Forbes* and himself a naturalized American of British and Canadian background, argues that immigration worked in the past in America only because earlier waves of nativist backlash succeeded in limiting it to a level that could be successfully assimilated into the dominant Anglo-Saxon American culture. Brimelow criticizes pro-immigration free-marketeers like Julian Simon for ignoring the issue of the skill levels of the immigrant labor force, and their likely impact on blacks and others at the bottom end of the economic ladder. But his basic complaint is a cultural one. Attacking the *Wall Street Journal's* Paul Gigot for remarking that a million Zulus would probably work harder than a million Englishmen today, Brimelow notes:

> This comment reveals an utter innocence about the reality of ethnic and cultural differences, let alone little things like tradition and history – in short, the greater part of the conservative vision. Even in its own purblind terms, it is totally false. All the empirical evidence is that immigrants from developed countries assimilate better than those from underdeveloped countries. It is developed countries that teach the skills required for success in the United States...it should not be necessary to explain that the legacy of [the Zulu kings] Shaka and Cetewayo – overthrown just over a century ago – is not that of Alfred the Great, let alone Elizabeth II or any civilized society.

Elsewhere, Brimelow suggests that culture is a key determinant of economic performance, and that people from certain cultures are therefore likely to do less well economically than others. He implies, furthermore, that some immigrants are more prone to random street crime because of their "impulsiveness and present-orientation," while others are responsible for organized crime which is, by his account, ethnically based. Finally, Brimelow argues that the arrival of diverse non-European cultures fosters the present atmosphere of multiculturalism, and is, to boot, bad for the electoral prospects of the Republican party.

A similar line of thought runs through Buchanan's writings and speeches, and leads to a similar anti-immigrant posture. Buchanan has explicitly attacked the notion that democracy represents a particularly positive form of government, and hence would deny that belief in universal democratic principles ought to be at the core of the American national identity.[1] But if one subtracts democracy from American nationality, what is left? Apparently, though Buchanan is somewhat less explicit on this point, a concept of America as a Christian, ethnically European nation with certain core cultural values that are threatened by those coming from other cultures and civilizations.

There is an easy, Civics 101-type answer to the Brimelow-Buchanan argument. In contrast to other West European democracies, or Japan, the American national identity has never been directly linked to ethnicity or religion. Nationality has been based instead on universal concepts like freedom and equality that are in theory open to all people. Our Constitution forbids the establishment of religion, and the legal system has traditionally held ethnicity at arm's length. To be an American has meant to be committed to a certain set of ideas, and not to be descended from an original tribe of ur-Americans. Those elements of a common American culture visible today – belief in the Constitution and the individualist-egalitarian principles underlying it, plus modern American pop and consumer culture – are universally accessible and appealing, making the United States, in Ben Wattenberg's phrase, the first "universal nation."

This argument is correct as far as it goes, but there is a serious counterargument that reaches to the core of last year's debate over "family values." It runs as follows:

America began living up to its universalist principles only in the last half of this century. For most of the period from its revolutionary founding to its rise as a great, modern, industrial power, the nation's elites conceived of the country not just as a democracy based on universal principles, but also as a Christian, Anglo-Saxon nation.

American democracy – the counterargument continues – is, of course, embodied in the laws and institutions of the country, and will be imbibed by anyone who learns to play by its rules. But virtually every serious theorist of American democracy has noted that its success depended heavily on the presence of certain predemocratic values or cultural characteristics that were neither officially sanctioned nor embodied in law. If the Declaration of Independence and the Constitution were the basis of America's *Gesellschaft* (society), Christian Anglo-Saxon culture constituted its *Gemeinschaft* (community).

Indeed – the counterargument goes on – the civic institutions that Tocqueville observed in the 1830's, whose strength and vitality he saw as a critical manifestation of the Americans' "art of associating," were more often than not of a religious (i.e., Christian) nature, devoted to temperance, moral education of the young, or the abolition of slavery. There is nothing in the Constitution which states that parents should make large sacrifices for their children, that workers should rise early in the morning and labor long hours in order to get ahead, that people should emulate rather than undermine their neighbors' success, that they should be innovative, entrepreneurial, or open to technological change. Yet Americans, formed by a Christian culture, possessed these traits in abundance for much of their history, and the country's economic prosperity and social cohesion arguably rested on them.

It is this sort of consideration that underlay the family-values controversy during last year's election. Basic to this line of thought is that, all other things being equal, children are better off when raised in stable, two-parent, heterosexual families. Such family structures and the web of moral obligations they entail are the foundation of educational achievement, economic success, good citizenship, personal character, and a host of other social virtues.

The issue of family values was badly mishandled by the Republicans and deliberately misconstrued by the press and the Democrats (often not distinguishable), such that mere mention of the phrase provoked derisive charges of narrow-minded gay-bashing and hostility to single mothers. Yet while many Americans did not sign on to the family-values theme, few would deny that the family and community are in deep crisis today. The breakdown of the black family in inner-city neighborhoods around America in the past couple of generations shows in particularly stark form the societal consequences of a loss of certain cultural values. And what has happened among blacks is only an extreme extension of a process that has been proceeding apace among whites as well.

The issue, then, is not whether the questions of culture and cultural values are important, or whether it is legitimate to raise them, but whether immigration really threatens those values. For while the values one might deem central either to economic success or to social cohesion may have arisen out of a Christian, Anglo-Saxon culture, it is clear that they are not bound to that particular social group: some groups, like Jews and Asians, might come to possess those values in abundance, while Wasps themselves might lose them and decay. The question thus becomes: which ethnic groups in today's America are threatening, and which groups are promoting, these core cultural values?

III

The notion that non-European immigrants are a threat to family values and other core American cultural characteristics is, in a way, quite puzzling. After all, the breakdown of traditional family structures, from extended to nuclear, has long been understood to be a disease of advanced industrial countries and not of nations just emerging from their agricultural pasts.

Some conservatives tend to see the third world as a vast, global underclass, teeming with the same social pathologies as Compton in Los Angeles or Bedford-Stuyvesant in Brooklyn. But the sad fact is that the decay of basic social relationships evident in American inner cities, stretching to the most intimate moral bonds linking parents and children, may well be something with few precedents in human history. Economic conditions in most third-world countries simply would not permit a social group suffering so total a collapse of family structure to survive: with absent fathers and no source of income, or mothers addicted to drugs, children would not live to adulthood.

But it would also seem *a priori* likely that third-world immigrants should have stronger family values than white, middle-class, suburban Americans, while their work ethic and willingness to defer to traditional sources of authority should be greater as well. Few of the factors that have led to family breakdown in the American middle class over the past couple of generations – rapidly changing economic conditions, with their attendant social disruptions; the rise of feminism and the refusal of women to play traditional social roles; or the legitimization of alternative life-styles and consequent proliferation of rights and entitlements on a retail level – apply in third-world situations. Immigrants coming from traditional developing societies are likely to be poorer, less educated, and in possession of fewer skills than those from Europe, but they are also likely to have stronger family structures and moral inhibitions. Moreover, despite the greater ease of moving to America today than in the last century, immigrants are likely to be a self-selecting group with a much greater than average degree of energy, ambition, toughness, and adaptability.

These intuitions are largely borne out by the available empirical data, particularly if one disaggregates the different parts of the immigrant community.

The strength of traditional family values is most evident among immigrants from East and South Asia, where mutually supportive family structures have long been credited as the basis for their economic success. According to Census Bureau statistics, 78 percent of Asian and Pacific Islander households in the United States were family households, as opposed to 70 percent for white Americans. The size of these family households is likely to be larger: 74 percent consist of three or more persons, compared to 57 percent for white families. While Asians are equally likely to be married as whites, they are only half as likely to be divorced.[2] Though dropping off substantially in the second and third generations, concern for elderly parents is high in Chinese, Japanese, and Vietnamese households; for many, the thought of sticking a mother or father out of sight and out of mind in a nursing home continues to be anathema. More importantly, most of the major Asian immigrant groups are intent on rapid assimilation into the American mainstream, and have not been particularly vocal in pressing for particularistic cultural entitlements.

While most white Americans are ready to recognize and celebrate the social strengths of Asians, the real fears of cultural invasion surround Latinos. Despite their fast growth, Asians still constitute less than 3 percent of the U.S. population, while the number of Hispanics increased from 14.6 to over 22 million between 1980 and 1990, or 9 percent of the population. But here as well, the evidence suggests that most Latin American immigrants may be a source of strength with regard to family values, and not a liability.

Latinos today constitute an extremely diverse group. It is certainly the case that a segment of the Latino community has experienced many of the same social problems as blacks. This is particularly true of the first large Latino community in the U.S.: Puerto Ricans who came to the mainland in the early postwar period and settled predominantly in New York and other cities of the Northeast. Forty percent of Puerto Rican families are headed by women, compared to 16 percent for the non-Hispanic population; only 57 percent of Puerto Rican households consist of families, while their rate of out-of-wedlock births is almost double the rate for non-Hispanics. In New York, Puerto Ricans have re-exported social pathologies like crack-cocaine use to Puerto Rico over the past generation.

Other Latino groups have also brought social problems with them: the Mariel boat lift from Cuba, during which Castro emptied his country's jails and insane asylums, had a measurable impact on crime in the U.S. Many war-hardened immigrants from El Salvador and other unstable Central American countries have contributed to crime in the U.S., and Chicano gangs in Los Angeles and other Southwestern cities have achieved their own notoriety beside the black Bloods and Crips. Half of those arrested in the Los Angeles riot last year were Latinos.

Such facts are highly visible and contribute to the impression among white Americans that Latinos as a whole have joined inner-city blacks to form one vast, threatening underclass. But there are very significant differences among Latino groups. Latinos of Cuban and Mexican origin, for example, who together constitute 65 percent of the Hispanic community, have a 50-percent lower rate of female-headed households than do Puerto Ricans – 18.9 and 19.6 percent versus 38.9 percent. While the rate of Puerto Rican out-of-wedlock births approaches that of blacks (53.0 vs. 63.1

percent of live births), the rates for Cuban and Mexican-origin Latinos are much lower, 16.1 and 28.9 percent, respectively, though they are still above the white rate of 13.9 percent.[3]

When looked at in the aggregate, Latino family structure stands somewhere between that of whites and blacks. For example, the rates of female-headed families with no husband present as a proportion of total families is 13.5 percent for whites, 46.4 percent for blacks, and 24.4 percent for Hispanics. If we adjust these figures for income level, however, Hispanics turn out to be much closer to the white norm.

Poverty is hard on families regardless of race; part of the reason for the higher percentage of Latino female-headed households is simply that there are more poor Latino families. If we compare families below the poverty level, the Hispanic rate of female-headed families is very close to that of whites (45.7 vs. 43.6 percent), while the comparable rate for blacks is much higher than either (78.3 percent). Considering the substantially higher rate of family breakdown within the sizable Puerto Rican community, this suggests that the rate of single-parent families for Cuban-and Mexican-origin Latinos is actually lower than that for whites at a comparable income level.

Moreover, Latinos as a group are somewhat more likely to be members of families than either whites or blacks.[4] Another study indicates that Mexican-Americans have better family demographics than do whites, with higher birth-weight babies even among low-income mothers due to taboos on smoking, drinking, and drug use during pregnancy. Many Latinos remain devout Catholics, and the rate of church attendance is higher in the Mexican community than for the U.S. as a whole as well. But even if one does not believe that the United States is a "Christian country," the fact that so many immigrants are from Catholic Latin America should make them far easier to assimilate than, say, Muslims in Europe.

These statistics are broadly in accord with the observations of anyone who has lived in Los Angeles, San Diego, or any other community in the American Southwest. Virtually every early-morning commuter in Los Angeles knows the street-corners on which Chicano day-laborers gather at 7:00 A.M., looking for work as gardeners, busboys, or on construction sites. Many of them are illegal immigrants with families back in Mexico to whom they send their earnings. While they are poor and unskilled, they have a work ethic and devotion to family comparable to those of the South and

East European immigrants who came to the U.S. at the turn of the century. It is much less common to see African-Americans doing this sort of thing.

Those who fear third-world immigration as a threat to Anglo-American cultural values do not seem to have noticed what the real sources of cultural breakdown have been. To some extent, they can be traced to broad socioeconomic factors over which none of us has control: the fluid, socially disruptive nature of capitalism; technological change; economic pressures of the contemporary workplace and urban life; and so on. But the ideological assault on traditional family values – the sexual revolution; feminism and the delegitimization of the male-dominated household; the celebration of alternative life-styles; attempts ruthlessly to secularize all aspects of American public life; the acceptance of no-fault divorce and the consequent rise of single-parent households – was not the creation of recently-arrived Chicano agricultural workers or Haitian boat people, much less of Chinese or Korean immigrants. They originated right in the heart of America's well-established white, Anglo-Saxon community. The "Hollywood elite" that created the now celebrated Murphy Brown, much like the establishment "media elite" that Republicans enjoy attacking, does not represent either the values or the interests of most recent third-world immigrants.

In short, though the old, traditional culture continues to exist in the United States, it is overlaid today with an elite culture that espouses very different values. The real danger is not that these elites will become corrupted by the habits and practices of third-world immigrants, but rather that the immigrants will become corrupted by them. And that is in fact what tends to happen.

While the first generation of immigrants to the United States tends to be deferential to established authority and preoccupied with the economic problems of "making it," their children and grandchildren become aware of their own entitlements and rights, more politicized, and able to exploit the political system to defend and expand those entitlements. While the first generation is willing to work quietly at minimum-or subminimum-wage jobs, the second and third generations have higher expectations as to what their labor is worth. The extension of welfare and other social benefits to noncitizens through a series of court decisions has had the perverse effect of hastening the spread of welfare dependency. Part of the reason that Puerto Ricans do less well than other Latino groups may be that they were never really immigrants at all, but U.S. citizens, and therefore eligible for social benefits at a very early stage.

As Julian Simon has shown, neither the absolute nor the relative levels of immigration over the past decade have been inordinately high by historical standards. What *is* different and very troubling about immigration in the present period is that the ideology that existed at the turn of the century and promoted assimilation into the dominant Anglo-Saxon culture has been replaced by a multicultural one that legitimates and even promotes continuing cultural differentness.

The intellectual and social origins of multiculturalism are complex, but one thing is clear: it is both a Western and an American invention. The American Founding was based on certain Enlightenment notions of the universality of human equality and freedom, but such ideas have been under attack within the Western tradition itself for much of the past two centuries. The second half of the late Allan Bloom's *The Closing of the American Mind* (the part that most buyers of the book skipped over) chronicles the way in which the relativist ideas of Nietzsche and Heidegger were transported to American shores at mid-century. Combined with an easygoing American egalitarianism, they led not just to a belief in the need for cultural tolerance, but to a positive assertion of the equal moral validity of all cultures. Today the writings of Michel Foucault, a French epigone of Nietzsche, have become the highbrow source of academic multiculturalism.

France may have produced Foucault, but France has not implemented a multicultural educational curriculum to anything like the degree the U.S. has. The origins of multiculturalism here must therefore be traced to the specific circumstances of American social life. Contrary to the arguments of multiculturalism's promoters, it was not a necessary adjustment to the reality of our pluralistic society. The New York City public-school system in the year 1910 was as diverse as it is today, and yet it never occurred to anyone to celebrate and preserve the native cultures of the city's Italians, Greeks, Poles, Jews, or Chinese.

The shift in attitudes toward cultural diversity can be traced to the aftermath of the civil-rights movement, when it became clear that integration was not working for blacks. The failure to assimilate was interpreted as an indictment of the old, traditional mainstream Anglo-Saxon culture: "Wasp" took on a pejorative connotation, and African-Americans began to take pride in the separateness of their own traditions. Ironically, the experience of African-Americans became the model for subsequent immigrant groups like Latinos who could have integrated themselves into mainstream society as easily as the Italians or Poles before them.

It is true that Hispanic organizations now constitute part of the multiculturalist coalition and have been very vocal in pushing for bilingual/bicultural education. There is increasing evidence, however, that rank-and-file immigrants are much more traditionally assimilationist than some of their more vocal leaders. For example, most Chinese and Russian immigrant parents in New York City deliberately avoid sending their children to the bilingual-education classes offered to them by the public-school system, believing that a cold plunge into English will be a much more effective means of learning to function in American society.

Hispanics generally show more support for bilingual education, but even here a revealing recent study indicates that an overwhelming number of Hispanic parents see bilingualism primarily as a means of learning English, and not of preserving Hispanic culture.[5] This same study indicates that most Hispanics identify strongly with the United States, and show a relatively low level of Spanish maintenance in the home. By contrast, multiculturalism is more strongly supported by many other groups – blacks, feminists, gays, Native Americans, etc. – whose ancestors have been in the country from the start.

Brimelow's *National Review* piece suggests that even if immigrants are not responsible for our anti-assimilationist multiculturalism, we need not pour oil on burning waters by letting in more immigrants from non-Western cultures. But this argument can be reversed: even if the rate of new immigration fell to zero tomorrow, and the most recent five million immigrants were sent home, we would still have an enormous problem in this country with the breakdown of a core culture and the infatuation of the school system with trendy multiculturalist educational policies.

The real fight, the central fight, then, should not be over keeping newcomers out: this will be a waste of time and energy. The real fight ought to be over the question of assimilation itself: whether we believe that there is enough to our Western, rational, egalitarian, democratic civilization to force those coming to the country to absorb its language and rules, or whether we carry respect for other cultures to the point that Americans no longer have a common voice with which to speak to one another.

Apart from the humble habits of work and family values, opponents of immigration ought to consider culture at the high end of the scale. As anyone who has walked around an elite American university recently would know, immigration from Asia is transforming the nature of American education. For a country that has long prided itself on technological superiority, and whose economic future rests in large part on a continuing technical edge, a depressingly small number of white Americans from long-established families choose to go into engineering and science programs in preference to business and, above all, law school. (This is particularly true of the most dynamic and vocal part of the white population, upwardly mobile middle-class women.) The one bright spot in an otherwise uniform horizon of decline in educational test scores has been in math, where large numbers of new Asian test-takers have bumped up the numbers.[6] In Silicon Valley alone, there are some 12,000 engineers of Chinese descent, while Chinese account for two out of every five engineering and science graduates in the University of California system.

Indeed, if one were to opt for "designer immigration" that would open the gates to peoples with the best cultural values, it is not at all clear that certain European countries would end up on top.

In the past decade, England's per-capita GNP has fallen behind Italy's, and threatens to displace Portugal and Greece at the bottom of the European Community heap by the end of the decade. Only a fifth of English young people receive any form of higher education, and despite Margaret Thatcher's best efforts, little progress has been made over the past generation in breaking down the stifling social rigidities of the British class system. The English working class is among the least well-educated, most state-and welfare-dependent and immobile of any in the developed world. While the British intelligentsia and upper classes continue to intimidate middle-class Americans, they can do so only on the basis of snobbery and inherited but rapidly dwindling intellectual capital. Paul Gigot may or may not be right that a million Zulus would work harder than a million English, but a million Taiwanese certainly would, and would bring with them much stronger family structures and entrepreneurship to boot.

IV

This is not to say that immigration will not be the source of major economic and social problems for the United States in the future. There are at least three areas of particular concern.

The first has to do with the effects of immigration on income distribution, particularly at the low end of the scale. The growing inequality of American income distribution over the past decade is not, as the Democrats asserted during the election campaign, the result of Reagan-Bush tax policies or the failure of "trickle-down" economics. Rather, it proceeds from the globalization of the American economy: low-skill labor increasingly has to compete with low-skill labor in Malaysia, Brazil, Mexico, and elsewhere. But it has also had to compete with low-skill immigrant labor coming into the country from the third world, which explains why Hispanics themselves tend to oppose further Hispanic immigration. The country as a whole may be better off economically as a result of this immigration, but those against whom immigrants directly compete have been hurt, just as they will be hurt by the North American Free Trade Agreement (NAFTA), the General Agreement on Tariffs and Trade (GATT), and other trade-liberalizing measures that are good for the country as a whole. In a city like Los Angeles, Hispanics with their stronger social ties have displaced blacks out of a variety of menial jobs, adding to the woes of an already troubled black community.

The second problem area has to do with the regional concentration of recent Hispanic immigration. As everyone knows, the 25 million Hispanics in the United States are not evenly distributed throughout the country, but are concentrated in the Southwest portion of it, where the problems normally accompanying the assimilation of immigrant communities tend to be magnified. The L.A. public-school system is currently in a state of breakdown, as it tries to educate burgeoning numbers of recent immigrants on a recession-starved budget.

The third problem concerns bilingualism and the elite Hispanic groups which promote and exist off of it. As noted earlier, the rank-and-file of the Hispanic community seems reasonably committed to assimilation; the same cannot be said for its leadership. Bilingualism, which initially began as a well-intentioned if misguided bridge toward learning English, has become in the eyes of many of its proponents a means of keeping alive a separate Spanish language and culture. Numerous studies have indicated that students in bilingual programs learn English less well than those without access to them, and that their enrollments are swelled by a large number of Hispanics who can already speak English perfectly well.[7] In cities with large Hispanic populations like New York and Los Angeles, the bilingual bureaucracy has become something of a monster, rigidly tracking students despite the wishes of parents and students. The *New York Times* recently reported the case of a Hispanic-surnamed child, born in the United States and speaking only English, who was forced by New York City officials to enroll in an English as a Second Language Class. Bilingualism is but one symptom of a much broader crisis in American public education, and admittedly makes the problems of assimilation much greater.

These problems can be tackled with specific changes in public policy. But the central issue raised by the immigration question is indeed a cultural one, and as such less susceptible of policy manipulation. The problem here is not the foreign culture that immigrants bring with them from the third world, but the contemporary elite culture of Americans – Americans like Kevin Costner, who believes that America began going downhill when the white man set foot here, or another American, Ice-T, whose family has probably been in the country longer than Costner's and who believes that women are bitches and that the chief enemy of his generation is the police. In the upcoming block-by-block cultural war, the enemy will not speak Spanish or have a brown skin. In Pogo's words, "He is us."

Notes

1 See, for example, his article, "America First – and Second, and Third," the *National Interest*, Spring 1990.
2 Census Bureau Press Release CB92–89, "Profile of Asians and Pacific Islanders."
3 Data taken from Linda Chavez, *Out of the Barrio* (Basic Books, 1991), p. 103.
4 Figures taken from *Poverty in the United States: 1991*, Bureau of the Census, Series P-60, no. 181, pp. 7–9; the percentage of people in families for whites, blacks, and Hispanics is 84.5, 84.8, and 89.0, respectively (pp. 2–3).
5 See Rodolfo O. de la Garza, Louis DeSipio, et al., *Latino Voices: Mexican, Puerto Rican, and Cuban Perspectives on American Politics* (Westview Press, 1992).
6 This same group of Asians appears also to have lowered verbal scores, though this is something that will presumably be corrected over time.
7 On this point, see Linda Chavez's *Out of the Barrio*, pp. 9–38.

19 Inclusion, Exclusion, and the American Civic Culture

Daniel J. Tichenor

Illegal immigration and the arrival of unprecedented numbers of asylum-seekers haunted American policymakers in the 1980s. Our nation's borders had become porous and inadequately regulated, and as always, racial issues loomed large in American immigration politics. By 1980 non-white newcomers from Asia, Latin America, and the Carribean dominated all forms of migration to the United States. Europe, once the origin of nearly all immigration to America, has accounted for only 10 percent of total immigration since the 1970s. The uninvited influx of asylum-seekers and illegal immigrants prompted a decade of polarizing debate among lawmakers over the entire structure of American immigration and refugee policy. Two major laws, the Immigration Reform and Control Act of 1986 (IRCA) and the Immigration Act of 1990, and their subsequent judicial and administrative interpretation, represent the culmination of this period of policy change. The treatment of aliens in this burst of policymaking reveals both a promising inclusiveness and a disquieting enervation of the responsibilities and perceived worth of citizenship.

A Break with the Past

The widespread support during the 1970s and 1980s for curtailing immigration was nothing new in American politics. Policymakers have long sought to restrict or bar outsiders of non-European races or ethnicities from entering the country. For example, the exclusion of the Chinese in the 1880s and the National Origins Quota system of the 1920s were both efforts to block entrance to all but Northern and Western European newcomers. Policymakers also historically have responded to worrisome illegal immigration by launching campaigns to seize and deport undocumented aliens (particularly Mexicans) *en masse*. Operation Wetback in 1954 led to the expulsion of over one million Mexican aliens, including a number of legal residents. The Hart-Celler Act of 1965 stripped away racist national origins quotas, but most reformers intended a new emphasis on family reunification to limit drastically the number of visas available to Third World immigrants.

Recent immigration reform represents a decisive break with this nativist tradition. The 1986 and 1990 laws made no effort to stop non-white, non-European migrants from dominating immigration into the U.S. Not only did these laws not restrict "new immigration," they also allowed significant increases in migration from these regions. The IRCA dealt with the illegal population residing in the country by granting legal status to over 3 million illegal aliens. The Immigration Act of 1990 granted stays of deportation to family members of aliens legalized under the IRCA. The 1990 law also raised the cap on legal immigration and allowed even that ceiling to be exceeded by relatives of citizens. In short, immigration reforms expanded alien rights and increased migration to the U.S., even though the original impetus for the law had been restrictionist.[1]

Immigration reform also produced an ideological convergence in favor of sustained immigration. This development was undergirded by two important forces in American politics: the legacy of the Civil Rights movement and the resurgence in the 1980s of free-market economics. The first extensive federal regulations on immigration were enacted amidst the drastic economic and social dislocations of the late nineteenth and early twentieth centuries. As ties between members of the national community assumed greater importance, an agitated society directed its venom against emancipated blacks and new immigrants both from Asia and from Southern and Eastern Europe. These were people whom white America largely saw as imperiling the American way of life. Although the Jim Crow laws produced by this racially exclusive nationalism were undoubtedly more pernicious than immigration restrictions, immigration policy was linked thereafter in the minds of progressive politicians and activists with the black struggle for full citizenship.

As 1980s immigration advocates on the Left sought to grant entry and protection to powerless alien groups (particularly non-white illegal aliens and refugees), free-market immigration advocates sought to unfetter the labor market and allow the labor supply to accommodate the demands of employers. Conservative think tanks and editorial pages encouraged not simply the free movement of goods, technology and capital, but the free movement of *people* across borders. Hudson Institute scholar Stephen Moore praised immigrants for "their propensity to start new businesses" and "their contribution in keeping U.S. businesses internationally competitive."[2] The key goal of the expansionist Right was to provide American businesses greater access to the immigrant labor market and relief from new regulations such as employer sanctions and job antidiscrimination protection for aliens.

Significantly, the ideological convergence in favor of sustaining robust immigration generated not consensual politics, but a new divide between market-oriented and rights-oriented expansionists. The locus of conflict seemed to shift from a question of *whether* there should be expansive immigration, to a struggle over *who* should benefit from an opening of the gates. In the legislative arena, free-market expansionists secured sharp increases in employer-sponsored and skilled-worker visas, as well as cheap alien labor for the agricultural, garment, and hotel sectors. Rights-oriented expansionists secured a generous amnesty program for illegal aliens, a new civil rights agency charged with combating job discrimination against aliens, new protections for temporary farmworkers, legal status for previously excluded refugee groups, generous allocations of family reunification visas, and the removal of many ideological and sexual-orientation restrictions.

Obscured among these initiatives was the original purpose of reform: to curb illegal immigration and regain control of porous borders. Instead of representing the centerpiece of immigration reform, the enactment of an immigration control mechanism in 1986 – employer sanctions – was clearly subordinate to the decade's expansionist reforms. Civil rights activists and market libertarians successfully opposed the creation of a new counterfeit-and-tamper-resistant employee identification system. When a pilot program was proposed by Senator Alan Simpson (R-WY) in 1990 to use driver's licenses in conjunction with employer sanctions, it was defeated on the House floor by members of the Hispanic Caucus who likened it to South Africa's apartheid system of passbooks for blacks. Free-market expansionists exempted small businesses from employer sanctions, which the Reagan and Bush administrations viewed as another regulatory burden on U.S. companies and never enforced strictly. Dampened briefly after the IRCA was enacted, illegal immigration soon returned to the peak levels of the pre-reform era.

Nothing New

These distinct rationales for expansive immigration are hardly novel. In his *Report on Manufactures*, Alexander Hamilton noted that it was in the national interest "to open every possible avenue to emigration from abroad." Consistent with his vision of commercial empire, Hamilton perceived aliens as "an important resource, not only for extending the population, and with it the useful and productive labor of the country, but likewise for the prosecution of manufactures."[3] Almost a century later, Andrew Carnegie praised open immigration as "a golden stream which flows into the country each year." He added crassly: "these adults are surely worth $1500 each – for in former days an efficient slave sold for that sum."[4]

Whereas Hamilton emphasized the financial empire to be reaped from open immigration, Thomas Jefferson's enlightened idealism expressed a special obligation to newcomers. Although he had opposed immigration as a young man, Jefferson wrote in 1817 that the U.S. should be a new Canaan where outsiders would be "received as brothers and secured against . . . oppression by participation in . . . self-government."[5] In contrast to Carnegie's economic pragmatism, Ralph Waldo Emerson exalted in 1878 that "our whole history appears like a last effort of the Divine Providence on behalf of the human race." He extolled American opportunity – "opportunity to civil rights, of education, of personal power" – which he saw as an "invitation to every nation, to every race and skin."[6]

The American political community is often characterized as lagging well behind the industrial democracies of Europe in terms of welfare rights. Sociologist Ann Shola Orloff, for instance, emphasizes that the American framers' penchant for dividing political authority has produced an attenuated, even anemic, system of social welfare that pales in comparison to its European counterparts. "Against the backdrop of European welfare states," Orloff writes, "the American system of public social provision seems incomplete and belated."[7] But the issue of how a nation treats those from outside its boundaries reminds us that inclusivity and benevolence encompass more than welfare provision. At the same time, the potential for immigration to erode feelings of mutual economic obligation in a political community and to hurt the nation's poorest citizens most, underscores the limits of viewing immigration policy as a measure of a polity's benevolence.

The European Comparison

The fact that the U.S. permitted increases in alien admissions and extended new rights to non-citizens is striking compared to the political response of many west European nations. European politicians struggled between "national identity" and obligations owed to foreigners residing and working within their borders. In the midst of stunning postwar economic growth, Britain, France, Switzerland, West Germany, and other nations recruited millions of foreign guestworkers (from the Middle East and Northern Africa) to prevent labor shortages and to keep wages in check. In the 1970s, a time of employment scarcity among citizens, anti-immigrant voices began challenging the presence of guestworkers. The politicization of immigration was fueled further by waves of asylum-seekers and illegal aliens seeking entry into these culturally homogeneous societies. Many people began to wonder whether European civic cultures were capable of assimilating new ethnic and racial groups. New restrictionists in Europe warned that aliens undermined the solidarity and loyalty that common ethnicity and historical experience engenders. As German scholar Kay Hailbronner notes, Germans "think of their nation not as a political unit but as a cultural, linguistic, and ethnic unit."[8]

Several political parties (most notably the National Front parties of France and Great Britain and the *Republikaner* party in Germany) emerged as standard-bearers of this new breed of nationalist politics. "These movements were built, not surprisingly, on the edifice of anti-immigrant, racist, and xenophobic appeals," writes political scientist James Hollifield.[9] Jean Marie Le Pen, leader of the French National Front, garnered at least 10 percent of the vote in elections throughout the 1980s, sounding the battlecry "La France aux Français" (France for the French).

As a result, the European mainstream was forced to accommodate the Right's attitude toward immigration. Le Pen's consistent appeal, drawing on nationalist subcultures of Jacobinism on the Left and Gaulism on the Right, prompted other parties in France to shift their immigration position. The National Front in Britain was weakened not only by a strong two-party system and stout resistance from Prime Minister Margaret Thatcher, but by the co-opting by the Conservative Party of the National Front's anti-immigrant stance. Britain's 1981 Nationality Act established gradations of citizenship for immigrants from former colonies. It also instituted conditional birthright citizenship; children born in Britain to parents without permanent-residency status are no longer guaranteed full membership. Even Sweden and Denmark, known for their generosity toward refugees, imposed strict denial rates on asylees. As immigration scholar Lawrence Fuchs notes, "Europeans generally [have] asked about foreigners, How can we get these outsiders to go home? or, failing that, How can we keep them outside the polity a while longer even as they work among us?"[10] Significantly, the resurgence of restrictive nationalism occurred when most of the migrants seeking membership were non-whites.

Though the U.S. is currently absorbing a similar influx of non-white, Third World nationals, nativist voices reminiscent of the Know-Nothings, American Protective Association, and the Immigration Restriction League were largely muted in the 1980s. Whereas European policymakers restricted the flow of immigrants and refugees to their countries, summarily deported illegal aliens and asylees, and denied full membership to foreign guest-workers (regardless of how long these "guests" lived and labored in their societies), their American counterparts increased alien admissions, made citizenship easier to gain, and expanded opportunities for and protection of illegal aliens and temporary workers.

One can overstate the generosity of pro-immigration reforms. After all, the new employer-sponsored and skills-based visas reflect more strongly a concern for labor-market demands than one for the well-being of newcomers. But pro-immigration reforms certainly reflect an inclusive vision of membership as well as self-interested economic calculations.

The Downside

If the recent expansion of alien admissions and rights demonstrates a promising inclusiveness of outsiders, it also describes an enervation of the bonds between Americans. During the Great Depression, John Dewey argued that freedom in the twentieth century required government to secure not only the natural rights of individuals, but also their economic well-being.[11] This new social contract, the heart of the New Deal, raises the question of whether certain obligations owed to disadvantaged members of the political community must be met before newcomers are granted admission and membership goods.

The agenda of rights-oriented expansionists focused resolutely on the compelling needs of individual aliens, yet ignored how increases in alien admissions might affect disadvantaged citizens. At its most absurd extreme, political champions of the special lotteries and "diversity" visas, which had been designed principally to benefit Irish aliens, defended these programs using civil rights language and described European immigrants as "disadvantaged" persons.

Absent from this calculus is any serious consideration of policy costs or trade-offs. The absoluteness of rights-based arguments often derails meaningful deliberation of contending claims: whether the presence of numerous unskilled and vulnerable foreign workers perpetuates a segmented labor force, for example, or whether it forces unskilled domestic workers to choose between low-wage jobs with poor working conditions or unemployment. These are questions that never figured prominently in policy debate. Nor were the civic merits of asking U.S. companies (or the state) to retrain citizens to fill skilled positions fully weighed by most policymakers.

The responsiveness of immigration-policy reformers to the rights claims of aliens and American employers also caused them to ignore how reforms affected some of the nation's poorest citizens, of whom a disproportionate number are African-Americans. As economists George Borjas, Julian Simon and others have demonstrated, immigrants have been anything but costly for American society when one examines *aggregate* economic information.[12] But while there is considerable evidence that immigrants contribute to our overall economic well-being, the economic picture is murkier when we consider their impact on the country's economic underclass. Whereas some econometrics evidence suggests that the incomes of native blacks are not adversely affected by new immigrant inflows, sociologists like William Julius Wilson detect a marked contrast in the attitudes of American employers toward Asian, Central American, European and Mexican newcomers, on the one side, and urban native blacks, on the other.[13] In particular, Wilson suggests that the loss of manufacturing jobs in Chicago affected native blacks and new immigrants very differently. Though less formally educated than native black workers, Mexican and other immigrants still lost fewer jobs. When displaced from blue-collar jobs, immigrant workers found new employment faster. Based on interviews with Chicago-area firms, Wilson suggests that employers viewed these groups very differently. Inner-city blacks (especially young black males) were seen as "unstable, uncooperative, and dishonest." Mexicans and other Third World immigrants, by contrast, were "perceived to exhibit better 'work ethics' than native workers" largely because they endured poor working conditions, meager pay, and few opportunities to advance. Wilson suggests that the unwillingness of many native blacks to tolerate these wages and conditions has shaped employer attitudes. His findings are reinforced by a General Accounting Office report claiming that janitorial firms of Los Angeles replaced unionized black workers with non-unionized immigrants.[14]

The preference for immigrant labor is not a new development. More than a century ago, Frederick Douglass lamented that "every hour sees the black man elbowed out of employment by some newly arrived immigrant." Studies of job competition in the expanding urban labor markets of the late nineteenth century suggest that new immigrants were preferred over southern blacks who had migrated north.[15]

Ironically, even as immigration reform drew residual energy from the civil rights movement, policymakers showed a profound inattention to the most intractable problems of African-Americans. This quality of immigration policymaking seems to exemplify a political community of citizen-strangers, in which many white members express a greater affinity for and identification with newcomers than with fellow black members. Moreover, the estrangement of citizens is reinforced by the flight of white citizens from cities to fortress suburban communities offering safe havens from urban problems. It is worth adding that those aliens whom black citizens most hoped to see admitted – Haitian refugees and African immigrants – benefited least from immigration reform.

All this is not to say that new immigration has to represent a zero-sum game, in which the economic and political ends of newcomers are at odds with native blacks. Far from it: Alliances between black and Hispanic leaders can yield important economic and political goals that serve both constituencies. But it is disturbing that policymakers never thoroughly examined so many fundamental questions about how immigration reform might affect the nation's urban poor.

Aliens as Scapegoats

Immigration restriction has emerged again as a prominent and divisive issue in American politics, stirring popular passions and raising the specter of nativist and racist traditions finding new programmatic expansion. Immigration policymaking in the 1980s was an insulated process, dominated by organized groups, professional lobbyists, and policymakers in Washington. Recently, however, policymakers have played to public fears about crime, welfare dependency, and overall economic uncertainty by using aliens as convenient scapegoats. Indeed, it has become a popular sport in Congress to propose amendments denying aliens (even legal, tax-paying aliens) income support, health care, educational benefits, disaster relief, and other forms of public support. Many legislators also have called for sweeping reductions in immigration. Despite having championed a foreign guestworker program when he was a senator in the 1980s, California's governor Pete Wilson has blamed immigrants for unemployment and budgetary woes in his state. Some California and Texas politicians have called for a wall of troops to guard the U.S.–Mexican border, while others advocate a constitutional amendment denying the children of undocumented aliens birthright citizenship.

Tellingly, this new burst of restrictionist populism has shown as much disdain for informed public deliberation as did the last decade of immigration politics. Recent political efforts to scale back total immigration and alien rights have discouraged discussion of several important questions concerning the nation's social and humanitarian goals. Given that most immigrant visas are distributed to relatives of American citizens and permanent residents, are we willing to sacrifice the social goal of family unity for that of having fewer immigrants? Are we willing to apply strict numerical ceilings on refugee admissions, regardless of the persecution asylees may be fleeing? The last time our nation stridently rejected humanitarian obligations to refugees, millions died at the hands of Germany's Nazi regime. Likewise, is it just to deny public benefits to *all* aliens, including those who are legally admitted and pay taxes? Do we owe special obligations to the children of illegal aliens, whom the Supreme Court has recognized as "innocents" and many of whom are U.S. citizens? And how far are we willing to go in denying health care to undocumented aliens? Would that include such necessities as prenatal or emergency care?

Recent immigration politics also have obscured important information that might elevate the debate. In their haste to reap political
gain at the expense of newcomers, "born-again" restrictionist politicians conveniently fail to make critical distinctions between the
economic and social characteristics of legal and illegal migratory
streams. Nevertheless, legal immigrants and refugees have been
held political hostage largely because of a continued failure to
curb illegal immigration.

Conclusion

Several observers see the latest wave of Third World newcomers
as a formidable threat to American culture. These observers often
focus their concerns on Latin Americans, drawing attention to
linguistic separatism and dramatically low levels of naturalization.
This is nothing new. Throughout American history, natural-
born citizens blamed new immigrant groups for failing to become
fully integrated members of society. Political scientist Rodolfo de
la Garza offers an alternative explanation for why Mexican-Americans and other Hispanics have been slow to embrace American
culture: "Mexican-Americans have retained a 'Mexicanness'
only because they were so long denied access to American institutions."[16] For most of the nineteenth century, new immigrants were
incorporated into the political community by Martin Van Buren's
compromise between republican virtue and modern democracy –
decentralized political parties. These imperfect "civic associations,"
to borrow a phrase from political theorist Wilson Carey McWilliams, linked the interests of immigrants to something larger than
themselves.[17] The civic educator of today's immigrants, by contrast,
has been a centralized, rights-based regime that teaches little about
obligations and the value of participation.

Scholarly debates concerning alien admissions and rights have
generally oscillated between national and global perspectives,
either challenging or vindicating the sovereign right of nation-
states to control their borders. On the one hand, Joseph Carens,
Judith Lichtenberg, and other proponents of an internationalist
view have stressed that the equal moral worth of individuals
trumps distinctions between aliens and citizens.[18] This perspective
reminds us that new migratory pressures are produced by a vast
disparity in wealth between First and Third World peoples. On the
other hand, political theorists such as Michael Walzer, Bruce Acker-

man, and Mark Gibney argue that open borders would render communal life meaningless and sacrifice essential bonds and duties between national citizens.[19] In both arguments the voices of local communities expressing their distinct needs and concerns are often neglected.

Recent immigration reform reflects this neglect and thus exposes an American political community with remarkably weak ties and obligations among citizens. Fragmentation of national institutions accentuated divisions between policymakers, producing contradictions and cross-purposes in the legislation. The failure to engage citizens and localities in policymaking may result in a strong political backlash against recent expansions in alien admissions and rights. By insulating meaningful policymaking from local communities and public deliberation, national decisionmakers have unintentionally provided a window of opportunity for irresponsible politicians to translate xenophobic appeals into votes. The new volatility of American immigration politics has increased the likelihood of dramatic policy changes if political pressure for new restrictions builds.

Engaging citizens and local communities in deliberation over immigration policy involves considerable risk for expansionists. Public opinion polls have usually found Americans generally opposed to large-scale immigration and refugee admissions. Yet the alternatives to public education and informed dialogue on this issue are hardly appealing. Centralized and insulated policymaking in the 1980s often ignored important trade-offs as well as the reasonable concerns of local communities. One residual effect of this process is that certain cities and states have unfairly been asked to absorb a disproportionate share of the initial costs of new immigration. In turn, the populist restrictionism of recent years has invited irresponsible politicians to perpetuate anti-immigrant stereotypes and to pay no attention to the potential economic, social, and moral costs of their knee-jerk policy proposals.

Requiring immigration policymakers to be attentive to the concerns of citizens and local communities might bring important costs and trade-offs to the surface, providing an opportunity for public officials and citizens to educate one another. It may also give aliens a greater incentive to pursue cultural and political membership so that they may participate in a meaningful deliberative process. Finally, it may enable American political communities to respond to the needs of citizens and newcomers of diverse ethnic and racial groups without diffusing the special commitments and obligations that foster attachments among members.

Notes

1 Daniel J. Tichenor, "The Politics of Immigration Reform in the United States, 1981–1990," *Polity* (Spring, 1994), 333–62.
2 Stephen Moore, "Who Should America Welcome?" *Society* (July/August, 1990), 55.
3 Alexander Hamilton, *Papers on Public Credit, Commerce, and Finance*, ed. Samuel McKee (New York: Liberal Arts Press, 1957), 194–5.
4 Andrew Carnegie, *Triumphant Democracy, or Fifty Years of the Republic* (New York: C. Scribne's Sons, 1893), 34–5.
5 Thomas Jefferson to George Flower, *The Writings of Thomas Jefferson*, ed. A. A. Libscomb and A. E. Bergh (Washington D. C.: Thomas Jefferson Memorial Association, 1903), 15: 139–42.
6 Hans Kohn, *American Nationalism: An Interpretive Essay* (New York: Macmillan, 1957), 143–4.
7 Ann Shola Orloff, "The Political Origins of America's Belated Welfare State," in Margaret Weir, Ann Shola Orloff, and Theda Skocpol, eds, *The Politics of Social Policy in the United States* (Princeton, NJ: Princeton University Press, 1988), 37–80.
8 Kay Hailbronner, "Citizenship and Nationhood in Germany," in William Rogers Brubaker, ed., *Immigration and the Politics of Citizenship in Europe and North America* (Washington D.C.: German Marshall Fund of the United States, 1989), 74.
9 James Hollifield, *Immigrants, Markets, and States* (Cambridge, MA: Harvard University Press, 1992), 171.
10 Lawrence Fuchs, *The American Kaleidoscope: Race, Ethnicity, and the Civic Culture* (Middletown, CT: Weslayan University Press, 1990), 477.
11 John Dewey, "The Future of Liberalism," *Journal of Philosophy*, April 25, 1935, 226–30.
12 Julian Simon, *The Economic Consequences of Immigration* (New York: Blackwell, 1989); and George Borjas, *Friends or Strangers? The Impact of Immigration on the U.S. Economy* (New York: Basic Books, 1990).
13 Econometrics evidence on the impact of new immigrants on native blacks is discussed by George Borjas, *The Changing Course of International Migration* (Organisation for Economic Co-Operation and Development, 1993). For a contrasting picture focusing on the distinctive attitudes of American employers toward native blacks and new immigrants, see William Julius Wilson, "The Plight of Black Male Job-Seekers," *Focus* (September, 1992), 7–8.
14 The GAO Report is discussed by Jack Miles, "Blacks vs. Browns," *Atlantic Monthly* (October, 1992), 41.

15 Stanley Lieberson, *A Piece of the Pie: Blacks and White Immigrants since 1880* (Berkeley, CA: University of California Press, 1980); and Arnold Shankman, *Ambivalent Friends* (Westport, CT, 1982).
16 Rodolfo de la Garza, "Mexican Americans, Mexican Immigrants, and Immigration Reform," in Nathan Glazer, ed., *Clamor at the Gates* (San Francisco, CA: ICS Press, 1985), 99.
17 Wilson Carey McWilliams, "Parties as Civic Associations," in Gerald Pomper, ed., *Party Renewal in America* (New York: Praeger Publishers, 1980), 51–68.
18 Joseph Carens, "Aliens and Citizens: The Case for Open Borders," *Review of Politics* (Spring, 1987), 251–73; and Judith Lichtenberg, "National Boundaries and Moral Boundaries: A Cosmopolitan View," in Peter Brown and Henry Shue, eds, *Boundaries: National Autonomy and Its Limits* (Totowa, NJ: Rowman and Littlefield, 1981), 70–100.
19 Michael Walzer, "The Distribution of Membership," in Brown and Shue, eds, *Boundaries*, ibid. 1–36; Bruce Ackerman, *Social Justice in the Liberal State* (New Haven, 1980); and Mark Gibney, *Strangers or Friends: Principles for a New Alien Admissions Policy* (Westport, CT: Greenwood Press, 1986).

Epilogue: Where the Maps are Not Yet Finished: A Continuing American Journey

Jamie Goodwin-White

Control over entry and exit of individuals, and the role of those individuals within a nation-state's borders, have been considered a fundamental requirement of a nation-state's self-determination. Thus, it is recognized that immigrants play a large part in constituting national identity. This is perhaps more true for the United States, a nation of immigrants from its very inception, where the children of immigrants continue to be joined by newer groups, than for any other nation-state. While other nations have chosen to determine their constitution through the inclusion and exclusion of certain groups and the rights and roles afforded immigrants and natives, no other nation has defined itself as a nation of immigrants in the way the United States has, and many have specifically avoided this classification.

The fact that there exist no ethnic criteria for an American identity means that the ideal member can be an immigrant. The "true American" standing at the podium with a politician is often not a third or fourth-generation American, but an immigrant who has naturalized and attained the American dream. They reflect what we want most of all to believe about ourselves; that Americans are hard-working entrepreneurs, who are always in search of (and eventually find) a better future for themselves. Indeed, it seems Americans are at least as likely to vaunt their immigrant stock as they are to proudly count how many "American" generations of ancestors precede them. Curiously, in this land of immigrants, to be the "other," the outsider, is somehow, counter-intuitively, to belong. One whose origins are elsewhere, who *now* lives in America, is an American. In some ways, all immigrants are Americans. The American character is based, after all, on an ideal of progress. To leave what is familiar (and often loved) in search of a grander ideal seems a particularly American myth. The other puzzle piece of the myth, that of the welcoming (specifically American) shore, the beckoning land of opportunities, is surely integral. The myth is more uniquely American if the grand ideal, the "green light shining across the water,"[1] is America. But simply through undertaking what is considered a particularly American behavior (leaving the old for a struggle toward the new is, after all, the first stage of the American dream), all immigrants are, in some sense, Americans. The fact that many of them come here, to a country where this restless, hopeful uprooting continues internally, should be no surprise.

Perhaps the restlessness of America is a function of the physical landscape of the country. We are bounded, for the most part, by two large oceans, and our land boundaries are largely vast desert areas (to the south) and remote wilderness (to the north). Internally, much of America is still wilderness, or only sparsely populated. The fact that the western states are still experiencing population growth, much of it from the older states, may be an indication that, to a certain extent, the American frontier has not completely disappeared. Americans exist in a somewhat "unfinished," unbounded space, where opportunities are always seen just around the next corner. While the open physical spaces of America may encourage constantly "on the move" Americans, it sometimes seems as if we are genetically encoded for such behavior. In a nation of immigrants, and children of immigrants, where everyone is from someplace else – is it ever possible in America to be truly at home? Or does home become nothing so much as a constant wandering? This particularly American conception of home is counterpoised with more stable models by filmmaker Wim Wenders:

> They have that in America: "Mobile Homes," "Mobile" is said with pride and means the opposite of "bogged down" ... (or) "stuck." "Home" means "at home," "where you belong" ... (whereas) what *makes* it a home in the German language is the fact that it is fixed somewhere. (Peck 1996)

This raises an important issue, in that rootedness, or belonging in place, has generally been presupposed as requisite for the existence of national identity and culture. Individuals must belong in some bounded space in order to have loyalty to it, and this "belonging" is critical to the formation of a national identity. The United States, even internally, is an uprooted society, where individuals never stay in place for very long. In any given year, one of every six Americans will change their place of residence (U.S. Bureau of the Census 1994). Those who are always on the move seem to find that, in the end, they really belong in no place. Their ties to place are transitory, rarely permanent, rarely fixed. In the words of Robert Burns:

> I've seen sae mony changefu' years,
> On earth I am a stranger grown;
> I wander in the ways of men,
> Alike unknowing and unknown

This is viewed as problematic, in that communities (on any scale) lose stability along with continuity when all of their members are strangers from somewhere else, and no one stays long enough to add to a sense of belonging. Internal validity is threatened when the constituents are constantly in flux.

These issues are perhaps best illustrated within the United States by the rapidly growing, high-mobility states of the American West. A recent special edition of the Arizona Republic, entitled "A look at who we are and what we like about living here" complains that Phoenix never feels like home. Everyone is from somewhere else, no one stays very long, and even those who do never feel Arizona so much to be their home as a previous residence. The introduction concludes, lamentingly, "The only constant is that each summer will be hotter than the next...," "The only constant...," the only certainty – an indication that one feels less than secure, that one is not, in short, at home (Lowe 1996). Home is the intersection of people and place. When one element is uncertain and constantly changing, so is the interrelated second element.

On a national level, however, this connection becomes paramount. No American state demands a singular loyalty from its residents. A highly mobile population which moves from one state to another is a concern for the states, surely, but on a more fundamental level is problematic only in that the individual constituents of the nation are uprooted. More important, more symbolic than state boundaries, are national borders. It is at this level that individuals must be connected, that place becomes a referencing point for a people. *This* place, and no other, is America; and it is ours – or perhaps, more correctly – it is us. This is where, most especially in America, a moral dimension is superimposed over ethnic, civic, or cultural aspects. The nation as an expression of a people invokes all sorts of normative aspects. Ideas on what America should be, and what its situation in the world should be, lead to questions of what Americans should be. How do we define who belongs in a nation of immigrants – where the dialectic of insiders versus outsiders is inextricably confused, and a significant element in the moral construction of American identity is contingent upon the suspension of this dialectic?

Citizenship and Naturalization

Citizenship remains the primary means by which a nation-state constitutes its membership. While immigrants residing within a nation-state undeniably affect it, they do not do so as members. When immigrants naturalize, then, they become Americans, with all affiliated rights and responsibilities. Only one aspect of membership remains reserved for native-born citizens; in that the president of the United States must be of native birth. Naturalized immigrants can exercise their membership, and through voting, determine the course of an America to which they now belong. Citizens have the ability to influence a democratic state in ways that non-naturalized immigrants cannot. In a country where debates about immigration and the role of citizenship have become the clarion call of political candidates, an influx of new "Americans" (however conceived) undeniably has the potential to enter into and alter the debate. And in fact, whether new citizens become politically active or not, they do have an impact by the very nature of their presence. With current Congressional legislation aimed at reducing immigration (legal and illegal), and states considering whether or not they have responsibilities to provide services for illegal immigrants residing within their boundaries, naturalization results in an immigrant population largely immune to these considerations. The American conception of equal citizenship renders naturalized citizens (virtually) indistinguishable from its native-born. As such, they cannot be deported (except in cases of treason), and are entitled to the same social services on the part of state and local governments as native-born citizens.

Perhaps the reason why these debates have become so contentious, so emotionally charged, is that just beneath the political and economic façades are deeper sub-texts of identity and belonging: of nations and individuals. For questions of citizenship and immigration are fundamentally questions of rights and responsibilities coded in relationships between individuals and society, and individuals and the state (in this case, the U.S.). Who has the right to enter – and the right to stay? What responsibilities does a democratic state have to those individuals living within its boundaries? What rights are reserved for citizens, and how does this delineation characterize the meaning of citizenship itself? What does naturalization mean for those who seek it – and for those who do not? The answers to these questions are critical for assessing the interplay of identity and space. While territory has often been considered the spatial context across which states exercise their power, it should also be explicitly realized as the context *within* which identity is created, experienced, and made relevant. These two elements are hardly indistinguishable – one element of a state's exercise of power is its very ability to designate a formal expression of national identity (following the idea that a nation is comprised of individuals). In doing so, the state must draw borders which include member-citizens and exclude others.

In this case, the borders are not drawn as lines in the sand, so to speak, not as a result of negotiations between two states to delimit realms of control. Rather, the lines are drawn internally, chimerically – invisibly etched as a result of highly discursive sets of negotiations between the state and individuals (native-born and foreign-born, citizen and alien, legal entrant and illegal) in an attempt to delimit spheres of belonging. Here, two fundamental points must be made. First, these discursively created borders are no less real than the physical ones, and an incomplete tracing of their evolution can be attempted through analysis of legislative and judicial histories. Yet their etching, as a discursive process, is permeable and endlessly mutable. Second, these borders, and the nature of their creation, are realized symbols of much larger idealities of the "being" of the state, and its relations to its inhabitants. Lines, tangible or not, are drawn to enhance and elucidate distinctions. Citizens possess certain rights that non-citizens do not, legal residents possess rights that illegal residents do not, and so hierarchical "strata" of belonging, of an American identity, are formed. At different times in the history of the United States, then, citizenship has had many different meanings, and the nation has constituted itself differently. The Chinese Exclusion Act, for example, engendered a construction of America where a certain group did not belong in the mix. Immigration and Naturalization Service preference categories still determine, on a yearly basis, who can enter, and thus share in the constitution of America. Yet citizenship is open to all who have resided legally in the United States for a certain period of time, precisely because American ideas of a democratic nation demand that all who are allowed to enter, must have available to them a means of integration.

Thus, the significance of citizenship is predicated upon what rights, or entitlements of belonging, should distinguish members from non-members (this idea, in turn, also means that the significance of citizenship entails a determination of what responsibilities states have toward members versus non-members). In order to clarify the meaning of citizenship, the reverse is also true – namely that rights and responsibilities of individuals residing within the United States are predicated upon their membership status.

And yet here we encounter a paradox faced by a nation-state which defines itself as a nation of immigrants. In that citizenship has meaning, that meaning is determined by what rights and responsibilities distinguish members from non-members. However, in recent American history, the distinctions have hardly been noticeable. Immigrants can live in the United States without naturalizing, and many do.[2] Indeed, all that separates legally resident immigrants who do not naturalize from naturalized citizens is the right to vote, work in some federal government positions, and a small cluster of social service benefits reserved for citizens. This proximity of legal-resident "denizen" status to full-fledged citizenship has been assessed as one of the reasons why the naturalization rate among immigrants in the United States has been low in recent years. Simply put, there are few incentives for an immigrant to naturalize, and some potential drawbacks. The adoption of American citizenship often means a severing of ties (on a practical as well as emotional level, in that former countries may deny the new American the right to return). Until recently, Mexican immigrants to the United States could lose property in Mexico if they became United States citizens. This has changed as the Mexican government has begun to allow and encourage dual Mexican–U.S. citizenship. Decreasing naturalizations, viewed as a response to the lack of significant differences between citizenship and denizenship, have led Jacobson (1996) and Schuck (1984) to conclude that citizenship, in the traditional sense, is being devalued.

A contemporaneous phenomenon has been the increasing importance of international human rights law. In that human rights have become recognized as an extension of an individual person, territorially based identities such as citizenship, in which rights have traditionally inhered, become less important. Quite simply, a national affiliation is no longer necessary in order to claim fundamental human rights, especially given the relatively recent, continuing emergence of an international human rights regime embedded in international organization. This has profound implications for immigrants, often resident in a country where they have no citizenship. It is increasingly possible for non-citizens, especially but by no means exclusively those recognized as having some permanent legal status falling short of citizenship (those individuals Tomas Hammar terms *denizens*) (Hammar 1986) to reside in the United States without changing their nationality, as the substantive differences between citizens and denizens are attenuated.

However, while rates of naturalization for immigrants to the United States have been low in recent years, Immigration and Naturalization Services offices are reporting unprecedented upswings in naturalization applications within the last few years (Pachon 1995). 407,398 persons naturalized in fiscal year 1994, and many more began the process – individual INS offices are receiving more than 2,000 new naturalization applications daily (INS 1995, Pachon 1995). For the first time, naturalization rates are approaching the record level of 442,000 reached in 1944. The 1944 INS Annual Report commented that the record for that year would represent the highest number of annual naturalizations for years to come (INS 1996). Fifty years later, naturalizations are for the first time nearing this historic level. In light of the preceding discussion, how can an unprecedented increase in the naturalization rates of immigrants be interpreted? It is perhaps too obvious, now, that large numbers of naturalized citizens could, if they so wished, drastically redirect the bordering process of "belonging". The greater question, then, becomes this: can this increase in naturalization be seen as a symbol of the new boundaries that have emerged? In order to answer this question, it must first be determined what factors are responsible for this increase in naturalization rates, and second, what this change indicates for citizenship in the United States.

Although citizenship has traditionally been considered an exclusive loyalty, there are increasing signs that, for many immigrants (especially in the United States) this ideal is increasingly elusive. Decreasing naturalization rates (prior to the recent upsurge), and an increasing emphasis on human rights as opposed to rights predicated on nationality seem to validate an idea that citizenship (measured as an exclusive loyalty tied to a territorial state) is, conceptually, on the decline. And in this most traditional sense, this is most certainly true. While reasons for the recent upsurge in naturalizations are not yet empirically determined, suggested causal factors are the product of individuals' different relationships to both "internal" and "external" spaces. In addition to the recent eligibility of the IRCA cohort (see Jacobson 1996, Ch. 1), the new possibility of dual citizenship in several countries and the increasingly immigrant-hostile political climate are believed to have played a role in the recent naturalizations. Also, the results of the changing political climate on immigration are such that the lines between citizen and non-citizen are becoming more deeply inscribed. Welfare reform and the increasing restrictions on green card holders serve to increase the differences between citizens and denizens. Citizenship, predictably, is increasingly necessary for immigrants to claim rights. The internal spaces of a nation of immigrants are constantly being re-mapped. The increasing importance of dual citizenship, and the expected correlation with increasing naturalization rates, point to the changing nature of external spaces as well.

The implications for individual rights are clear: citizenship (with regard to rights) is no longer as critical as it once was. The implications for American citizenship and an American identity are somewhat more opaque. Etienne Balibar considers the factors necessary to produce a national identity, especially in cases where nations have been formed through immigration:

> That ideological form must become an *a priori* condition of communication between individuals (the "citizens") and between social groups – not by suppressing all differences, but by relativizing them and subordinating them to itself in such a way that it is the symbolic difference between "ourselves" and "foreigners" which wins out and which is lived as irreducible. In other words, to use the terminology proposed by Fichte in his *Reden an die deutsche Nation* of 1808, the "external frontiers" of the state have to become "internal frontiers" or – which amounts to the same thing – external frontiers have to be imagined constantly as a protection and projection of an internal collective personality, which each of us carries within ourselves and enables us to inhabit the space of the state as a place where we have always been – and always will be – "at home." (Balibar 1996)

In that identity is defined territorially, ideas of "home" are specific to those who belong within the borders. Outsiders become (at best) guests, or (at worst) invaders. In any case, following Balibar's argument, there must be a consistency between the external and internal borders of identity. Those who are not part of the collective whole, yet remain within the physical external boundaries must be (in some way) "marked off" – and this demarcation has traditionally been associated with citizenship, and the different packages of rights and roles – the different "parcel-ings" as it were, of citizens and non-citizens – in order that the meaning of identity (tied so nicely by Balibar to the residence of a space called "home") be preserved.

Yet once again the specific case of the United States presents a dilemma; a dilemma which only serves to illustrate how strangely apt the current increasing reliance on non-territorially based human rights is *here*. From the very beginning, American citizenship was to be available to all who had legally entered the United States, and resided legally for a period of time. This extension of citizenship required very little of the individual immigrant – very little that was unattainable, at least. The reason for the extension of the "right" of citizenship to virtually all was the idea that a democratic, American ideal required that all resident in the country have available some means of incorporation (whether they opted to take advantage of this or not). The formation of a civic society required the incorporation and participation of those living in a democracy. And when so many of those residents are immigrants, and the American identity is to a large degree based on an immigrant past, this was even more critical. Recently, international law has begun to conceive of nationality as a human right – on a strikingly similar basis: that *wherever* individuals live they should have some fundamental rights (which are often, still, tied to citizenship). Thus, while emphases on citizenship and human rights are often counterpoised, in the United States the increasing deterritorialization of rights is somehow oddly correct.

The emphases on human rights for immigrants is not necessarily in opposition to an American identity, for in America, as argued above, the "internal borders" are somewhat difficult to ascertain. The ideal of incorporation, the age-old "melting pot" analogy reflects a fervently constructed American identity based upon little more than open spaces of belonging. With few other criteria for membership, ironically, the idea of an open membership with spaces for all who seek it becomes critical to national identity. Theoretically then, even if recent practice illustrates the tenuously constructed nature of this national model, it is difficult to determine what implications for American identity a territorial disengagement of rights will produce. And, by extension of the earliest ideals of extension of citizenship to all, and the subsequent realization by the international community of nationality as a universal human right, recent trends are rather curiously situated in the United States.

Perhaps then, it should be argued that while citizenship, as a traditional model, is still being "devalued," there are increasing indications that perhaps we should look to a differently constructed model of belonging. The context for rights, as well as for individual identities, is increasingly transnational. Immigrant communities and networks, as well as the increasing propensity for dual citizenship can be seen as evidence. If we can look at citizenship as a measure of "belonging in space," perhaps we should consider that the realm of imagined spaces is now (or soon to be) quite different from before?

Traditionally, immigrants were believed to sever ties with home countries and assume a "new" American identity. The old was discarded, and an American home quickly embraced. Indeed, the founding fathers agreed that citizenship ought to be chosen. Immigrants could (and still can) live fairly easily in America without opting to "become Americans." To become a member, one had to make the choice to do so. And the choice, still today, involves forsaking any other affiliations and loyalties. The idea of American citizenship, as an exclusive membership which must be freely chosen, thus reflects earlier Puritan themes.

And yet, increasingly, to base identity on place of birth and current residence is misleading – the myriad in-betweens mark kaleidoscopic possibilities for individual spatial identities. As the kaleidoscope glass turns, tiny objects fall into place – creating a "snapshot" of an endlessly altered mosaic. So each immigrant's experiences, whether in residence, or indirectly via immigrant networks and thoughts of home, begin to shape as an identity the collection of unpredictable interactions of many places. In the words of Edmond Haraucourt: "To go away is to die a little, it is to die to that which one loves: everywhere and always, one leaves behind a part of oneself." And as is illustrated in America, there is an equilibrium to the system: place and people, even in a world which has advanced to transnational spaces and identities, are connected yet. As surely as one "leaves behind a part of oneself," one also takes various pieces with them – and new spaces become connected with the old in quite intangible ways, but through quite tangible movements. We see this especially in the "transplanted" communities of immigrants in the United States.

Immigrant Communities: Transplanted Spaces, Transplanted Identities

Citizenship entails a specific form of "belonging in space." Immigrant communities too, are examples of this – serving as "transplanted" spaces where identity and all other connections are referenced back to a point of origin. For this reason, immigrants residing in these concentrations maintain connections with those things which link them to a previous "home" – co-ethnics, cultural and linguistic practices, even forms of spatial organization. Well-established immigrant enclaves may reflect a spatial organization (so far as house placement and spacing and personal space, for example, are used) which gives the area an appearance of being unlike the host country – and very much like the country of origin. It is conceivable that this local sense of spatial relationships, determined by a circumscribed enclave, manifests itself on a larger scale. Immigrants' ideas of migration possibilities within the United States may be a function of ideas and information extended from a spatially ordered settlement, and thus (whether settled or in motion), immigrants add to the landscape of an America where "home" is difficult to define – and always, somewhere else: either grafted, in the case of immigrant communities, onto foreign soil or displaced in the case of perpetual movement.

These spatial patterns have a critical link to identity, especially for immigrants in the United States. Much research has focused on the spatial concentration of immigrants, and the reasons for and consequences of this concentration. Castles and Miller (1993) discuss the importance of micro-structure migration networks, whereby origin and destination specific paths are constructed over time. These networks serve the primary purpose of providing information about destinations to potential immigrants. Chain migration ensues, whereby earlier immigrants have established routes and mechanisms which facilitate the immigration process for later migrants from the same country of origin. These processes produce (at least initially) spatial concentrations of immigrant populations, as networks by definition encourage entry at certain common points. As these shared paths become familiar, migration networks also serve to provide support services which allow for continued migrations, and establishment (or re-establishment, given the site-specific nature of the process) of community for those who have arrived in the United States. Migration networks provide vital connections among immigrants in a new community, as well as ties to the country of origin. Immigrant communities address the difficulties which individuals often face in an unknown setting: linguistic, educational and employment barriers, as well as cultural differences. Immigrant communities are thus believed to play an important role in determining movement patterns, concentrations of immigrants, and their integration into a new country.

Citizenship also serves as a measure of an individual's place of orientation. This is true on a practical, as well as theoretical level. Naturalization has often been considered an indicator of an individual's successful adaptation to a new country (Karst 1989). Becoming a citizen entails a certain degree of acculturation with regard to the host country. On the most basic level, an immigrant has had to demonstrate competence (in most cases) in the English language. Some familiarity with the United States is necessary in order to pass sections of the exam requiring knowledge of U.S. government and history. The process of preparing for naturalization usually involves the assistance of immigrant social service groups (some of which now work directly with the Immigration and Naturalization Service in an attempt to increase naturalization rates), and U.S. citizens, either native or foreign-born. These steps arguably increase an immigrant's connections with the host society.

It is a logical assumption that as immigrant communities maintain ties with place of origin, the effect of these ties on movement is bi-directional. Thus, if communities establish routes whereby immigrants are brought from certain origins to certain destinations within the United States, these communities should also facilitate movement back along these same routes. There is some evidence that immigrants residing in concentrations within the United States have a greater propensity for return migration than do their more dispersed counterparts (Pachon and De Sipio 1994). Conversely, those immigrants who have abandoned the "myth of return" are more likely to live outside of immigrant clusters. This makes sense in that an immigrant living in an immigrant community still has a spatial referent, per earlier discussion, to "back home." This referent would encourage, and perhaps be necessary for, return migration.

In addition, those immigrants who plan on return migration tend not to seek naturalization (Pachon and De Sipio 1994). The consideration of return migration thus provides further support for the connections posited between secondary migration, immigrant enclaves, and citizenship. Citizenship would entail the adoption of a new spatial referent, one which would not allow for return to a place of origin outside of the United States. This re-orienting, however, might encourage an identity tied to a larger scale of possible destinations, and dilution of the significance of movement – constraining *in situ* support networks.

If then, citizenship is (or was) a "belonging in space," today's immigrants are much less capable of assuming it. In a transnational world, where ties to family and home can be more easily maintained, and where return migration looms as a possibility, ties to previous homes are not so easily severed. The Irish immigrant of a century ago firmly planted his feet on new American soil – the homeland soil (often by necessity) reconciled to an unattainable past, a memory fragmented by the impossible costs of return. Soil, once, may have been the important tangent. Immigrants simply planted their feet firmly on the ground in two successive spaces. Once the first connection was lost, roots were established where one's feet now rested. Sustenance, on physical and emotional levels, was site-specific – dreams of home (although undoubtedly still important to an immigrant's identity) were perhaps less real in their unlikelihood. But in the age in which bodies travel in jets from one node to any of a thousand, and communications criss-cross the space above our heads at unimaginable speeds – is it any wonder that the human mind also races about the globe at will – unsatisfied with an unrealistic stolidity? Should it be a surprise that modern immigrants rarely follow a linear assimilatory path toward an exclusively American identity when they communicate daily with family in a far-away home, or live in border communities where quotidian life is somehow inextricably American and Mexican? And is there, any longer, in this nation of immigrants, such a thing as an identifiable, uniquely American identity? Has there ever been?

Further, it must be realized that diasporic individuals are, with increasing frequency, more than once removed. We now see diasporic communities and individuals in the truest sense – rather than being away from a specific home, the system, constituted as it is by relentless, multidirectional motion, is one in which notions of home become individually meaningless figments of identity. Space, in the traditional sense, loses relevance. Identity becomes deterritorialized – a product of many different relationships to many different spaces, rather than a fixed moment in one past space. And yet, the notion of a homeland, and the possibility of return to one special place are enduring myths, even among immigrants who have realized the American dream.

Simply, immigrant communities and the transnational nature of these communities have two paradoxical functions. On one level, they serve to continue multifaceted identities and connections to different places. In that they do so on any soil (and not necessarily, in fact, with any connection to soil at all) challenges the relevance of "real" spaces. Transplanted spaces (Mexican barrios and China-towns, for example) in America and all over the world mean that immigrants can live on foreign soil and still maintain aspatial tangents to a deterritorialized "home." This home then, hangs in the balance as memory. The paradox is that it is perhaps even more real in this imaginary, disconnected form. Human beings, it seems, have emerged into new transnational spaces, where one can adapt to a shift of physical space. Cognitively, psychically, the shift may never have occurred.

When we think of a nation, then, as an entity constituted by individual constituents, citizen or non-citizen, we must consider the individual constituents themselves as constituted. Individual identities, however, are not as simply constituted as in the past. Where once a multiplicity of hyphenated identities: Irish-American, Mexican-American, Italian-American, were celebrated, we now find individuals linked through myriad connections to myriad "homes." Former places in space somehow all find their expression in a new space. Intricately synthesized places of being have shaped immigrants who must see the exclusive loyalty of citizenship as an anachronism, carried from an age in which all of existence occurred on a much smaller, more contained scale.

Notes

1 The reference is to F. Scott Fitzgerald's *The Great Gatsby*.
2 Of the immigrants who were admitted to the United States in 1977, 41.5 percent had naturalized as of 1993. For the entry cohort of 1982, 37.6 percent had naturalized by 1993. Naturalization rates vary with age group, visa category, occupation, and country of birth. The rate for all 1977 immigrants reflects a high for immigrants from the former Soviet Union, of whom 63.3 percent naturalized, and a low for Canadian immigrants, of whom only 14.5 percent naturalized (Immigration and Naturalization Service 1996).

References

Balibar, Etienne. 1996. "The Nation Form: History and Ideology." In Eley, Geoff and Ronald Grigor Suny, eds, *Becoming National: A Reader*. Oxford: Oxford University Press: pp. 132–49.

Castles, Stephen and Mark J. Miller. 1993. *The Age of Migration: International Population Movements in the Modern World*. London: Macmillan.

Hammar, Tomas. 1986. "Citizenship: Membership of a Nation and of a State." *International Migration* 24: 735–47.

Jacobson, David. 1996. *Rights Across Borders: Immigration and the Decline of Citizenship*. Baltimore: The Johns Hopkins University Press.

Karst, Kenneth L. 1989. *Belonging to America: Equal Citizenship and the Constitution*. New Haven: Yale University Press.

Lowe, Sam. 1996. "A Place In Search of a Community." *The Arizona Republic*, September 22, 1996. Special edition: p. 30.

Pachon, Harry and Louis DeSipio. 1994. *New Americans By Choice: Political Perspectives of Latino Immigrants*. Boulder: Westview Press.

Pachon, Harry. 1995. "Prop. 187 isn't all that's propelling Latinos to INS." *Sacramento Bee*, May 22, 1995.

Peck, Jeffrey M. 1996. "Rac(e)ing the Nation: Is There A German 'Home'?" In Eley, Geoff and Ronald Grigor Suny, eds, *Becoming National: A Reader*. Oxford: Oxford University Press: pp. 481–92.

Schuck, Peter H. 1984. "The Transformation of Immigration Law." *Columbia Law Review 84*, I: 1–90.

U.S. Bureau of the Census. 1994. *Current Population Reports 1993–1994: Geographic Mobility of the Population*. Washington, D.C.: U.S. Government Printing Office.

U.S. Immigration and Naturalization Service. 1996. *Statistical Yearbook of the Immigration and Naturalization Service, 1994*. Washington, D.C.: U.S. Government Printing Office.

Index